Stirling Moss

'I reckon that as a racer one should go for it, as fast as possible . . . I liked to have a dice, a real old tear-up . . . to me that's the name of the game . . .'

Stirling Moss

My cars, my career

Stirling Moss

with

Doug Nye

Foreword by Five Times
World Champion
Juan Manuel Fangio

PSL

PATRICK STEPHENS
Wellingborough, Northamptonshire

British Library Cataloguing in Publication Data

Moss, Stirling
    Stirling Moss: my cars, my career.
    1. Moss, Stirling   2. Automobile racing
    drivers —— Great Britain —— Biography
    I. Title   II. Nye, Doug
    796.7'2'0924   GV1032.M6

ISBN 0-85059-925-3

For Elliot,
who I hope will never
want to feel the
magic of ten-tenths

Patrick Stephens Limited is part of the Thorsons Publishing Group

Printed and bound in Great Britain

10 9 8 7 6 5 4 3 2 1

Contents

PROLOGO

Es para mí una gran distinción que el rival que más he respetado en mi vida deportiva me haya solicitado escribir el prólogo de su autobiografía.

A mí me preguntan muchas veces cuáles fueron los corredores con más capacidad en mis tiempos. Y siempre te he tenido en cuenta a vos y a Ascari. Dos personas, quizá, con el mismo temperamento. Pero, mientras Alberto le daba mucha importancia a la prueba de clasificación, para largar de la cuerda y tomar la punta, sin que nadie lo moleste, vos demostraste no tener una estrategia tan rígida y te convertiste en un tipo de luchador que también sabía ir a buscar la punta corriendo desde atrás.

Escribir este prólogo no me resulta difícil porque en mi biografía, recientemente editada en la Argentina y titulada: "Fangio: cuando el hombre es más grande que el mito", vos y Ascari han merecido un capítulo entero.

Yo te vi correr por primera vez en Monza, cuando eras un jovencito, y me sorprendió tu manera de conducir creo un Cooper. Más tarde te vi sobre otro coche inglés, de Fórmula 2, y ya andabas muy fuerte. Desde ese momento fui siguiendo tu trayectoria y siempre te consideré uno de los mejores pilotos de la época. Llegado a este punto no podría olvidar que, siendo tu un piloto particular de Maserati, ponías en aprietos al equipo oficial de fábrica y que fue ello, quizá, una de las causas que disturbó a mi protegido, Onofre "Pinocho" Marimón, aquél sábado de clasificación para el Gran Premio de Alemania en 1954, en Nurburgring, cuando encontró la muerte en un despiste.

Al año siguiente fuimos compañeros de equipo. Yo digo siempre que se conoce a una persona cuando se convive. Y, una vez más, lo que yo había pensado de tu persona lo demostraste no solamente como piloto sino como compañero: sano, honesto, con unas cualidades sobresalientes en cualquier circunstancia y en cualquier coche que hayas corrido.

- 2 -

En mi libro cuento de tu capacidad como piloto al relatar tu llegada al equipo Mercedes-Benz, en 1955, y en qué terminaron unos ensayos privados realizados en Nurburgring, antes de que comenzara el campeonato de ese año, cuando me bajaste el tiempo en la mañana y tuve que dar tres vueltas realmente fuertes por la tarde para mejorar lo tuyo.

Eso, sin contar las carreras que hicimos "a cara de perro" desde la primera a la última vuelta, hasta el Gran Premio de Bélgica, en Spa, después del cual se aceptó mi criterio de que la lucha entre nosotros debía durar hasta que tuviéramos una determinada ventaja sobre el equipo contrario. En ese momento, Neubauer haría que nos mostraran el cartel de "Lansa" (andar más despacio) y quien de nosotros estuviera adelante en ese momento, seguiría adelante, y quien segundo, segundo.

Y también puede contar de tu capacidad el hecho de que ese año, con el Mercedes-Benz 300 SLR ganaste en la Targa Florio y en las Mil Millas, dos carreras en que yo no pude ganar.

En mi criterio, siempre sobresalieron tu fuerza de voluntad, tu perseverancia. Cuando tuviste tu grave accidente en Goodwood yo fui a visitarte en el hospital. Y creí que nunca te ibas a recuperar. Sin embargo lo lograste. Si los médicos hicieron por tí, también vos hiciste mucho por tu recuperación.

Es ese espíritu, más tus cualidades en todo sentido, los que te llevaron a ser uno de los mejores pilotos. Lamentablemente, no pudiste ganar un campeonato. Pero no de gusto te llaman "el campeón sin corona".

JUAN MANUEL FANGIO

03/87

Foreword by Juan Manuel Fangio

Five Times World Champion Driver

*I*t is indeed a great honour that the rival I respected most during my sporting life has asked me to write the foreword to his autobiography.

Many times I am asked who I considered the most talented racing drivers of my time and I always think of you and Ascari — two people with the same kind of temperament. But whilst Alberto gave much importance to qualifying, reaching the corner and taking the lead, so that he was always way ahead of the other, you did not have such a rigid approach, but became a fighter who knew how to take the lead, even when all seemed lost.

It is not difficult for me to write this foreword because in my biography, recently published in Argentina under the title '*Fangio: cuando el hombre es mas grande que el mito*', I have dedicated a whole chapter to you and Ascari.

The first time I saw you drive was at Monza, when you were a mere youngster. Even then, I was surprised at the way you handled the car — I think it was a Cooper. Later, I saw you in another English car, a Formula 2, and you were very fast indeed. From that moment I followed your career and considered you one of the best drivers of the time. Having said that, when you drove your privately-owned Maserati, you shook up the works team and, who knows, this could have been one of the factors that made my protégé Onofre 'Pinnocho' Marimon press too hard during that qualifying Saturday for the 1954 German GP at Nürburgring, when he was killed.

The following year we were in the same team, and I always think that you get to know someone by working with them. Once again, the qualities you demonstrated as a driver, you also demonstrated as a colleague; you were honest and genuine, with certain outstanding traits in any circumstances, and in any car you drove.

In my book, I recount your capacity as a driver when you joined the Mercedes-Benz team in 1955 and when we had several private tests at the Nürburgring before the actual start of the Championship that year. You improved on my time in the morning, and I in turn had to drive three hard and fast laps to better your time.

Then there were the times when we raced each other from start to finish, until the Belgian GP at Spa, when you finally agreed with me that the battle between us should only last until we had gained a certain advantage over the competition. Then Neubauer had to show us the 'Lansa' pit signal [slow down] and whoever was in front stayed in front, and whoever was second stayed second.

I can also recount the time in 1955 when, with your Mercedes-Benz 300 SLR, you won the Targa Florio and the Mille Miglia, two races I never actually won

In my opinion, your willpower and perseverance were your dominant characteristics. I remember when you had your serious accident at Goodwood, and I came to see you in hospital, I thought you would never recover. But you did. You must have done almost as much as the doctors to pull yourself through.

That kind of spirit, together with your outstanding qualities, made you one of the finest drivers of your time. You never won the Championship, but it is not without reason that they call you 'The Champion without a crown'.

JUAN MANUEL FANGIO

15 June 1958 — Spirit of
Grand Prix racing; The first
corner of the Belgian GP at
Spa-Francorchamps high in
the Ardennes, with Stirling's
Vanwall leading (briefly) from
eventual winner Tony Brooks
in the second Vanwall, Olivier
Gendebien's yellow Ferrari
Dino, Jean Behra's BRM, Peter
Collins's Dino et al . . .

Introduction by Doug Nye

Stirling Moss was the greatest road-racing driver never to win the World Championship title. And as one of his favourite catch-phrases (left) suggests, racing has been far more than just his chosen sport — the word itself describes his entire lifestyle.

During the early years of Fangio's truly front-line career from 1954 to 1957 only he seemed consistently capable of greater feats of driving skill — and even then only in Grand Prix cars. Even in Fangio's presence, Moss seemed to have the edge in sports car racing, which the great Argentinian *maestro* claimed not to enjoy.

In the four seasons which Stirling completed following Fangio's retirement from full-time competition, he maintained a superiority which only three other post-war drivers lucky enough to win the World Championship title — one of them being Fangio — have ever managed to emulate.

No other post-war driver, arguably bar the supreme Argentinian, has ever proved greater, and certainly none who could approach Stirling's demonstrable class — Jimmy Clark or Jackie Stewart — could match either his inclination or his ability to perform so majestically (and with such dedicated frequency) in such a bewildering diversity of cars. Arguably, Moss at his peak would have been superior to Fangio, for whereas Stirling drove many obsolescent and inferior cars during the height of his career, the great Argentinian's best years had generally been spent driving the best available cars.

These are considerable claims to make, but their truth is indisputable. No other driver regarded as the standard-setter of his time has been so successful while also being so consistently denied that elusive World Championship title. The very fact that Moss was Championship runner-up in four consecutive seasons, 1955-56-57-58, and was regarded by his rivals as The Man to Beat in 1959-60-61, and on into 1962, speaks volumes. . .

Once Fangio retired in 1958, Stirling seemed to be his natural heir, but the Championship title still eluded him as Mike Hawthorn pipped him by just one solitary point. Under the scoring system it made no odds that Stirling had won three Grand Prix races to Hawthorn's one. In fact Stirling's plea on Mike's behalf against disqualification from the Portuguese GP effectively gave the title away. But those were nothing if not sporting days. Such a gesture was typical. It was the sport that mattered, not something so ephemeral as the Championship itself.

Stirling certainly did not feel that way immediately after it had again been lost. He was deeply disappointed. He felt robbed of his life's ambition. He was sad, perhaps bitter, but explains how within a few days this perfectly natural reaction simply evaporated . . .

He wrote subsequently (during the winter of 1960-61); *'Looking back on it now in a far more philosophical frame of mind, I realise that to work myself up into the sort of state that I had done in the month preceding this race was absurd and from that point when I lost I have relaxed. I have always enjoyed my motor racing, except for that period, and although the World title is still something that I would like to win, I learned a valuable lesson; that if I don't, there is nothing much I can do about it . . .'*

In effect this was his true coming of age. He had become, indisputably, the most talented and capable racing driver of his era. He represented the standard by which all others had to measure themselves. Having achieved such a level a Championship title or two would have been nice, but really it was unnecessary. Just as in Fangio's day, every other front-line driver knew who was the boss . . . who was the man they had to beat, whose was the first name their eyes would search for when a new list of practice times was published . . . S. C. Moss — none other.

Once Fangio retired, Stirling could be quietly confident that in equal cars over a full race distance he had the measure, man for man, of all contemporary rivals. At his peak, at least until the emergence of Jimmy Clark in the latest Lotus chassis, one could even delete that requirement for 'equal cars' . . .

Throughout the sporting world Stirling Moss became simply 'Mr Motor Racing' — the complete professional — and he has remained so to this day, despite his front-line career having been so savagely terminated against that Goodwood bank in 1962.

His often intense professionalism brought some criticism, but his racing philosophy had always been perfectly simple, and consistent. He would explain: 'Right from the start I was never in racing for the money. I went professional to make the money to be able to race, it was very much that way round. If I hadn't got money coming in, I wouldn't have been able to race at all . . . and I loved to go racing, so I had to ensure first that the money was coming in . . .'

In short, he not only lived to race, he also raced to live. Since it was his livelihood he would drive anything, anywhere, provided the money was right and he could fit an engagement into his hectic schedule.

So he might race his Formula 1 Maserati against Fangio's Mercedes-Benz or Ferrari one weekend, then drive a 500 cc chain-driven Formula 3 car and a Standard Ten saloon in a minor meeting the next! He frequently drove Formula 1, sports, saloon and GT cars all in a single day's race programme, and he was usually The Man to Beat in each of them.

In effect there were two Stirling Mosses; one the energetic, keen, very friendly, open-minded and wonderfully talented *enthusiast* who enjoyed every moment of everything he tackled — and the other the hard-nosed commercial businessman single-mindedly intent upon paying his way. Little has changed today!

American writer Dennis Shattuck distilled the man's style and stature very nicely in 1960, when Stirling was at the peak of his prowess. Shattuck wrote for *Road & Track*; '*Moss not only is a slight, balding Englishman with an eye towards money, women and fine racing cars; Moss is the quickest way through a corner, the fastest way around the course and the ultimate performance of any racing machine. Moss is either victory or mechanical destruction . . .*'

He was not a car breaker, but no lack of skill every lost him a goal.

He always committed himself totally to any event he tackled, and he raced throughout Europe and in North America, South America, Africa and Australia. The only continents never to witness his prowess were Asia and Antarctica . . . yet even then at Invercargill, in New Zealand, he came as close to the South Pole as any racer can.

He paid enormous attention to detail in the equipment he drove and its preparation, and might make himself 'a pain' by the demands he made of a major team — like Vanwall for example — in which if his contract gave him choice of equipment he would if necessary exercise it to the Nth degree. He rationalized this perfectionism quite reasonably as being necessary to give himself and his team the best possible chance — that, after all, was what he was being paid for.

The record shows he was often right. By the figures given in this book, throughout his career he competed in 501 events, finished in 382 of them, and won 173, one win for every 2.9 events, or remarkably one win for every 2.2 times he finished. That's class, indisputable class . . .

His career reached its height in its final three and a bit seasons, not with a major factory team in Formula 1 but with his friend Rob Walker's private organization. In his last two full seasons — 1960-1961 — he had no less than 96 races, in all kinds of car, all over the world, and he won 46 of them . . .

By that time he was indisputably on top of the pyramid. There was no other driver he need fear in an equal car. Indeed he generally felt able — apart from the case of one exceptional newcomer — to give them all a short-head start in better equipment and still feel fairly confident in his own ability to make them Go — all the way — if they were actually to beat him. Any factory team would have gladly snapped him up, but he preferred instead to drive Rob's privately owned customer cars, simply because he enjoyed and respected the way in which that great gentleman enthusiast went racing. Thus he cast himself in his favourite role of under-dog, taking on the factory cars in a private entry.

It was entirely a role which Moss the fully-fledged Maestro truly relished and one which he twice played to a sensational degree in two immortal motor races during his final full season of 1961 — the Monaco and German GPs — in which he humbled Ferrari, a team which for years since an unfortunate incident in 1951 he had loved to beat.

Into 1962 he would finally bury the hatchet with Mr Ferrari, preparing to drive Italian cars entered by the Walker team, but the Goodwood accident that Easter Monday put paid to all such plans.

In later years Stirling would return to competition driving, 'just for fun', racing and rallying predominantly saloons but also accepting guest drives in a wide variety of historic racing cars like those in which he had built his glittering career. Even through the mid-'80s he kept his hand in with his own Chevron and Elva historic sports cars, 'Paying for my own racing, and finding it jolly expensive I can tell you . . . but I do it because I still enjoy it. I just love to race . . .'

As you would expect of Mr Motor Racing.

Now in these pages he describes in detail every car he drove in competition during that long professional career, and tells what many currently accepted classics were really like to race in earnest, through that hectic period, really from 1948 to 23 April 1962, when the story ends at Goodwood. The sections on each type of car are arranged chronologically, using his début-date in the car to decide the order in which we present them. There is a small degree of duplication in some details between the different sections, but we hope the reader will accept this as it is intended, to make each section stand on its own, and to make this book ideal 'to dip into'.

Here Stirling and I have tried to do more than merely tell the truth of what so many great cars — and many more humble and a few just plain awful ones — were really like. You will also find the life story of this most active and successful of all British racing drivers woven into the tale which follows. I hope you enjoy reading it as much as I enjoyed recreating it with one of my boyhood heroes . . . the greatest British racing driver; one of the greatest the world has ever known.

Doug Nye,
Lower Bourne,
Farnham, Surrey
July 1987

Acknowledgements

The publishers wish to thank the following for their assistance in kindly providing photographs to illustrate this volume:

Edward Eves
Geoffrey Goddard
Guy Griffiths
Denis Jenkinson
Tom March
Otis Meyer 'Road & Track' Librarian, Newport Beach, California
Steven Tee and Liz Payne of LAT Photographic

*Young Moss, the 'two-way'
Cooper, 1949.*

Young Moss

1923 JCC 200-Miles Race, Brooklands Motor Course, Weybridge, Surrey — Alfred Moss, Stirling's father, ready to race his Crouch — waiting by the paddock stalls.

My father Alfred was a dentist. He had quite a chain of dental surgeries around London, mainly in the poorer areas where the patients did not expect the dentists to spend much time generally chatting to them, but rather just do the job. 'In quick, yank and out, next please — that's the basis of good business,' he might have said.

Dad was also a very enthusiastic motorist; he raced at Brooklands and when he got the chance to study dentistry in the States he made the opportunity to race there, at Indianapolis and on minor board tracks.

My mum, Aileen, was another keen sporting motorist, driving in trials and rallies. When I was a kid, about six or seven, she would often let me steer the car along our driveway at The Long White Cloud, our small farm beside the Thames at Bray. Then, when I was about eight or nine, my father bought me an ancient Austin Seven. I was big enough to reach the pedals when Dad brought the seat right forward. It was completely stripped with no windscreen, but had a box affair at the back, and I drove it round and round in our fields.

That's where my mother kept horses. She was very keen on them, and I had a pony which I enjoyed riding round the fields, pretending I was a redskin like those I had seen at the movies, trying stunts like hiding from the US Cavalry by hanging out of the saddle sideways, that kind of thing. I enjoyed the fun of it, and then mother suggested I should go in for competition. After a while I decided that was less fun, because the jumps looked too bloody high to me!

On a horse my threshold of fear is pretty close. But I had a very good 14.2 hands pony, called Brandy, who could jump five feet and I had been brought up in a competitive family so I had quite a bit of success in gymkhanas. My young sister Pat saved the day for me. She began riding in a basket arrangement when she was only three. By the time she was six she was really quite good

15

Above *December 1935, Stirling's mum Aileen Moss does the driving while Alfred passengers the Singer on 'Juniper I' hill during the North-West London Motor Club's London-Gloucester Trial.*

Right *Sunny Margate for a Moss family holiday in the '30s; Aileen, young Stirling, and Alfred — what a future lay ahead . . .*

and that took the pressure off me a bit as Mum concentrated on her. By the time I was sixteen, Pat was really a very good rider indeed, and so it wasn't such a drag for my mother when I said I was not really that interested in progressing further from junior to senior. I had done pretty well as a junior, I had won a lot of competitions and really enjoyed winning, but I simply was not that keen on horse riding . . .

Dad had always encouraged competitiveness and physical fitness. He had me swimming, running, even boxing virtually from the day I was able to walk, and riding gymkhanas stoked-up my competitive sense. I enjoyed trying to beat the other kids, even when I might lose. At school I was quite a good sprinter, I boxed and played rugby. Recently my six-year-old son Elliott was watching me doing press-ups. I did twelve, then he wanted to have a go, and promptly did thirteen. I got down again and did fourteen or fifteen, he came back with a couple more; competitive little feller. Competitive family, I guess . . .

I went to the Haileybury Junior School of Imperial Service College at Clewer Manor, in a suburb of Windsor. It was a fine sporting school, and I moved on for senior education to Haileybury in Hertfordshire. I was fine at sports, but pretty hopeless academically. I also made myself a reputation for standing up for schoolboys' rights, better food, all that kind of thing. My housemaster christened me The Agitator!

Unfortunately, despite being naturally pretty athletic I had some childhood health problems and missed a lot of schooling. The worst thing was nephritis, a kidney affliction, which took me ages to fight off but left me in my late teens medically unfit for National Service. I believe Mike Hawthorn had a similar problem, only much worse than mine, and when he went to drive for Ferrari in 1953-54 a poisonous campaign started against him in the yellow press which claimed he was driving for the Italians to shirk National Service call-up. It even involved questions being asked about both of us in Parliament, and when that happened Dad had copies of my medical reports run off and circularized every MP to put them in the picture about why I wasn't serving two years in the Forces. It was odd, really, because I felt fit as a flea, but rules is rules and we complied with them.

During childhood I was also exposed to considerable pain, other than from the kidney problem, and I believe perhaps this became significant later in my career as it gave me pretty high tolerance, particularly in my ability to regain fitness rapidly after injury. I could exercise and do physiotherapy and largely

Gymkhanas and horseshows sharpened not only the Moss children's competitiveness, but also their natural reflexes and sensitivity; younger sister Pat and Stirling (aged 11) here, with four-legged friends . . . Stirling won over £200 on horseback — cash put towards his first car.

ignore any associated pain or discomfort. There's a saying that exercise is not doing you any good unless it hurts. If you don't mind it hurting too much, you can exercise harder, longer . . .

For years as a kid I suffered terrible ear-ache, which is no joke at all, I can tell you. There was also one time when I was playing with some friends in a tree house; we had a paraffin lamp up there, hanging on a rope — my cousin hit it with a broom, it swung crazily and splashed burning paraffin into my lap — that made my eyes water for quite a while . . .

Dad had hoped I would get my matriculation exams and go on to qualify as a dentist and join the family business but I was so hopeless academically there was no chance of passing. So I left school at sixteen, tried a 'crammer school', but then at seventeen decided to go into the hotel trade as a trainee manager with Associated British Hotels.

I went to work at the Palmerston Restaurant in the City as commis waiter, then the Bayswater Hotel where I remember during one dramatic stint as night-porter hearing a pop-pop-pop noise in the foyer which turned out to be a couple of characters yanking up the carpet, popping out its fixing tacks as they prepared to roll it up and pinch it!

Working behind the bar in the Eccleston Hotel at Victoria I then discovered graft. By pouring the dregs from splits like bitter lemon or tonic water into an empty bottle you would quite quickly end up with a full bottle of your own to be sold for clear profit . . .

Meanwhile I had become increasingly interested in motoring and motor cars. I read the specialist press and had at last begun driving on the open road. My progression in wheeled transport had been from my first pedal car, at age four, to the Austin Seven at around nine, then a motor bike during the war followed by the deep joy of a Morgan three-wheeler at fifteen, which was only legal because I managed to obtain a pre-dated licence!

When I was riding the motor bike — a Coventry Eagle I believe — I was too young to use it on the public road, but my father was in the LDV, the Home Guard, and I was attached to them as a despatch rider if needed. If the Germans had invaded I would have been allowed to ride it on the road. Therefore I was possibly the only kid in Britain who hoped that the Germans would invade . . .

When the Morgan appeared on the scene I could drive it as a 'non-reversible tricycle' on a motor cycle licence, minimum age for which was sixteen. The Morgan was a 1936 model with a Matchless vee-twin, air-cooled engine and I think we brought it for £50. I was dead keen to get out and about in it, so I applied for my licence two or three months early. I filled in my date of birth correctly — 17 September 1929 — but they obviously didn't study the application closely because they immediately sent me back a licence. So, despite being a couple of months under-age, I had incorrectly been provided with a legal licence. And if they were daft enough to send me a licence, I was daft enough to use it!

The Morgan was wonderful, but I hankered after a 'proper' car, and at seventeen I was thrilled when dad let me take over a 1940 MG TB Tickford Coupé which he had bought. This was even more exciting. Naturally there was an enormous ulterior motive — it wasn't all merely motoring enthusiasm. My early amorous adventures had already been assisted by the three-wheeler because when you're the only cat in town with something other than a motor bike it does help. And now the MG — marvellous!

Father had laid up several nice cars during the war. Two I recall would be fabulously valuable today — a 2.3 supercharged Alfa and a magnificent V12 Lagonda with a cocktail cabinet in the back. When the war broke out nobody wanted cars, so my father had bought these two cheaply and stored them on blocks in what we called the summerhouse.

Then in the winter of 1947-48 he bought Victor Biggs' BMW 328 and that became the car in which my competition career began . . . so read on . . .

BMW 328 *(1947)*

'My introduction. A very nice little sports car . . . for the road.'

Sprinting the faithful green BMW in the Poole Speed Trials, 1947 — Dad permitted young Stirling to drive bare-headed at that time. He wouldn't allow it when the open-wheeled Cooper came along . . .

Compared to my very first experiences of motoring in my Morgan three-wheeler and then the MG TB Tickford Coupé, the BMW 328 which my father let me drive in my first competitive events was certainly the fastest and best-handling car I'd driven at that time. It was essentially a long-legged proper sports car, great on smooth roads. It had quite good power and really excellent handling for its time, a good but fragile little gearbox and marvellously direct steering which gave plenty of 'feel' and confidence. Unfortunately we ran it largely in off-road trials, a type of event for which it was quite unsuited. Its ground clearance was never enough, and in deep mud it would snap its half-shafts at the drop of a hat. But it was fun, and it gave me a taste for motoring competition.

BMW of Munich had introduced their 2-litre *Typ* 328 sports cars in 1936 and they demolished all opposition the very first time they raced them, in the Eifelrennen at Nürburgring. With their blended-in front wings and aerodynamic styling they were really very pretty, and also technically advanced for their time. They had independent front suspension, generally good handling and marvellous rack-and-pinion steering. Their 6-cylinder engine used an advanced cylinder head design with inclined valves in hemispherical combustion chambers, operated by a complex system of cross-pushrods from a camshaft in the block. They gave about 80 horsepower and in 1946 this design was taken by Bristol as war reparation to launch their new car business. The BMW-derived 'Bristol' engine then provided power for many of us in both sports and Formula 2 cars into the 1950s.

In England immediately post-war we had no circuit racing until the aerodrome perimeter-track courses were invented. We certainly had nothing like the Nürburgring or the Mille Miglia where the 328s had shone pre-war. Through the summers of 1946-47 we had only very short-distance tarmac-surfaced hill-climbs like Shelsley Walsh and Prescott, occasional sprints like Elstree or the Brighton Speed Trials, and then in the winter the off-road trial reigned supreme.

I had begun to read *The Autocar, The Motor* and *Motor Sport* magazines, and I had seen an advertisement for a new type of racing car using the rotary-valve Aspin engine. I was wildly excited by this idea and promptly ordered one, enclosing my cheque for £50 from money I had won show-jumping. But my father noticed the cheque counterfoil and demanded to know what it was for.

I admitted I had ordered a racing car, and found myself in terrible trouble.

He went through the roof! He contacted the company, explained that S. C. Moss was under age and cancelled my order. They returned the deposit, and for the moment my dream of owning my own racing car was over.

But Dad then relented a little, and said that if I was really that keen to get into competition then I could borrow the BMW which he had just bought.

We used it mainly in trials that year. For example, on 2 March 1947 I drove it in the Harrow Car Club's Moss Trophy Trial, donated by my mother who had competed pre-war. The former owner of our BMW, Victor Biggs, won in his new 1½-litre HRG, but I got my name in *The Autocar*'s results as winner of the Cullen Cup. Then on Easter Sunday we went down to the West Country for the North-West London MC's Inter-Club Trial, and this time *The Autocar* reported '*The second test was a stop-reverse-restart where young Moss's green 2-litre Type 328 BMW (Harrow Club) was easily fastest in 17⅗ sec . . .*' I was famous!

It was then that I discovered, when in sticky mud, that the slightest over-enthusiasm on the throttle would snap a half-shaft like a carrot. What we did not perhaps appreciate was that the best people's 328s used special heavy-duty axles.

In June I drove the BMW in the JCC Eastbourne Rally, which was virtually a gymkhana on the prom. I won the 'easy starting test' — 12.8 secs — and the 'steering test' slalom — 18 secs — taking a first-class award overall . . . It was my first 'big win'.

I ran in the standing-start kilometre Brighton Speed Trials in September, managing seventh quickest in the 2-litre standard sports car class, and at the Poole Speed Trials over a half-mile winding course at South Lytchett Manor I had my first brief taste of competition on a virtually normal road. My car might not have been very quick compared to the HRGs and Tony Crook's lightweight 328 but I had improved — to fourth in class.

At the end of that month I ran in the Chichester Speed Trials over half-a-mile of Merston aerodrome's perimeter track with just one fast curve joining two straights. *Motor Sport* reported how '*. . . at the corner, Moss blipped his BMW's throttle . . .*' but did not record where I finished. Certainly not in the first three. But by that time I was eighteen, and a Cooper-JAP 500 had been ordered to replace the BMW in the new year . . .

My most vivid memory of the 328 comes from a trial in the West Country, where — sure enough — we'd broken a half-shaft, and a chap named Dave Price towed us all the way home behind his Allard, on a very short rope and at one *hell* of a speed. My father said he would steer, because he had more experience, so I crouched petrified in the passenger seat, feeling as if we were going quicker on that tow rope than the BMW had ever gone on its own! I realized then that I had a very low threshold of fear . . . and I believe that in the formative years of my career that could well have been an advantage.

In the BMW I was competing against good people like Tony Crook and Gillie Tyrer in similar cars who did most of the winning. Yet Ford V8-engined trials specials were beginning to dominate on those muddy hills, and for the first time I realized that the car mattered as much as the driver. It was important to have the right equipment and to prepare it well for whatever type of event you had entered. Given equal driving skill, the driver whose car had more power or was better suited would nearly always win. That was an eye-opener for me. I learned the importance of being properly equipped.

In retrospect, I must say that when I drove that BMW I really was a total novice. I never really approached its limits. Driving on the road wasn't suitable to learn just how fast corners could be taken, while hard-surfaced sprints and speed trials were so short there was no chance to get to know your car well enough. I was totally inexperienced and the BMW really was the start of it all, my introduction, not at all specialized enough for what we tried to do with it, but for me an addictive first step into competition . . .

Cooper 500s *(1948-54)*

'I drove nothing but air-cooled Coopers in my first two seasons, and they were the cars in which I learned the rudiments of racing, and discovered the satisfaction of winning . . .'

My first Cooper 500 was more or less a present for my eighteenth birthday, although my father ensured I paid something towards it. The very first time I sat in the car it felt very strange; so unlike anything I had ever driven before — a tight, spartan little centre cockpit, exposed wheels front and rear and the only instrument a rev counter. There was no padding so I was badly thrown around that first season and I held myself upright by gripping the cockpit side with my arm. But that little Cooper was delightfully responsive. It would dodge and dive instantly wherever you steered, and I found early on that the way to make it perform with that single-cylinder motor cycle engine was to work away at the gearbox and keep it revving somewhere near the top of its torque curve.

I think perhaps some other, older, contemporary drivers handled their 500s like conventional cars without appreciating that once the revs had been allowed to die away you were lost, for there was never the power low down to recover lost momentum. This remained characteristic of 500s throughout my seven seasons' driving them, during which most of my cars were Coopers.

John Cooper and Eric Brandon built their first 500 cc sprint car in 1946 at the modest Surbiton garage owned by John's father, Charles. The British 500 cc 'poor man's motor racing' movement had been founded by some Bristol enthusiasts. John and Eric wanted all-independent suspension on their car, so they took two Fiat Topolino front ends — which had simple wishbone-and-transverse-leaf-spring independent suspension — and welded them together back-to-back. They installed an air-cooled single-cylinder JAP speedway engine in the rear, chain-driving to a solid rear axle, and then clothed it all in a neat aluminium single-seat body. This Cooper-JAP Mark I was driven by both its creators until a sister was completed for Eric Brandon's use in 1947.

These two Cooper-JAPs were so successful that other enthusiasts — including my father and me — were soon asking John and his father to build replicas for 1948. Through the years until 1954 I would drive air-cooled Coopers Marks II to VII and ultimately end my 500 career in the very special Cooper-Norton Mark VIIA owned by master-tuner Francis Beart and developed by him and his colleague Ray Petty.

But in the beginning my earliest outings in our cream-painted original car ought to be described in some detail . . .

By 1948 life in post-war Britain was desperately grey and dull. Everything worthwhile still seemed to be rationed, including petrol. Then when the Government cancelled the 'Basic' petrol ration private motoring was effectively banned. Unless you had a business allowance you had to use public transport, or somehow fiddle the fuel for your private car. In fact, the motoring public seemed more determined than ever to travel and find some fun, despite the gloom. Several go-ahead motor clubs planned a full season regardless.

We still had no mainland race circuits. Brooklands was derelict and part-demolished. Donington Park, near Derby, was an enormous military transport depot, and London's Crystal Palace was abandoned and overgrown. So we relied on private-road sprints and hill-climbs, until later in the year the idea of using abandoned aerodromes provided circuits at Brough, Goodwood, Silverstone and Dunholme Lodge. They were generally bare and barren, but it was near enough to proper road racing to thrill enthusiasts starved of sporting spectacle.

On the bright side, 'Basic's' cancellation didn't affect the competition cars themselves, because they burned methanol which *was* available, although expensive.

During 1947 we had seen and read about the new Cooper-JAPs. They fascinated me — real racing cars with single-seater bodies and open wheels, and affordable!

I discovered Cooper's Garage in Surbiton, and one day that autumn contrived to drive past with my father in the car. One of the prototype 500s was in their little showroom. We stopped. 'Gosh Dad look at *that*, wouldn't it be *terrific* to have one of them for next season?'

He had always been interested in mechanical things and the Cooper was neat and ingenious, and impressed him. He knew Stan Greening of J. A. Prestwich — who made JAP engines — and felt sure we could obtain a decent one. A tiny horsepower advantage in such a class meant at least you started in good shape. He eventually said I could order a Cooper and agreed to help to some extent, but I had to find most of the price — about £575 — myself.

My parents had always taught me that if I wanted something I must first be able to afford it, which usually meant sacrifices to find the money. I had a fair amount saved from gymkhana prizes, but to pay for the Cooper I now had to sell my tent, radio, camera and so on. I think that Dad bought them, but he had made his point, and believe me he drove a hard bargain!

I fell short of the mark, but my eighteenth birthday was coming up in September '47 so my parents made up the difference and the order was confirmed. Dad had told me 'If you're really determined, try it for a season and I'll help you all I can . . .'

That winter we watched our new car being built. I proudly sent off my entry for the important Shelsley Walsh hill-climb in May '48. But they were already over-subscribed and returned it . . .   That was a blow.

Second attempt, an entry for the Bugatti Owners' Club hill-climb at Prescott near Cheltenham, on 9 May 1948; and they accepted.

Dad had arranged a decent JAP engine through Stan Greening. We had a German prisoner-of-war named Don Müller working on our farm at Bray who had been a BMW fitter pre-war and was a very nice guy, and keen. He would act as our mechanic. For transport we knocked out the centre partition of our horse-box trailer, and Dad would tow it with the Cooper inside behind his elderly estate-bodied Rolls-Royce. My mother would normally come along, often with a rather rebellious Pat, my younger sister, who would rather be on her horses. By this time she was already a brilliant rider and was enjoying great gymkhana success.

Our car was finished at last, just one week before Prescott. With Eric Brandon along to help, we tried it out at Cippenham not far from home, on the site of a new housing estate where only the service roads as yet existed. We fired-up the engine and I drove a real racing car for the first time in my life . . .

It was fantastically exciting. It felt really good, very compact, light and responsive. Compared to the BMW I was sitting incredibly low. It felt very quick. But the vibration from that single-cylinder engine was fantastic!

Cooper tried to insulate it from the rest of the frame by mounting the JAP on two transverse seven-leaf springs, but I could cup my open hands around the steering wheel rim, and then just by blipping the throttle make it blur between thumb and forefinger, hitting them both!

This was very off-putting, but one just had to adapt to it. Eventually, improved engine mounts would damp its worst effects.

These initial test runs ended when I narrowly missed a cyclist who wobbled into my path. In any case we were making so much noise it was inevitable we should soon be chased away . . .

At least I then started my first racing car event at Prescott with around four miles' experience.

Prescott was only a half-mile climb and everybody had two practice runs, then the downhill return, before the competition proper. I was determined to do well, and my second run in anger clocked 50.01 seconds which at that moment was a new 500 cc class record, but the stars of the class were still to

Above *9 May 1948 — Dawn of a superlative career — S C Moss, Prescott hill-climb, in his very first competitive event with the Cooper-JAP 500 Mark II. The elbow over the cockpit coaming was necessary to steady himself because the early Cooper's seat offered such poor support.*

Above right *6 June 1948 — The first victory — Stirling corrects a power slide in the tiny Cooper-JAP on his way to a class win at Stanmer Park hill-climb, Brighton.*

go and they promptly put me in my place, pushing me back to fourth.

I was still thrilled to see the next issue of *The Motor* declaring that '*S. Moss and R. M. Dryden, both on Coopers, are promising recruits to Class 1 racing . . .*' while *The Light Car* gave me more space; '*Eighteen-year-old S. Moss, whose mother used to handle the white Marendaz in trials so well, wrote his name in the book of folk to watch . . .*' The following month's issue of *Motor Sport* reported '*Moss drove his Cooper really stirringly . . .*' Such praise, just for fourth-fastest time, was really heady stuff for any ambitious teenager in his first event.

Second time out, on 5 June, we ran at Brighton's Stanmer Park hill-climb. It was a brand-new venue and my father told me 'Here's your chance. The others all knew Prescott, but here you all start level . . .'

Sure enough, our 500 class became a battle between Eric Brandon and me. Eric rushed his 'works' Cooper up first in 61.02 secs, and I responded with 59.88. Eric fought back at 59.30, but I finally took the class in 58.78. This was my first outright win and my first 'racing car' trophy.

My first circuit race followed on 4 July at the Blackburn Aircraft company's Brough aerodrome. These were only the second 500 cc-movement circuit races ever run, and I paid my five shillings entry fee with enormous anticipation — for this was going to be 'The Real Thing'.

We took the car up by train. It poured with rain and there were only nine starters, arranged in three heats with only three starters each. I won heat three, but averaged only 48.9 mph due to the rain and the loose-surfaced and tight 0.65-mile circuit. It rained harder for the final, but I won again, this time at 52 mph. The organizers finally staged an eight-lap handicap, with me on scratch and apparently forgotten by the starter long after he had flagged the others away. I managed to take the lead on the third lap and notched my hat-trick by winning at 51.5 mph.

To my astonishment *The Daily Mail* splashed the story under a headline reading BROUGH CAR RACE WON BY BACKMARKER, and their breathless report made a big production of what had really been a grey and miserable — though undeniably satisfying — day's sport. It ran: '*Road-racers hurtled their machines round the treacherous surface of the rain-sodden track . . . for the first time the crowd were able to see midget 500 cc cars in neck-and-neck duels instead of beating lap records or racing against the clock . . . it was a new thrill, and the handling of his car by 18-year-old S. Moss of London brought him out ahead . . .*'

I won £13, plus a presentation pint tankard and we flew home from Brough with the car in an Anson. Such success was intoxicating.

At this time, having had the Cooper for just two months, I had not only won my first hill-climb but also my first three circuit races (admittedly very minor ones), and now we sailed to Jersey for the Bouley Bay 'climb where I won the class again.

After practice at a hill-climb, having climbed and returned to the paddock twice, the Cooper would have run only a couple of miles. We used practice above all just to verify the gearing because we could change the drive sprockets for others with a different number of teeth. Initially we would simply change the sprocket on the engine, but we later became really sophisticated and began changing the sprocket on the clutch. The engine sprockets had something like 16, 17, 18 or 19 teeth, whereas the ones on the clutch had more like 42 or 43 so changing them enabled us to gear the car far more precisely, going up or down in finer increments. We would juggle with alternative Lodge R49 or R50 spark-plugs and experiment with tyre pressures, and between practice and the actual event we would also lift the cylinder head, touch-in the valves and generally polish it all up inside with Duraglit — our demon tweak!

I believe this was my father's idea, 'Look, we'd better see how it's going inside there . . .', and it seemed quite a reasonable thing to do. He told me 'OK, you haven't done any distance but you have used the revs', so with Don and myself he would check the valves and springs and wield the Duraglit.

The standard JAP had five studs retaining its cylinder head, so the advent of a four-stud version was a big deal purely because it meant one less to undo. We had to adjust the total-loss lubrication drip properly, and then we would put it all back together and tackle the class runs.

We did not merely run the car as completed by Cooper. From the beginning we paid great attention to its development and improvement, to give ourselves an edge over our competitors. Dad's influence showed itself as we drilled the pedals, chassis and body-framing to save weight. We fitted aviation-style Simmonds self-locking nuts everywhere in place of ordinary lock-nuts, and wired or split-pinned everything necessary to resist vibration. We remounted the Newton telescopic dampers, lapped-in each individual brake drum and marked each wheel so it would always be replaced in the same position. We added small cooling ducts to the front drum brakes, and our four-stud JAP engine eventually used a slightly over-size inlet valve — thanks to Stan Greening — and a Specialloid J29 piston with its ears turned-off where we found they tended to pick up when run hard. We normally used an aircraft-pattern Lodge R49 spark-plug, and generally the engine was quite reliable.

The first exception was Bouley Bay where, despite winning the class, my engine was badly damaged. We were due at Prescott within 48 hours for another 'climb and didn't have a spare engine. Don went with the car on the boat, while my father and I flew home, collected necessary parts, then drove to Southampton to meet the ferry. While Dad drove the tow car, Don and I lurched around inside that narrow horse-box, stripping the Cooper's damaged engine. We finished it in time, and my three class runs at Prescott were all sub-50s — 49.86 secs, 49.88 secs and 49.51 secs for another win. This time *The Daily Graphic* headlines read ACE DRIVERS BEATEN BY 18-YEAR OLD: WON RACE IN CAR HE REBUILT ON THE ROAD. The piece was written by Kay Petre, Britain's most famous pre-war lady racing driver, and she quoted Raymond Mays — father of the ERA and of the new BRM project and a real hill-climb superstar — as saying of S. Moss Esq; *'He is the most promising of our young drivers . . .'* I was thrilled.

That July the RAC announced that it was taking a one-year lease on the disused aerodrome at Silverstone to develop its perimeter tracks and runways as a racing circuit. An international Grand Prix would be staged there in October, with a 500 cc race in support. In Sussex, the Duke of Richmond and Gordon planned to run races round the perimeter track of what had been the Westhampnett fighter aerodrome on his Goodwood estate; another opportunity to go circuit racing . . . which I relished.

At September Prescott it poured with rain, the programme dragged as crashed cars had to be recovered from the hill and I later told Robert Raymond — who wrote the first Moss biography — 'It was the only time I have ever been really tensed-up. I was wet and miserable, and people kept rushing past saying so-and-so's pranged, and so-and-so's gone off the road, until when my turn came, two hours late, I made a mess of it . . .'

My best climb was only third fastest, which rather brought me down with a bump . . .

The following weekend on 18 September, the British Automobile Racing Club — which pre-war had been the Brooklands ARC — ran its inaugural race meeting at Goodwood. I celebrated my nineteenth birthday there on the practice day by setting fastest 500 cc time, but grid positions were decided by ballot and I started in mid-field on race-day.

I managed to take the lead into the first corner and led to the end with dad frantically waggling 'SLOW' signals at me every time I came past the pits for fear of my breaking the engine. It was only a three-lap race, but that was over seven miles which was reckoned to be a *long* way for a methanol-burning 500. First prize was 30 guineas, fabulous for those days and for a driver of my inexperience. It more than compensated for Prescott in the rain.

The RAC's major 500 race at Silverstone then went bad for us, as my engine drive sprocket came adrift while leading.

One final, very minor, aerodrome race remained, at Dunholme Lodge near Lincoln, which I managed to win, so overall my 1948 season included fifteen individual events of which I had managed to win eleven, adding a third place, two fourths and only one real failure. We had earned some prize money, but certainly hadn't broken even: a win at Prescott, for example, was worth £10 but the entry fee was a fiver!

Through Stan Greening, JAP had been generous with engine spares, and I will never forget the day Dad came home from his dental surgery with a free drum of Sternol Oil. One of his patients was Sternol's Managing Director and he'd agreed to back us in kind. I guess few people will argue with their dentist!

The little Cooper had thus given me my entrée into a more serious form of competition in which one no longer merely raced one's road car. Here you arrived with a specialized competition car, checked its tyre pressures, warmed-up the engine on a soft plug, put in a harder one for the climb or race, used practice to optimize tyre pressures and gear ratios, and only then began to drive in real earnest.

Of course, there was a debit side. The Cooper-JAP was far more temperamental than any road car. We mixed its methanol fuel from methyl alcohol with an additional two per cent acetone and a dash of castor oil. The JAP's air-cooled finning was not particularly deep and since the engine ran enclosed in the Cooper it would surely have overheated had we not run it enormously rich with carburettor jets like drain-pipes so that the alcohol could cool the engine internally.

Really one could virtually 'think' all these cars around a course; they were so light and nimble you simply turned the steering wheel just so much and that's exactly where the car would go.

I was just beginning to learn some of the black arts, such as the dazzling discovery that by increasing front tyre pressures we could decrease understeer. I had not learned at this stage to scrub-in brand-new tyres to achieve optimum grip, but we always warmed-up the oil most carefully, running the engine in gear with the little car's rear wheels jacked-up and whirling round, just like the ERAs around us in the big-car class. Only later did we realize they did this purely to warm-up their pre-selector gearboxes, which we did not possess!

Above all, I had begun to learn the rudiments of competition driving in a tailor-made competition car. One of the big problems with that first Mark II

Cooper was location within the cockpit. You will see from old photographs how I hooked my elbows over the cockpit coaming, and I would press them in hard to hold myself secure in corners.

Ending 1948 we sold that original cream-painted Mark II to Austen May, and during 1949 we ran our replacement long-wheelbase Cooper Mark III only five times in 500 cc form instead of with its usual alternative twin-cylinder 1,000 engine. Cooper's built-in several extra features for us, like long-range pannier tanks, rack-and-pinion steering and a special seat with extra location around my rib cage and shoulders, and with slot-in leather-upholstered curved side panels against my hips and thighs to wedge me in tight.

Our 1948 record enabled my father to wangle a little sponsorship from the trade, and Dunlop tyres, Lodge plugs and Mobiloil each offered bonuses for selected events if we did well on their products. A Bedford van replaced the horse-box, and we sold advertising space on its sides for small but useful sums.

The new Mark III was anodized pale green instead of painted because spilled methanol fuel was a marvellous paint-stripper. We had a lucky horseshoe motif sign-painted on its headrest, with seven studs, my mother's lucky number, a superstition which rubbed off on me.

The Mark III's debut came at the maiden Easter Monday Goodwood meeting, in 1949. We ran it first as a 500 with a JAP single installed but the piston failed on the opening lap. We then fitted the new 1,000 cc twin for a handicap, and won.

In 500 form I won at the second Silverstone British GP meeting in May, at

19 April 1949 — Equipe Moss at Easter Monday Goodwood with their brand-new 'two-way' Cooper-JAP Mark III; Alf, Stirling, Don Müller, and Aileen holding 'The Boy's' Herbert Johnson helmet. Note the lucky horseshoe with its seven holes and evidence of Mobil sponsorship.

31 July 1949 — Pedestrian problem for Moss at Zandvoort where John Habin's unfortunate mechanic was on the grid as the starting flag fell and stepped into the Cooper's path. Stirling knocked him flying. He went to hospital with bruising and shock; SM went on to win.

Blandford hill-climb and at Zandvoort in Holland. There and at the International Trophy Silverstone meeting in August, I ran a 'sloper' JAP engine which was actually the vee-twin crankcase with its rearward barrel, rod and piston removed. This wasn't such a good idea. It was down on power compared to the conventional 500s and Brandon beat me by 0.2 sec.

In 1950 the FIA recognized 500 cc racing as International Formula 3. I used a new Mark IV Cooper that year with our special Connolly hide upholstery — from which it was easy to wipe oil that would have stained cloth permanently — and with liberal cadmium plating. First time out at Brands we had the piston seize . . . shades of the Mark III.

I won my heat in the major 500 race supporting the British GP at the 'Royal Silverstone', but when leading the final into the last corner of the last lap I had another piston fail which let Frank Aikens' Iota-Triumph whip by to win with my crippled car just second by 0.2 sec from Peter Collins.

A week later we visited Monaco for the first time. JAP provided a new 'sloper' engine with its single cylinder leaning forward this time. It was nothing special, revving to only 5,600 instead of the normal 6,800-7,200 rpm but it had plenty of torque even then, and on such a tight circuit I was able to win regardless.

This was my first success on what would become one of my favourite Grand Prix circuits. The Monte Carlo crowd is always very close to the action. As a driver one was always conscious of their proximity, and this gave Monaco a uniquely intimate atmosphere which I found very stimulating.

I won five races in a day at Brands Hatch on 25 June, but the following month saw my first damaging crash in the HWM at Naples. Two weeks later, on my first day out of plaster, I raced the Cooper again at Brands Hatch, winning my heat but suffering gearbox trouble in the final. John Cooper lent me his spare works car to win another heat that day, but in the final it, too, failed after setting fastest lap.

It was at this point that some people began to suggest that, although I was pretty quick, I was also 'clearly' a car-breaker, a criticism which stayed with me throughout my career but which, needless to say, I emphatically deny.

Meanwhile, during 1949, Cooper drivers 'Curly' Dryden and young Peter Collins — two years my junior — had begun using twin-overhead camshaft

Norton road-racing engines instead of the usual Speedway JAP, and now into 1950 'Big Bill' Whitehouse and former motor cycle speedway star Alf Bottoms were also using Norton power and became hard to beat.

Norton themselves didn't really want to know about four-wheeled racing, and their 'double-knocker' engines were virtually unobtainable unless you were prepared to buy a complete motor cycle and cannibalize it. The Norton offered around 50 horsepower compared to something like 45 from the very best pushrod JAP, but that was a ten per cent gain, and it felt a better kind of power, more torque, smoother; more sophisticated.

As the big International Trophy Silverstone meeting approached in August, we had been trying to obtain a good Norton engine for several months. Power was vital there and, finally, just five days before the meeting, our 'double-knocker' arrived from the Bracebridge Street factory. Ray Martin was recommended to us to convert our Cooper to the new engine and he managed it just in time, even to the extent of welding-up a suitable oil tank from an old drum the night before. We were running on Shell by this time so the Castrol badge still visible on that new oil tank caused some amusement.

I hadn't even heard my Norton run before practice began, when it was fine-tuned for us by Harold Daniell of Norton TT fame and his assistant Hermann Meier. It made a fantastic difference; I set fastest time by a clear three seconds but on race day my clutch wouldn't disengage so ten minutes before the start it was all in bits.

No way could I keep the new engine running on the line, so I waited instead at the back of the grid for my father and Ray Martin to push-start me after the rest had gone. In two hectic laps I managed to take the lead and become the first 500 driver to score two victories on the full Silverstone GP circuit. I was lucky. That makeshift oil tank split, and I finished with more oil swilling around the undertray than inside the Norton's plumbing.

My 21st birthday was on the day following my first TT win at Dundrod — which was my first in any major road race — and I spent it at Brands Hatch racing the Cooper 500. Unfortunately its gearbox refused to enter into the spirit of things after I accidentally changed direct from top into first. After winning a heat, I was out.

By the end of that 1950 season I had accumulated sufficient points to win my first BRDC Gold Star as British road racing champion driver of the year. Formula 3 results accounted for a good share of those points and in some quarters I was criticized because of it. Some members of the Establishment still regarded Formula 3 with disdain, not 'proper cars' at all, but my view was that the Gold Star was there to be earned by winning motor races, and you couldn't win races unless you started in them, so what was wrong with racing in Formula 3? I was by this time a professional racing driver, and the harder I worked — which meant the more races I drove — the more I could earn. Certainly the 500 cc class had been good to me, and it would continue to be so . . . but if anybody who had never tried 500 racing believed it was *easy* to win there, I felt they were welcome to try, because it really was fiercely competitive; a terrific training ground.

We had come far from those early days. Now everything about the car set-up could be vital, purely because we had so little power to play with. Therefore any advantage one could gain in reduced rolling resistance or mechanical drag or better braking or traction could pay off handsomely. At its height 500 cc Formula 3 was a *very* demanding class.

In November 1950 my friend and business manager Ken Gregory, who also ran the Half-Litre Club and was an occasional 500 driver in his own right, invited me to join him in a Kieft record attempt at Montlhéry. Our F3 Kieft project of 1951-52 — see pages 000-000 — developed from this attempt, and when it finally ran out of steam in mid-1952 I returned to the Cooper fold.

When I made that decision two Kiefts had been virtually written-off, and my borrowed car — owned by Derek Annable — had been roundly beaten at Prescott by Les Leston's latest Cooper-Norton Mark VI. This finally convinced me I needed a Cooper again, so Ken arranged the loan of John Cooper's works car for Boreham the following Saturday.

My goggles broke there, and I was happy to salvage third place behind Alan Brown's Cooper and Don Parker's Kieft. I then drove Derek Annable's Kieft for the last time at Brands Hatch, before my first big win with John's Mark VI at Zandvoort, and another win at Turnberry in Scotland. We then took the car to the blindingly quick Grenzlandring on the German-Dutch border where I placed narrowly third. John Cooper was uncatchable in his special streamlined Cooper, while Eric Brandon's standard car just pipped me at the flag.

That was actually a fascinating experience, and possibly my most vivid memory of Formula 3. Until then I hadn't realized how economical it could be to slipstream another car. While tailing Eric I found I could back right off the throttle without losing any speed and therefore not burning very much fuel, which was a great revelation to me. Perhaps my being so enthralled by this discovery caught me out at the finish, when I just mis-timed my final lunge for the line, and Eric beat me by a short head, dammit!

I won twice more that season, at Goodwood and Castle Combe. Finally at Charterhall I was chasing John Coombs' Cooper for the lead when it lost a wheel. I spun in avoidance and had to settle for second behind Brandon — again.

In 1953 I drove nine 500 events in my own new Cooper Mark VII. Francis Beart had been preparing my Norton engines for some time, and now in the Mark VII we were burning new nitro-methane fuel which unleashed a few more vital horsepower. I was able to win at Crystal Palace, Nurburgring, the British GP supporting event and at Charterhall, and finally Castle Combe. But after winning the F3 heat there in Wiltshire, I used an 1100 JAP-twin engine in the Cooper for a *Formule Libre* event and it was then that I had my accident with Tony Rolt — see page 33.

By 1954 I was at last on the verge of genuine Formula 1 success with the Maserati 250F, but I still ran in Formula 3 because it remained highly competitive, and was fun.

Cooper had just introduced their Mark VIII all-tube chassis, but during 1953 the pace of Francis Beart's own specially modified Cooper Mark VIIA had always impressed me when driven by Alan Brown and, particularly, by Stuart Lewis-Evans. This car had a Beartized all-tube chassis, restyled bodywork, a 3-inch lower driving seat and had its engine mounted further forward. Beart and Ray Petty were most capable engineers, and I raced their ultra-light special eight

2 October 1954 — Daily Telegraph meeting, Aintree — Stirling's farewell appearance in a 500cc Formula 3 car; Francis Beart's very powerful, very light, 'Cooper-Norton Mark VIIA. Straight arms, lucky horseshoe, pole position, fastest lap and first place — typical Moss.

Stirling Moss: My cars, my career

times in 1954, winning the first four races on the trot, then two more to make it six in all, including Nürburgring again where Lewis-Evans had the wretched luck to break down when leading comfortably, almost within sight of the finish. I had been baulked badly behind another car, which I eventually displaced for second, but my eventual win at Stuart's expense was entirely fortuitous.

When it had first appeared, the Beart-Cooper's megaphone exhaust was welded to the chassis to eliminate vibration, being connected to the cylinder head via a length of flexible pipe which could easily be disconnected for engine removal. When I drove it at Aintree in May '54 we used a special new Robin Jackson cylinder head — another famous name in the British tuning world. It carried three spark-plugs but we only used two of them with dual ignition. Its new exhaust position meant we had to run a second megaphone, while leaving the original disconnected but still of course welded to the frame. This complicated-looking twin-exhaust 500 puzzled many people, and it was the quickest I ever raced, but also, as far as I was concerned, the end of the 500 line.

I drove my last 500 cc race in it at Aintree on 2 October 1954, when I was able to win again and shared fastest lap with new star Jim Russell. In all I had run the little motor cycle-engined air-cooled car in over eighty events, and had won over fifty of them, more than I could ever have dreamed possible on that distant day in 1948 when I had first driven my brand-new Cooper-JAP on the unfinished estate at Cippenham.

Cooper 1000 and 1100s (1949-53)

'In its class that car was so fast the others could hardly compete — and its acceleration was really staggering up to 100 mph . . . But so far as the chassis was concerned, I shudder to think how ignorant we were!'

*A*lmost from the start, the Cooper 500 chassis had been able to accommodate a twin-cylinder 1,000 cc engine instead of the original single-cylinder 500, enabling owners to run in serious Formula B races amongst the 2-litre unblown cars. The Cooper in this form was so fast and so nimble, that on any reasonably twisty circuit which wasn't dominated by a really long straight we could be extremely competitive. This was true at Garda in 1949, when I drove in my first Continental road race on a genuine road circuit and where I first made my mark internationally . . .

*B*y 1949 Cooper's basic 500 had evolved into their Mark III design which had cast magnesium wheels which were lighter than the cast aluminium originals, and a new combination fuel and oil tank above the engine. An extra 8½-9 gallons could be carried in a scuttle tank above the driver's legs and if necessary others could be inserted beneath the seat or slung alongside in a pannier. The seat back was raked to give more cockpit space and for those who wanted to fit a 1,000 cc twin-cylinder engine there was a stretched-wheelbase chassis option.

Three cars had been fitted with 1,000 cc twin-cylinder engines the previous year, and now my father and I ordered one of these improved Mark III chassis. We closely followed Cooper's progress on our car, which was to be fitted with rack-and-pinion steering, an improved bucket seat and pannier tanks.

The Vincent-HRD Black Lightning engine was at that time the most potent 1,000 available but they wouldn't sell us one. Stan Greening of J. A. Prestwich let us have an alternative 1,000 with dry-sump lubrication. It was worth about £200 and Stan also promised spares support. Dad then talked Dunlop, Mobiloil and Lodge into offering a small retainer each, plus result bonuses. We acquired a Bedford van transporter, and with the alternative 500 and 1,000 cc JAP engines for our new 'two-way' Cooper we planned a full 1949 season, which would include my first Continental outings.

We changed engines between races on the new car's debut at Easter Goodwood, where I beat George Abecassis' sister Cooper-Vincent-HRD to win a handicap event.

Gregor Grant — who founded the weekly racing magazine *Autosport* the following year — wrote in the 500 Club journal *Iota*: *'Stirling Moss' . . . runaway win in the handicap event with the Cooper 1000 proved conclusively that the Berkshire lad is approaching the star class. Apart from Reg Parnell, there was nobody to come anywhere near young Moss for sheer handling skill. There was a touch of Rosemeyer in the way he tackled the tricky Woodcote Corner; the same fire and certainty that the car was always under control. The only criticism that I can make is that young Stirling still has a fondness for racing gear-changes, which are essential in sprints, but play merry hell with the transmission in actual racing. The TT boys in the top class don't go in for the straight-through-throttle-wide-open stuff, unless they are risking everything on saving split seconds for an outright win . . .'*

I can only claim that that is precisely what I was doing . . . and it paid off.

The JAP twin was really a very simple engine, extremely easy to maintain in the field. It had steel cylinder barrels, but weighed only 125 lb, which allowed the car to be very light overall and well-balanced. It's a tribute to the stability of Cooper's original concept that the same chassis could perform as well as a 40-horsepower 500 as it could with twice that power in 1,000 trim. The twin-cylinder engine was obviously much smoother than the vibratory single. It was ostensibly air-cooled by the flow of air round its finned barrels, but really just like the 500 single it was effectively liquid-cooled by the alcohol fuel which we cascaded through it. Carburettor jets were enormous for this reason.

We added big air scoops each side of the engine cover to ensure adequate cooling flow, but I remember that when the engine broke behind me one day the smoke came billowing forwards out of these supposed 'intakes' when I was travelling at quite high speed. We really were blundering around in a black art there.

The 1,000's extra power meant that I had to learn about proper throttle control for the first time. Rather unexpectedly the hard-pressed gearbox — which was common to both 500 and 1,000 — remained reliable. This was probably because with the larger engine I now had sufficient torque to cut out some gear-changes. I no longer had to work hard with the gear-lever to keep within the narrower rev range of the 500 single.

After Goodwood, we sailed to the Isle of Man for the Manx Cup on the Douglas circuit and I charged away from the field, only for the magneto drive to shear with three laps still to go . . . I broke the Shelsley hill-climb record, climbing in 38.57 sec with the 1,000, and then set off in great anticipation for Garda.

This first Continental foray was a real eye-opener for me. I was still only 19 and this was my first race on a proper Continental road circuit. A tricky and demanding one it was, too, passing through villages as it rose and fell through the hills. I was up against Villoresi, Tadini and Count Sterzi in V12 Ferraris, although they were in the larger class. I managed third fastest time overall in practice — quicker than Tadini — and then placed third in the final behind the surviving two Ferraris after Sterzi had crashed, my Cooper finishing four minutes ahead of the second-placed 1,100 cc car . . .

The Italian crowd gave me a fantastic reception. They were fascinated by our spidery-looking air-cooled Cooper and for some reason they christened it *The Jukebox*, which I suppose was an in-word at the time, rather like *Sputnik* a few years later.

I won £200, which was my first experience of really worthwhile start and prize money, and believe me it was a large sum for those days . . . This really was the next logical step in my development from being an enthusiastic amateur towards proper professionalism. In fact the Italian motor racing establishment accepted me after that performance, whereas at home I tended still to be regarded with something approaching suspicion. It seemed that many influential

10 July 1949 — IX Circuito del Garda — Stirling's introduction to full-scale European road racing and he took to it like a duck to water in the 'two-way' Cooper-JAP 1,000. Here before the start the Mark III displays its anodized pale-green finish, long-range tank, added seat support and engine cooling 'ears'; Stirling, his body belt, and 'COOPER'-lettered overalls, with that coveted BRDC badge just below the breast pocket.

people believed I drove on too fine an edge to be quite acceptable . . .

We ran the 1,000 at Reims in sweltering heat but the conventional 1100s overwhelmed it on the long straights there and it quickly broke a chain.

When we had first considered the car, we reckoned on a dry weight of 620 lb and an output of 84 bhp, giving a power-to-weight ratio of 303 horsepower per ton. According to contemporary publicity, Ferrari's 2-litre V12 weighed 1,294 lb and developed 140 bhp, so in comparison its power-to-weight ratio was a measly 242 bhp per ton. At that rate we should have left any Ferrari for dead. In practice, this may well have been true under acceleration up to about 100 mph, but frontal area and drag in aerodynamic terms meant that no 100 horsepower car weighing half-a-ton could ever keep up with a 200 horsepower car weighing one ton unless it also had half the frontal area, or about twice the cornering power. So the Cooper 1,000 had a real advantage low-down on initial acceleration, but on any decent straight, and on top-end acceleration, and ultimately around a complete race-circuit lap as at Garda and particularly at Reims, the more conventional contemporary Ferraris would always leave us for dead.

On the way home from Reims I finished third at Bouley Bay, Jersey, which put me into third place in the RAC British Hill-Climb Championship, a position I held to the end of the season.

At Zandvoort, we put the 1,000 engine into the car for me to practise for the major Dutch Grand Prix. I hoped the organizers would let me start in it but they would not, so we re-worked the engine as a 'sloper' 500 and I won the supporting event after bowling over John Habin's mechanic on the startline. I felt sure I'd killed him — he stepped straight in front of me as I took off and was thrown way up into the air. But apart from being somewhat shocked he survived unscathed.

In August we raced at Lausanne in Switzerland where engine trouble ended another good run, but the organizers awarded me a Gold Cup 'for the most meritorious performance'. Back home I set a new Prescott hill-climb record at 44.77 sec and then won my final two events of the season, the Madgwick Cup at Goodwood and the Shelsley hill-climb, where I lowered my June time by 0.38 sec.

Into 1950, John Heath and George Abecassis gave me a Formula 2 drive in their new HWM team, so our hybrid Cooper twin became redundant. J. A. Prestwich developed an enlarged 1,097 cc dry-sump '1100' version which others would use and which would ultimately dominate the British hill-climb and sprint scene. Meantime we sold our 'two-way' Cooper to Jim Burgoyne, and bought a new Mark V for 500 cc Formula 3.

I would not use an air-cooled JAP twin engine again until the final meeting of 1953, at Castle Combe, where I felt that it could make the Formula 3 Cooper chassis a good bet for the *Formule Libre* race. Alf Francis, who was my mechanic by that time, wasn't at all keen and wanted me to use my Formula 2 Cooper-Alta instead, because he felt the smaller car would be vulnerable amongst the heavy cars under braking.

He was absolutely right. I briefly held the lead, and then as I braked hard for Quarry Corner the Cooper slowed with its usual efficiency but that proved too much for the braking ability of Rob Walker's Connaught, which was right behind me driven by Tony Rolt. He was taken by surprise and was quite unable to avoid running into me, which sent my little Cooper somersaulting off the road. It threw me out on the way. I picked myself up and ran to safety before collapsing with a broken shoulder, damaged arm and twisted knee.

My twin-cylinder Cooper career thus ended with me in Bristol Hospital, followed by physiotherapy under Dr Philip Bauwens at St Thomas's in London. I was able to drive my automatic Jaguar Mark VII five days after the shunt, but it took 12 weeks for the fracture and muscle-tissue to heal, which was a bore . . . something the cars themselves had never been.

3 October 1953 — Joe Fry Memorial Formule Libre race, Castle Combe. Stirling cuts past Tony Rolt's Rob Walker-owned Connaught in pursuit of Bob Gerard's Cooper-Bristol. The Connaught clips the Mark VII Cooper-JAP 1100 which somersaults, throwing its driver on to the verge. His shoulder broken, Stirling instinctively runs clear. That photographer taking avoiding action is Geoff Goddard who took many of the shots in these pages . . . but missed this incident.

'Offset-seat' HWM (1950)

'I learned more about racing in HWMs than in virtually all my other cars put together. The great thing about the original HWM was that it was so stable and so forgiving that one could over-drive it to a quite ridiculous degree, and it would respond by giving quicker lap times than seemed remotely possible on paper . . .!'

*T*hese cars in which I began road racing seriously in Europe were created by John Heath and George Abecassis, partners in Hersham & Walton Motors at Walton-on-Thames. In 1950, John and George not only gave me my very first professional works team drive, they also introduced me to top-level European racing and to an entirely new and dazzling sporting world whose surface I had formerly barely scratched.

I learned an enormous amount about driving from these HWMs, and almost as much about living from my older and widely-experienced team-mate Lance Macklin! The team and its cars thus played a profound role in my development as a racing driver, and have a very special place in my affections.

*H*eath and Abecassis were both enthusiastic drivers, George being the more capable in a racing car. He had made his name immediately pre-war in an Alta built at Tolworth by Geoffrey Taylor.

Post-war the partners raced and sprinted various Altas and a magnificent Type 59 Bugatti, and then in 1948 John built himself an Alta-engined enveloping-bodied sports special. He replaced it for 1949 with the cycle-winged 2-litre Alta-engined HW-Alta which was so successful — including some Continental races — that for 1950 he laid down a full team of three broadly similar cars using the same four-cylinder engine, and he named them HWMs after his motor business's initials.

At the end of that season, Denis Jenkinson of *Motor Sport* wrote in his annual *Racing Car Review*: *'The team of HWM cars has appeared at the majority of Formula II races, and has invariably given a very good account of itself and has always been a worthy representative of this country. Pronounced as 'harsh doobler-vay em' by the continentals, these neat green cars have made an impressive sight wherever they have appeared . . . To see a full team of three English racing cars on the starting line of the major Formula II events has been most heart-warming and every possible congratulations must be given to John Heath and his team for making a very praiseworthy attempt to get Britain's name on the motor racing map . . .'*

The HWMs had all-independent transverse leaf spring suspensions using Standard 12 front wishbones and hubs. Their offset-seat body could be rigged with cycle mudguards and lights for sports car events, or stripped to run in 2-litre Formula 2. John actually had an entry for Le Mans, but as the season developed it could not be fitted into the programme and so was dropped and the cars never did compete in sports car form that year.

Their twin-cam Alta four-cylinder engine gave around 140 bhp at 5,500 rpm, and drove through an Armstrong-Siddeley pre-selector gearbox. Its gear-change was a simple steering column stalk operating in a quadrant. The driver simply selected the next gear he would require and once the selection had been made he could engage it when needed merely by kicking the clutch pedal. This left both hands free to steer the car under braking and cornering. This system had appeared in ERAs and MGs pre-war, and I found it an advantage on tight and twisty circuits where the disadvantages of its weight and power-absorption were minimized.

I had first been invited to test one of these new HWMs at Odiham aerodrome in the winter of 1949-50. It was bitterly cold. George drove first and promptly spun off — typical George, but in fact the car was not set-up properly; it was a handful.

Tall John Heath appreciated this and implored me to take care as I trundled off, feeling most uncomfortable. The car felt bulky and heavy, very strange compared to my tiny Coopers. Then suddenly there was a terrific thump underneath, I'd hit a runway light and smashed the sump!

After the initial dismay John was very decent about it, and he and George signed me on for — as I recall — 25 per cent of 'my' car's start and prize money.

I made my HWM début on 10 April 1950, at Easter Monday Goodwood. The new car's handling had been transformed by raising its steering box to correct a geometry fault. It still felt big compared to the Coopers, but against any other sports car I had ever driven it was very light, nimble and quick.

We ran two cars in several short races that day. George had a punctured carburettor float sink and John spun in the first, but I then drove the latter's car in a five-lap *Formule Libre* event alongside George and we finished sixth and seventh amongst F1 cars, the irrepressible George having spun again.

He retired from the F1 race after running fifth and then I reappeared in Heath's car for the Third Easter handicap, finishing second behind Duncan Hamilton's Maserati.

Heath's chief mechanic was a Polish ex-serviceman named Kovaleski who had adopted the English name 'Alf Francis'. He was amazingly inventive and resourceful, and would play a major role in my career, long after HWM's demise.

Our first Continental trip was to Montlhéry for the Prix de Paris on 30 April, where I ran third until my Alta engine broke a con rod. George also retired so HWM retreated in temporary defeat . . .

They found my broken rod had been cracked for some time but since the crack hadn't grown the rod had simply been rebuilt into the Montlhéry engine. The partners would not let that happen again.

We reappeared at Mons in Belgium, running the three team cars plus a sister which had been sold to 'Buster' Baring. They were all wrongly geared, but we finished 6-7-8-9 with the Belgian Grand Prix driver Johnny Claes ahead of me, then Heath and Baring. Obviously Claes could command good start money from the Belgian clubs, and this was the way John would run the team, fielding a local driver whenever possible to attract good money.

Johnny Claes then notched our first win in the *GP des Frontières* at Chimay, while John Heath and I ran two other cars at Aix-les-Bains, without success. I had stupidly enjoyed the local gateaux too enthusiastically and poisoned myself. I managed to drive in one heat but my car failed and John — who was not a very fast driver — did little better.

I had really been looking forward to the Swiss GP on the tremendous Bremgarten circuit, but I developed some form of jaundice and missed the trip. I wasn't doing very well . . .

Then, fortunately, I redeemed myself in the Rome GP at the Baths of Caracalla circuit, teamed with Heath and the Swiss driver Rudi Fischer who had driven 'my' HWM at Berne. I was delighted to re-establish myself, and the HWM's agile handling, good Alfin drum brakes and pre-selector gearbox were all well suited to the Roman circuit. It had become an extremely stable and forgiving car, good fun to drive and in fact it allowed one to 'over-drive' it fearfully hard to compensate for its relative lack of power. It you did that, it would respond by lapping faster than — by any sensible standards — it really should.

This enabled me to give the works Ferraris of Ascari and Villoresi quite a fright, which was marvellous because one was driving close enough to the crowds to sense their excitement. HWM versus Ferrari was rather like Christians versus the lions all over again, if essentially as one-sided. This was a different world from driving in tiddly little five or ten-lap races on one of the bleak aerodrome circuits at home. Here in Europe we were racing over 200 miles or more, between tall kerbs, trees, walls, houses and people, with yellow straw bales or pole-and-sandbag barriers leaving no margin for error. It taught precise driving and prevented the novice from developing the bad and untidy driving habits that he might get away with on an airfield.

I had a wonderful time dicing against the Ferraris in that Rome GP. But I was running third and had set fastest lap when a front stub axle snapped and I lost its expensive Borrani wire wheel complete with brake drum, and skated to rest on the other three wheels.

After my Garda appearance the previous year in the Cooper, this performance cemented my growing reputation in Italy. We would race there three times more that year, and every time we were very warmly received, as a little British team doing a competent job with modest equipment.

At Reims, myself, John Heath and Lance Macklin finished 3-4-5 on a very fast circuit for which HWM's sports car sized bodies and modest engines were far from ideal. Alf Francis and the mechanics then had to haul the cars back over the Alps, way down to Bari where, after our showing in Rome, the local club had invited us to run against the works Alfa Romeos in their F1 race the following weekend.

We followed in John's beloved Citroen Light 15, and after enormous dramas, which included one of the trucks getting lost in darkest Italy and then a fire in our garage at Bari, Lance, Fischer and I still got to the start on time.

After all the dramas I was well pumped-up, and as Jenks wrote at the time '. . . *Moss drove as he had never driven before, chasing two 158 Alfa Romeos for the whole race and finishing third only some three minutes behind, after racing for nearly 200 miles. In doing this Moss had outpaced the rest of the field, which included 4½-litre Talbots, Formula 2 Ferraris and 4CLT Maseratis . . .'*

I feel to some degree I was lucky, because the other HWMs retired, but that was my first wheel-to-wheel meeting with the top contemporary Formula 1 teams, and I was thrilled with that result. The only way it could have been better would have been for me to be driving a British Grand Prix car capable of matching the Alfas horsepower for horsepower.

The Naples GP followed on the very tight and twisty Posillipo street circuit, ideal for our cars. The opposition came from short-chassis F2 Ferraris which could not exploit their power advantage there, and I was able to lead Rudi Fischer's sister car to finish 1-2 in our heat — my first F2 win and my first for HWM — while Lance was second in his heat.

Just before the start of the final, Alf noticed my car was leaking water. I decided I'd have to build sufficient lead to top-up the radiator in a pit stop, but as Cortese led in his Ferrari I was baulked behind a slower runner and could not get by. Lance closed on to my tail, before we both managed to barge ahead.

We then caught and passed Cortese and were running comfortably 1-2 when I came up behind Berardo Taraschi, a back-marker in his supercharged 750 cc Giaur. He had seen me and waved me by on the outside as he pulled over in a very fast curve. But just as my HWM's front wheel came alongside the Giaur's tail, it broke away and slid out and his hub cap burst my tyre. The HWM had been balanced in a drift so I now completely lost control and rammed a sturdy tree at about 85 mph.

It was my first bad crash . . .

My knee was broken against the dash and I knocked out two teeth and broke two more against the mirror mounting. I had an almost sub-conscious memory of reading about Dick Seaman's death at Spa in 1939, sitting stunned in his crashed Mercedes as it caught fire. Now I jumped from the HWM almost by reflex, and ran a couple of yards before collapsing.

Lance had seen me crash, and let Cortese through to win while Fischer retired so John Heath ended that day with one driver second but another in hospital.

Back home, Reuters press agency informed my father that I had crashed and he flew out and took me back to England with my broken knee in plaster. As a practising dentist he fixed-up my teeth in his own surgery.

For the next couple of weeks I drove my Morris Minor with a hand clutch and with my plastered leg parked on the passenger's seat, before beginning to race again the moment the plaster was removed.

I rejoined HWM at Silverstone in August, teamed with Fergus Anderson, the

Above *26 August 1950 —
Goggles down in a despairing
attempt to see which way the
road goes during the BRDC
International Trophy race at
Silverstone, Stirling hammers
on in the 'educational' HWM.
Despite his expression he
still manages to look
relaxed.*

Right *15 October 1950 —
High above Lake Garda, the
HWM is about to snap one of
its desperately over-worked
front stub axles and throw a
wheel. Racing on such roads,
lined by massive marker
posts, trees, drops, walls and
houses, taught Moss precision
and sharpened his fine
judgement.*

racing motor cyclist. He finished seventh in his heat, I was fourth in mine, soaked by rain because in the 1950 HWM one sat right in the firing line of spray from its offside front wheel.

Dad borrowed a visor for me to wear in the final. After goggles it seemed like wearing a bay window! Conditions were atrocious for the final but amongst the F1 field I managed to finish sixth . . . which pleased me and impressed some good people.

Tommy Wisdom for one made the fabulous offer of his recently-introduced Jaguar XK120 for the Tourist Trophy race at Dundrod and two days before that important opportunity Lance and I drove our HWMs at Mettet in Belgium, facing four 2-litre Ferraris including Ascari and Serafini, and a flock of the little French Gordinis. It was wet again, conditions which never particularly bothered either of us, and we finished 4-5 in heat one and then 1-2 in heat two, the Ferraris having broken under pressure. On aggregate time, however, Robert Manzon won for Gordini with our HWMs placed second and third.

After the TT win, also in the rain, we returned to Formula 2 with HWM at Perigueux in France, where again the Ferraris failed and Manzon's Gordini won from Andre Simon's with me third.

At Goodwood, I finished seventh, and then managed to beat Ken Wharton's blown 1½-litre ERA in a 2-litre racing car event at Castle Combe before returning to Garda in Italy. There, unfortunately, I had another stub axle break and this time the wheel flew off and knocked a hole in a new wall, whose irate Italian owner refused to return HWM's wheel until HWM arranged to repair his wall!

Lance had hurt himself there in a practice crash, so our acting team manager Tony Hume raced the hastily repaired car, simply to guarantee its start money. Afterwards as we began to push this car to the truck, Tony suggested I should perhaps have driven it instead of my own which had just lost a wheel 'as it would have been safer'. At that moment one of its front wheels fell off! Another stub axle had snapped . . .

At the London Motor Show, John, Lance and I visited suppliers and prospective sponsors, looking forward to 1951. I remember John talking to somebody from Standard, telling him that their Vanguard stub axles were too fragile, and could they supply better? This turned out to be the man who had designed them, and he protested that they could not possibly break, whereupon John produced a snapped-off stub from his coat pocket and proved his point!

In fact we had been subjecting these components to far greater cornering loads than they had ever been intended for, so it wasn't really fair — but it was amusing. You should have seen that engineer's face as John produced the evidence!

Cooper-MG *(1950)*

'This was the first front-engined, water-cooled Cooper that I ever raced — pre-dating the Cooper-Altas by a couple of years — but I drove it in only one five-lapper at Goodwood and, do you know, I can't recall a thing about it . . .'

17 June 1950 — BARC Goodwood meeting — Moss's first true sports car race, but a terribly minor one, in John Cooper's under-powered works prototype Cooper-MG. See the company's trade-plate, '307 PD'.

John Cooper had built a light but conventional prototype sports car during the winter of 1948-49, using a 48 bhp Vauxhall Ten 4-cylinder engine mounted up front. This Cooper-Vauxhall had quite a pretty cycle-wing body, but when it proved under-powered John spent part of the 1949-1950 winter uprating the basic concept to carry a 1,250 cc MG engine, tuned to produce around 75 bhp. The archives tell me I was invited to drive his new factory prototype Cooper-MG in a BARC Members' meeting at Goodwood on 17 June 1950, but it wasn't in very good form and I could only finish fifth — though it cleared its throat just long enough for me to set fastest lap, at 74.5 mph. John took over for a five-lap handicap later that day, actually wearing my crash helmet, and he finished second and again set fastest lap. I expect it was quite an agile and nice-handling little car, in the best Cooper tradition, but under-powered like all the MG-engined specials of that period . . .

Jaguar XK120 (1950-52)

'A stunningly beautiful road car which gave me enormous pride in the vehicle; a sensational new twin-overhead camshaft engine . . . In 1950 it was the epitome of British excellence . . .'

*T*hese cars were absolute stunners when they were first announced. It's difficult these days to describe the impact they had. In 1948 life generally was grey, and then at the London Motor Show we saw a flood of new cars with this breathtaking twin-overhead camshaft sports Jaguar the star.

What impressed me most was its sheer beauty. I think all the William Lyons Jaguars have been really beautiful, and the XK120 made such an impact that everybody wanted one but they were nearly all for export so you couldn't buy one for love nor money. Because of this, being given the chance to drive such an exclusive car in my first big long-distance race when I was still only 20 gave me a marvellous charge . . .

I vividly remember the enormous pride I felt in the vehicle, even though my subsequent experience of racing them proved some of the limitations of racing a road car. It had quite soft, long-travel suspension, a lot of smooth power for the time and though people have since criticized its gearbox, steering and brakes, believe me they were all good enough by the standards of their time!

Despite its considerable weight, the XK120 never handled heavily. You had to show it who was master sometimes as it tended to lift its inside rear wheel and wag its tail under power, but it was — and remains — a particularly special car for me . . .

*T*owards the end of 1950 I had driven my own Cooper and John Heath's HWMs in some 19 events. I had won 11 times and finished second in three more. The RAC Tourist Trophy was being revived, at Dundrod on Ulster on 16 September. Dundrod was a superb, very daunting public road circuit which was being used for the first time. To me it became one of the world's finest driver's circuits.

I was desperate to drive in the TT but no manufacturer wanted to know. They probably feared I would have an accident and bring them bad publicity, because here in Britain I was perhaps regarded as driving too quickly for my own good, even though my only accident thus far had been plainly through no fault of my own. I tried Aston Martin, Jaguar, even down to MGs, for a TT drive, but nobody would give me a car.

Tommy Wisdom was motoring correspondent of *The Daily Herald*. He and his wife had both driven at Brooklands pre-war, and he still raced sports cars as often as he could. He knew my parents and had seen me race, and he had more faith. He called one day to say he'd been offered a Jowitt Jupiter for the TT and that his personal XK120 'JWK 958' — one of a batch of six works-prepared cars with aluminium (not steel) bodies, all but one of which had been sold to selected owner-drivers — was vacant. Would I like to drive it at Dundrod? He said 'It's a sensational car, you drive it and we'll go 50/50 if you win anything'. I said 'You bet.'

This was a wonderful opportunity, really quite fantastic, and fortunately I made the most of it.

Tom persuaded Jaguar to lend me a blue XK120 for a few days prior to the race so I could get to know it. I raced the HWM at Mettet in Belgium then flew straight to Belfast for my first look at Dundrod. Practice began on wet roads following a cloudburst and Leslie Johnson set fastest time in his sister XK120 'JWK 651', lapping in 5:39.0. I managed 6:05 and felt very depressed. I told Leslie 'It's no good, I just can't go any faster . . .' He just grinned and told me 'You'll go faster,' and do you know I did . . .

Next day in the dry I clocked 5:28, 81.39 mph, which was five per cent faster than my RAC handicap time. It was most unusual for a big car to equal its handicap, never mind exceed it, but Norman Culpan's Le Mans Frazer Nash had

16 September 1950 — The day before his 21st birthday saw Stirling win his first major International sports car race — the RAC Tourist Trophy at Dundrod. Here he is in Tommy Wisdom's special XK120, lapping John Buncombe's HRG. This shot typifies Dundrod — Moss grew to love it.

bettered its handicap by 3.6 per cent, and my HWM team-mate Lance Macklin had just shaved his Aston Martin's given time by 0.6 per cent . . . it looked like a good competition.

Just before the start a real downpour began, driven by a howling gale, which lasted throughout the three-hour race. Leslie led, but I passed him on the second lap and just drew away to win. Racing in the rain never really bothered me as much as it did some drivers, and with the Jaguar I feel it was a positive advantage because it lightened the steering and saved the brakes.

The gale blew down the press tent, and I had such a long lead I was able to ease back a little until on the penultimate lap my father in the pits heard a rumour — untrue as it turned out — that Bob Gerards' Nash had caught me on handicap. I suddenly saw him signalling me to go all out on the last lap which I didn't really understand but I managed to raise the lap record that time round to 77.61 mph. And then we'd won . . .

Peter Whitehead's XK 'HKV 500' — another in that special private owner-driver batch — was second on speed and handicap and Leslie Johnson third on speed but only seventh on handicap.

It had been my first real sports car race, on a really daunting road circuit, and I had led most of the way and won in pouring rain. It was the most worthwhile race I'd won at that time. It was worth about £1,400 in prize and bonus money, quite something in 1950, and it really launched my professional career. That evening Bill Lyons asked me to lead his Jaguar works team for 1951.

Leslie Johnson was keen to compensate for Jaguar's XK120 débâcle at Le Mans where the works cars had all gone out with brake and clutch troubles. He persuaded Bill Heynes, the chief engineer, to prepare 'JWK 651' for a 24-hour record attempt at Montlhéry Autodrome that October, and invited me to co-drive. Our target was 100 mph for 24 hours, and we managed it, averaging 107.46 mph, putting 112.40 miles into the last hour, and Leslie lapping the banked speedbowl at a best of 126 mph. We shared three-hour stints, and for the thirteen hours of darkness had only the car's head- and spotlights to show the way. It's amazing how short headlight beams become on a steeply banked speedway!

The following April I had my first works Jaguar drive in another '120, this time in a really serious road race — the Mille Miglia . . . Italy's one-lap thousand-mile race was a daunting prospect. You couldn't possibly learn the course, you just had to attack it like a rally special stage and go as hard as you dare, realistically driving at, say, seven- or eight-tenths maximum effort, all the way.

I drove 'HKV 500' and my diary for 29 April 1951, read: *'Today is Mille Miglia day so up at 3 am. Cold and wet. Went to start, tremendous set-up, with thousands of bods organizing things. Pouring rain when I left at 4.32 am, 3 minutes after Leslie Johnson. Caught the Ferrari saloon which started 1 minute ahead in about 4 miles. Car going well considering, getting along at about 115 mph, in darkness! Then after 15 miles it happened. Chap waved me down, applied brakes, nothing happened, turned wheel, same effect. On oil! Hit Fiat which Leslie and Ascari had done, and bent wing on to wheel. Went to garage and reversed, gearbox jammed in reverse, took 2 hours to repair. Also bonnet wouldn't close, so had to retire, damn it.'*

Back home I won in the first steel-bodied '120 'JWK 675', with a 196-horsepower engine, at the big *Daily Express* Silverstone meeting and then for Le Mans that year the aerodynamic-bodied spaceframe-chassised C-Types appeared — and no longer were we trying to race production road cars . . .

I rallied an XK120 with Gregor Grant, Editor of *Autosport* in the 1952 Lyon-Charbonnières; inconsequential fun which earned a second in class. Then at May Silverstone the BRDC organized what they called 'The Race of The Champions' which involved six new and supposedly identical XK120s, for which Johnny Claes, Prince Bira, 'Toulo' de Graffenreid, Paul Pietsch, Tony Gaze and I — representing Belgium, Siam, Switzerland, Germany, Australia and Great Britain — drew lots. We were given just enough practice to get the feel of the cars and then raced for five laps. Three of my rivals had made their names racing pre-war. I had a fairly easy win . . .

Then in mid-summer Leslie Johnson had another of his ideas. Having averaged 100 mph for 24 hours at Montlhéry he now talked Jaguar into attempting 100 mph for a week!

We used an XK120 Coupé, Leslie and I sharing the driving with Jack Fairman and Bert Hadley, the pre-war Austin OHC Racer star. We again drove in three-hour spells. The speedbowl lap was under a minute at 120 mph, so it was quite a strain. After each straight we hit the banking high up near the lip, then plunged off, twice every fifty seconds, night and day. In each spell we would cover about 200 laps. It was impossible to keep one's mind occupied on a job like that. We had a two-way radio which helped keep boredom at bay. We talked all the time, called each other names, even told stories.

5 May 1951 — BRDC Silverstone 'May Meeting' — Moss masters the 1-Hour production sports car race, helping Jaguar to take the Team prize with this, the first steel-bodies XK120.

One dare not let the mind wander, because we were running within four feet of the banking lip at around 120 mph. One had to concentrate on something. I worked out how many million revs the engine made in a day, how many times the wheels turned, things like that.

The weather did not help; hot by day, cold at night. Night driving was a strain, too, because we couldn't afford the drain on the battery of extra lights. The headlights had to be set very high to let us see the top of the banking when we were on it, and this meant that on the short straights we could see nothing at all because the beams were playing in the air.

We hit several hares, rabbits and birds, and Leslie swore at one point that he'd seen a huge ten-foot tall figure in a long cloak, wearing a tall pointed hat, striding towards him along the verge. Next time round the figure had gone . . .

It worried the life out of him for the rest of his stint.

In fact I had donned a Shell fuel funnel, pulled a tarpaulin around me and sat on Jack Fairman's shoulders as he strode along the verge. After Leslie had whizzed by we ran away and hid . . . All very childish, but good fun in the circumstances. Leslie then had an extraordinary idea to get his own back during one of my stints. I came whistling off the banking to find him sitting with Jack Fairman in the middle of the track, playing cards!

Then he took the pit signal board and put it out on the track, so that my natural line past the pits took me between it and the timekeeper's hut. He was lounging beside the hut so I waved to him as I shot through the gap.

Next time round the board had been moved closer to the hut. The gap was narrower, but I couldn't leave the fast line so I shot through it again. Next time round, he'd moved the board closer still. Each lap he narrowed the gap which made me concentrate harder to pass through it. Eventually he gave in, and the board went back to its proper position, hung on the hut. At least it passed the time . . .

The run ended on 5 August and the timekeepers confirmed that we had covered 16,851.73 miles at an average of 100.31 mph. This proved indelibly the stamina and speed of that beautiful Jaguar, and apart from a final fun run in another Coupé in the RAC Rally that November it was the last time I drove an XK120 in anger — a car which I recall with admiration, and gratitude.

12 August 1952 — Montlhéry Autodrome, Paris — The bronze XK120 Coupe after completing its seven-day run. Left to right on car are Bert Hadley, Leslie Johnson, SM and Jack Fairman, team manager 'Mort' Morris-Goodall is in shirt-sleeves behind, along with David MacDonald — 'Dunlop Mac' — in braces, hand on car. Jaguar importer Delecroix is on the extreme right.

Driving Techniques 1

Learning by Experience

Right at the start of my driving career I was really the greenest of green novices. I was terribly young, my experience even of normal road driving had been limited and virtually the only things going for me were — I suppose — my naturally competitive nature and a fair degree of athleticism. Perhaps crucially my eyesight, co-ordination and reflexes were all pretty good.

Now, looking back forty years to my earliest drives in the BMW 328, I remember having what today seems like an inordinately low threshold of fear. I never really approached that car's cornering limit because I believed that if it skidded, or even worse spun, then it must surely overturn. I simply did not appreciate that most relatively low-built competition cars will only roll over if they hit an obstacle or are tripped up by something like a kerb or a soft verge or ditch.

I had minimal experience of driving hard on the public road. It wasn't really suitable and I never really tried to explore the cornering limits of any of my early cars — the Morgan, MG or BMW. I do not believe I have ever been a reckless driver (despite what the occasional magistrates' bench may subsequently have concluded to the contrary!), but in those earliest days bravery was not my strong suit.

When I progressed to the Cooper, I realized several things. Firstly, there was so little power to play with I had to make best use of what there was. That meant trying to keep the car tracking comfortably along the line of least resistance, minimizing power-absorbing tyre-scrub, over as much of the course as possible. I also appreciated that I should only interrupt the delivery of power to the rear wheels as briefly as possible when gear-changing — hence the 'racey' straight-through changes for which I was often criticized during those early 500 days. The older experts would all shake their heads gravely and say 'Young Moss will never learn — he will break his car driving it like that . . .,' but in fact we had very little gearbox trouble, and the fractions saved on each gear-change quickly added up into winning times.

Nobody ever coached me — as such — in driving technique.

My father gave me some general advice. I watched some of the other chaps, the good ones like Eric Brandon, but above all I simply soaked up experience. Even then, it was all on a very inconsequential level until 1949 when we first took the Cooper 1,000 abroad — particularly to Garda — and I had my first taste of full-blown Continental road racing. Then John Heath and George Abecassis invited me to join HWM for a full European season in 1950 and that was like being taken from infants' school and hurled straight into university!

I found myself driving a proper racing car behind a sizeable water-cooled genuine car engine mounted in a really substantial chassis with a far-back cockpit. I was racing mainly on public roads which had merely been closed and barricaded against normal traffic for the race weekend, and they were lined with all the natural hazards of the open road — houses, trees, telegraph poles, bridges, walls and ditches, sometimes a river or even the sea!

Back home the British vogue for using aerodrome perimeter track and runway circuits was just beginning, but I was already aware of just how hard you could drive on such a course with very little chance of getting hurt should you over-cook it. The wide open spaces around those aerodrome circuits taught many British drivers bad habits. Boy, did they have to un-learn them rapidly the instant they ventured on to the Continent! Some could never adjust to the hazards they found on genuine road circuits, and consequently they were never as quick there as they might be at, say, Silverstone or Snetterton.

Another awful thing for British racing was so many organizers' insistence upon running even quite major races over piddling little distances of five, eight, or maybe twelve laps. Though such races were good for the public, they didn't do much to advance a driver's development. On the Continent we were virtually just warming up as the 100-mile mark went by . . .

Fortunately, HWM took me abroad before I might have developed any aerodrome-racing bad habits, and after being thrown in at the deep end at the likes of Naples, Bari and Mons I took to proper road circuits and their obvious hazards like a duck to water. I had sufficient confidence in my own abilities to convince myself that no way would I slide wide enough to hit that tree or that wall. I made damn sure I did not, while otherwise driving just as fast as I possibly could, and obviously to my great delight I discovered that on most circuits I could lap competitively with the HWM while keeping that kind of margin in hand.

Rather like the little Cooper 500s, the HWM had no power to spare so keeping it neat and avoiding power-absorbing slides paid real dividends. Fortunately the HWM chassis handled quite well and it enabled me to 'overdrive' those cars terribly hard but in a balanced way which paid off — both short-term for myself and the team but very significantly long-term in my development of a smooth and fluent driving style which I found to be the quickest way . . . And the sheer racing mileage we accumulated meant I learned a great deal in a short time.

I believe that about the only bit of hard advice I was given during this formative period was merely a warning to 'watch out for Farina'.

He was certainly very tough, he was Italian, they didn't wear crash hats, and had a reputation for being forceful and literally 'pushy' at the least provocation. You could see it by looking at him — he simply looked mean and hard as nails. He had been racing since the early '30s, was already deeply scarred from countless racing accidents, and he had obviously come up the hard way. No kid — particularly no *English* kid — was going to get any help from him!

At Bari, he and Fangio lapped my HWM in their works *Alfettas,* Farina going by first in a corner, out of which he then ran rather wide towards the straw bales. This forced him to back off, but my HWM was well on song so I promptly aimed up the inside with my foot hard down and repassed him. He got pretty upset about that, and after sorting himself out went booming past properly, leaving me in his dust, but Fangio had been right behind him and had seen what had happened and as he shot past on Farina's tail we glanced across at each other and I saw he was laughing like a drain!

Farina had not shunted me, but then by the standards of his *Alfetta* I was not a competitor. I was still rather in awe of these people. I had met Nuvolari at Garda; by then he was quite old, but I knew perfectly well who and what he was, the Fangio of his era, and I certainly held him in total awe.

Now I was beginning to hone my technique by driving in company with the Italian stars, even though with the HWM we could not really hope to keep pace with them except on the most favourable of circuits.

Perhaps the most useful legacy of this road racing training affected my braking technique. I learned very quickly not to rely upon trackside markers as braking points. One might choose something prominent as a braking mark only to find it had been moved next time round. Therefore I came to rely almost totally upon distance perception to judge my braking point, and this survived throughout my career.

I never consciously used markers on either side of the track, other than to quote some reference to co-drivers or perhaps team-mates in later years if they asked where I was braking. In my formative years I doubt if the organizers of most Continental road races even considered erecting accurate 100- or 200-metre marker-boards, so I had to choose my own cues and decided that both the simplest and surest way was to rely totally upon my visual perception of distance, which fortunately seemed very accurate.

By the time I left HWM I had certainly accumulated a great deal of experience in double-quick time, and it was to prove a priceless asset in the years to follow.

Frazer Nash 'Le Mans Replica' *(1950-52)*

'One of the most unlikely-looking proper racing cars you would ever see, but . . . it really was very good in all respects . . .'

I raced these Bristol-engined cycle-winged cars only five times during 1950-52. Each time I had difficulty gearing them properly, also having to acclimatize to their incredibly high-geared steering. But once you were used to them they were excellent. I really do have warm admiration for these cars. The Le Mans Rep Frazer Nash really was a jolly good racer, a real wolf in sheep's clothing whose performance belied its rather antiquated appearance. On first acquaintance that very direct steering could catch you out, but it made driving a real finger-tip job without the car ever feeling in any way delicate. The cockpit floor was very high so that, even though the actual seating position was quite straight-legged, you had a commanding view. The cockpit was also very slim and confined, despite its two seats.

Those Bristol engines had quite a decent power band and were smooth and forgiving . . . not too touchy about being mildly over-revved. The 'Nash really was a well thought-out, nicely balanced car with a decent engine and good brakes and, cycle wings and all, it really was very quick in its class.

H. J. Aldington was the business and driving power behind AFN Ltd when its chain-driven sports cars really made their name pre-war. Although they were certainly never cheap, his Frazer Nashes were very stark and uncompromisingly sporty with good power-to-weight and very nimble handling. From 1934 Aldington became the British BMW importer after finding that their management and engineers all shared his enthusiasm and appreciation for the finer things in motoring. They understood balance and handling and flair in a sporting car, things which the Lords of the British motor industry never could figure out.

Post-war — with BMW out of the game — it was natural for AFN to begin building a new generation of Frazer Nash sports cars using their BMW experience. They used the latest type of BMW 328-based 2-litre engine which Bristol had begun to make in England. 'H.J.' persuaded them to build him a special Frazer Nash Specification (FNS) version guaranteeing 100 or 120 bhp, in place of the 85 hp standard unit. Bristol then developed their own BS1 and BS4 competition engines which eventually gave 140 bhp, and the entire series became nice smooth units with good usable torque although always below the best Italian designs on horsepower.*

H.J. used the earliest of the Bristol FNS engines in his prototype 'High Speed' or 'Competition' model Frazer Nash in 1948. He shared the third of these cars with its new owner Norman Culpan to finish third overall at Le Mans in June 1949. Subsequent cars were then sold as the 'Frazer Nash Le Mans Replicas'.

I had my first race in one of them at Castle Combe in October 1950. It was a typical minor meeting for me, driving HWM in Formula 2, my own Cooper in Formula 3 and then the 'Nash in the sports car race. I became accustomed to its high-geared steering, and beat Tony Crook's car by a few lengths, which was nice. The following June I drove Sid Greene's 'WMC 181' in the British Empire Trophy race at Douglas, Isle of Man.

You could hardly imagine a circuit better suited to the 'Nash's direct steering

---

* SM recalls these engines this way. Today they are considered top-endy, pulling really well only within a narrow rev-band. One of Moss's greatest natural skills was to drive a car on its strengths, and while others might have struggled he would have kept the Bristol engine in the meat of its torque curve, most of the time! DCN

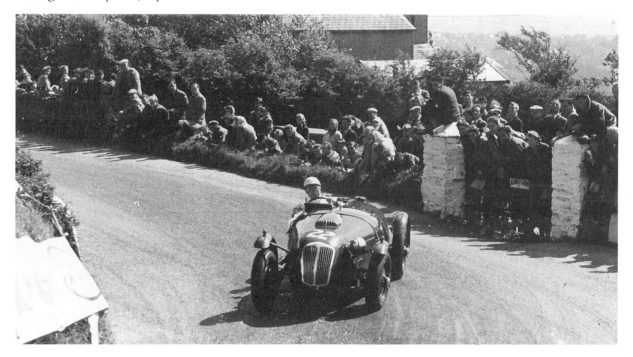

14 June 1951 — British
Empire Trophy race, Douglas,
Isle of Man — only the
offshore islands gave British
drivers the opportunity to
practise genuine road racing
on 'home' soil. Stirling in Syd
Greene's 'Le Mans Rep' uses
all the road on his way to first
place. Note the abundant
safety precautions . . .

and nimble handling, but in practice it was way under-geared and its engine felt feeble between 3,500 and 4,300 rpm. I was quite despondent and wrote in my diary 'We cannot possibly win this race, and I doubt if I can even be 1st among the Frazer Nashes. I don't know the car's or the brakes' capabilities yet, still, press on!'

It was a handicap race, with the 1500 class given a three-lap credit over the 2-litres. This made two Lester-MGs our main problem. I had to lap them three times. But the 'Nash felt much better in the race and I averaged 67 mph. Pat Griffith's Lester-MG was lapping at 62 mph to hold the lead on handicap. I took second place behind him with just two laps remaining. He was still three minutes clear on handicap, but then his engine seized and my father signalled 'take it easy' so I toured round for a rather lucky win; rotten luck for Pat Griffith, who had driven very well.

On Easter Saturday 1952 I shared Roy Salvadori's car in an informal relay race at Castle Combe and then back in Douglas in Sid Greene's car for the 1952 Empire Trophy it was my turn for an attack of gremlins which knobbled its electrics and put me out. Then I was asked to drive a works car in the Prix de Monte Carlo, a 2-litre sports car race supporting the Monaco Grand Prix which that year was run for over 2-litre sports cars. I had a factory C-Type Jaguar for the main race.

The 'Nash felt good on the street circuit, apart from its bottom gear being too high, but in the race I couldn't do much about Bordoni's OSCA which left me to dice for second with Manzon's Gordini. It was all quite exciting until a rear wheel came loose — the stud holes had elongated and eventually I had to retire. As you'll see from the C-Type section, that just wasn't my day.

Aston Martin DB2 *(1950)*

'A good-looking proper Grand Touring car which made all the right noises for two young chaps, posing in a Rally whose outcome didn't mean much to either of them . . .'

*L*ance Macklin and I shared this DB2 Coupé in the 1950 *Daily Express* 1,000-Mile Rally organized by the MCC. I believe we borrowed the car from the factory and for us the Rally developed into an open-road race in which we competed against each other to see how many hours of sleep we could get at each control before the rest arrived! We didn't take it terribly seriously.

I quite liked the old DB2 Aston Martin although, in common with all Astons in my experience, its engine was rather highly strung and would not put up with being really thrashed. It was also rather a heavy car although it handled quite well, but our habit of arriving at the controls hours before we were due and then hanging around to clock-in didn't make us very popular with the organizers. Eventually we came to a terrific traffic jam climbing Bwlch-y-Groes in Wales and after waiting at the tail of the queue we decided we had to have a go and passed the lot on the outside with two wheels scrabbling along on the verge. By this time we were quite unpopular with the other competitors as well as the organizers, but we still completed the road section without losing any marks.

Then they all had the last laugh, because we made an unholy mess of the special reversing and parking tests at the end — which in those days tended to decide such rallies — and thus ended my 1950 season . . . inauspiciously.

Morris Minor (1951)

'A really nice road car with extremely good handling, a nice little floor-change gearbox, and no power . . .'

I ran my own Morris Minor on the road and drove it extensively throughout Europe on the way to races with HWM when I wasn't travelling in John Heath's Citroen. I got into trouble in it early in 1950 when somebody took exception to the sight of me cornering it rather quickly on the public road and reported me to the police. I was fined £15 and had my licence endorsed and suspended for a month. That meant my competition licence was also invalid so I was effectively unable to work. I appealed but the suspension was confirmed and that meant pleading my case before the RAC Competitions Committee. Fortunately they decided I'd been hard done-by and they let me go on racing regardless, even though I had to be driven to and from the circuits.

Later in 1950, when I broke my knee at Naples, I had my Minor fitted with a hand-operated clutch so that I could drive it while my leg was still in plaster. The Minor had been designed by Alec Issigonis, who later produced the Mini, and I was a great fan of its excellent suspension and really terrific cornering abilities. I only did one competitive event in a Minor, and that was the 1951 Chiltern Night Trial, when I shared a friend's Minor Convertible. We lost 50 marks through mis-reading a map reference, but enjoyed ourselves regardless . . .

Kieft 500s *(1951)*

'Of all the cars I have ever driven, that Kieft was the greatest step forward I have ever experienced — miles ahead of its class.'

*T*he Kieft 500 began life as a co-operative project involving myself, Dean Delamont of the RAC, John A. Cooper — who was Sports Editor of *The Autocar* and formerly a BRM design engineer — and Ray Martin — who was a practical mechanic and fabricator. It was intended to provide me with a better F3 car than I could buy off the shelf, along with everybody else, from the Cooper Car Company.

It had a very far-forward driving position and low-pivot swing-axle rear suspension. Its inherent understeer made it a terrific little car to drive, far easier than a Cooper, far more forgiving and very, very quick. It really was a very sophisticated and advanced design. As far as I know, it was one of the earliest fully adjustable racing cars. In that respect it was far ahead of its time.

Cyril Kieft was a Welsh industrialist attempting to break into racing car production. Now he underwrote this project for us, afterwards modifying the design for customer production in his own factory. I joined his company as a director, but the production Kiefts were never as good as our lovingly built prototype and quite soon I found myself returning to Coopers.

*F*or 1951 I had the Formula 2 drive with HWM, and a new place in the Jaguar works team. I was only 21, and although life was becoming very complicated as I tried to fit sports cars, F2 and F3 dates into my schedule I still wanted to continue racing 500s. I needed someone to help organize my affairs and invited Ken Gregory to act as my business manager. He was a personal friend and one of the prime movers behind The 500 Club — which has grown into today's British Racing & Sports Car Club.

John *'Autocar'* Cooper was another good friend, and through him I had met Ray Martin the previous August when he had converted my Cooper very quickly and effectively from JAP to Norton power. The Cooper was good, but I felt

14 May 1951 — Whit Monday winner — Stirling greets the chequered flag at Goodwood in the big-race debut of his brand-new Kieft-Norton C51, as Cyril Kieft subsequently described it.

it could be better, less twitchy and much more stable. So John, Ken, Ray Martin, Dean Delamont and I discussed the possibility of building a new Norton-engined F3 car of our own for 1951. Coincidentally, following the Montlhéry 24-hour record attempt with Leslie Johnson in his XK120, Cyril Kieft asked Ken and me to attack some 500 and 350 cc class records there in one of his production F3 cars, which until that time had not been very impressive.

After taking the records, Kieft then asked me to drive for him in 1951. I didn't think his existing F3 chassis was particularly good but I suggested that we could produce a prototype of our own which Ray Martin would build and which Kieft could then produce, paying us a royalty on each one sold. He accepted and so the project began.

I had explained what I wanted in a 500 chassis. John brain-stormed ways of achieving it, Dean did the drawings and Ray made the parts. We would use the double-knocker Norton engine from the Cooper and it progressed rapidly, with me acting as progress chaser, ordering bits, collecting them, bawling out suppliers for late delivery . . . I quite enjoyed it.

I think this was the first time that serious theoretical thought had been applied to a 500. I wanted it to be stable, unlike a Cooper which was essentially easy and quick to correct once it had started to slide, but which would begin to slide very easily. Cooper cornering tended to be a series of lock-on lock-off stabs instead of a smooth, stable sweep.

John and Ray argued we should start with near equal weight distribution on all four wheels. The rear should have no roll resistance, so that on entering a corner the front wheels would accept all the transfer of load from inner to outer wheel. This would decrease the front tyres' cornering power so the car would enter a stable understeer while the rear wheels, free from roll, would have maximum traction against the road surface and so could accelerate the car without spinning.

Dean sat me down on the floor of his flat while he placed books around me to represent wheels, engine, gearbox, pedals, etc. This decided a sensible layout and showed how far forward I could go to balance the engine/gearbox/rear suspension mass behind me. To limit the change in camber angle — or 'lean' — of the rear wheels as they rose and fell on their swing-axles, the universal joints which drove the axles were coupled back-to-back on the centre-line, so

Below right 22 July 1951 At attention for The Queen after winning the Dutch GP 500cc race at Zandvoort; Mum holds refreshment, Ray Martin (bespectacled) is just beyond SM, on right are Cyril Kieft (cravat) and Zandvoort's creator John Hugenholtz.

Below 11 May 1952 — Stirling had an engine problem in the trusty prototype Kieft which prevented him running clear of the pack at the start of the 500cc Brussels GP in the Bois de la Cambre. He ran into a multiple collision, overturned, and the wreck was then rammed again . . . here his worst fears are confirmed, the Kieft's a write-off.

The much-loved Kieft prototype was very severely bent, as shown in these Guy Griffiths photos taken outside Ray Martin's workshop after the crestfallen team's return from Brussels. Note the chassis frame distortion within the cockpit. The production Kiefts were never to prove anywhere near as good as it had been.

allowing the maximum possible swinging length. To save weight we used rubber springs, bushes at the front, and a single central one at the rear actuated by wires and pulleys. It was actually a straight crib from Joe Fry's *Freikaiserwagen* Champion hill-climb car. By varying the number of rubber strands in the rear 'spring', different suspension rates could be achieved, the same trick being possible at the front by adjusting the rubber bushes used there in torsion. The rear radius arm locations could also be varied to alter rear-wheel toe-in.

It was all terribly technical, and we didn't really know how we would adjust it in practice, but I suspect our Kieft 500 might have been the first racing car in which the need for different easily adjusted suspension settings on different circuits had been properly appreciated and provided for.

Three Girling drum brakes were used, a single inboard drum going on the rear against the chain-drive sprocket.

Ray Martin did a superb job. I remember watching spellbound as he folded up steel sheet over a former, then welded it to form front wishbones which were as light and stiff as could be.

The 'Kieft' prototype was designed and built in fourteen weeks from scratch and was completed just in time for its first race at Whit Monday Goodwood, on 14 May 1951.

I had driven a 1950 model in the Luxembourg GP on 3 May, and didn't rate it very highly at all. On 13 May I drove my HWM at Monza, Ken having practised the new Kieft for me at Goodwood, then I caught the night train from Milan to Zurich, and used two 'planes to get to Shoreham Airport next day where I met my father who drove me to Goodwood. I arrived just half an hour before the Kieft's first race, which was a flop because we left a soft warming-up spark plug in its engine! I finished eighth, and only just qualified for the final.

Eric Brandon won that heat in his Cooper and he said to me 'I don't give much for that new car you've got . . .'. I told him 'Well, you know, there are reasons . . .'

We then put the right plug in for the final and starting from row four I was third ending lap one, and second ending lap two. Steaming on into Madgwick Corner, which was all but flat-out in a Cooper at that time, I relished every glorious moment as I was able to stuff the Kieft in there absolutely flat and drive right round the outside of Eric, gesturing to my car and mouthing across to him 'You're going to have to buy one of these'.

His face was a picture . . .

At Silverstone I found I could take Stowe absolutely flat-out, quite impossible with the Cooper, because I was able to select the optimum speed by balancing it against tyre drag from the Kieft's understeering front wheels.

I raced it six times but had some other problems, including the rear suspension bungee snapping, which collapsed the suspension and put me into a spin at 80 mph. But it was the first car to get below two minutes for the Silverstone lap at the British GP meeting, and my F3 win there was one of the easiest of my career.

At Nürburgring I led by forty seconds at the end of the second lap, then a steering arm broke. At Freiburg mountain climb the Kieft's class-winning time was 8:18, against Ken Wharton's best of 8:49 with the Cooper-JAP 1000. We won again at Brands Hatch ending that season, and Ray Martin modified the car somewhat for 1952. But I only raced it four times more, because at Brussels on 11 May 1952 I rolled it avoiding a multiple pile-up. Others thudded in behind me and by the time the dust had settled our beloved Kieft was a write-off.

Derek Annable loaned me his production car but the factory-built article from Bridgend was never as good as our original, and this one threw a wheel at Nürburgring, but I then won at Silverstone after Don Parker's car broke on the final lap when just inches ahead.

Cooper had closed the gap with their new Mark VI, so I then obtained a new Kieft from the works. It was very short-lived. I ran it at Fairwood Aerodrome in Wales and a JBS spun in my path at the first hairpin, I rammed it and then an Arnott piled in from behind, which then ran up the Kieft's sloping tail and over my helmet and crashed down on my car's front suspension, which it smashed to pieces.

Derek Annable lent me his car again for Prescott the following day and I managed second fastest time of the day but Les Leston's Cooper was quicker. I tried John Cooper's Mark VI at Boreham and liked it, and then drove Derek's Kieft for the last time in the big Brands Hatch meeting on August Monday, throwing the rod in the final. I had finally decided there was no future in the Kieft, there'd never been one as good as our prototype, so I returned to Coopers for the rest of my 500 career, resigned my directorship of Kieft, and that was that.

HWM Formula 2 *(1951-52)*

'When John Heath decided to build proper centre-seat HWMs for 1951 he gave me my first experience of what real Grand Prix cars might feel like — unfortunately we never recaptured the form of our rather quaint-looking offset cars of 1950 . . .'

*J*ohn's mechanics at Walton-on-Thames, under Alf Francis, began HWM's 1951 programme by building a prototype, which was then set aside, followed by four team cars, the prototype being completed later. Only the Alta engine and pre-selector gearbox remained from the 1950 design, these cars using all-new tubular chassis and suspension.

They had basically MG coil-spring and wishbone front suspension, with Morris Minor rack-and-pinion steering and a de Dion rear axle mounted on splayed-out quarter-elliptic leaf springs and tubular radius arms. They never achieved the success of their offset-seat predecessors, but they added greatly to my education as a racing driver.

*L*ance Macklin and I tried the first new HWM at Goodwood on 9 March 1951, but due to bad machining it bent its valves which ruined the cylinder head so our trip was wasted. Next day Alf Francis' men had it running again and we both drove.

I noted in my diary *'It seems far better than last year's and I could take the second curve after the pits flat. I spun it at Woodcote, going too fast. You can now spin its wheels. Took Minor round. Very good, beat J2 MG!'*

Testing there again on 17 March the new car was going well once more. I lapped at 1:47 in pouring rain but then George Abecassis spun it tail-first beneath a concrete barrier at Woodcote, which crushed him against the steering wheel. It looked terrible, but he escaped with a broken shoulder and ribs and a very minor skull fracture. He was well enough to spectate nine days later, on Easter Monday, when we ran two cars in the Lavant Cup.

In those days even major Goodwood races were laughably short, still pre-war Brooklands style. This one lasted just five laps, so you can see why I preferred man-sized 200-mile road racing in Europe.

I was not entirely happy with the HWM's handling but I was able to beat Brandon's new Cooper 1100 by a bare 0.8 sec, and Lance was fourth in his sister car. We then ran in the Richmond Trophy, finishing fifth and sixth.

After this curtain-raiser we travelled to Marseilles for the season's first Continental F2 race. The course was incredibly bumpy and dusty, very tiring indeed. I did 29 practice laps and found my new car pattering badly under braking and picking-up poorly out of the many slow corners. I bought a body bandage, binding and string. My father, who had travelled down with Lionel Leonard, bound my steering wheel.

Villoresi's Ferrari won from Trintignant's Gordini and my HWM, with Lance sixth.

In San Remo practice, two cylinders misfired and I could not rev beyond 5,000 rpm, while Lance had 6,000. We finished practice fifth and sixth fastest, but this was a combined Formula 1 and 2 race and Ascari and Villoresi ahead of us had the new 4½-litre Ferraris and 'Bira' his 4½-litre Maserati-based OSCA V12. We finished fifth and seventh amongst this strong field, but it wasn't a good day. I wrote *'I spun twice, and had a couple of trying moments when put on accelerator instead of brakes, and when selected second instead of fourth gear!'* Everybody else seemed thrilled by my fifth place, but perhaps I was simply learning to aim higher.

At Silverstone my Alta engine again misfired and the car slid around too much. The race was run in two heats and a final, and I managed to finish sixth in my heat, the first 2-litre home. Then the skies darkened before the final and the most fantastic rainstorm began, completely flooding the circuit. We were flagged away into a wall of water left by the leaders, and then great gusts of hailstones added to the rain. I tried as hard as I could to get amongst the big cars, making

HWM on tour in Europe, 1951 — Lance Macklin, Stirling's long-time girlfriend Sally Weston (niece of Granville Weston the biscuit tycoon), that great enthusiast John Heath and SM himself checking the tightly-bound wheel of his latest Formula 2 HWM.

the most of their power embarrassment in such a flood, but the spray from every car I tried to pass nearly drowned my engine, and me!

Reg Parnell led the Alfas in Tony Vandervell's *Thin Wall Special* Ferrari, while I lay fourth. Just then, Geoff Richardson's RRA hit a marker tub at Stowe Corner and rolled it into my path. I knocked it up into the air, and it dumped sand all over me before wedging in my HWM's front suspension. I had to stop for a marshall to kick it free — losing fifteen places. I was classified fourteenth overall when the stewards abandoned the race.

The Monza Autodrome GP on 13 May then introduced me to motor racing's spiritual home north of Milan. The HWM again refused to rev cleanly, peaking at only 5,400 halfway along the straight, and I was 7 secs slower than Ascari and Stuck's V8 AFM.

It was a two-heat race decided on aggregate time, and once it was over I would write '*Most fantastic dice of my life . . .*'

I disputed fourth place with the Gordinis of Trintignant and Simon, which boxed me in, one ahead, one alongside. Down the straight on one lap I sawed at the steering and dropped the second Gordini which left me free, latched-on behind the other one. I lacked the power to pass him but finished fourth, behind an Ascari and Villoresi Ferrari 1-2.

In heat two, Villoresi muffed his start, which allowed me to get ahead of him. Halfway round the opening lap, he stormed past, nipped in front of me and tried to draw away, but it was at that moment that the blinding light of 'slipstreaming' burst upon me . . .

In the previous heat, running with the Gordinis, we had all had virtually the same horsepower but their cars were lighter and smaller than mine so offered relatively little aerodynamic effect. Although we were clearly capable of running faster in close line-astern than individually, the effect was not very noticeable. Now with this powerful Ferrari just a yard ahead of my HWM, which was tucked completely into its aerodynamic shadow, I saw higher rpm than I'd seen all weekend — 5,900 instead of only 5,400 — and I even found I could lift off the throttle and *still* maintain contact, at undiminished speed. I was literally being sucked along in the Ferrari's slipstream and the sensation was fantastic.

Villoresi did not try to shake me off. He just hammered round with me latched on behind him, and although I couldn't pass him because the Ferrari was already running far beyond my car's unaided maximum speed we made terrific progress through the field!

Eventually Gigi decided to lose me. He ducked from side to side along the straights and each lap dived deeper and faster into the daunting *Curva Grande* beyond the pits, but to his credit he never jabbed his brakes. Such an option never entered our heads in those days.

Meanwhile the Gordinis had latched on to my tail and were slipstreaming me, so all four of us were hurtling round Monza in a long sixteen-wheeled snake. I had to shake them off without losing my tow and I finally managed it by surging wide into one bend as if to overtake Villoresi on the outside. The Gordini immediately behind followed me, until at the last possible moment I snapped back on to the Ferrari's tail, leaving him committed to the corner on the wrong line so he had to back off.

Villoresi's experience finally told as he left his braking desperately late in lapping someone into a curve and I was just unable to follow, having to brake hard and stay behind the backmarker instead. I did not see Gigi again until after the race, when he slapped me on the back.

I finished third in the heat and on aggregate, and this formative experience made sleep impossible that night . . . it was perhaps the most significant lesson of the many I learned with HWM.

Genoa's harbour-side circuit was then ideal for us and Lance and I were able to lead Ascari and Villoresi from the start — the first time genuine British-green cars had led Italian-red since long before the war.

In fact it was unusual for our HWMs to make such a good start, because with the pre-selector gearbox you cannot slip the clutch, but this time both Ferraris had hung fire. Lance led with me on his tail and we could actually *hear* the crowd when we arrived at the first turn ahead of the home team!

I took the lead, while Lance had to stop, but soon after quarter-distance a horrible grinding noise announced diff failure. I really think I might have won that race.

John had been invited to enter two HWMs in the Formula 1 Swiss GP at Berne, which I had been so disappointed to miss the previous year. We were absolutely the pygmies there, against 4½-litre V12 Ferraris and Talbots and the twin-stage supercharged 400-horsepower works *Alfettas*.

The Bremgarten really was a circuit which sorted out the men from the boys. I regarded it as a terrific challenge. Again my engine misfired, but fuel consumption turned out to be 7 mpg, so at least we would not need to refuel. Someone timed me through a twisty section second fastest, 1/5th second slower than Fangio.

It was grey and drizzling on race day and initially I ran eleventh amongst the 21 starters, using the HWM's fine roadholding to compensate for its lack of power as the rain intensified. Suddenly my aero screen shattered into a cloud of flying splinters.

My face was blasted with flying glass, and wind and rain nearly ripped off my visor and helmet. I had to hold my helmet down against the wind for the next thirty laps, but I just held seventh place until — only 300 yards from the finish — I ran out of fuel.

This was a frustrating end to a desperately hard day's work, and George had retired our other car. My introduction to the Bremgarten was character-building . . .

At Aix-les-Bains, I was fastest in practice but felt ill that night. In my heat I was lining up to take the lead from Cortese's Ferrari when he spun and we all ran into each other behind him. I just managed to catch Manzon's leading Gordini to win, but the HWM handled peculiarly and before the final Alf discovered its track rod and steering arm were bent, giving the front wheels 2½ inches toe-out! John gave me his car for the final; I could hardly reach its pedals, but as they pushed me to the grid we found its engine was broken. So I had to return to my toed-out special, and I trailed Rudi Fischer's private Ferrari closely until my engine went off and I finished a distant second.

By this time, our starting money was usually around £200-250 per car, but after our showing at Caracalla the previous year the Rome club offered £350 for us to return. John made a lone HWM entry there for me, while Lance raced another in Angoulême that weekend. In Rome I had only covered the first 450 yards of practice when my engine's timing chain broke, smashing the valve gear and pistons. I was ill again next day, as was the rebuilt car, and on race day I made a terrible start — caught out by the starter's tiny flick of the flag — but initially I ran second behind an indecently quick OSCA until my throttle jammed open. I stopped to correct that, then the plugs oiled up, causing a second stop, the magneto began to cut at high revs and finally the gearbox played up. I finished fourth to general disappointment, not least mine.

After my Le Mans début for Jaguar, I returned to HWM at AVUS, Berlin, but as soon as we saw the circuit with that immense banked North Turn we realized we could not possibly gear our cars high enough to be competitive.

Then Ken Gregory telephoned to tell me a telegram had arrived from Mr Ferrari inviting me to drive one of his 4½-litre cars in the *GP d'Europe* at Reims that Sunday, but I decided I could not possibly desert John Heath and must drive at AVUS — thus rejecting my first chance to drive a Ferrari.

At AVUS, with HWM's highest 3.7:1 back axles installed, we could pull no more than 5,400 rpm, while the streamlined BMW-engined German cars were pulling 160 mph along the straights and passing us on both sides! Some of them were averaging something close to our maximum speed . . . In the race both our cars destroyed con rods, pistons and crankshafts; mine after 2½ laps, Lance's after 15.

Rouen was another farce. The organizers banned push-starts, but we had no electric starters. We asked them how could we restart after refuelling? Could we keep our engines running? No! That's forbidden! I led initially, stopped to refuel and push-started my car myself, driving off with a marshal flouncing along behind bawling *'C'est interdit!'* My gearbox broke to end a perfect day, while Yves Giraud-Cabantous in our second car had its back axle break.

The strain of racing all over Europe was beginning to tell. Alf and his mechanics were flogging themselves into the ground merely to put our HWMs on the grid.

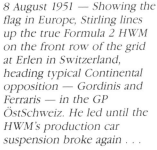

8 August 1951 — Showing the flag in Europe, Stirling lines up the true Formula 2 HWM on the front row of the grid at Erlen in Switzerland, heading typical Continental opposition — Gordinis and Ferraris — in the GP ÖstSchweiz. He led until the HWM's production car suspension broke again . . .

*23 September 1951 —
Showing Ferraris the way on
their home ground, Stirling
wheels the HWM through the
Aerautodromo chicane during
the Modena GP. It would not
last long . . .*

There was never the time nor the money to prepare them properly to survive to the finish, and I'm afraid that was becoming frustrating.

But then at Mettet, John gave me Cabantous's Rouen car which really impressed me. I described it in my diary as being '. . . *very good, with wonderful brakes and good motor, except that No 3 piston ring broke and plug oils up'*. It oiled-up when I was lying second and after two pit stops I could only finish fourth.

Two days later I drove the V16 BRM for the first time at Folkingham. So that was how real Formula 1 power felt! It really put our HWMs in perspective . . .

John gave me a new Alta engine which was lighter and had more power than the older type for the Dutch GP, where the entry was poor. I diced with Fischer's Ferrari for third place, behind the Talbots of Rosier and Etancelin. With fifteen laps to go Etancelin burst a tyre which left me running second and I hung on, in mounting excitement, until with just two laps to go my car's magneto fell off so I shot into the pits. Alf fixed it and I rejoined without the bonnet before Etancelin could repass. But my engine was stammering and popping and Etancelin boomed by on the very last lap, shouldering me back to third. I wrote in my diary, '*I drove better than ever before I think . . . ice cream and bed at 2am'*.

We ran both the HWM and my Kieft at Freiburg hill-climb, finishing fourth F2 behind quick German cars whose drivers knew the long climb intimately. We tried German Dunlop tyres and I wrote that night, '*Nearly crashed three times. Tyres N.B.G.!'*

Over the cobbles at Erlen I had set fastest practice time in the HWM when a telegram arrived from the Marzotto team, asking me to drive a 1½-litre Ferrari at Bari. I could not accept due to my HWM commitments, but next day another telegram arrived, this time from Enzo Ferrari himself.

I led the Erlen race by 9 secs until a front wishbone snapped at around 100 mph, the wheel folded inwards and retired me again.

On my way home I stopped by Modena to meet Mr Ferrari in person. John had decided against entering the HWMs for Bari so I was able to make my début in the Italian car, a most exciting prospect — but one which turned to dust (see page 70).

We then returned home, and headed west to the Curragh in Ireland where

I won both the scratch and handicap races run concurrently for the Wakefield Trophy, even though the HWM would only pull 121 mph along the straight.

One final Italian foray remained, the Modena GP on Ferrari's doorstep, where I ran fourth amongst the Ferraris and Gordinis before more magneto trouble and finally No 3 plug blew out of the head. Lance drove brilliantly, finishing third behind Ascari and Gonzalez in one of his best-ever races.

That ended HWM's 1951 European programme and we then finished the season at Goodwood, and Winfield in Scotland. In Sussex I led Lance and George home in a rare HWM 1-2-3 in the Madgwick Cup, and then led the Third September Handicap until the last few yards when Farina's Alfa Romeo inevitably roared by. I finished fifth in the 'big' 15-lap *Daily Graphic* Trophy, which Farina also won. In fact that was quite a day for me as I had won in the HWM, and twice in a C-Type Jaguar.

At Winfield, George and I and Duncan Hamilton put up a show of passing and repassing on the way to another HWM 1-2-3 in a 2-litre race run concurrently with *Formule Libre*.

It was then time to look towards 1952.

Alf Francis argued that all HWM needed was more power in the existing well-proven chassis. But John Heath was intent upon sweating out an entirely new car, which meant starting all over again. Alf resigned, to join Peter Whitehead's private team, and I also decided to take my chance elsewhere. I would drive for HWM only three more times.

I had enormous respect for what John in particular had achieved, but now I had to progress. Leslie Johnson had attracted me to his sophisticated-sounding new G-Type ERA, but I offered to drive for John again in any race for which the ERA might be unavailable.

Early that year everything seemed to go wrong. The G-Type was late, and I destroyed my beloved F3 Kieft prototype at Brussels. On the way home our caravan, on which my manager Ken Gregory and I had lavished so much time and money, broke away from behind my XK120 Coupé, nearly overtook us downhill and demolished itself before our very eyes.

So I was happy to accept John's offer to drive an HWM in the Swiss GP at Berne on 18 May. We had a minor argument just before the start over spark-plugs. I maintained the ones fitted were too soft. John insisted they were not. They were, and after running third behind the Ferraris of Farina and Taruffi they cooked and at the end of the third lap I had to stop for a complete new set. George was running fifth in his car when a rear axle-shaft sheared, the wheel flew off and he crashed heavily, escaping unhurt but destroying his car.

Peter Collins — my full-time replacement in the team that year — saw George's crash as he drove by and within a few hundred yards an identical failure struck his car, fortunately in a slow corner, where he spun to a standstill. As soon as John heard what had happened, he called in Lance and myself, explained the problem and suggested we should withdraw, which we did, feeling very dejected about the whole thing.

John immediately had new parts made and loaned me a 1951 car for the Eifelrennen at Nurburgring the following weekend, where Duncan Hamilton would drive a 1952 model. Meantime the rest of the team took three other cars to Montlhéry — HWM were working as desperately hard as always to earn their keep.

At the 'Ring I lost a handsome lead in the 500 race when my borrowed Kieft lost a wheel, but the seven-lap F2 race saw me lead Fischer's Ferrari for a couple of laps until the onboard extinguisher began rattling around my feet and I lost time ditching it overboard. I was frankly worried about losing another wheel but I managed to finish second, feeling enormously pleased and relieved. It felt wonderful just to finish anywhere at all . . .

Subsequently, after my ERA blew up and caught fire in the Belgian GP, I was still stiff and shaken in the hotel when I saw John and he offered me an HWM for the French GP at Reims the following weekend. I was not in a good frame of mind. My ERA incident had occurred at very high speed and now, maybe unfairly, I was almost expecting the worst every time I even sat in a racing car.

At Reims I did eight practice laps in the HWM. It was leaking oil badly so I decided not to do any more, to save its engine. Just before the Grand Prix I won the sports car race in the C-Type Jaguar, which was the first-ever major victory for a car using disc brakes, a marvellous tonic. But it was fearfully hot in the sun and I made a bad start in the HWM, nearly stalling. I had a private race with Mike Hawthorn's Cooper-Bristol for sixth place but the HWM just simply was not quick enough, and eventually I had to make a long stop for plugs, oil and water, rejoining thirteenth.

The oil leak grew worse. First pints, and then gallons of oil were being pumped all over me, the pedals became slippery and the airstream was blowing oil up over my chest and face 'til I was drenched in it from head to foot.

Meanwhile the sun was roasting down, the engine and gearbox were blisteringly hot so you can imagine the discomfort and stench of it all. I had to stop several times for refills of oil, and rags to clean my goggles. Still the car kept going and I was determined to stay with it as long as it would run. We finally finished tenth . . .

It was abundantly clear that the HWM was no longer the best British Formula 2 car — that mantle had passed to the new Cooper-Bristols.

The first, long chapter in my road racing education had ended, but HWM had given me a wonderful grounding . . . something for which I will always be grateful to John Heath and George Abecassis, and to their long-suffering mechanics.

Jaguar C-Types *(1951-53)*

'To me the C-Type Jaguar was another stunningly beautiful car, and although today it hasn't the same charisma as its successor, the D-Type, it was actually a nicer car for road racing . . .'

*I*recall the C-Type — in common with all the Jaguars that I raced — with considerable affection. They called it the XK120C — for 'Competition' — but really only its engine and front suspension had much in common with the production car. Its spaceframe chassis was designed for racing, unlike the XK120's which behaved like a touring car being driven fast, quite nice and soft and comfortable, rather floppy in fact. The racing C-Type changed all that. It was taut. Comfort was completely compromised to performance and road-holding.

Those 3½-litre XK engines had nice, smooth power and made a lovely noise. But I do remember how Jaguars never had good seats. The XK120's weren't that good, and when the C-Type came along they built racing seats which were not much better.

Of course one great advance was Malcolm Sayer's new aerodynamic all-enveloping body, because it helped to make the C-Types fast for their time.

*I*first saw the C-Type, which Jaguar intended to introduce at Le Mans, on 16 May 1951 when I wrote in my diary: *'Up early and left for Coventry and Jaguar's. Met Leslie* (Johnson) *and Peter Walker and saw new Le Mans car. Later Peter and I went to Motor Industry Research Association track and tried it. Car is very rapid (about 150mph +) but has an oversteer, which may be due to shock absorbers. Brakes* (still drums at this time) *not very good, but no fade during try-out . . .'*

For Le Mans, team manager Lofty England teamed me with Jack Fairman. We were faced by Ferrari and Talbot but most impressively in terms of sheer hardware by Briggs Cunningham's American team. I wrote of them on the Tuesday night before practice, *'Fantastic! 76 packing cases, 3 spare Chrysler Rocket engines, 3 race cars, 1 spare car, a caravan, charging plant, etc!'*

Just like the XK120 in the previous year's TT, I felt enormous pride for the C-Type as we presented it for scrutineering or ready for the start at Le Mans. It was the most modern, futuristic, potent-looking device and my pride in it was doubled because it was finished in British Racing Green. We really did feel as if we were showing the flag, and that counted for a lot . . .

In second practice it was raining and misty, and I found the C-Type's lights were inadequate, despite being the maximum wattage allowed by the regulations. I couldn't see a thing. Lofty gave me the job of pacemaker, to break the quickest Talbot. He believed the Ferraris and Cunninghams would both trail us, but Gonzalez in the Talbot would try to build a time cushion in the lead before his change-over. I had to see what I could do about Gonzo and his brakes!

Sure enough, first time down the Mulsanne Straight I took the lead and Gonzalez came honking past under braking for the ninety-degree right-handed Mulsanne Corner. I repassed on the run back up past the pits, then let him outbrake me again into Tertre Rouge at the end of the Straight. The C-Type wound up to 150 mph as I repassed, and I could see he was getting all hot and bothered. He promptly tried to outbrake me again at Mulsanne Corner, and after five laps of this he dropped way back, his brakes cooked.

I then found the C-Type's shape was good enough for me to hold 5,700 rpm — about 150 mph — on half-throttle down the straight, and to conserve my own drum brakes I was applying them at 600 yards into Mulsanne. I managed to push the lap record up from under 100 mph to 105 mph during this spell, taking the curve on the brow before White House at 130, the White House ess itself at 120 and the curve beyond the pits — which was just 'on' without braking — at 115-120 mph.

Then Jack took over. During practice we had discussed shut-off and braking points round the circuit. The only one upon which we could not agree was for the right-hander at Arnage, which followed a succession of fast sweeps after Mulsanne. The road was lined by trees, leaving few clear distinguishing marks and making it difficult for us to define to each other exactly where we did what. I finally selected the tree beside which I believed I was lifting and John Cooper found some whitewash somewhere and we painted the trunk as a marker. Then rain washed out the last session before the race, so we couldn't check it.

When Jack finished his first stint in the race he was convinced that I really was some kind of driving genius because he found that he could only get round Arnage if he braked as hard as he possibly could when he first *sighted* that tree, never mind drawing level with it! Only then did he find I'd left a note for him saying, '*Arnage white tree much too late. I am braking 50 yards after curve past Mulsanne*'. I'm told poor Jack turned the air blue for about ten minutes, without repeating himself once!

After four hours Jaguars lay 1-2-3, leaving everyone for dead. All went well until the Johnson/Biondetti car broke and then Jack and I were well in the lead after eight hours when we suffered an identical failure. The culprit was a copper oil-delivery pipe in the sump, which was fractured by vibration, starving the bearings of oil so that they broke up. Steel pipes were adopted subsequently, preventing any repetition.

Fortunately for the two Peters, Whitehead and Walker, there was no opposition left when they inherited the lead in our last surviving C-Type, so they could

A few seconds before 06.19am, 4 May 1952 — start of a very wet Mille Miglia — This rare shot shows a pair of interesting 'Jaguars' ready to go in Brescia's Viale Rebuffone. Stirling is just easing his goggles (either for comfort or to prevent misting) in the works' latest disc-braked C-Type 'XKC 003' on street level, while on the ramp Pezzoli/Cazzulani in the rebodied Biondetti Jaguar Special ('620') look on with interest. Norman Dewis — Moss's passenger — shows no obvious emotion whatsoever.

ease off to limit vibration, their copper pipe survived, and they went on to win.

After Le Mans I did not drive for Jaguar again until September when I won the Dundrod TT for the second time. I used my Le Mans car again — chassis 'XKC 002' — and I took the lead on the opening lap and was never headed. Lofty then entered me in a single car for the closing Goodwood meeting where I drove it in two short races and won them both. Le Mans, Dundrod or Goodwood — super-smooth and fast public road circuit, rough and winding but quick country-road course or aerodrome perimeter track — all seemed to suit the C-Type Jaguar . . .

I was named as Jaguar's number one for 1952, and they let me have a beautiful XK120 hard-top Coupé in my green-and-cream colours for use on the road.

We ran 'XKC 003' in a minor handicap race at the Easter Monday Goodwood meeting but the handicappers were pretty harsh and I could only finish fourth. That car was fitted for the first time with Dunlop disc brakes and this was effectively a very minor shake-down before my second Mille Miglia . . . there we met the Mercedes-Benz works team of super-light 300SL Coupés.

I quickly wished we could have prepared the way the Germans did. Their whole team had been in Italy for months to learn the course, perfect their cars and to choose refuelling and service stations. In the race Jaguar's works test driver Norman Dewis rode with me and we set off in pouring rain at 6.19 am. The only car modifications for the race were a full-width screen, and a tool-kit and drinking flask in the cockpit. After a couple of hours the rain eased and finally stopped and we'd overtaken several good runners when a thump and lurch announced a thrown rear tyre tread. While we were changing it Karl Kling's Mercedes went by, and he had started four minutes behind us, which was worrying . . .

I trailed him into the Ravenna control, and passed him soon after, then caught Caracciola's 300SL and passed him only to catch myself out going into a right-hander. We knocked down some posts on the verge before I was able to regain the road, and Norman used up a whole box of matches trying to light a cigarette!

We lay seventh at Rome, but the rear dampers had gone and the fuel tank was leaking. Then in Siena we drove through the flames from Biondetti's Ferrari which had ignited while being refuelled. Fortunately our leaks didn't catch fire as well. Stopping for more fuel in Florence, a dope in a Fiat opened his door just as I came haring in, and our Jaguar chopped his door straight off! Norman picked it up and gave it back to him, but received no thanks.

Unknown to us, we were virtually assured of fourth place until on the descent of the Raticosa, with only 145 miles to go, I lost the front end and understeered into a rock. This broke the steering rack away from the frame, so with steering gone, dampers gone and fuel tank split we had to retire.

Significantly during that race, while trying to hold the Jaguar straight at 150 mph down the Ravenna straight in pouring rain and against a terrible cross-wind, and thinking nobody could possibly go any faster, one of the 300SL Mercs rocketed straight by. I repassed it later but it really shook me at the time, and it shook Jag's when we told them about it . . .

They were clearly going to be very quick at Le Mans. In fact I sent a telegram to William Lyons reading '*Must have more speed at Le Mans*' — and that sowed the seeds of disaster . . .

We ran the cars at the May Silverstone meeting, and I won in '002' again on disc brakes. Then Lofty took '003' down to Monaco for me, the Grand Prix that year being run for sports cars over 2 litres. I qualified on pole but tight street racing like this wasn't really the Jaguar's forté. Robert Manzon's lighter and smaller 2.3-litre Gordini was more at home. He took a second a lap out of my lead and passed me along the seafront. Then at Ste Devote Corner, the right-hander at the foot of the hill up into the town, Reg Parnell's Aston Martin blew-up and spread oil on the road. Stagnoli spun his Ferrari and rammed the Aston and then Manzon and I arrived and we both slid into the wrecked Aston,

2 June 1952 — Monaco GP, Monte Carlo — His first outing in this classic event, but it was run that year for sports cars. Here Moss whips his Mille Miglia C-Type through the Tabac with not another car in sight. But at St Devote, Reg Parnell's Aston Martin DB3 has thrown a rod, spun in its own oil and off go the Jaguar, Robert Manzon's Gordini and Tony Hume's Allard ('84') as well. Stirling rejoined the race, but only after receiving outside assistance . . .

and Tony Hume followed in his Allard. A couple of English holidaymakers hopped over the bales to help me pull the Jaguar's crumpled bodywork from its tyres, then I limped round to the pits where some more expert work got me back into the race. I recovered fifth place before the organizers black-flagged and disqualified me for receiving outside assistance.

The Gordini's pace against the C-Type seemed to emphasize what I had told Jaguar after the Mille Miglia, so they hastily developed a sleeker, long-nosed and long-tailed small-radiator spec for Le Mans. The radiator header-tank was moved back separately to the bulkhead, but in Le Mans practice this system just didn't work. Hot water seemed to be circulating straight from the engine to the header tank and by-passing the small radiator, so it inevitably boiled. Finally Bill Lyons himself ordered two of the three cars back on to standard radiators, even though that meant hammering bulges into the bonnet to accommodate them.

I made quite a good start, from fourteenth to fourth by the Dunlop bridge but after ten laps I didn't like the car's handling. Its drum brakes (we had rejected discs for reasons I'll explain shortly) were giving out, then after 24 laps it boiled itself into retirement. Ian Stewart's sister car had already fallen and Duncan Hamilton's soon followed, neither of the Peters — the previous year's winners — getting to drive.

It was an unmitigated Jaguar disaster.

Next day I was off to Spa for the début of the G-Type ERA in the Belgian GP. 1952 was not an easy year for me . . .

I felt sure Jaguar could regain credibility in the Reims GP sports car race, and Tommy Wisdom loaned me his car — 'XKC 005' — for it and I talked Bill Heynes — Jaguar's chief engineer — into fitting it with disc brakes.

Now they didn't just happen upon the scene like the greatest thing since sliced bread. Today all production cars use them and they cause hardly any problems, but that's because we had all the problems in 1952!

We would run them at one circuit, like Reims, say, where there were long straights along which the brakes could cool quite comfortably, and they'd give no trouble. But if we then ran them on a tighter circuit with less space between the corners, enormous heat would build up and vaporize the fluid as soon as we began braking hard.

Next time you braked the pedal would hit the floor. Then we'd get knock-off, a condition in which when you cornered hard, the wheel assembly would flex and the disc would push the caliper pistons back. When next you applied them, the pedal's initial movement would be lost in merely popping the pistons back out again into contact with the disc, without really clasping it tight. They corrected this by putting balance pipes across the top of the caliper, but until they did that we quite often found the pedal going suddenly straight to the floor so we'd go whistling up the escape road. We didn't understand what was happening, and by the time we got back to the pits to tell the engineers that the brakes had failed, the pedal would have come back again and the system would be working.

'Can't find anything. Are you sure the pedal went to the floor?'

'Listen, I've just been up the escape road at 130!'

Anyway, Reims was ideal for the embryo disc brake but after making the best start in the fifty-lap race I was passed early on by our old friend Manzon's Gordini. It led until a stub axle broke and it crashed, leaving me to an easy win. It was a fantastically hot, typical Reims day and I was almost heat-stroked by the time the race finished. That was actually my first win in twelve races, the first since Silverstone, and it did a lot to recoup Jaguar prestige after the débâcle of Le Mans.

I won again in '005' at Boreham, then the works team re-emerged for the inaugural Goodwood 9-Hours day-into-night race where I shared a new car '011' with Peter Walker and we held a comfortable five-lap lead until the A-bracket locating the rear axle failed. We lost half an hour while it was replaced and

13 June 1953 — Le Mans 24-Hours — Moss (3.4-litre Jaguar 'XKC 053' Lightweight co-driven by Peter Walker) leading Ascari (4.5-litre V12 Ferrari 375MM Berlinetta heavyweight co-driven by Luigi Villoresi) early in the GP d'Endurance. Both led. Ascari set the new lap record and retired. Moss/Walker finished second.

finished fifth. Three minor races in Tommy Wisdom's by this time rather tired car completed my C-Type season.

Through 1953 I raced the cars eight times, and won the Reims 12-Hours.

We tried much harder to prepare for the Mille Miglia and I covered around 6,000 miles in reconnaissance but all within two weeks of the race. Mort Morris-Goodall was my passenger in '011' but a rear axle tube twisted in the diff housing and put us out before the first control at Ravenna. It was a miserable Mille Miglia, my third for Jaguar ending in my third retirement, and it was the last they ever attempted.

I had a new works car — '037' — for May Silverstone and on the first practice day I was convinced it was possible to take the very fast left-hand kink at Abbey Curve flat out. Then on one lap I had to change my line because another car was in my path. I then made the mistake of keeping my foot down, anxious not to spoil a 'hot' lap. The car went into a savage oversteer and dropped a wheel off the edge of the road; it dug in to the soft verge at about 110 mph and the car rolled . . .

Fortunately I escaped with only bruises and shock but I was anxious to test my reactions to such an accident and reported for practice next day. The car was rebodied in time for the race and I finished only seventh. None of the C-Types was on form and the first four places fell to Ferraris and Aston Martins.

Bill Heynes had developed three special lightweight cars for Le Mans, each running Weber carburettors instead of SUs, plus disc brakes with transmission-driven servo assistance. Lightweight, conventional-shape bodies were fitted, and these were the ultimate C-Types, with 220 horsepower. Despite the absence of Mercedes-Benz we faced the strongest-ever Le Mans entry.

I was to share 'XKC 053' with Peter Walker, and I led in the early stages until after twenty laps my engine began running rough. They changed the plugs and it was no better, but after another couple of laps I had the fuel filter removed which did the trick for it was blocked. From there on it was plain sailing. After our delays Tony Rolt and Duncan Hamilton won at record speed in '051', Peter Walker and I were second — 29 miles behind — in '053' and Peter Whitehead/Ian Stewart came fourth behind a Cunningham in '052'.

It was my best result yet at Le Mans, but by this time I knew the *Grand Prix d'Endurance* well enough to know I didn't like it. You must never confuse Le Mans with a motor race, at least not in those days when reliability was generally so much poorer than today. Le Mans was always a great *event* but no way was it a great motor race.

Elsewhere we might run up to 6,000-6,100 rpm, but for Le Mans we'd be limited to something like 5,600-5,700 which was frustrating. It was one of the few races in the world in which we weren't really allowed to dice, and to me that's the name of the game. I reckon that as a racer one should go for it, as fast as possible. For that reason I was never a Le Mans driver. I liked to have a dice, a real old tear-up.

The worst thing there is the morning fog, and then the speed differential between the fast cars and the tiddlers. It was always one of the few races which I felt was really dangerous because of factors beyond your control. Imagine at night, closing on two pairs of rear lights at 150 mph, without knowing if the rearward pair was about to pull out to overtake the guy in front of him. My future wasn't in my own hands there; too many possibilities for another driver to do something stupid.

Le Mans involved something like 120 drivers, of whom only forty or so would be really competent, and they would be in the faster cars when their skills were needed in the slower ones, since when you were hurtling along the Straight and your closing speed on the tiddlers ahead might be 80 mph they needed to be competent to see you in their mirrors.

Yet going there as part of the Jaguar works team or of Mercedes-Benz's was always a source of great pride. Both cars were the envy of everybody, and that charge of adrenalin helped compensate for what I didn't like about the race until later in my career, when only one thing could persuade me to do Le Mans, and that was money . . .

That 1953 Le Mans 1-2-4 finish was a terrific achievement for Jaguar, and Bill Lyons was never bothered about other races. He knew simply that winning Le Mans sold sports cars, and that was all that mattered. Still, they ran '011' for me in the last British Empire Trophy race to be run on the Isle of Man, and I finished second to Reg Parnell's lighter and more nimble new Aston Martin DB3S.

Peter Whitehead and I shared '012' — the Le Mans practice hack — in the Reims race which was a 12-hour midnight-to-noon affair for the first time that year. After pacing the leading Ferrari and Cunningham early on, we went ahead and won by four laps. That was the day my Cooper-Alta Special tried to cut my feet off in the French Grand Prix, and Mike Hawthorn in his works Ferrari beat Fangio . . .

We then ran my Le Mans lightweight car in the Lisbon GP in Portugal but I wasn't very happy because its brakes would lock as the car went light on the bumpy circuit and I was beaten into second place by Bonetto in a Lancia.

For the second Goodwood 9-Hours Peter Walker and I shared '012' and we led Tony Rolt and Duncan Hamilton's sister car in a Jaguar 1-2, I'm told with our disc brakes glowing in the dark. With an hour to go all seemed settled, but at 11.04 with a 27-second lead our car's engine seized and three minutes later the second-placed car's did the same, I think due to oil surge on Goodwood's long corners. On distance covered we should have placed ninth and tenth but of course we hadn't passed the chequered flag.

We then encountered more trouble in the Dundrod TT, where the gearboxes broke, and I waited just short of the finishing line to limp across third on distance but fourth on handicap behind two of those DB3S Aston Martins.

Lofty and I and Tom French of Dunlop then went off to Mexico to recce the Carrera Panamericana race route, but Bill Lyons ruled out entering on the grounds of cost — estimated at £30,000 — and I never did get to drive in it. At least that gave me my first sight of the USA, which I had always wanted to visit — I had a picture of it as a real land of milk and honey; I mean they had sweets and no rationing! I wasn't disappointed.

I did not drive for Jaguar in 1954 until the all-new D-Type emerged at Le Mans, but the C-Type had given me enormous pleasure and a lot of valuable experience and success in an extraordinarily wide range of events.

Ferrari 166 *(1951)*

'My memories of this car are coloured by the background to my driving it, but essentially I discovered a very impressive, incredibly smooth engine . . . in a dangerously untrustworthy chassis . . .'

*T*his contact with Ferrari, very early in my career, was a most unfortunate episode which put me right off perhaps the world's most famous racing team, until it was too late . . .

*A*t Bari, in September 1951, I had my first drive in a foreign car. It was not a very pleasurable experience. Ever since my first Italian race in the Cooper 1,000 at Garda in 1949 I had perhaps been better recognized in Italy than at home, at least until my 1950 TT win at Dundrod. During 1950 and '51 I did pretty well with HWM, and now Ferrari had invited me to drive for him at Bari.

I had just had a front wishbone snap on my HWM at Erlen in Switzerland, and on the way home in my Morris Minor I took a big detour to visit Ferrari in Modena. French was our only common language and mine wasn't very good, but we seemed to get on well enough.

He said he would like me to drive his new 4-cylinder 2 ½ -litre car at Bari if it was ready in time, or failing that definitely in the Italian GP on 16 September. He then made me an enormously tempting offer to accompany Ascari and Villoresi to the Argentine Temporada series early in the new year, and asked me to join his team exclusively for 1952. This was the year before he made a similar offer to Mike Hawthorn, which Mike accepted.

It was a terrific honour. To be offered a place in one of the world's top teams was a dream for any English racing driver. So far only Dick Seaman had achieved it, to join Mercedes-Benz in 1937. Make no mistake, I was very excited, but Raymond Mays was still making noises to me about BRM and I really wanted to do my best with a British car. Perhaps the as-yet-unproven BRM would become the car Ferrari had to beat?

So, rather cautiously, I agreed only to driving the Ferrari at Bari so long as my HWM commitments would permit. John Heath confirmed he would not be entering the race, so that was my cue — I was going to race a foreign car for the first time.

The Bari club confirmed an attractive starting money deal for me in a Ferrari, so my father and I went off to Italy by air and train, the sleeper from Rome to Bari proving a dreadful experience. At Bari we met Peter Whitehead, the English privateer who was running his own Ferrari, and also Villoresi who was driving for the works. There in the garage was the new 4-cylinder car all set up ready to go, and I went to bed happy.

Next morning when we got to the garage I sat in the 4-cylinder to see how it fitted and a mechanic asked me abruptly what I was playing at. It wasn't my car, it was going to be driven by Piero Taruffi — I was out of a drive.

I was stunned. In effect I was reduced to bumming round the town to find an alternative, and I was very grateful when David Murray — the Scots privateer who subsequently founded the Ecurie Ecosse Jaguar team — offered me his Ferrari, which was an ancient ex-Peter Whitehead short-chassis model rigged for Formula 2 with an unsupercharged 2-litre V12 engine in place of its original 1 ½ -litre supercharged F1 unit. It wouldn't have a chance in the race but at least it was a runner and it was mine if I wanted it.

I approached the organizers and persuaded them to increase David's start money if I drove his car, but even this makeshift plan collapsed in practice.

The car was rigged with the Continental pedal system, with the throttle in the centre and brake pedal to the right instead of vice versa. I had never driven a car equipped that way, and I found it very confusing. The swing-axle rear suspension was lethal; it had enormous and almost instantaneous oversteer the moment one even thought of entering a corner, and I was just building up speed as practising began when the brakes appeared to fail and I crashed into the straw bales. I had hit the centre accelerator instead of the right-hand brake pedal. David's mechanics repaired it sufficient to practice again next day but its engine disintegrated, and that was it . . . goodnight.

Fangio won for Alfa Romeo, his pace breaking up both Ferraris of Ascari and Villoresi, leaving Gonzalez second in the only surviving 4½-litre Ferrari and Taruffi third in 'my' new 2½-litre car. That either proved Mr Ferrari's wisdom in preferring Taruffi to me or suggested that perhaps I could have done at least as well.

I battled with the organizers to give David Murray 200,000 lire for his efforts on my behalf, and I came out of it with another 100,000 lire for myself, but none of that was any thanks to Ferrari who had really dropped us all in a hole. I did not forget, and I would not forgive, and because of that it would always give me great pleasure to beat those red cars — Grand Prix, sports and GT alike . . .

7 July 1949 — Prix du Leman, Lausanne, Felice Bonetto's already elderly Ferrari 166 is harried here by Stirling in his 'two-way' Cooper. Two years later Stirling will drive David Murray's similar Ferrari (briefly) in practice at Bari and the experience will not impress him . . .

Sunbeam-Talbot 90 *(1952)*

'My rally cars — very under-powered but well-balanced, easy cars to overdrive desperately hard, surprisingly good on slippery or loose surfaces and quite exhilarating really, considering how gutless they were!'

20/27 January 1953 — the Monte Carlo Rally saw the Sunbeam-Talbot 90 carrying its service back-up inside and on top! Stirling at the wheel, Desmond Scannell by his side, John A. Cooper in the back, not quite able to repeat their previous year's fine second overall . . .

*I*n the early years of my career, until I began racing in the southern hemisphere, I had the annual problem of what to do during the winter. I earned my living as a professional racing driver, so when there was no racing during the closed season my living dried-up. Then at the end of 1951 Norman Garrad, who was sales and competition manager of the Rootes Group, invited me to join his team for the 1952 Monte Carlo Rally, and from success in that grew a series of further international rallies for Rootes, spread over three seasons, which yielded some success . . . and a lot of fun.

I regarded my début in the 1952 Monte Carlo Rally as a considerable adventure, a fun thing to do. We believed a crew of three would be ideal and I was joined by two friends, John Cooper of *The Autocar* and Desmond Scannell, Secretary of the British Racing Drivers Club. We started from Monte Carlo itself because that gave us the chance to recce vital parts of the route. After a hectic drive down there through deep snow, we started the rally itself at 10 pm on a bitter-cold night. I was to drive the tricky sections, John and Des would share the links between.

We had a reasonably easy run until we reached the Luxembourg-Liège section where the roads were appallingly rough and covered in sheet ice. Back in France, on the Saint Flour-Le Puy section many competitors crashed as we drove through blizzards and low, dense cloud. I found on the ice with chained tyres that the best way was simply to keep on as much power as the Sunbeam could offer. We were travelling at 70-75 mph most of the time, near the car's maximum and it paid off.

We were among only fifteen crews to arrive in Monte Carlo penalty-free, and then came the regularity test on the snow-covered Col de Braus. Des calculated our times and average speeds against our targets, for we could lose points both by arriving early at controls and by being late. We were 6 secs behind time at the first control, I drove hard to arrive at the next virtually spot-on, and we soon found the odometer was useless for judging distance covered — due to wheelspin.

Down towards a tunnel near Castillon we were within 3 secs of our target time relative to the route map, but here I ran on to sheet ice and the Sunbeam slithered nose-first into a deep snow-bank. We hauled it out and set off to regain lost time down the Col de Castillon. Trouble was, none of us had thought to time how long it had taken us to get going again. John and Des first told me I had to make up two minutes, then declared I should *lose* two minutes. I suggested we try the 'Boy Scout's Average'; each of us should estimate how long we had been stationary, we would add the estimates together, then divide by the number in the group — three. We agreed a final figure, and I toured slowly along to the final control, with John counting off the seconds against his stop-watch.

We had finished, and then came the four-hour wait for the organizers to declare the result. Sid Allard had won in one of his own cars, but we were declared runners-up by just four seconds! It was a marvellous result for me as a novice rally driver, for all of us as a novice crew. Perhaps it also proved something about the 'Boy Scout's Average'?

Norman Garrad and the Rootes brothers certainly seemed delighted. I'm not surprised — my fee was a flat £50 . . .

We ran a similar car and the same crew in the 1953 Monte, but that was an anti-climax. The weather was so mild it was like a long drive in the country. Over 200 crews arrived unpenalized, so the outcome was dictated by sheer horsepower in the acceleration and regularity tests, and we finished sixth but Rootes also won the prestigious Team Prize. It was not half as dramatic as '51, nor a quarter as much fun.

In July 1952 I joined a strong Sunbeam-Talbot team in my first Alpine Rally, sharing my car with John Cutts. Mike Hawthorn joined us — after I had told him what a terrific way this was of earning fifty quid! — and he was navigated by John Pearman. Sunbeam's most experienced rally driver, George Murray-Frame, shared with 'Chippy' Chipperton, and Nancy Mitchell, Leslie Johnson and George Hartwell drove other Sunbeams.

This latter trio struck trouble, but for the rest of us it was quite an entertaining and challenging few days. The rally covered 2,057 miles through France, Italy, Austria and Switzerland, and the organizers calculated it involved 120,250 ft of mountain-climbing. Our class had to average just over 36 mph, there was very little time in hand for food, refuelling and tyre changes so we all tried to gain as much time as possible to ward off the unexpected. In other words this was a good free-for-all charge around the Alps.

It was hard going but we survived penalty-free. Far into the event, between Menaggio and Pre St Didier, my car shed its exhaust system which had to be replaced, giving me 26 minutes to make up which I managed with John Cutts hanging on for dear life.

We survived, amongst only thirteen crews unpenalized from 31 still running, while by Aix-les-Bains only 27 cars entered the *parc fermé* and only ten of them could still qualify for a *Coupe des Alpes,* awarded for a clean-sheet run. The final day sent us over famous cols, the d'Iseran — Europe's highest where our already meagre horsepower died away due to the thin air — Galibier, Glandon to Castellane, then over the minor cols to Grasse and the finish in Cannes. The cars were then painstakingly scrutineered to ensure they were as specified at the start, and George, Mike and I each won a coveted *Coupe,* we placed 8-9-10 overall and won the Team Prize.

Next time in the Alpine we would run the convertible Sunbeam-Talbot Alpine model, which would be a much more pleasant prospect after these hot and rather claustrophobic saloons.

Harford III *(1952)*

'. . on the first hill or two we both bounced like mad to help the rear wheels grip, but we didn't really synchronize our bounces although we still managed to beat the other celebrities, which was our main aim.'

*M*ud-plugging trials form the only branch of motor sport in which the cars run with virtually flat tyres, keep largely in bottom gear and very rarely go much above 10 mph. Like so many specialist sports it sounds dead easy, though it is actually anything but. The co-ordination, throttle control and sensitivity demanded from the driver are quite fantastic. The object is essentially to climb further up an impossibly slippery or loose-surfaced hill than your opposition. You have a separate hand-operated 'fiddlebrake' lever for each rear wheel which you can apply to prevent that wheel spinning and dissipating power. To work these fiddlebrakes effectively while steering the car on to the least slippery route makes your brain work overtime. I drove the Harford only once, but it was quite a demanding winter's day out.

*C*uth Harrison was a great enthusiast and one-time ERA racing driver from the North. He had also driven in rallies and became a leading trials driver. The Kitching Trophy Trial was one of the sport's major events, and in February 1952 Cuth invited me to enter it, driving the Harford III, one of his side-valve Ford-engined specials. He put Reg Parnell into Harford II and John Bolster — who became famous as a deer-stalkered pit-lane foil to Raymond Baxter's television motor racing commentaries — in a Dellow.

We attracted the biggest crowd ever at a club trial, with 1,600 cars parked in the lanes nearby, while TV newsreel cameras covered the event. John *Autocar* Cooper came along as my passenger/bouncer/ballast and, although we didn't get that bouncing business together, we were the best of the visitors.

And I still swear it really is not nearly as easy as it looks . . .

Jaguar Mark VII *(1952-54)*

'What a fabulous car. I have the warmest affection for the old Mark VII because, although it looked like a great waddling dumpling and it made such a business of going round corners, it was actually very well-balanced and light to drive.'

9 May 1953 — Stowe Corner. The mighty Jaguar Mark VII at Silverstone gave Stirling enormous enjoyment and victory in the May meeting touring car races of 1952 and '53, then third place in 1954 after the starter pinion had jammed at the Le Mans-type start and he had to leap out and rock the great car in gear to free it before trying again!

*T*he great and apparently gormless Jaguar Mark VII saloons found their way into racing in the annual *Daily Express* Silverstone production touring car races. They were powerful enough to pull 110-115 mph on the straight and were so softly suspended that through the corners they would lean over to the most *enormous* degree. Inside they retained the standard seats which gave the driver no location whatsoever, so in tight corners I had to stretch my leg across to brace myself against the opposite door, otherwise I would slide across the seat like the carriage on a typewriter!

Despite such antics the cars would go so well, yet made such a business of doing so, that it was a real achievement to keep them going as fast as they could go. Despite all that body roll, they really did hold the road extremely well, and you could push them a long way before they would finally let go and gently slide beyond control.

The body seemed to fly out behind the rest of the car like a scarf, yet they were actually very light to steer, they had good power brakes, and really were as much fun as anything. Once you could accept the lean, they gave great confidence and, particularly in the wet, I found you could change their attitude on the throttle in a most well-mannered way to balance out that basic understeer.

I first did battle with a Jaguar Mark VII in the May Silverstone meeting of 1952, which was the first to use the current start-and-finish location just after Woodcote Corner. In practice Ken Wharton had lapped 3 seconds faster in his Healey saloon, but I made the best start and led throughout, beating Ken by 6 seconds. Apparently the tyre squeal accompanying me round Woodcote, right in front of the grandstands, on every lap prompted someone to suggest it should be recorded and played at the next Dunlop shareholders' meeting.

My trusty steed was 'LWK 343' a veteran of the Monte Carlo and RAC Rallies, and I would use it again for the corresponding race the following year, with the same result.

In practice for that 1953 meeting I rolled the works C-Type Jaguar which knocked me about a bit. But although bruised and stiff, I still managed to make the best Le Mans-type run-and-jump start in the touring car race. Again I led all the way, which proved to my satisfaction I hadn't lost my nerve after the accident.

When the 1954 May Silverstone meeting came round I was on a hat trick in the Mark VII, and Jaguar again prepared 'LWK 343' for me, plus 'LHP 5' for Tony Rolt, while 'assisting' Ian Appleyard with his car 'SUM 7'. But my car's starter jammed, which let Ian Appleyard get away to win from Tony and me, though all three of us shared fastest lap at 77.48 mph.

For 1955 I joined Mercedes-Benz, so my Jaguar-driving days were over. For sheer fun and entertainment value I think I missed the old Mark VIIs more than the Cs and Ds!

BRM V16 *(1952)*

'Without doubt the worst car I ever drove . . .'

This is the classic example of a small concern convincing itself it was Mercedes-Benz and going into the high-technology racing car business deeper than either its competence or its finances would allow.

BRM's V16-cylinder car had good drum brakes, quickly replaced by the first disc system in Formula 1, and quite a good gearbox, but I believe that was cribbed from pre-war Mercedes-Benz drawings . . . Its V16-cylinder centrifugally-supercharged 1½-litre engine was a fantastic device, which produced a lot of power along with a sensational, ear-splitting noise, but its power characteristics were totally unsuited to Grand Prix-style road racing.

Its chassis and suspension design was not really capable of putting its power through to the ground, its steering was simply dreadful and its cramped-up short-arm driving position was straight out of the ark. When the car was first announced it *sounded* absolutely stunning. Here at last was a British Grand Prix car which could take on the world, but its management was a shambles.

Extraordinary things happened; they would repair anything once it had gone wrong, yet seemed incapable of preventing similar failures recurring. When it was running on song it was fantastically powerful and far and away the fastest thing I had yet driven, but they expended all their energy persuading the engine to keep running and hardly any on making the chassis handle. It seemed to me that the driver wasn't meant to know too much, he was merely there as a necessary evil, and after just one race for them — and interminable testing — I took myself elsewhere.

The British Racing Motors project was created by driver Raymond Mays and engineer Peter Berthon, who had been primarily responsible pre-war for the very successful English Racing Automobiles project, better known as ERA.

Ray was a charming man, very much the sponsorship king of British competition during the '20s and '30s when he put together a long and highly successful career. In 1945 he contacted British industry with proposals for a co-operative project to build an astounding new Grand Prix car designed by Berthon. He attracted sufficient support for the British Motor Racing Research Trust to be formed, and with components being made for them throughout the industry he based his new team in the old ERA works behind his home at Eastgate House in Bourne, Lincolnshire.

From the beginning, the project was under-financed and Ray's vision of running a kind of British Daimler-Benz racing department became a nightmare. Industry at large was being told to 'Export or Die' by the Labour Government and there were endless delays and material shortages. The first car wasn't even completed until 1949 and it didn't race until 1950, and even then its début was premature.

All this time the Trust's PR machinery had been a great deal more effective than the racing car they were building, and the newspapers, magazines and radio had been pumping out BRM propaganda which raised public expectations to the sky.

Therefore, when this potential world-beating masterpiece broke its transmission on the startline at Silverstone first time out, people threw pennies in its cockpit and one newspaper headline screamed '*Blooming Rotten Motor*' with the words arranged one above the other so the initials down the page read 'BRM'.

Irrespective, that engine made a spine-tingling noise and the car itself, hardly any part of which stood higher than the tops of its wheels, really did look stunning.

While BRM were enduring all this agony, John Heath and George Abecassis of HWM simply got on with motor racing. My success in their cars, and the little Coopers and of course the TT XK120, had helped to make my name. I had gone to Folkingham Aerodrome in Lincolnshire in December 1949 when the first BRM had been unveiled to the press. Raymond Mays drove it round the aerodrome perimeter track a few times and it really did make a fabulous noise.

Ray had been the very first established motor racing figure to declare that perhaps this young chap Moss had some talent, and soon after that disastrous BRM début at Silverstone he contacted my father about the possibility of my trying the car.

Vague approaches continued through the winter of 1950-51, but it wasn't until the summer that I really followed them up. By that time two BRMs had finished in the British GP, and on 17 July I drove up to Folkingham to try one of the cars.

The silly thing about the aerodrome perimeter track which BRM used for testing was that its surface was disintegrating and in places strewn with gravel. The BRM engine's centrifugal supercharging went on producing more and more boost the higher the revs rose, unlike conventional Roots-type superchargers — as used by Alfa Romeo, Maserati and everybody else at that time — which ran up to a peak pressure somewhere high up in mid-range and then dropped away again beyond a certain point.

The Rolls-Royce centrifugal supercharging which BRM adopted had been developed in wartime aero engines to maintain high power outputs at high altitudes where the air was thin. Aero engines ran at near constant speeds, so the efficient centrifugal blower was ideal. Its only serious use in racing cars up to that time had been in American track racing. There again, the engines ran at almost constant speed, so they were being boosted at almost constant pressure.

But road racing was a totally different proposition. Here the engines had to rev through a very wide range, and were constantly accelerating and decelerating. With the BRM the higher the revs the greater the power output. On the narrow, hard road racing tyres of the time this spelled runaway wheelspin the moment the driven wheels broke traction, because as they began to spin the engine revs would climb, and that would mean higher boost going to the engine, which then meant even more power coming out of it to spin the wheels some more. The result was chronic wheelspin, until either the driver backed off, in which case the revs would fall completely out of bed and you'd have no power, or the engine probably went bang. Testing a car with such characteristics on a loose and slippery test track where the car could spin its wheels constantly was not going to teach them anything of value.

But I was the relative novice. I could discover nothing about the car at Folkingham except what great power it had, so I suggested to Ray they should take it to Silverstone or Goodwood where we would have some target lap times.

He agreed but, as became standard practice at BRM, many decisions were agreed but never acted upon. Peter Berthon especially was obsessed with secrecy, and I suspect there was a strong element of not wanting everybody to know how slow the car would be round a proper circuit in contrast to much more humble machinery . . .

The moment I got out of the car Ray offered me a contract for 1952, but I wasn't so sure. There was a vast difference between the BRM and any other car I'd yet driven. When I opened the throttle, even at high speeds in top gear, the whole thing shuddered with an almost frightening surge of power. It could spin its wheels effortlessly at speeds equal to most other cars' maximum. I wasn't used to such forces knocking my head back against the headrest under acceleration, and when I applied its powerful three-leading-shoe Girling drum brakes I was slammed forward against the steering wheel.

I could live with such engine and braking power, but I couldn't stand the car's driving position and general handling. I was so cramped against its steering wheel it was quite impossible to adopt my natural almost straight-armed driving stance. The car needed steering all the time, even on the straights. It felt very unstable and alarming.

I went to Bourne again on 26 August for a long technical discussion with Mays and Berthon. I told them I wanted to drive only British cars, which meant that the BRM was my only chance of a competitive Formula 1 ride. Ray offered me a drive in the Spanish GP at Barcelona, which after some thought I accepted with the proviso that I would require several hundred miles' serious testing and practice in the BRM before starting my first race in it.

Before Barcelona, however, both BRMs failed humiliatingly during Grand Prix practice at Monza, and they were withdrawn from the race. There was hell to pay, a storm of bad publicity at home and the Trust put its foot down and told Mays and Berthon to keep the cars out at Monza for a comprehensive test programme until they got them right.

I stopped off there the day after racing my HWM at Modena, and Bourne's chief mechanic Ken Richardson warmed up a car for me, but after only a lap and a half a piston went. The V16 was so complicated it then took the mechanics a couple of days to get it ready again. I was due to race at Goodwood so couldn't hang around. I returned home, then reported again at Monza and finally got to drive a car on 6 October. I did about ten laps before a piston popped again.

Fangio was testing an *Alfetta* at the same time. Team manager Guidotti let me have a go in it while the BRM mechanics began another long repair. The Alfa's brakes seemed bad compared to the BRM's, but its roadholding was good and stable. In comparison the BRM felt huge.

Two days later I got to drive the V16 again, lapping in 2:06 before overheating set in. Next day it boiled again and they changed the radiator in the lunch break. Finally the supercharger failed. Another day's testing saw me get down to 1:58.8, 2.1 secs outside Farina's *Alfetta* lap record. On the fifth day I saw 11,400 rpm on the straight, which was I believe 184 mph — then the engine failed again.

I had another minor race engagement, and a telegram was awaiting me at home from Mr Ferrari asking me to sign up with him exclusively for 1952. After my Bari experience of the mysterious ways in which his team worked, I politely refused. It was a great honour, but I still hoped there was promise in the all-British BRM.

I didn't have to return to Monza short-term, because Ray then brought the cars home, and the Barcelona entry was scratched amid another storm of disappointment, and some derision.

Ray had asked me to submit a written report on my impressions of the car at Monza, and this is what I wrote, dated 12 November 1951:

'All the following remarks are based upon facts and findings and not theories.

'1. The real difficulty in handling this car springs from the fact that it becomes unbalanced very easily, ie, when it is put into a drift or slide. No sooner has this begun than the car gives a flick sideways, in a small but troublesome oversteer; this characteristic is made worse if the surface is bumpy.

'2. The car has a dangerous trick of understeering excessively on a trailing throttle which, although undesirable, is sometimes unavoidable. This was found to decrease if the anti-roll bar was made thinner, or completely done away with.

'3. The car's handling definitely improved a lot in the wet if the anti-roll bar was removed, but when tried in this condition in the dry it was bad. When a very thin anti-roll bar was fitted, the cornering in the dry on slow (up to 70 mph) bends was improved over the thicker bar; but when it came to fast curves (over 120 and up to 165 mph) a high-pitch patter developed and the other bar was found superior.

'4. On fast curves the front of the car drifts out too far, showing that the wheels do not grip sufficiently. This makes it difficult to steer the car accurately while drifting.

'5. On watching the front wheels closely while cornering, I found that they wobbled sideways, as well as the usual up and down suspension movement. This wobbling was apparent on the track rods as well as the wheels and, although considerable, no judder whatsoever was felt at the steering wheel, pointing to the fact that there must be considerable play in the layout. In actual fact I found that one could move the steering wheel 5″ to 7″ without the car's direction being affected. While the car was on ramps I turned the steering wheel 10″ with only 1″ movement of the road wheels due to slack in the steering joints.

'Could a rack and pinion steering be tried?

'6. With the driving position as it is now, the steering ratio is too low, as proved by the fact that one's arms get tied up before a correction can be effected. This fault may be corrected when the driver has more room between himself and the steering wheel.

'7. The driving position is bad because:-

'a) The driver is much too close to the wheel.

'b) Brake pedal and throttle are too far apart; this could be corrected simply by turning the brake pedal pad round.

'c) The seat back is too erect and I think it would be more comfortable and a better layout if it was leant back 5 to 10 degrees more. The padding round the shoulders is very good but I should like a little more in the small of my back and stronger sides to the seat. Pedal distance is excellent for myself.

'8. I think the rear end of the car is excellent, also the brakes.

'9. The top gear seemed to be about right for Monza, as far as I could judge. It would be an advantage if 3rd gear was lowered a bit so that both Lesmo and the Pave could be taken in this gear. 4th could be a fraction higher, I think, but until we get the car's road-holding improved it is difficult to say what speed one can get round the Curva Grande in that gear.'

The upshot of this report, which I think was quite detailed and constructive, was that Bourne carried out a number of modifications, mostly to the seat and driving position. My main gripe, about the hopeless steering, was apparently ignored.

A further period of Monza testing in November was ruined by continuous rain, and then in February/March 1952 there was a six-week period of BRM testing at Monza, in the middle of which I drove the XK120 in the Lyon-Charbonnières Rally. An early disc brake system was now fitted to the car, the first in Formula 1. The whole period was punctuated by the usual mechanical problems but

21 March 1952 — Testing the BRM P15 V16-cylinder at Monza Autodrome, outside Milan. Here Stirling negotiates one of the two Curva di Porfido *turns before opening-up Britain's fractious white hope along the start-and-finish straight. Note Dunlop's experimental disc brakes visible through the wheels.*

we all felt things were progressing. The Trust made noises about entering the Turin GP on 6 April, which would have been great, because Formula 1 looked set to die from lack of competition since Alfa Romeo had just retired, which left Ferrari with no opposition other than BRM. The V16s simply had to run in Turin to disprove the team's reputation for unreliability and non-starting. If they non-started again, then race organizers across Europe would turn to the bigger fields and better racing offered by Formula 2, and that would leave our 'world-beating' Formula 1 car high and dry because it wouldn't be eligible for a World Championship run for Formula 2 cars.

The Turin organizers offered BRM £1,500 start money for just one V16 to face Ferrari, a fabulous sum in those days. When I went off for the Lyon-Charbonnières, Ken Wharton took my place as test driver, then I returned and everybody was working towards Turin. Suddenly, with just days to go, the Trust ordered both cars back to England and scratched the entry.

It was shattering.

I felt so sorry for development engineer Tony Rudd and his mechanics. Mays had been trying to get Fangio, the reigning World Champion, to drive the car and now he'd received confirmation from Argentina that Fangio and Gonzalez were both coming to Folkingham and wanted to test a car there on 5 April, the day before Turin.

Anxious for publicity, Ray was simply dazzled by the prospect of the World Champion driving for BRM, so the team opted out of Turin, leaving Ferrari with a dull walkover. Race promoters throughout Europe got the message that BRM entries really could not be relied upon, so Formula 1 died and Formula 2 became the Championship class.

BRM had got its charismatic drivers, but they no longer had a Grand Prix car . . . just an outdated Formula 1 and *Libre* machine which still wasn't raceworthy.

We had all tried to persuade Ray on the 'phone from Monza of the importance of racing at Turin, but he argued that it was better to let Fangio test the car than

7 June 1952 — Ulster Trophy, Dundrod, Stirling is push-started from the pit-lane as he takes his already-ailing disc-braked BRM out in preparation for his first and only V16 race. Note all the extra cooling louvres cut in the couple of months since pre-season testing at Monza. Here in Ulster they were still insufficient to save the day.

risk another public fiasco by racing. I had been all teed-up to drive in Turin and was bitterly disappointed. Fangio subsequently told me that if he'd known of the date clash, he would gladly have come over after Turin, but nobody told him.

The first Formula 1 entry of the season eventually came at Albi, but the BRMs were driven there by Fangio, Gonzalez and Ken Wharton because I was involved that day wearing out a Frazer Nash and crashing a C-Type at Monaco.

That Albi race was in southern France on 1 June, and the Trust had already publicly promised the Northern Ireland Prime Minister that they would run three V16s in his Ulster Trophy race at Dundrod on 7 June, the following weekend.

In those days you could not reliably airlift an entire team from one circuit to another in mere hours, and BRM with their perpetual shortages could not possibly rebuild engines and properly prepare their cars in time between these two events.

Anyway, Fangio and I were to drive at Dundrod and we found the entire team arriving there almost out on their feet, and the two V16s which were flown in very late were also 'rather tired'.

Only one car was available for first practice and Juan did a few laps in it to learn the circuit before I tried my car. The handling seemed better than when I had last driven it at Monza, but on this circuit the car felt more dangerous than ever! I realized it was because Monza is 100 feet wide with broad verges. Here at Dundrod, I was driving along a really good and difficult country-road circuit, between banks and trees. The car still wandered and twitched on the straight, and you can imagine how the banks seemed to be darting out at me all the time. And its engine would not fire cleanly on all 16.

That night Ray decided, without telling Fangio or me, to fix my car as being the least unhappy of the pair, and to give it to Fangio, a move which — since Juan was number one — I had already agreed to in early negotiation. But nobody told me it was happening.

When I went to collect my car in Belfast next morning, I knew it wasn't mine as soon as I sat in it. It had my race number, and my seat, but it wasn't my car. It was Fangio's with a new radiator fitted overnight to stave off the overheating experienced in practice. One of the mechanics owned up to the switch when I asked him. Ray said nothing to me, so I kept quiet and just drove up to the circuit behind him in the other V16.

By the time we arrived, my car was already boiling. Ray told me not to worry. 'It will probably be all right in the race,' he said. Actually I was quite relieved that it probably wouldn't last the distance, for Dundrod was damp after heavy rain.

Fangio and I lined up on the back of the grid, and it was raining again as the engines were started with two minutes to go. Then my engine stalled, and had to be restarted, and as the starter held up the thirty-second board I put the clutch out and selected first gear. With about ten seconds to go, the clutch began to take up and the car began to creep . . .

There was nothing I could do to stop it as I had the clutch right out. I had to heel-and-toe with my right foot on brake and accelerator together to keep the engine running yet hold the car stationary. The clutch was taking up more and more, so I had to brake harder and harder, and of course just as the flag was about to fall the clutch burned out and the engine stalled.

I glanced across at Fangio and saw that he had stalled as well! So as the field roared away it left our two BRMs behind. The mechanics rushed out to push-start us, and we screamed off, Fangio first, then me.

My clutch was slipping dreadfully, and he quickly lost me. Then I came to the left-hander before the hairpin and there he was facing back towards me, going down the road backwards, so the two V16s were nose-to-nose, careering down towards the hairpin in most unconventional style! He had taken avoiding action when 'Bira's' OSCA had flown through the hedge, and spun. He seemed to be going faster backwards than I was forwards.

He rolled beyond the hairpin and stopped, while I crawled round with the clutch slipping, and he then rejoined behind me. By the end of that first lap, apart from the bad clutch — which didn't matter too much as the gearbox really was so good — I couldn't get full revs, and the engine was already boiling again.

On the second lap, after I'd passed some of the slower cars, the gear-lever knob came off in my hand. I slung it at somebody as a souvenir.

By this time Fangio and I were both having trouble getting round the hairpin. We had to slip our clutches and with mine already practically burned-out this didn't help. The V16 was so high-revving, with such poor torque at low revs, that we had to keep it running between 10 and 12,000 rpm to get results . . . it would be like trying to hold an ordinary car at between 4,000 and 5,000 rpm in London traffic.

After the second lap I came into the pits with chronic overheating. They told me to keep going. Frankly I wouldn't have minded if they'd called it off right then. As it was, I crawled round to complete four laps, then they pushed the car away. Fangio suffered persistent fuel starvation and kept stopping at the pits before finally calling it a day.

Ray issued a statement after the race, saying in part 'We are ashamed. But we had extremely bad luck. If the race had been a day or two later the result would have been different.'

BRM always wanted an extra day or two to make the result different; but their car was so complex and under-developed, and their organization so chaotic, that they never got it . . . and there are no 'ifs' in motor racing.

I thought it over, and wrote to tell him I didn't really want to drive the BRM again. I didn't either, but when seven years later I had the chance to drive their replacement 2 ½ -litre unsupercharged car, that would be a different matter. In contrast to the V16 being by far the nastiest car I ever drove, the 1959 4-cylinder would be one of the nicest — by some way.

ERA G-Type *(1952)*

'Leslie Johnson told me David Hodkin was a genius, and I believed him . . .'

*T*his post-war ERA wasn't a patch on the pre-war cars of the same name, but I discovered that rather late in the day. It was intended to combine the best Bristol 2-litre Formula 2 engine with an outstandingly stiff yet light chassis, plus sophisticated suspension and weight distribution and a low centre of gravity. The naturally tall Bristol engine was lowered by fitting a dry-sump lubrication system with its oil carried in a separate tank instead of a conventional sump underneath. Hodkin then made the car low overall by offsetting the driver's seat, so I sat beside the centre-line prop shaft instead of above it, in a broad virtual sports car body which left only the wheels unclothed. It was all intended to generate so much cornering power that it could compensate through the corners for what the Bristol engine's modest horsepower lost to Ferrari and Maserati along the straights. But the car was just over-clever and simply didn't work. I had wanted desperately to find a competitive British Formula 2 car, and this wasn't it . . .

*I*n 1948, my former Jaguar team-mate and friend Leslie Johnson had bought moribund ERA Ltd from its pre-war co-founder and sponsor Humphrey Cook. Leslie based it in Dunstable, doing automotive R & D work, and employed some excellent people. His first chief engineer was the pre-war technical head of Auto Union's GP team, Prof Dr Robert Eberan von Eberhorst. When he moved on, he was replaced at Dunstable by Cambridge engineering graduate David Hodkin.

Formula 1 died through lack of support before the 1952 World Championship season began, so the CSI ran its World Championship instead for 2-litre unsupercharged Formula 2 cars. Of course the Italian teams had tailor-made cars ready and running. We Brits tried to wave the flag with a variety of mainly Bristol-engined specials.

Leslie Johnson told me David Hodkin was a genius, and described their plans for an ultra-sophisticated new G-Type ERA. I was persuaded that it would be far superior to anything that Cooper could blacksmith together.

I was wrong.

Eberan had proved the efficacy of 'big-tube' chassis construction, and now Hodkin developed a remarkable frame built from two massive tubes made from magnesium sheet rolled into an oval section, and joined by four cross-members. It weighed only 95 lb and had a stiffness of 3,000 lb per degree deflection per inch, which was a combination which would not be bettered for ten years, until the arrival of the monocoque Lotus 25.

High polar moment of inertia was the object of Hodkin's preferred weight distribution, which he achieved by splitting the great masses of engine and gearbox apart at each end of the frame, like the weights on a dumb-bell, to make the car inherently stable.

Its rear wheels were located by a de Dion axle system whose links could be adjusted to induce understeer or oversteer at will as the car rolled in corners. Its wheels were cast light alloy with hollow spokes to promote airflow over the front brake drums, while the rear drums were mounted inboard to reduce unsprung weight.

I drove this car seven times after its début in the Belgian GP on 22 June 1952, and it never made the grade. It braked and steered very nicely, but first time out at Spa a piston seized in practice and the team had no spare engine. They had to fly one out from Dunstable and even then it had to be converted to dry-sump lubrication in the garage overnight. Just after the start a gudgeon pin broke, the new engine locked solid and I found myself careering off the road into a kilometre post. The car caught fire on impact and I baled out to ponder just what I had let myself in for . . .

In the British GP the rebuilt ERA overheated and misfired, I tried too hard to compensate and spun. While I was having these problems Mike Hawthorn was making his name in his cheap and cheerful — and uncomplicated — but effective Cooper-Bristol, fourth at Spa and third at Silverstone behind the all-conquering Ferraris.

The ERA then went better at Boreham, where I finished third, behind Mike. We didn't survive the Dutch GP, then at the end of the year at Goodwood, I set best 2-litre time in practice before being shunted at the first corner of one race by Dennis Poore's Connaught, but managed to run again later that day. In October at Castle Combe I led the 2-litres for five laps until the steering broke, and finally at Charterhall the steering again gave trouble — all probably stemmed from the Goodwood shunt.

At last the G-Type was proving itself one of the quickest F2 cars in Britain, but that wasn't worth much when it was still obviously no match for Ferrari or Maserati internationally.

Its broad body, though low, created more aerodynamic drag than the conventional centre-seat style used by everyone else. It had very powerful brakes but at that time they tended to come on in a grabby way, and that spoiled the delicate touch necessary on the steering wheel and in balancing the car which I knew was vital to corner competitively.

ERA failed to capitalize on their chassis' light weight because the car was not noticeably lighter overall than its opposition. Its basic understeer gave a feeling of secure stability which probably cost us dearly, since the front tyres were scrubbing against the track surface and that dissipated horsepower which we couldn't afford, being already some 30 horsepower down on the Italians.

What was nice was to be able to see the wheels go up and down with nothing else flexing. Even when I spun it in the wet and it seemed to go on revolving for an eternity I still felt a curious confidence, and I was able to gather it all up and press on virtually regardless.

It was, above all, a project which made an awful lot of fuss about doing very little. By this time I was very disillusioned by the Clever Professor approach to racing car design. I would eventually learn that even the most brilliant concept can fail if the team concerned lacks the manpower and organization and money to develop the inevitable bugs out of it. Even Maserati took a year to sort out a design developed from a preceding model, while it took the titanic resources of Mercedes-Benz to produce a winner from the drawing board, and even they promptly lost a race or two through teething troubles. Against those examples, what chance did poor little ERA stand?

Before the end of the year Leslie Johnson sold the entire G-Type project to Bristol, who adopted its virtual two-seat layout as the basis for their aerodynamic Le Mans Coupés of 1953-55. In the 24-hour race's medium-capacity classes, David Hodkin's baby finally found its niche . . .

4 October 1952 — Trying to give the unloved and unlovely G-Type ERA every possible advantage, Stirling cut corners tightly during the minor Formula 2 event at Castle Combe. It was more wasted effort — the car's steering broke soon after.

Connaught A-Type *(1952-53)*

'The Connaught was really an educated Cooper . . . which meant, unfortunately, that it was not as quick . . .'

*I*drove the Formula 2 Connaughts only three times in 1952-53. They were beautifully-made and sophisticated but compared to the blacksmith Cooper-Bristols were always overweight. They handled well enough, but then under-powered cars often do, and they were never as easy to drive as the Cooper, though more nimble in some ways than the rather bastardized front-engined Coopers which I would use. Although it was larger than the Cooper and you sat more in it than on it, the Connaught never felt like a big car. It was a car of reasonable finesse but not that easy to drive, fairly rewarding but never a fun car, you couldn't hurl it into a corner, it was not forgiving in that way. Its basically Lea-Francis engine was pretty responsive, but you had to show respect on revs. If they said 6,000 rpm, boy they meant it; 6,100 and you were in trouble!

*R*odney Clarke was another of those great British car enthusiasts who virtually threw all sensible business caution to the winds post-war to begin building racing cars. He was actually a very bright engineer and many features built into his Connaught cars were very advanced. You can judge how good they were if you appreciate that their cast-alloy wheels — which were a very expensive and exotic rarity in the early '50s — are still accepted in historic events today, whereas Cooper's original cast wheels have long since been banned because they developed fatigue cracks in the poor-quality magnesium alloy of which they were made.

Rodney Clarke was able to turn his Continental Automobiles business at Send, in Surrey, into Connaught Cars thanks to the financial backing of Ken McAlpine who was not only heir to the building company fortunes but also an enthusiastic amateur racing driver.

I first drove one of their A-Type Formula 2 cars in the 1952 Italian GP at Monza. Leslie Johnson's G-Type ERA had really flopped by that time. In fairness, its form had been improving, but compared to Ferrari and Maserati and even to Mike Hawthorn's GP record with his humble Cooper-Bristol I had realized it was a no-hoper.

I talked it over with Leslie and we agreed we wouldn't attempt to run at Monza, where the long straights and fast curves put the emphasis on power and straight-line speed which the G-Type did not possess. If it had had a forte at all it *should* have been its cornering power, which didn't really count for much at Monza.

Therefore, I arranged to drive a Connaught there instead. Although it obviously lacked the power of the Italian cars, it might be quicker than the G-Type through the air.

Connaught used to transport their cars in an old cut-about bus. It arrived late in Milan and for some reason we had to unload the three cars and drive them on the open road from the city centre out to Monza, in the dark, and of course without lights! McAlpine, Dennis Poore and I drove them behind a police motor-cyclist who hammered along at 70-plus, going for gold, with us roaring along in his wake anxious not to lose our guide.

Perhaps of more importance to Mike Hawthorn and me than the Grand Prix itself was our battle for BRDC Gold Star points. This rather took precedence over our final placings overall, which against Ferrari and Maserati would be of fairly academic interest.

Mike was 0.2 sec quicker than me in practice until I managed to slipstream Ascari along the back stretch to pip him by 1.4 secs. Then in the race my engine broke a rocker, and Mike's engine snapped its magneto drive so it all proved completely academic anyway.

I next drove the Connaught in the Ulster Trophy at Dundrod the following May. Mike was in the works Ferrari team by that time and he was also entered.

7 September 1952 — SM's Italian Grand Prix debut in the works A-Type Connaught stopped short with engine failure after a hopeless attempt to match the home-grown products of Ferrari and Maserati.

The race comprised two heats and a final. We started in different heats, I lost 30 secs with gearbox trouble in mine and rejoined sixth. Duncan Hamilton was leading in his HWM, I managed to get back into second place but he won by nine seconds — despite bounding high off a bank along the way. My car's gearbox was still sick, so they put me instead into Roy Salvadori's sister A-Type for the final, where I would meet Mike who had won his heat for Ferrari. The Clerk of the Course decided that swopping cars was agin the rules, so I wasn't allowed to start. What had been promoted as a great Moss v Hawthorn confrontation therefore never happened . . . I was annoyed about that, even though I doubt I would have stood any chance against Mike in that Ferrari.

My final Formula 2 Connaught drive followed in the Dutch GP at Zandvoort where I had more trouble and finished a dispirited ninth. They were not lucky cars for me, and I had to look elsewhere to find the competitive British-made Grand Prix car which I desired.

Humber Super Snipe *(1952)*

'No don't be silly, of course I didn't race it, it was a publicity stunt for the Rootes Group, fifteen countries in five days . . . and not a bad car for that kind of jaunt . . .'

2 December 1952 — Leslie Johnson, SM, David Humphrey and John Cutts enjoying the space and comfort of the Humber Super Snipe during their epic, virtually non-stop, European tour.

The idea was to demonstrate this big, luxurious 4-litre car's ability to cope with all types of weather and road conditions while visiting as many European countries as possible within a very strict time schedule. It was a winter run, made in late-November/early-December 1952. The crew comprised, inevitably, Leslie Johnson (again) and myself, navigated by John Cutts and with David Humphrey of Rootes as riding mechanic. We started from Oslo in Norway, and visited Sweden, Denmark, Germany, Holland, Belgium, Luxembourg, France, Switzerland, Liechtenstein, Austria, Italy, Yugoslavia, Spain and Portugal, just nipping across the borders and out again in appalling weather — snow, ice, blizzards almost everywhere.

We had a super-target of four days, which meant averaging 35 mph, and we went into our fourth 24 hours aiming to do the final 1,200 miles to meet it. I had done most of the mountain driving, always making up time downhill, but finally Leslie had to average 64 mph for the last three hours across Spain to Portugal. He did it, and we had covered 3,280 miles in 3 days 17 hours 59 minutes . . . which was 900 miles a day with only the German *Autobahnen* as modern-type motorway.

The only trouble was one puncture; not at all bad, considering.

Sunbeam-Talbot Alpine (1953)

'The only car in which I ever won by cheating . . . after so much effort I really felt I deserved it, never mind some piffling regulation . . .'

16 August 1953 — Marseilles. Battered but unbowed — SM and his regular Rootes factory team navigator John Cutts with the Sunbeam after another gruelling and very successful International Alpine Rally.

*I*nto 1953 I was retained by the Rootes Group. We did the round-Europe run in the big Humber — see page 88 — and when the Sunbeam Alpine convertible was developed, with an eye on the American market and named in honour of our success in the previous year's Alpine Rally, they asked Sheila van Damm and me to do some high-speed runs with it. Sheila did 120 mph on the Jabbeke-Aeltre record stretch in Belgium, and then at Montlhéry Leslie Johnson put 112 miles into one hour and I lapped at 116. Then came the serious business of the Alpine Rally . . .

*N*orman Garrad entered a team of the new Alpine convertibles in the 1953 event, which fell between the French and British GPs. John Cutts and I struck early trouble with wheel nuts working loose. Next morning on the timed 30-mile climb, including the Falzarego, Lana and Pordoi Passes, I had to stop twice, once when a plug lead came adrift and secondly when my rally plate dropped off. I was trying so hard I still managed fastest Sunbeam time.

The rally thereafter was rather easier than predicted. At the finish in Cannes 25 of us remained unpenalized, so John and I had won our second consecutive *Coupe*, our team-mates Sheila van Damm/Anne Hall won the *Coupe des Dames* plus a *Coupe des Alpes*, and George Murray-Frame/John Pearman and John Fitch/Peter Miller also took *Coupes*. Peter Collins and Leslie Johnson both retired their cars, with back axle and engine trouble, but now with two consecutive *Coupes* to my name I was in line for a *Coupe des Alpes en Or* — the much-coveted Gold Cup — for three consecutive penalty-free Alpine Rallies. This would be quite a feat, as so far only one had ever been awarded — to Ian Appleyard in his legendary Jaguar.

George Murray-Frame, Rootes' rally specialist, was also in the running, and he already had a Silver Cup on his sideboard for three non-consecutive unpenalized Alpines.

Obviously we were very keen when the 1954 Rally came round. But weather conditions were appalling; it was July but they would have suited a 'Monte'. The Alps were snowed-in and some of the most demanding early Cols had to be by-passed. This reduced tyre wear and the usual Alpine problems of overheating and fuel vaporization. The problem instead was keeping warm in our convertible Alpines.

After the first twenty hours on the road the night stop at St Moritz saw 62 of the original 82 starters still running. Sheila van Damm lost 80 secs on the Dolomite circuit which ultimately cost us the Team Prize.

Then in a ridiculous 1 km straightline speed test I pumped up the tyres to 50 psi, and had the normal oil drained out and replaced instead with thin spindle oil to reduce drag. Others didn't bother to this degree and they missed their target times by a fraction, which proved crucial.

The Rally then had a sting in its tail with the final 29 hours from Cortina to Cannes. It was fantastically demanding. We tackled the slow Dolomite roads first, then the newly-cleared Stelvio, the Petit St Bernard, Iseran, Glandon, Croix de Fer and Galibier and finally the Col de la Cayolle and down into Cannes.

It was almost impossible to keep to schedule down the la Cayolle and we were all running terribly close to the permitted hour's lateness. Sheila bounced her Alpine off a bridge but carried on. I tried so desperately hard to stay unpenalized that we covered the last few miles to one control utterly flat-out downhill with John Cutts counting off the time beside me. We just made it to the split-second . . . keeping our chances for that Gold Cup still alive.

For the first and only time in my life the sheer release of tension after driving that hard overwhelmed me. I burst into tears; most extraordinary.

The car had suffered. Only second and third gears survived, but we still entered Grasse on time. Eventually 37 crews reached Cannes for the final test, most of their cars battered and quite a few crippled.

Scrutineers were to verify that every finisher had all mechanical features intact — 'as they had started'. We were penalty-free, but they were looking at us — somebody had tipped them off about my gearbox problems.

That Gold Cup was tantalizingly within my reach and rightly or wrongly I felt I bloody well deserved it!

The scrutineers asked me to demonstrate that the car still had all its gears. First and top had gone for ever, but with a scrutineer beside me I drew away from rest in normal second, chattering to him all the time, '*Voila! Le premier!*' He nodded. I accelerated, and changed up with much waggling of the steering column gear-change, surreptitiously flicking the overdrive button as I did so into overdrive second, '*Voila,*' I said, '*Deuxieme!*'. He nodded again, then another waggly change flicking the overdrive button off to select normal third, '*Troisieme!*' — at least that was the truth — and then, with a final flourish, overdrive-third masqueraded as top gear — '*Quatrieme!*'

To my enormous relief he nodded and beamed '*Bon, merci Monsieur Moss . . . felicitations!*' I had won my third consecutive *Coupe* with John Cutts and secured that coveted Gold Cup . . .

It is the only time I can ever remember having cheated.

George had lost his chance by 1/5 second in the speed test, but Sheila and Anne Hall won the *Coupe des Dames* again and our Sunbeam Alpines finished 3-4-5-6-7 in the 2,600 cc class.

Later that year, in November, Norman Garrad took me over to the States for the American Mountain Rally, driving an Alpine navigated by Ron Kessel and although I didn't do particularly well we won the Team Prize again which was Rootes' main objective. It was while in New York on that trip that Ken Gregory telephoned to tell me of Mercedes' fabulous offer for 1955.

Rallying for the Rootes Group was the last thing on my mind as I hurried back to Europe . . .

Cooper-Alta Special (1953)

'It took twelve weeks to build. It was the first Formula 2 car to run disc brakes. And it was a catastrophe . . .'

*T*he idea was to build an all-British Grand Prix car for 1953 using the best proven equipment available, mounted in a light and simple chassis with quite sophisticated suspension and powered by an Alta 4-cylinder engine using Weber twin-choke carburettors. It was a dog. Quite a good-looking dog in fact, but a dog nonetheless . . .

*T*he success of our prototype Kieft 500, largely designed and built for me by John *Autocar* Cooper and Ray Martin, persuaded me to become involved in a Formula 2 car project which John mooted around the time of the 1952 Motor Show. He suggested that chassis parts could be supplied by John *Racing Car* Cooper, and that Ray Martin could build them up assisted by Alf Francis, former chief mechanic of HWM, and Tony Robinson.

I favoured using a 6-cylinder Maserati engine, but they would only sell us a complete car. What we all really wanted was a British car so I accepted Alf's suggestion that we should use an Alta 4-cylinder instead. He had considerable experience of them at HWM, using Italian Weber carburettors. They already gave 140 bhp — the equal of a Bristol 6-cylinder — and he felt there was more to come, so we went with that.

The original deal with Cooper Cars was for our car to use their frame tubes, wheels and body panels so that it would look externally like their latest front-engined Cooper Mark II, but *Autocar* Cooper wanted to use coil-spring-and-wishbone front suspension instead of their standard transverse leaf-spring, and his design also required different front stub axles to carry Girling disc brakes, plus a de Dion rear axle with coil-springs and inboard-mounted drum brakes instead of the normal Cooper-Bristol set-up.

The idea, as in the Kieft, was to eliminate basic oversteer and substitute stable understeer instead, a feature which I now realize is not a good idea if the driver has the ability to cope with oversteer.

It became obvious that we could not use a complete Cooper frame because so many tubes had to be resited to pick-up John's new suspension, so Ray Martin and Alf Francis worked at fantastic speed to get the new frame to Surbiton only eight weeks after the design began, ready for the body panels to be made for it. We had the engine on order from Geoffrey Taylor's little factory at Tolworth beside the Kingston By-pass, but when it arrived, with only eleven days left before our target début at Easter Goodwood, they found it was bigger than the mock-up around which they had built the car. It fouled the rack-and-pinion steering, which had to be resited and that ruined the steering geometry.

The car was dropped off the trestles on to its wheels for the first time at 4 am on the Monday preceding Goodwood. Its front suspension promptly collapsed because the coil-springs were far too weak. Three hours' work put supplementary coils inside them to jack it all up, and then they found the car was too big to fit into our brand-new transporter!

After some surgery and a lot of cursing they got the car to Goodwood, where I drove it briefly. It was entered in three races, ran badly in the first and we scratched it from the rest.

There were so many problems it's hard to recall them all. We could not balance the front disc brake effect against that of the inboard rear drums. Oil leaking from the final drive affected the drums mounted on its cheeks. Oil and brakes never mix happily!

While the G-Type ERA frame had impressed with its extreme stiffness the previous year, this one demonstrated the torsional rigidity of a wet bus ticket. It flexed and whipped and vibrated under braking and, despite John's aim of designing-in stable understeer, it was actually extremely twitchy if I tried to corner at all quickly.

5 July 1953 — French GP, Reims-Gueux — Shortly before the clutch disintegration which could so easily have cut short SM's career there and then, his specially-built Cooper-Alta Spl hurtles along the Soissons road, towards the city of Reims . . .

This twitchiness was exacerbated by preposterously high-geared steering, which felt even higher than the Frazer Nash and which simultaneously demanded so much strength yet so much sensitivity to prevent over-correction that it was quite impossible.

We all worked hard and at Silverstone I ran second to a Maserati but with its chassis faults no longer obscuring all other facets of its performance I now realized how under-powered that Alta engine really was. The car carried me through the Eifelrennen at Nürburgring, finishing a distant and uncompetitive sixth, at Rouen I finished last with trouble in the Alta gearbox, and finally in the French GP at Reims I was hammering down the straight at peak revs when the flywheel disintegrated between my feet. Flying pieces burst the bell-housing and shrapnel gashed my leg . . . it could have been much worse. That was the final straw.

I watched Mike Hawthorn win his great battle with Fangio's Maserati to become the first Englishman since Seaman to win a *Grande Epreuve*, and then decided we should abandon our misbegotten Cooper-Alta special. For the German GP in four weeks' time we would fit the Alta engine — which had improved quite considerably under Alf's attentions — into a standard Cooper Mark II frame which we would buy from *Racing Car* Cooper . . .

It was the end of my competitive relationship with Ray Martin, and tragically my long friendship with John *Autocar* Cooper did not survive long before he died in a head-on road accident behind the wheel of a Le Mans Rep Frazer Nash.

Cooper-Alta Mark II Special *(1953)*

'The Alta engine running on nitro-methane produced an awful lot of power, so much that it destabilized the near-standard Cooper chassis we were using and at Monza it peeled-off tyre treads as easily as peeling a banana . . .'

*A*fter the final collapse of our own Cooper-Alta project we had to come up with something fast to replace it, and dropping the Alta engine into an off-the-shelf Cooper chassis seemed the answer. Only when we started on the project did we find it wasn't going to be that simple, and when we found more power from the engine by running it on nitro, the standard frame was simply overwhelmed. We ended up with a car which went like a rocket down the straights, so fast that Cooper's 15-inch wheels — the only size available — centrifuged their tyres to destruction. It demanded great finesse through the corners; it had a very narrow band of cornering performance and would not forgive small mistakes. It was a challenge which I didn't really enjoy, because despite all the drama — and some minor success — it was still not competitive with the best.

*A*lf Francis was in charge of building-up this car for me along with his assistant Tony Robinson. We decided to mate the Alta engine this time with a pre-selector gearbox and then found that the assembly wouldn't fit into the standard Cooper Mark II chassis. So we had a pile of bits, Charlie Cooper — John *Racing Car* Cooper's father — let Alf use his chassis jig suitably modified in the Surbiton works, and Alf set about building me a Grand Prix car in eleven days.

I had discovered the horrors of the under-developed V16 BRM four years after its inception; of the G-Type ERA after a year's construction; of the Cooper-Alta Special after twelve weeks; and here we were tackling the replacement Cooper-Alta in under twelve days — you might observe that some people never learn . . . but it worked out on balance better than expected.

However, we got in deeper still. John Morris of SU persuaded me to try his company's fuel injection, and I thought there might be some advantage because the modified Hilborn-Travers injection system used by Connaught on the A-Types had worked quite well. Rodney Clarke's thinking was very advanced for the time, and he had also mixed nitro-methane into the Connaught's fuel which unleashed more power than his basically Lea-Francis engine had any proper right to.

Alf couldn't cure misfiring in time for us to use the injection system in Germany, so we reverted to SU carburettors and then tried Rodney Clarke's nitro fuel tweak instead and on the dyno at Barwell Engineering in Chessington the result was *amazing!* The Alta ripped out 200 bhp, and 100 bhp per litre at that time was very good indeed . . .

The new car was completed in eleven days from Alf cutting the first metal, and at Nurburgring after jamming in second gear while warming-up before the start it behaved well enough for me to finish sixth. At Sables d'Olonne a week later I was third. Alf installed injection for a minor race at Charterhall, where we retired, then refitted the carburettors for the *Libre* event that same day in which I diced with Tony Rolt in Rob Walker's Connaught until my hastily fitted carburettors drifted off tune.

Back at Barwell's Alf refitted injection, and although nitro corroded the fuel pump's internals we took the car to Monza on nitro fuel to frighten the Italians. With the car running stationary its exhaust fumes set everybody's eyes streaming and if they inhaled some of the gases they had to fight to catch their breath.

We weren't allowed to warm the car up before the race because of this, and had to start from cold on the line . . .

26 September 1953 — Moss's favourite number '7' on the Cooper-Alta Mark II 'eleven-day wonder' car, seen here at Goodwood's Woodcote Corner during the circuit's final major meeting of the year where, in its three races, the nitro-fuelled special finished second, fourth and retired.

On lap two of the Grand Prix I lay fifth, trailing two Ferraris and Maseratis, and for twenty laps I made Felice Bonetto's life in his Maserati a misery. But I was pulling 135 mph across the finish line and just beyond that point where the apron merged into the road circuit there was a surface change from cool concrete to dark asphalt which got hot in the sun. I remember vividly running on to that surface change and *whish*, off would come a complete tyre tread. Each time one separated we had laboriously to change one of those little 15-inch wheels, which entailed undoing four studs because we didn't have proper knock-off centre-locks. The fuel tank also sprang a leak so I had to top it up four times instead of the scheduled three, and at the end of the day I finished thirteenth, but at least both car and engine had survived a full GP distance.

For the first time — apart from the BRM V16 — I had experienced real power in a single-seater, and I subsequently won both heats of the London Trophy at Crystal Palace in it, and next day took the F2 class at Prescott hill-climb! In the closing Goodwood meeting I was beaten into second place by a works Connaught which handled more easily on that circuit, I was fifth in the *Libre* race behind the *ThinWall Special* and two V16 BRMs, and finally, in a third race that day, I retired with magneto drive problems. That was the last time I drove the car, loaning it to Eric Thompson for the very last race of that season at Snetterton, where he crashed mildly on the opening lap.

If we could have had that nitro engine in the G-Type ERA chassis, and if the team could have been properly organized, we might perhaps have made our mark that season. As it was I had tried almost everything and had learned fast, and what I had learned was that there was nobody in Britain at that time who was capable of building a competitive Grand Prix car.

The only answer, sadly, was to buy foreign . . .

OSCA MT4 *(1954)*

**'A fantastic little car,
a real little jewel —
even when it had no
brakes . . .'**

*I*t had been a major ambition of mine to race in America, and when the
millionaire enthusiast and team patron Briggs Cunningham gave me the
opportunity I jumped at the chance. He invited me to join his team in Florida
to share his new 1,452 cc Italian sports car with his son-in-law Bill Lloyd in the
1954 Sebring 12-hour race. I was incredibly impressed by what turned out to
be a real little thoroughbred of a car. It was powerful and well-balanced and
very nimble, and it survived the 12-hours in quite good health, which is more
than can be said for the big works Lancias, and purely as the icing on the cake
— we won outright!

*O*SCA stood for *Officina Specializzata Costruzione Automobili,*which was
a company founded in Bologna in 1947 by the surviving Maserati brothers
after they had sold their original business to the industrialist Adolfo Orsi and
his son Omer. They were essentially very good, practical engine men and their
twin overhead camshaft sports car engines were really crisp and powerful. As
I discovered with the Cunningham-entered car at Sebring, the rest of the car
— apart perhaps from its drum brakes — wasn't at all bad either.

*7 March 1954 — Sebring
12-Hours — Stirling in the
little American-liveried Briggs
Cunningham-owned OSCA
which impressed him so
much on the desolate
Hendrick Air Base circuit.
What's a complete lack of
brakes between friends?
Sharing with Bill Lloyd, this
was Moss's first Sports Car
World Championship race
win.*

At the time I was asked to drive it, I didn't know anything about these cars
at all, but I did have a burning ambition to race in America. Here in England
life was still pretty hard. Wartime-style rationing was only just ending and life
was still rather grey and austere. The wealth evident in the Cunningham equipe's
turn-out each year at Le Mans seemed fantastic, and obviously as a film buff
I had a vision of the high life in the Land of the Free . . . they had no rationing,
they had good food, and no ration-coupons were necessary to obtain it.

I had asked Jaguar to enter a car for me at Sebring but they said no, and then
Briggs Cunningham made his offer which I accepted. The English party included
Reg Parnell, Roy Salvadori, Peter Collins and Pat Griffith for Aston Martin, and
leaving at the same time were Fangio, Ascari, Taruffi and Villoresi who were
to drive for Lancia.

With the little OSCA in such company we would clearly be the underdogs, but that was a situation I would always relish. That way you can only do better than expected . . .

The Lancias just wiped the floor with everybody for sheer speed, but Briggs' OSCA was quite amazing. It was very like a Cooper in character. You could drive it as hard as you liked, slinging it sideways was no trouble, and that was a good thing because as the race progressed we found it had little or no brakes and we had to put it into a slide to slow it down. Typical Italian, it was designed to go, not stop.

It was an extremely well-balanced little car and I noted in my diary '*I really must say this car really is a little beauty — 5,900 in top and 5,600 in gears — faster than the 'Nashes'*. After the first two hours the Lancias were way ahead but it became a real 'ten little nigger boys' race. The Lancias began to break, Taruffi eventually leading alone, with our OSCA second though miles behind. Then Taruffi's car packed up, two miles from the pits, and he began desperately to push it.

His task was hopeless, so we gleefully inherited the lead with the OSCA still healthy, apart from a clutch which had given trouble all day and the fact that it was almost totally brakeless. By broadsiding the car to slow it for the turns I managed to bring it to the finish, so Bill and I won this American endurance classic both outright and on handicap, and naturally we won our class by miles. It was a most unexpected success and for me a wonderful American début. The OSCA's Fren-do brakes really were awful and in the pit lane after the race we could floor the brake pedal really hard and still push the car with one hand! Never mind, otherwise it was a little gem, a superb little sports car.

Leonard-MG *(1954)*

10 April 1954 — British
Empire Trophy meeting,
Oulton Park. Lionel Leonard's
handsome little MG-engined
'special' in the paddock. The
British Empire Trophy event
had just been transferred to
the mainland after the end of
road racing for cars on the
Isle of Man.

*V*ery much one of an early '50s genre of MG-engined small-capacity sports cars, a special without being very special . . .

*L*ionel Leonard was a good friend, a tulip bulb importer and a great racing enthusiast who travelled with us when we were racing the Kieft in Europe in 1951. That year he was racing a Cooper-MG sports car of his own, which he bodied as a copy of the contemporary Touring-styled Ferrari *Barchetta* sports car. He later sold it to Cliff Davis, who fitted a better engine and really made it go. Cliff then bought a Tojeiro which had a twin-tube chassis instead of Cooper's fabricated channel type, to which he fitted a similar body. AC bought the Tojeiro chassis design with Lionel's body style as the basis for their AC Ace sports car, which eventually became the AC or Shelby American Cobra.

Meanwhile, Lionel had built his own MG-powered sports specials and he had a new GRP-bodied one on the stocks which he asked me to drive in the 1954 British Empire Trophy handicap at Oulton Park. Unfortunately the body was late so I had to drive his older car. I finished third in my heat but retired in the final. My diary tells me the car handled nicely but lacked power, and when the crank broke in the final I was lying second in class behind Peter Gammon. *C'est la vie.*

The Maserati 250F (First Phase) *(1954-56)*

'To make my mark in Grand Prix racing I had to swallow my possibly misplaced patriotism and drive a foreign car. We chose the Maserati, and it proved to be a beautiful, stable, lovely car to drive . . . It was just a pity it was not more reliable.'

*T*he Maserati 250F was derived from their 1952-53 six-cylinder 2-litre *Tipo A6 GCM* and as developed in full 2½-litre Formula 1 form from 1954-58 it became one of the most beautiful of all classic Grand Prix cars. Maserati effectively put the 250Fs into production for customer sale and, having been encouraged to invest my future in such a car, friends and family ordered one for me, and at top level it made my name.

*D*uring 1953, Mercedes-Benz developed a new Grand Prix car for 2½-litre Formula 1 racing which was to begin in 1954. Unknown to me, my father, Ken Gregory, and some other friends including the late Laurence Pomeroy — the prominent British technical journalist who knew the Mercedes people well — had suggested to the German company's racing manager Alfred Neubauer that I merited a place in their new Grand Prix team.

Neubauer was not convinced. I had yet to prove myself in a competitive Grand Prix car, and he had already arranged for Fangio to join as number one, supported by the company's pre-war ace Hermann Lang who was still not too old, and by Karl Kling who had served the factory sports car team nobly since 1952. The young blood was supplied by another German, Hans Herrmann.

Neubauer told Ken that I had no experience of cars with more than 200 horsepower — which was not strictly true — and that I had yet to finish better than sixth in a Grand Prix, which — regrettably — *was* true. He advised that I should first obtain a really good competitive Grand Prix car, perhaps a Maserati, and prove myself with it amongst the big boys.

It was sound advice. I had always wanted to succeed in a British car, but the unpalatable truth had to be faced that none was competitive; even against Ferrari and Maserati, never mind Mercedes-Benz! The HWMs had petered out, the G-Type ERA had sunk without trace and my Cooper-Altas had flopped. I did not fancy Ferrari, so Neubauer's recommendation of Maserati made good sense.

I was in America when I heard from my family that they were ordering me a brand-new Maserati 250F for 1954, my father guaranteeing the cost of around £5,500 in my absence, though it would be my money which would pay for it. This news was both thrilling and a little disturbing. Inevitably I had some doubts. Had my family and friends more faith in my ability than I had myself? Would I measure up to the investment in such a car?

Alf Francis was to maintain and prepare it, assisted by Tony Robinson, and The Rootes Group provided a Commer transporter in which Alf set off for Modena on 20 March 1954, having already used it to collect 200 gallons of BP fuel and 60 gallons of oils, plus sufficient Dunlop tyres for a half-dozen races, and four cases of Lucozade. Even then, there was money to be made from product endorsements!

In Modena, Alf discovered Maserati had not even started on our car. This upset me greatly but I had yet to learn the ways of Italian racing teams in general, and of Maserati in particular.

My insistence on having a right-side throttle pedal instead of the traditional Italian central arrangement also caused Alf some grief, chief mechanic Bertocchi understandably protesting 'We have been building racing cars for over thirty-five years and surely we know what is best for the drivers? Is Mr Moss so different from the Champions of the World? . . .'

Finally they grudgingly agreed to change, and then Alf requested a better seating position, because I liked to sit back from the steering wheel — unlike

Maserati's standard position. This time Bertocchi agreed to move a chassis cross-member, and to mount the dash a little further forward, with a more reclining seat. In fact, Alf told me he had crept in and cut the tubes at night, presenting Maserati with a *fait accompli* next morning to settle the argument! We had also arranged to run Dunlop tyres instead of Maserati's usual Pirellis, which brought another grumble from designer Bellentani — 'If Pirelli are good enough for us, why aren't they good enough for your Mr Moss?'

As the car progressed, Tony Robinson and I travelled to Modena. The car — chassis '2508' — was eventually ready to test at the city's Autodrome on May 5, Bertocchi insisting Alf should try it first, then driving it harder himself. When I arrived I did twenty or so fast laps — and loved it.

The engine developed around 240 bhp at 7,500 rpm, but in view of the tough programme planned I intended to observe a strict limit of 7,200. This might not have been very bright, because unknown to us it coincided with an engine vibration period. The unit breathed through three twin-choke Weber carburettors, and was mounted well back in a robust tubular semi-spaceframe chassis, driving to a combined gearbox-cum-final drive unit at the back. It had coil-and-wishbone front suspension, a de Dion rear-end with transverse leaf spring, and powerful heavily finned drum brakes.

We made our début at Bordeaux on 9 May 1954, where I was dismayed to find the car a handful on Dunlop tyres on a damp track. During the race it began to rain, so Alf promptly bought four Pirellis behind the pits and called me in to fit them. They transformed the car, and I finished fourth, the only surviving Maserati.

We proudly brought our new car home for May Silverstone the following Saturday. I finished third in heat one, aiming purely to preserve the machinery

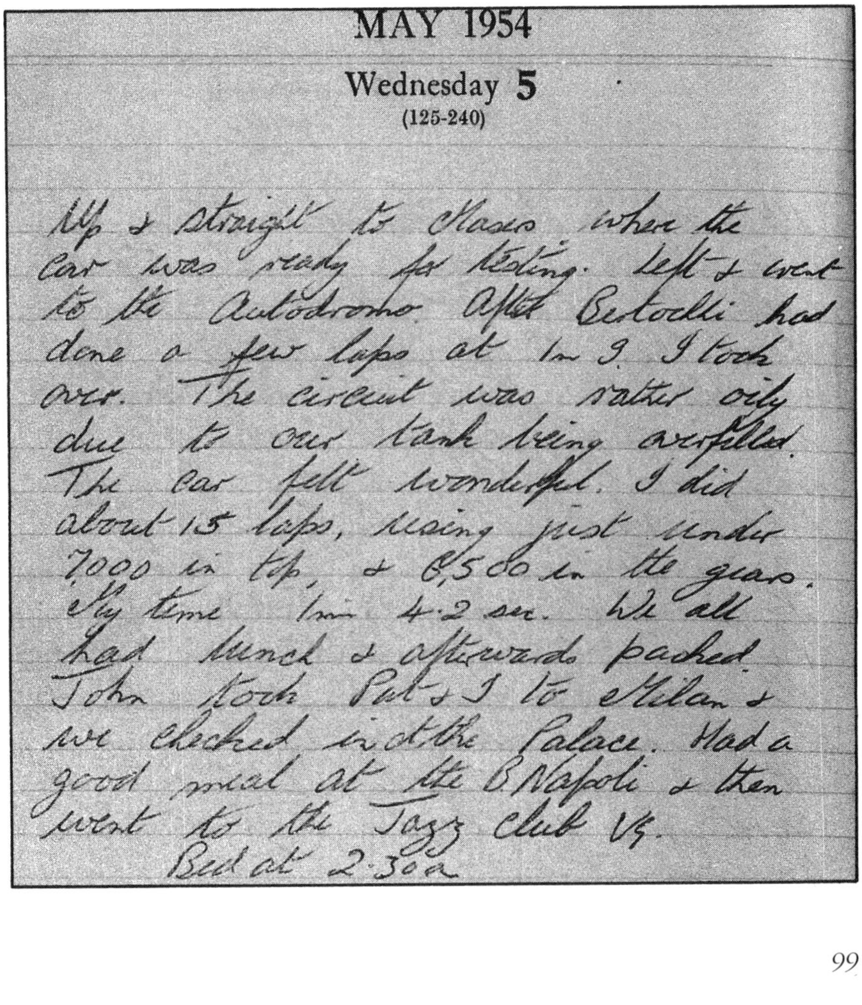

MAY 1954

Wednesday 5
(125-240)

Up & straight to Maser where the car was ready for testing. Left & went to the Autodromo after Bertocchi had done a few laps at 1m 9. I took over. The circuit was rather oily due to our tank being overfilled. The car felt wonderful. I did about 15 laps, using just under 7,000 in top, & 6,500 in the gears. My time 1m 4.2 sec. We all had lunch & afterwards packed. John took Pat & I to Milan & we checked in at the Palace. Had a good meal at the o Napoli & then went to the Jazz club VG. Bed at 2.30a

---

29 May 1954 — the inaugural Aintree '200' — Running anti-clockwise round the rain-swept Liverpool circuit, Stirling scored his first race win in '2508'. Always adept in the wet, here he holds a slide at Tatts Corner, ahead of Etancelin's obsolescent Talbot-Lago. Note the lucky horseshoe, and the filler cap for the car's early-spec engine-bay oil tank — soon to be updated.

for the all-important final, and there I kept religiously below 7,200 rpm and ran second behind Gonzalez's works Ferrari until lap 25 when my de Dion tube broke.

Alf repaired and reinforced it, and rebuilt the engine in time for the inaugural Aintree meeting on 29 May, when we used the new circuit for the first and only time anti-clockwise. I finished third in my heat using the Bordeaux and Silverstone choke and jet sizes, but they were too small for Aintree, concentrating torque too low down. Alf and Tony then changed them for the final, and the Maserati went like a bird, beating Reg Parnell by 48 secs to score my first win in a Maserati.

Back in Italy, the Castelfusano road circuit replaced the Baths of Caracalla for the Rome GP. There, I ran second behind Onofre Marimon's works 250F until a pinion gear in my back axle failed and I pushed across the line to be placed sixth.

Bertocchi told Alf there was a modified type of gear on the way, which we could have before the Belgian GP. This followed Le Mans, two weeks away, and would be my maiden Maserati *Grande Epreuve*.

The new gears were delayed, so Alf and Tony simply rebuilt our damaged transmission at Maserati's with standard parts and a new casing. At Spa my initial practice time was a poor 4:46.

I was very despondent, until Alf spotted Fangio had been using 8,100 rpm, 900 more than me. Naturally, a works engine for Fangio was very different from one for a customer, but this news cheered me up.

Bertocchi then urged us again to use Pirellis instead of Dunlops. He lent us a set and I promptly lopped 6 secs off my time without revving any higher. Our new-type gears arrived and were fitted after practice, and on race day I finished third behind Fangio and Trintignant . . . and in a Championship Grand Prix! It was terrific.

Perhaps Neubauer had been right. *Now* we were going places . . .

I really had taken to the Maserati. Obviously it had more power, and higher performance, than any of the British cars I had been struggling with, but above all it was just a lovely car to drive. It steered beautifully, and inclined towards stable oversteer which one could exploit by balancing it against power and steering in long sustained drifts through corners. It rode well on the normal type of relatively smooth-surfaced course, although its small coil-springs and leaf spring rear-end would use up available suspension movement over the bumps at Nurburgring.

We planned to miss the French GP for Alf to prepare the car carefully for our home race at Silverstone. Omer Orsi, Maserati's MD, seemed impressed by the way we operated, and he allowed Alf to do the work in the factory. But one day Orsi summoned him to ask if we would loan our car to the works team for Villoresi's use at Reims.

The new Mercedes were making their début there, Fangio had left Maserati to lead the German team, and Lancia had loaned Ascari and Villoresi to Maserati since their own cars were not yet ready.

I'm not sure I knew of this loan idea beforehand, but Alf knew the Italians well and subsequently argued it was no bad thing for them to feel obliged to us. Villoresi drove my car at Reims, and finished fifth, while I drove a works Jaguar in the preceding 12-hour race.

Maserati then rebuilt our car free of charge, fitting the latest-type cylinder head, cutting a specially low first gear, fitting a new-type rivetted fuel tank and replacing its early-style engine-bay oil tank with one at the tip of the tail in latest works car style. We bought a set of Pirelli tyres, costing 65,000 Lire, which seemed an awful lot for tyres at the time — over £30!

Orsi also encouraged me to use more revs, by offering to pick up the cost of any engine failure. This was enormous encouragement, removing a major inhibition and enabling me to race the Maserati for the first time in earnest.

At Silverstone I qualified on the front row and our new extra-low first gear helped me get away second behind Gonzalez, and although Fangio and Hawthorn subsequently passed me I was able to battle with Mike, using 7,800 rpm. I got away from him, and took second place from Fangio's poor-handling streamlined Mercedes, which I must say was a *big* moment for me.

There was nothing I could do about Gonzalez out in the lead, and with only ten laps to go I had settled for second place, when one of the final-drive reduction

Friends and rivals — Stirling in civvies as entrant chatting with a pensive Mike Hawthorn over '2508' at Crystal Palace; habitually crew-cut Alf Francis looks on. By this stage of its career '2508' had the later-spec tail-mounted oil tank — see its second filler cap . . .

gears came loose on its shaft, and slid lengthwise out of engagement. This left my Maserati with a perfectly healthy engine, connected to a gearbox working just fine, but with no connection between it and the rear wheels, so — agonizingly — my British GP was over.

This was the first time a Maserati had suffered such a failure, and it just had to be mine in my home Grand Prix.

Life went on. We now faced a succession of five Formula 1 races in five weeks in France, Germany, England, Italy and Switzerland.

At Caen I had led for about 45 of the 60 laps when it began to rain and on Dunlop tyres, as in Bordeaux, I could find no traction so 8 secs lead became minus 3 secs behind Trintignant. I managed to fight back but then the Maserati's rear dampers failed and Maurice won.

My engine was rather tired when we arrived at Nurburgring for the German GP. Alf set the car's ride-height high for the bumpy 14-mile mountain circuit. After first practice, in which I set fastest time 8 secs inside Ascari's lap record, Maserati team manager Nello Ugolini offered me a place in the works team, which I accepted with delight.

They took the body apart that night and hand-painted it red, apart from the nose which we kept green. Onofre Marimon, their likable Argentinian driver, watched what was going on and welcomed us to the team, but next day in practice he overshot a corner above Adenau Bridge and was killed. They withdrew the second works car for Villoresi in respect, which left our car to defend Maserati's reputation alone.

I had over-revved in practice, yet the works mechanics — still grief-stricken — worked all night to fit a new cylinder head. Ending lap one I lay third, but my engine's big-ends ran on lap two.

Maserati agreed to repair the damage, and loaned us a factory car for Oulton Park the following weekend. We missed practice, so I started from the back of the grid, but was able to win quite comfortably. I ran again in the *Formule Libre* race, and also won that. Although these were only minor events, they were my first in a proper works Maserati, and I was really bucked to have won them both on home ground.

Pescara's 17-mile road circuit down on the Adriatic coast of Italy is a world away from modest Oulton Park, but I was reunited there with my own 250F — now effectively a works car — the following week. Unfortunately they had modified the lubrication feed to its back axle's top reduction gear, and one of the steel feed pipes which they used cracked on lap four. Oil began spraying into the cockpit, so I retired rather than risk a back-axle seizure. Believe me, Pescara was no place to allow that to happen.

The Bremgarten owed me better luck for the Swiss GP, and Maserati now effectively regarded me as their number one. On the second practice day there it rained and I set fastest time, which not only boosted my confidence enormously but also impressed Neubauer on a circuit and in company which he respected. Still Fangio and Gonzalez had lapped quicker in the dry so I lined up third on the grid.

Early in the race I took second place from Gonzalez's Ferrari and settled down 6 secs behind Fangio's Mercedes. But I noticed my car's oil pressure falling and eased back, letting Hawthorn by, before finally retiring when the oil pressure vanished. Ugolini called in Harry Schell for me to take over his car, but when he stopped his engine had no oil pressure either so our race was over.

Our cars' tail-mounted oil tanks were using new-design filler caps with a spring-loaded internal collar retained by a small nut. On both cars that nut had vibrated loose, dropped into the oil tank and had been washed right through to the pressure pump, which it wrecked.

Maserati had two weeks in which to rebuild the engines before Monza. Brand new oil tanks were fitted from a new supplier, and there I managed to qualify on the front row beside Ascari's Ferrari with Fangio's inevitable Mercedes on pole. Only 0.3 sec separated our times.

I ran third early on, Ascari took the lead, and Villoresi then passed me in his Maserati, and two laps later displaced Fangio to trail Ascari — before his car broke. Soon after, while slipstreaming Fangio and Ascari into the *Curva Grande,* I saw my chance and slingshot past them both to take the lead. Ascari came back at me, but his engine broke almost immediately, so next time round I found myself holding an increasing lead as Fangio's Mercedes was slowing!

In the pits Omer Orsi asked Alf to slow me down. Even though I eased off a couple of seconds a lap, Fangio still fell away so my lead continued to grow.

This was absolutely wonderful while it lasted — leading the Italian Grand Prix as effective number one for a major Italian works team — but twelve laps from the end my car began to trail a haze of smoke. Its oil pressure started to fluctuate, and I stopped at the pits for three gallons of oil to be added under pressure. But as I accelerated away those three gallons lay on the pit apron where the car had been standing, and by the *Curva Grande* all the oil had gone, pressure had zeroed and I knew my race was over.

I tried to limp on, but at the old *Curva di Porfido,* which would disappear beneath the new speedbowl that winter, my engine seized. I coasted as far towards the pits as I could, then hopped out and began to push the last half-mile. Alf came to meet me, but of course dare not help, and Neubauer patted me on the shoulder as I panted past behind my oil-smeared car. I sat on its tail waiting for Fangio to win, and then pushed across the line to be classified tenth.

Fangio — as the great sportsman he was — greeted me as the moral victor, and Pirelli even paid me a winner's bonus. Although I was bitterly disappointed to have lost yet another race so near the finish, I was still elated by the knowledge that I had taken on all the stars on equal terms, and had led a major *Grande Epreuve* on merit. It seemed that in the eyes of the Grand Prix fraternity, I had at last 'arrived'.

The culprit that day was a broken aluminium oil pipe, which had been clipped too rigidly against the chassis and had cracked through vibration.

The engine was completely wrecked, so it was fortunate that Maserati

25 September 1954 — Turning it on at Goodwood's Madgwick Corner with '2508' now in factory colours, its rear wheels sliding under power while a touch of opposite-lock maintains the balance. Pole position, fastest lap and first place are the result, in the Goodwood Trophy.

themselves would foot the bill. Only the bare crankcase could be re-used and Orsi detailed four of his mechanics to help Alf and Tony repair the car in time for two minor British races, at Goodwood and Aintree, before the season's finale in the Spanish GP at Barcelona.

I led the Goodwood Trophy throughout, then had a terrific dice with Mike Hawthorn's new Vanwall in the *Formule Libre* Woodcote Cup, behind Peter Collins' 4½-litre *ThinWall Special* and Ken Wharton's V16 BRM which were uncatchable. I took third place by about six feet from Mike, having completely worn out the Maserati's brake linings.

At Aintree I was able to lead the F1 race throughout, lapping the new circuit clockwise this time, while in the *Libre* race I won again, leading Sergio Mantovani's works 250F for a Maserati 1-2. Alf had been working on me to be kinder on my brakes and Bertocchi had emphasized how I used up far more brake lining than Fangio. I was gaining experience and refining my driving technique all the time, and at Aintree I finished with lining to spare, and told everybody as much!

Only the Spanish GP remained, but there in Barcelona I was slapped down to size again. I crashed the works' spare car in first practice after Alf was late arriving with my own. That works car had a centre throttle and I had muddled-up the pedals and hit the accelerator when I needed the brake. I never could adapt to a centre-throttle position and I swore I would never again drive a car with such a layout. My own car's oil-scavenge pump packed up in the race, a real come-down after the promise of Monza and those minor successes at home.

But Neubauer at last was convinced of my ability, and he asked me to join Mercedes as Fangio's number two for 1955. It was a marvellous offer I could not possibly refuse, but I know that Maserati were deeply disappointed, having lost first Fangio, then me to the German giant.

I retained my 250F, and under the terms of my Mercedes contract remained free to drive it in events they did not enter. Alf fitted experimental SU fuel injection and Dunlop disc brakes and in testing at Silverstone early in 1955 it felt good. However, when I practised it for the Easter Goodwood meeting I found it oversteered too much on that tighter circuit, it was unmanageable in corners and would pull only 7,200 instead of its normal 7,800 rpm down the Lavant Straight. It had become a real handful and I could finish only third in the *Libre* race and retired in the F1 event.

With fuel injection, its torque characteristics had become very peaky, which upset what had been its exemplary handling. Next day Alf put the engine back on to carburettors and I lapped Goodwood in 1:31, whereas the previous day on fuel injection I had been unable to break 1:33.

We ran at Bordeaux in the middle of Mercedes' Mille Miglia preparations, and harried Jean Behra's works 250F until a fuel-tank strap broke, losing me four minutes, but I eventually finished fourth and set a new lap record.

At Silverstone my engine overheated when a liner sank, allowing exhaust gases to pressurize the water system. The engine seized. Alf took it back to Modena where we were no longer exactly the flavour of the month.

Maserati's people were not unfriendly, indeed they had assured me of a place in '56 should Mercedes not continue, but now we were very much mere customers . . . and nothing more.

We entered the car for Lance Macklin, Mike Hawthorn, Bob Gerard and John Fitch to drive when I was committed elsewhere and I did not race it again until 13 August at Snetterton where the immense difference in character between my Mercedes and this traditional Italian oversteerer seemed really vivid.

I was slower in practice than the Vanwalls of Wharton and Schell and on race day found myself in a huge dice with an Australian named Jack Brabham driving a centre-seat Bobtail Cooper with a rear-mounted 2-litre Bristol engine. He spun at the Hairpin with four laps to go, and I finished third. A plug electrode had fallen into No 1 cylinder and we had the axle ratio wrong. At least I managed to set fastest lap, despite the problems.

Up at Aintree Parnell set fastest time ahead of me in the new aerodynamic Connaught, and we began a terrific dice as the race started only for my engine to burn a piston with four laps to run. Reg's Connaught broke two laps later, so Salvadori won in Sid Greene's 250F.

By this time my old car was very tired, and its development had completely stagnated relative to the latest-spec works cars, despite its use of disc brakes in place of their well-developed but increasingly outmoded drums.

However, we shipped it out to the *Formule Libre* 1956 New Zealand GP after Christmas, and on Auckland's Ardmore aerodrome circuit I held a good lead and had lapped everybody else when a fuel line began to leak and I had to refuel. Alf got me away again in thirty-odd seconds, and so I managed to win my first NZ GP.

Mercedes-Benz had now withdrawn, so I rejoined Maserati officially for 1956, and would use their cars during the major part of the new season. Still my old faithful '2508' remained in harness, and when the factory could not spare me a car for the Aintree '200' on 23 April 1956 I drove my own.

By that time its disc brakes had been removed and replaced by drums ready for sale, and its engine was very tired so it was a real bonus when I won after Connaught and BRM had driven each other into the ground!

My final outing in what by this time should have been an uncompetitive and obsolescent car was another minor success, as I won both heats of the London Trophy at Crystal Palace, on Whit Monday, 21 May. We then sold the old car. It had played a crucial role in my career, and in three seasons' service had won seven Formula 1 races in my hands and — most significantly — had helped me into the Mercedes-Benz drive in 1955.

Jaguar D-Type (1954)

'Yet another beautiful Jaguar, perhaps the most charismatic of them all, but very much a precision instrument tailor-made for Le Mans, and not at all a rough-road nor aerodrome circuit racer . . .'

12 June 1954 — Le Mans 24-Hours — Stirling sweeping his works Jaguar D-Type through the esses, but he and co-driver Peter Walker are heading towards retirement. Not his favourite Jaguar . . .

Bill Lyons was determined to build on his Le Mans wins with the C-Types in 1951 and 1953 by arming himself with a bullet-proof works sports car which could set new standards there. With Bill Heynes' rigid and rugged new monocoque chassis, more power from the 3.4-litre XK engine and an even more stunning aerodynamic body from Malcolm Sayer, this was it.

The last of my four seasons as a Jaguar works driver came in 1954, and as they concentrated on Le Mans I was denied the chance to accumulate anything like as much experience of the D-Type as I had of the generally lovely old 'C'. I raced the D-Type only three times, at Le Mans, Reims and in the Dundrod TT where, respectively, I retired with brake failure, retired with back axle trouble and pushed over the finish line with the oil pressure gone to salvage eighteenth place. Possibly, therefore, my opinion of the 'D' versus the 'C' is a wee bit coloured . . .

It was certainly stiffer, quicker and more precise than its predecessor, and its ultimate performance was considerably better. But on an undulating road circuit such as Dundrod it was neither as responsive nor as manoeuvrable as it was on the smooth and very fast expanse of Le Mans or Reims.

What launched the car's reputation was Tony and Duncan's incredible battling drive through the rain at Le Mans in '54, when they were beaten only very narrowly by Gonzalez and Trintignant in the big 4.9 Ferrari. Then came the model's 1955-56-57 Le Mans hat-trick. I watched that happen from the cockpit of rival cars. This was particularly difficult to swallow in 1955 when our Mercedes 300SLRs had Jaguar by the throat — leading by almost three laps — until our own management ordered us to withdraw from the race following the 'Levegh' accident. Because of that, I feel that they did not so much win that race as finish first . . . and there is a significant difference.

Lister-Bristol *(1954)*

'I only drove this car once but it was a very impressive little 2-litre, the lightest Bristol-engined car I ever drove.'

25 September 1954 — Hardly the most beautiful sports car ever made. Here at Goodwood, Stirling gave Roy Salvadori and the Gilby Engineering Maserati A6G a hard time with the works Lister-Bristol. It was a typical day's work for him — four races, one win, two second places and a third with three very different cars.

Brian Lister asked me to drive what was normally little Archie Scott-Brown's works car in the big September International meeting at Goodwood '54. I was driving my own Maserati 250F in the Formula 1 Goodwood Trophy and Woodcote Cup races that day, and the Cooper 500 in Formula 3.

I remember enjoying that little green-and-yellow Lister, but it had a tendency to lift its inside rear wheel when I turned into the fast corners at Woodcote and Madgwick, which rather spoiled acceleration on the way out because I couldn't get back on the power early enough without wheelspin kicking the tail round. I would not really come to grips with Listers until four years later, by which time they had Jaguar engines and had become so potent that they were capable of giving the works Aston Martins a very, very hard time . . .

Connaught ALSR (1954-55)

'I raced it twice and won twice, a one hundred per cent record, yet I can't really remember this car at all . . .'

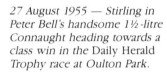

27 August 1955 — Stirling in Peter Bell's handsome 1½-litre Connaught heading towards a class win in the Daily Herald *Trophy race at Oulton Park.*

Just like the A-Type Formula 2 cars, the sports Connaughts were beautifully made, but within their class — which in this case was 1,500cc — they were a little bit big and heavy, although in common company not under-powered.

The particular car which I drove was owned by Peter Bell and I raced it twice, in October 1954 in the *Coupe du Salon* at Montlhéry and then in August '55 in the *Daily Herald* Trophy at Oulton Park. In the French race its engine misfired at high revs due to the French idea of 95-octane fuel but I made a good start and held the class lead to the end. At one stage I was passed by Peron's OSCA, but I thought it was a 2-litre!

At Oulton Park I won the 1,500 class again, and was seventh overall amongst the big cars. It was a nice-handling, good-looking car, but really rather big and certainly expensive for its class.

Mercedes-Benz W196 (1955)

'Driving for Mercedes in Fangio's wheel-tracks was like studying in a motor racing master-class . . . our cars represented the pinnacle of contemporary technology, but that didn't make them any easier to drive — certainly they were never that . . .'

4 December 1954 — First Mercedes-Benz test-drive for a thrilled Moss at a dank and chilly Hockenheimring. Here he is push-started before a crowd which includes the bulk of Alfred Neubauer (in hat and tie), beyond Moss are Rudolf Uhlenhaut, 'Pa' Moss, Mercedes' Baron von Korff, and pushing (right) is hefty senior mechanic Erwin Grupp.

Mercedes-Benz had dominated Grand Prix racing during the 1930s when they built a legend for no-holds-barred motor racing at the highest level which simply steam-rollered all opposition. When they decided to re-establish this reputation post-war they made an immense investment in money, men and material and their new 2½-litre Formula 1 cars, with the desmodromic-valved straight-eight, fuel-injected lay-down engines, set new standards which the opposition could not match. It seemed that the only way to beat them would be to join them, and after taking racing manager Neubauer's advice to prove myself in a Maserati in 1954, he fortunately invited me to join their team for 1955.

I was in New York when I heard the news of the Mercedes offer, on 22 November 1954. I was on my way to drive a Sunbeam in the American Mountain Rally and I had just called into Rootes' New York office when Ken Gregory telephoned with the details. It was such a fantastic opportunity I couldn't sleep that night just thinking about it. One word in my diary tells it all — 'Wow!'

After the rally I flew to Cologne where Ken and I were met by Mercedes who took us to Hockenheim to try a W196 for the first time. On a damp track I eventually equalled Karl Kling's record, and was very impressed with the fuel-injected engine, but not so much with the hefty car itself. But, after all, this was Mercedes-Benz. This was my opportunity to drive in the same team as Fangio, and I was not about to say 'No'.

My ambition was still to win the World Championship in a British car but none was competitive, especially not against this massive German organization. Consequently, as a committed professional racing driver I had no option but to accept a German offer should one be made.

What really impressed me was that as I clambered out of the car, rummaging in my pockets for a handkerchief or rag to wipe my face, a mechanic suddenly appeared, bearing hot water, soap, a flannel and a towel! Out there in the middle of the desolate Hockenheimring this was forethought I could hardly credit. I thought then that to be associated with such an organization could not be bad . . .

They made me a handsome offer, which I accepted, to drive both Formula

4 December 1954 — The Mercedes deal has been agreed — Neubauer, Alfred Moss and Stirling drink to the future.

DECEMBER 1954

Sun rises 7.47 **Saturday 4** Sun sets 3.53
(338-27)

Up at 10am & out to test the cars. 1st I learnt the Circuit with a 220 & then a 300 SL. This was quite fantastic for a saloon. Max was 145, but only because of the rev limit. I then tried the G.P. car. It is difficult to drive. Very flighty, has a nice gearbox. My best time (for Hockenheim in the damp) were 2.35 SL 300, & 2.15 G.P. Kling also did 2.15 but it was slightly dryer (I hope). We all (press Mercs Alf & then us) had lunch & then they took us to the airport & we took off at 4.30 a PAN-AM. To London, Ron met us. Later Sally came up & Ellen & Rob, SW & I went to the Colony.
Bed at 4am

30 January 1955 — Hot stuff; about to see the chequered flag waved at him for the first time in a Mercedes-Benz, Stirling takes a drink during the Buenos Aires City GP. For Formule Libre his W196 has a 3-litre engine under that bonnet bulge. Note the wide-open cooling intakes and hot-air deflector shields for the driver's comfort. Stirling won Heat Two — second to Fangio overall.

1 and sports cars in 1955, but left me free to drive elsewhere provided commitments did not clash.

With Fangio in a sister car as number one, I knew I might not be able to win the Championship just yet, but whatever else might happen, I should certainly gain enormous experience.

Our season began with the Argentine Grand Prix, and on the long flight down there in something like a DC-6 I had my first experience of Neubauer the joker. He was an amazing character, who could have anybody snapping to attention if necessary, but would also show great thought and understanding and in relaxed moments could have us all rolling about with laughter. That long flight had become incredibly boring when suddenly there was a terrific roar from Neubauer *'Der Moss! Der Herrmann! Hier kommt!'.* The twin toilet doors on that airliner were cramped together in a kind of vee-shaped lobby — Neubauer was famous for his roly-poly figure and we rushed back to find him pretending to be stuck between the toilet doors . . .

Mercedes had developed a 14 cm shorter-wheelbase W196 chassis for that season, and two were available for Fangio and Kling in this race, while Herrmann and I drove old 1954 long-chassis models.

I qualified mine on the inside of the third row of the grid for the Grand Prix, yet my time was within a second of Fangio's and Ascari's — Alberto driving for Lancia — in the front row. Only 1.8 secs covered the first ten cars. I was simply staggered by the heat of the Argentinian high-summer, well over 130 degrees on the track. Our cars had extra cooling holes cut in the bodywork and hot-air deflectors rigged to minimize cockpit temperatures.

I ran in a third-place bunch with Ascari and Farina's Ferrari early on, chasing Fangio and Gonzalez (Ferrari). After three laps Ascari passed Fangio, and Gonzalez and I were trailing them. I was very fit, but the heat was still too much for me. Ascari spun and crashed, and even Gonzalez was overcome — handing over to Farina.

This presented me with a lonely second place in Fangio's wake, but at thirty laps my engine suddenly starved and cut out due to a vapour lock in its injection. I was groggy from the heat, but not as much as the ambulance-men and marshals who immediately surrounded me seemed to think. Despite my protests, I was bundled into an ambulance, and only set free when we found an interpreter. I walked to the pits where Neubauer called in Hans, and I took over his car to finish fourth. Meanwhile the implacable Fangio just drove on and on, ignoring the heat, to win from the Ferrari driven in relays by Gonzalez, Farina and Trintignant.

Juan's stamina in such conditions was virtually super-human. He had built it up in his early days in *Carretera Turismo* open-road racing, many of these events covering 2,000 miles a time, a few nearly 6,000! He had also, however, arranged a little medical help, having some specially formulated pills made up locally to combat heat and fatigue. Fangio's pills became celebrated amongst his rivals but he was not averse to sharing them with team-mates if the occasion arose, as I discovered come the Mille Miglia . . .

Two weeks later, the Buenos Aires City GP for *Formule Libre* cars was run in two heats on a more twisty circuit at the Autodrome, giving the local specials a chance to face the visiting GP teams. We used the 3-litre (actually 2,992 cc) engines being developed for the 300SLR sports car, mounted in three 1954 long-chassis cars. These new engines had cast-alloy cylinder blocks instead of the welded-steel water jacket type used for the 2½-litre (actually 2,496 cc) F1 units.

Heat one became a battle between Fangio, myself and Kling for Mercedes, and Farina's Ferrari, but we were on specially hard-compound Continental tyres to resist the heat and they offered no grip at all. Farina's Pirellis were more effective, and he beat Fangio and me by a clear ten seconds.

We had had some trouble with a locking front drum brake — inboard of course on these early-season long-wheelbase cars — and since there was no time to strip it between the heats, its linings were simply squirted with oil. Obviously braking was diminished, but at least it cured the locking. There was a servo in the system anyway, so very heavy pressures could be applied, which would wear down the high-spots in both the brake linings and the drum liner as the heat burned the oil away. From this Argentine expedient Mercedes rapidly developed the push-button brake-oiling system which subsequently handled locking brakes on the 300SLRs.

Starting heat two, Farina then spun his Ferrari and promptly handed it to Gonzalez which presented us with a clear lap's lead, too much even for him in front of his home crowd. I followed Fangio until Trintignant's Ferrari grew large in my mirrors. I could not risk that, so I cut past Fangio and won the heat by three seconds. It was my first — minor — win for Mercedes but Fangio won overall on aggregate, having placed second in both heats. My third and first place times gave me second overall for our first Mercedes-Benz 1-2. These 3-litre W196 *Formule Libre* cars really had performed with 340 bhp against the normal GP car's 290-odd, but this would be their only race.

It had quickly dawned on me that there was nothing easy about driving the world's finest racing cars. The W196's broad, flat body reflected the lengthy straight-eight engine reclining ahead of me. My feet were splayed wide to pedals separated by a massive clutch housing between my shins. The car rode very comfortably, but everything about it felt heavy. It undoubtedly possessed great performance. Its engine was terrific, safe at high rpm with its mechanically-closed 'desmodromic' valve gear taking care of the top end should one inadvertently over-rev. It had good torque and a very wide usable power band, and the chassis put its power down well.

But the gear-change pattern was the reverse of what I was used to, selecting second and fourth by backward movements, third and fifth by pushing forward, so down-changes under braking tended to be pulling the lever backwards instead of punching it forwards, which under normal deceleration felt unnatural. It was a difficult change to handle, and even worse to remember. My recollection of racing the Mercedes is of having to concentrate like hell, all the time!

I would later find that it was also quite difficult in the wet, and prone to weaving under power — wet or dry. It always felt a big car — almost patently Teutonic — and, although it was very strong, and fast, it always demanded intense respect and I never developed the affection for it that I did for, say, my Maserati 250Fs although it was certainly a better-engineered racing car.

After our great day in the 1955 Mille Miglia, the European World Championship season began at Monaco, for which Mercedes had again flexed their muscles and provided two brand-new short-wheelbase cars — 6 cm shorter than the 'Argentine 55' spec — with the front brakes now conventionally outboard in the wheels, doing away with the need for brake coupling-shafts and allowing the chassis frame to be simplified to save more weight. Fangio and I were given these cars, his having its engine mounted further forward than mine. It handled rather better and he and Ascari both qualified at 1:41.1 while I put my car on to the outside of the front row 0.1 sec slower. Juan and I raced round nose-to-tail to build a considerable lead until at half-distance — fifty laps — Fangio's car broke its engine and retired. I could hardly believe it. Surely this didn't happen to a Mercedes?

But, with only twenty laps to go, the same thing happened to mine. An adjusting screw in the valve gear had broken, jammed under the camshaft and punched a hole in the cambox which gushed oil on to the exhausts. I eventually pushed across the line for ninth and last place. Ascari dropped his Lancia in the harbour, and Trintignant won for Ferrari. What a race!

We aimed to make amends at Spa, where Fangio tried a new medium-wheelbase W196 with outboard front brakes and the lightweight chassis mods and I took an 'Argentine' standard car with inboard brakes. Mercedes had the will and facilities to try *anything*. I felt that if I asked engineer Uhlenhaut to try square wheels he would either have a car ready for testing next day or would explain very earnestly how they had tried that idea in 1936 and found it made the ride bumpy! This time, the new car was soon rejected, and Fangio fell back on an original-style long-wheelbase inboard-brake car.

Poor Ascari had been killed in a Ferrari testing crash at Monza only days after his Monaco immersion, so young Eugenio Castellotti ran a lone Lancia which suddenly set fastest time. That shook us rather, but we felt we should oust him on the final day of practice, until bad weather ruled that out.

Race day was fine and dry, and Fangio cut out Castellotti instantly and I followed him through. We pulled away and I contentedly followed the master, beginning another lesson in how to drive a Grand Prix car. We finished comfortably 1-2 again, re-establishing the Mercedes image after the Monaco débâcle.

The horror, and in my case the added gross disappointment, of Le Mans intervened before the Dutch GP at Zandvoort. There we qualified 1-2-3, Fangio in a Monaco short-chassis car, me in a standard medium-length '55 model, then Kling in the outboard front brake 'Spa Special'. It is interesting to reflect that while, as a Mercedes team member, I was proud to be involved in that impressive line-up, only three years later I would be prouder still as our three green Vanwalls lined-up in the same dominant formation . . .

Fangio went into his usual immediate lead but I muffed my start — concentrate on that gear change pattern, Moss! — and was passed by Musso's Maserati, which stung. I quickly got ahead of him again, passed Kling and took up my customary second place for another instructive master-class from Fangio. We ran that way throughout the remainder of the race, generally just two or three metres apart in what became known as 'the train', and we lapped every other runner. It was our third 1-2 finish of the season, our second in World Championship races, and it was clear that as long as our Mercedes survived they were uncatchable. Everybody else was racing just to be the first non-Mercedes home. We developed enormous faith in everything about the cars, and the team.

The German and Swiss GPs were cancelled following the Le Mans catastrophe, but the British GP was held for the first time at Aintree, on 16 July. There, Juan and I, as well as new team-member Piero Taruffi, each drove Monaco-style short-chassis outboard-braked cars, mine having a new one-piece front body section which hinged forward clamshell-style — unusual in F1 at that time. We also had a new rear torsion bar adjuster provided in the cockpit, which allowed us to reset the rear suspension to compensate for the lightened fuel load around half-distance. Mercedes had also tried to make their gearchange foolproof —

16 July 1955 — The first Moss victory in a World Championship-qualifying Grand Prix, the 'British' at Aintree. Stirling kept just ahead of Fangio to the line to reverse 'The Train's' normal running order. His W196 has a new one-piece hinge-forward bonnet. Compare its shortened wheelbase to the Argentine Libre car's on page 111. **Right** *As Aintree owner Mrs Mirabel Topham presents the laurels, the racing peers Lord Selsdon (profile) and Earl Howe (almost hidden beyond Stirling) seem to approve.*

or Mossproof? — by adding an interlock mechanism to the exposed cockpit gate so that in each position only the next gear ratio one-above or one-below could be engaged. Uhlenhaut's men had developed it on the 'SLR in which I had been tending to change from second straight into fifth.

I took pole position in practice and without any formal team discussion or orders for the race I followed Fangio for some time before moving ahead, with Juan for once following me. I feel fairly confident that he could have turned it on and reversed the order had he really wanted to, but I certainly felt that I would at least make him work hard for it because here I was at last — leading my home Grand Prix . . .

As it was, I got away from him in the latter stages by leaving him a backmarker to pass just before a corner, and I led on my own — sensing rather than really seeing the spectators' delight. At fifty laps I was some 12 secs ahead, but Neubauer was signalling 'PI' — 'Piano', gently — to us, so I had to slow down. I still managed to slip in a quick 88th lap to break the record, but Fangio was now very close, and one lap later he was on my tail. I just led to the chequered flag by 0.2 sec, with his car's nose about level with my steering wheel. It was our fourth 1-2 finish for Mercedes, I had just won my first *Grande Epreuve* and became the first Briton to win the British Grand Prix, but don't ask me if Juan could have taken it from me . . . because I believe he could — he was the very best.

Kling was third, 1 min 11.8 secs behind us, and the new addition to the team, Piero Taruffi, finished fourth one lap down, to complete an emphatic Mercedes demonstration, starting four cars and having them finish 1-2-3-4. Only in retrospect has this win palled a little for me, relative to some I scored later in my career. One's first win is always special, and at the time that Aintree success was a magical moment.

The Daimler-Benz board had already announced their intention to withdraw from Grand Prix racing at the end of the season, because it was diverting too much experimental department attention from production car programmes.

At that time we thought we would be continuing with the sports cars in 1956, but after Aintree our opposition couldn't wait to see the silver cars' withdrawal because nobody else had the facilities nor organization to combat Stuttgart's might.

Only the Italian GP remained, at Monza. We drove in a lengthy test session at Nurburgring, followed by another at Monza in August when we tried the newly-completed speedbowl section for the first time. Its inclusion with the road circuit caused all kinds of tyre problems. We tested cars of three different lengths, streamlined and unstreamlined, and also experimented with an 'SLR-style air brake. We decided that a streamlined medium-wheelbase car was best suited so Mercedes built two specially for this one final Grand Prix race . . .

As insurance we returned to Monza with a new long-chassis streamliner, a short 'Monaco' model and a medium-wheelbase outboard-braked open-wheeler in addition to the two new tailor-made cars, but we soon discovered that Mercedes science had out-fumbled itself. Since our August testing, the Monza authorities had smoothed many of the new bankings' bumps and now the best of our cars was the old long-chassis streamliner, but even that was bottoming over what humps and dips remained.

Consequently there began what at Mercedes might be classed as a panic, with the solitary long-chassis steamliner's suspension being hastily jacked-up while the racing department in Stuttgart feverishly built two new long-chassis frames because all the experimentation had left them with only one long-chassis on the inventory. By the end of the second official practice day at Monza the two new chassis were ready and they were whisked down to Milan on Mercedes' fabulous high-speed transporter which had been built for just such an emergency. This remarkable vehicle was an open-platform truck, big enough to carry one car, powered by a 210-bhp sports car engine and capable of cruising at over 100 mph.

Obviously, against this background, our Italian GP practice resembled musical chairs but eventually Fangio ended up in a long-chassis latest-spec streamliner, I had a similar chassis clothed in the taller, more bulky 1954 streamlined bodywork, Kling had a long-chassis open-wheeler and Taruffi a short-chassis 'Monaco'spec car. We still filled the front row of the grid, with Taruffi on row four, and then I managed to take the lead from the start and held it until we went on to the banking. There Fangio hurtled by on the low line, with me preferring to run a little higher, and soon Mercedes were zooming round 1-2-3-4 and totally dominating their farewell Formula 1 race; Fangio, myself, then Taruffi and Kling. Our nearest challenger was Castellotti for Ferrari while Mike Hawthorn in another Ferrari lay sixth.

It seemed a trouble-free race, everything going to plan, until lap nineteen when Fangio's tyres flung up a stone which smashed my aero screen. I swept into the pits and to my astonishment — I should have known better — the mechanics had a replacement available which they whipped on to the car and sent me away again amazingly quickly. I drove really hard to catch up, setting a new lap record, then equalling it, and I was about to take sixth place on lap 27 when a piston collapsed and my Mercedes F1 career was over. Kling's ended on lap 33 with transmission failure. But the remaining two cars proved reliable; Fangio won from Taruffi, with Castellotti third, and John Fitch brought my private Maserati to the finish, albeit ninth and last. Fangio had clinched his third Drivers' World Championship title with this win, his second in succession, and I was runner-up, my best-ever placing.

The team's season ended for me with some exciting drives in the 300SLR sports cars, but then the Mercedes-Benz board announced that all its objectives had been achieved, it would not continue even in sports car racing for 1956, and that the party was over.

The question for all of us was where to next? And after Mercedes-Benz, the only way was down . . .

Austin-Healey 100s *(1955)*

'Good-looking, very British sports car which even in its 'small' 2.6-litre form was surprisingly effective as a long-distance road racer . . .

13 March 1955 — Car entrant Donald Healey, Moss (in typical lightweight hot-weather race wear for the time) and the debonair Lance Macklin celebrate their appearance at Sebring. They finished sixth.

*I*n the 1954 Sebring 12-hours my old friend and former HWM team-mate Lance Macklin did wonders for Austin-Healey's American sales drive when he and George Huntoon finished third behind my winning OSCA in the prototype Healey 100S. Few could buy an OSCA, but anyone could buy a Healey.

They then produced an improved 100S spec for 1955, with over 140 horsepower, and I was asked to share one with Lance at Sebring. He drove it down from New York, arriving with an interesting collection of speeding tickets!

In practice our car was easily the quickest of seven 100Ss entered, and we covered 106 miles, using 4.5 mm of tyre tread and averaging 10-11 mpg US. Five of the Healeys finished the 12-Hours, with ours placed sixth overall and class-winner behind a D-Type Jaguar, two Ferraris and two Maseratis. I managed one of my best-ever starts, second across the timing line from 33rd place in the line-up.

Unfortunately, at Le Mans Lance's Healey was involved in 'Levegh's' catastrophic Mercedes accident, and after involvement in another fatal crash at Dundrod in the TT he retired from racing.

I drove a Healey again — just for fun — in the Bahamas Speed Week at the end of the year, finishing sixth in the Governor's Trophy, while a top wishbone broke in the Nassau Trophy. Not a bad car, but such a humble engine — mine was only pulling 4,400 rpm on 5.50 × 15 tyres at Nassau . . . and that is hardly the stuff of racing legend.

Beart-Climax (1955)

'One of my more obscure drives — the other end of the spectrum in my Mercedes-Benz season . . .'

7 May 1955 — May Silverstone, with Stirling helmetless warming-up the little Beart-Rodger sports car in preparation for his second outing in it — a far, far cry indeed from works team racing in the World Championship, but still fun for a real 'racer'.

*F*rancis Beart prepared and entered what turned out to be my ultimate Cooper 500 in 1954. Into 1955 F3 racing was in decline, while interest in 1,100 and 1,500 cc sports cars increased. Mainstay was the new Coventry-Climax FWA four-cylinder engine which was an all-aluminium single-cam unit made originally for a Home Office civil defence fire pump contract. They had required a very light engine offering good power, exactly what motor racing demanded. So the fire pump engine began appearing in sports cars, starting with Kieft in 1954. The Beart car was a rather unsophisticated sports special built for him by Bernie Rodger, who'd worked on my old Cooper-Alta after Eric Brandon had bought it from me. I only drove it twice.

*T*he first time was at Easter Monday Goodwood, 1955, when it was completely new and unpainted, finished at 6 am that morning. Its clutch slipped and it wanted to lift its inside rear wheel and oversteer all the time, but I was lying sixth and leading my class on lap three of the race when the throttle broke, putting me out. I then drove the car again, painted this time, at the May Silverstone meeting, but its ignition played up, the catch on the drop-down driver's door broke so it dropped-down and I finished rather unhappily — last. Not every team could be Mercedes-Benz . . .

Mercedes-Benz 300SLR *(1955)*

'The 300SLR was, without doubt, the most rugged and unbreakable competition car I ever drove — it felt like a big car and always handled rather like a big, soft American roadster, with supple suspension capable of soaking up tremendous punishment, but never, ever, flabby . . .'

The 300SLRs took part in only six races during 1955, but they won five of them and only failed to win the remaining event — Le Mans — after one had been involved in a terrible accident which persuaded Mercedes' board in Stuttgart to withdraw the others when well in the lead and in perfect health. My personal record in the cars was six starts, three wins, two second places and one 'withdrawn (under protest) when leading' . . .

The 'SLRs were effectively sports-bodied versions of the W196 Grand Prix car. They were the W196S model to the engineers who created them, and they used 3-litre cast-block versions of the Formula 1 straight-eight desmodromic-valve gear engine. They were tested exhaustively prior to their début in the 1955 Mille Miglia, and they ended that remarkable season by clinching the Sports Car World Championship in the Targa Florio, taking it from under Ferrari's nose. I was proud to be a member of the Mercedes-Benz Grand Prix team, but to drive their fantastic sports cars as well really was the icing on the cake.

I suppose the story of our 1955 Mille Miglia victory in the 300SLR is a familiar part of motor racing legend now. I was navigated throughout the 1,000-mile Italian classic by Denis Jenkinson, Continental Correspondent of *Motor Sport* magazine. He had been Eric Oliver's passenger when they won the 1949 motor cycle sidecar racing World Championship, and he quickly proved to me not only his apparent fearlessness but also his very clear, quick mind which enabled him to relay his 'pace notes' virtually faultlessly throughout the ten-hour drive. 'Jenks' had previously logged landmarks all round the course on to 15 ft 6in of roller-notes. We perfected a hand-signal system so that he could keep me informed, regardless of the noise, of hazards — or lack of them — round the next blind corner or over the next brow . . .

We had compiled these notes during the most comprehensive reconnaissance, test and preparation period I would ever experience for any race.

Mercedes-Benz were implacably determined to win the Mille Miglia, and they spared neither expense nor effort to do so. The entire programme occupied three months of practice, test and development for this one race. The first two 300SLRs to be built were flogged mercilessly round the course, and then repeatedly to and fro over smaller, exceptionally punishing sections of it. We learned the course in 220 saloons and 300SLs as well as the practice 'SLRs, and for the race on May Day, 1955, the four works race cars — and their crews — were as well prepared as any have ever been for any motoring event. Jenks and I felt that among our team Kling and Fangio would lead the way — we might beat Herrmann . . .

We had each tested our new race cars the week before — on Tuesday 26 April — at Hockenheim. I was to drive '0004/55', Fangio drove solo in '0003', Kling solo in '0005' and Hans Herrmann was accompanied in '0006' by mechanic Hermann Eger. Our car was geared to over 170 mph at 7,400 rpm in fifth, but we were bothered by wind buffeting in the cockpit. Various screen and baffle changes were tested to prevent it. Jenks had been bothered by motion sickness in practice but had a pill prescribed to suppress it whose only side-effect was constipation. He felt that might be a positive bonus! Then dear old Fangio offered us each one of his famous 'stamina pills'. We were both rather suspicious of them but I took mine; Jenks saved his.

Mercedes had placed service depots in Ravenna, Pescara, Rome, Florence and Bologna. The starting order from Brescia was drawn by ballot; ours was 7.22 am so that was the number painted on our car.

I started the pre-warmed engine thirty seconds before we were due to be flagged away, then set off down the Brescia ramp into the rising sun.

April 1955 — Fine tuning the Mercedes-Benz 300SLR at Hockenheim before the Mille Miglia. Engineer Uhlenhaut listens as Jenkinson and Moss comment on cockpit comfort after high speed testing with the tall windscreen, side screens and that sheet-metal baffle visible between the 'SLR's twin headrests. The cockpit was still far too turbulent — a much cut-down windscreen without side screens finally did the trick.

My confidence in Jenks' pre-arranged hand-signals slowly grew as he read his roller-notes. We felt we might finish third behind Kling and Fangio. Any better would be a bonus. Essentially, the idea was to shut out the Ferraris, to dominate for Mercedes-Benz.

On the initial straights towards Verona the SLR was cruising at 7,500 rpm in top, some 175 mph, yet we were caught by Castellotti, who had started after us in his big six-cylinder 4.4 Ferrari. I was driving hard but taking no real risks, keeping the wheels away from the verges and kerbs. But entering Padua at around 150 mph I braked too late for the right-angle corner at the end of the main street, I held the car straight as long as I dared, then released the brakes and had to let the front end slide wide. It thumped its left front wing against the straw bales, bounced off straight and I accelerated away, cursing my carelessness and watching the gauges intently to see if the water temperature was going to rise, or the oil pressure fall.

The readings stayed steady. The thin bodyshell might be dented but mechanically the car was perfect. During our 'moment' Castellotti had roared by and grinned over his shoulder, which I didn't appreciate. He was over-driving that Ferrari terribly. I quickly realized there was little point in racing him — he could not last long. He was slithering into kerbs and over gravelly verges, burning shards of rubber off his tyres and smashing the car through the gears so roughly we could see it twitching and bucking on every change.

It was very spectacular, but not very impressive — remember, not long before in Buenos Aires I had for the first time followed Fangio at a similar distance in a similar car, and that had been watching real artistry in action . . .

The Ferrari left the 'SLR for dead under initial acceleration but we kept him in sight for many a mile, flinging up billowing clouds of dust and gravel as he careered from verge to verge along the winding road.

Approaching the Ravenna control Jenks brandished the route-card board for its official stamp. We stopped, the stamp thumped down, and I accelerated away, noticing the Ferrari there, having its wheels changed. We were not surprised . . .

We roared along the Adriatic coast at 170-plus towards Pescara. Jenks signalled me 'flat' over a blind brow, and I hit it as directed at 7,500 rpm in fifth. This was far faster than we had ever tried in practice, and the hump was harsher than we had suspected. The 'SLR took off like an aeroplane. I kept the steering wheel loose but straight and after an awfully long pause as we flew through the air the wheels touched down, thankfully in line — and down went my foot again.

Over the slippery level-crossing into Pescara I brushed some straw bales in quite a moment which came close to finishing our race against the petrol-pumps in a roadside filling station. About a mile or so further on, I then braked heavily for the second passage control stamp. Just beyond the control was the Mercedes pit, where eighteen gallons of fuel were added, just enough for the next leg to Rome. The windscreen was cleaned, Continental tyres checked and somebody handed us a slice of orange and a peeled banana. I was shown a note reading '*Taruffi, Moss 15 secs, Hermann, Kling, Fangio.*' We had been second at the previous control, 15 secs behind Taruffi and the leading Mercedes.

I was quite excited by this, too excited perhaps, for almost immediately after leaving the pit I totally misjudged a right-hand turn and slid straight on with the wheels locked up. Fortunately there was nothing hard hidden behind the straw bales through which we burst, before slithering over the pavement as I grabbed first gear and then thumped back down on to the road again, and away. Another worried scan of the instruments. Again the 'SLR seemed entirely unperturbed.

All we had lost was time so I concentrated hard driving up into the hills. The last six miles into Rome were, frankly, disturbing. We should have been doing 150 mph but the roadway was thronged with spectators, solid rows both sides. I eased back 20 mph or more, just as moral insurance, but then the final mile before the control was properly fenced and policed. Our card was stamped again and I braked at the Mercedes pit, killing the engine for the first time since leaving Brescia.

By this time I was bursting, so I leaped over the pit counter to relieve myself. I think Jenks was pretty bushed; he'd been sick over the side and had lost one pair of spectacles in the slipstream, but being very efficient and organized he had a spare pair just in case. While I was relishing my comfort stop they handed him a note reading '*Moss, Taruffi, Herrmann, Kling, Fangio*'. We had taken the lead! I bounded back into the car, the hot engine fired immediately and as he shouted the news into my ear I took off determined to maintain it, but really very worried. I'm a superstitious chap, you see, and there was an old Mille Miglia saying that he who leads at Rome is never first home.

Almost immediately we saw Kling's car piled into the trees, so he was out from fourth place. It was a warning of what could happen. Soon after, approaching a tricky right-hander, the newly filled tank splashed petrol over the back of Jenks's neck and being distracted he missed his signal, for the first time. Fortunately I recognized the corner and as we went through it very near the limit I grimaced at him — *Concentrate!*

As we climbed the Radicofani Pass one front brake began to grab, and then entering one sharp left-hander just beyond the summit it grabbed badly and caught me out. We spun to a stop, broadside with our tail in a shallow ditch, fortunately without hitting anything hard. I smacked it into first and to my relief was able to drive out of the ditch, but the road was so narrow I had to reverse twice before getting the nose round into the right direction, catching Jenks's finger in the reverse lock-out mechanism as I did so. He was only trying to be helpful. We pulled faces at each other, and now I had to make up for that little lost parcel of time . . .

Down into Florence the roads were appallingly rough at the speeds we were doing, but the 'SLR never complained, it took everything meted out to it and sat there ready for more. I had long cherished the minor ambition to cover the Florence to Bologna stretch in an hour, including the winding Futa and Raticosa Passes. Now was my chance.

First we had the card stamped at the Florence control, and the Mercedes pit crew there told us we were still in the lead. In fact, unknown to us, Taruffi's

Ferrari had already broken and Fangio had limped into Florence to have a broken injector pipe repaired. He was there hidden from us behind a scrum of people.

The Futa was slippery with rubber, melted tar and oil, and over its crest we saw Herrmann's 'SLR stationary but externally undamaged. Down from the Raticosa we tore into Bologna at 150 mph, card stamped at the control, and away before our pit could tell us the situation. Now my sole goal was Brescia — I just wanted to finish it.

The long straights along the edge of the Po Valley were virtually 170 mph all the way. We saw 7,600 rpm in places, 175 mph, and the engine was running more sweetly than ever. We zoomed past Cremona, and there was a special prize for the Cremona-Brescia leg which I was keen to win now that we had the perfect chance. We had some villages to negotiate as well as the final control in Mantua. In one village some fifty miles from the finish we had a big slide, perilously close to a very hard-looking wall, but got away with it again. Then we were into the outskirts of Brescia, past Jenks' last mark. He relaxed at his roller map, I turned into the finishing straight at 100 mph and we both began waving to the crowd for all we were worth.

We had finished, and finished well. That much we knew, but we did not yet know how well. I said to Jenks 'Do you think we've won?' as we edged the hot, battered and travel-stained 'SLR towards the finisher's paddock area; we didn't know how Fangio had done, nor what time Taruffi might yet set. Then the news was broken to us — it was one of the greatest moments of my motor racing life . . .

After a long soak in a hot bath, followed by dinner at Maggi Castle, I could not relax and still felt wide awake, so overnight I took my 220A saloon and drove off direct to Stuttgart for lunch with the Daimler-Benz board next day, then back to England. Fangio's pill was fantastic! Jenks had kept his and my father subsequently had it analysed in England, but there were apparently a couple of weird South American compounds involved which the chemists were very wary of attempting to reproduce.

We had averaged 97.95 mph for the 1,000 miles. The car's engine cover had never been raised. Back in Stuttgart the engine, when tested, gave identical power to when it had been built — 296 bhp at 7,400 rpm. What a testimony to Mercedes-Benz engineering . . .

Three weeks later we ran the 'SLRs again, in the minor Eifelrennen at Nurburgring. Fangio, myself and Kling finished 1-2-3, to the delight of a vast German crowd.

May Day 1955 — Glorious moment to end his fourth Mille Miglia — Stirling brings the 300SLR roaring across the Brescia finish line to shatter all existing course records in perpetuity. Every dent and scrape in that majestic motor car tells a story . . .

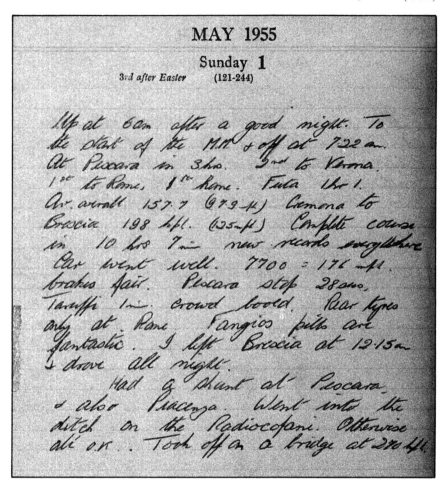

For Le Mans the cars were all rigged as single-seater sports cars with tonneaux and single headrests — as they had been at the 'Ring — and to save our drum brakes and combat Jaguar's discs we had hydraulically-actuated air-brake flaps fitted across the tail, moulded into the headrest shape. As well as providing additional — and extremely effective — retardation free of the danger of locking a wheel, we also found this device increased rear-tyre adhesion due to aerodynamic download.

I first discovered this download effect as the flap was on its way down after I had used it to slow into the tricky White House bends. With it still lowering and loading-up the rear wheels I found I could apply the power earlier and harder than normal. I wrote in my diary, '*The airbrake was fantastic!*' Our car had pulled 7,300 rpm along Mulsanne and we could outbrake the D-Types at the end of it. I wish we had had air-brakes in the Mille Miglia, it would have made that drive one hell of a lot easier! Another tweak — developed from a temporary expedient in the Argentine *Libre* race at the beginning of the year — was a row of four cockpit plungers to squirt oil into a locking drum brake, on the basis that no brake at all was better than one locked-up.

I shared car '0003' with Fangio, who took the opening stint, and he actually drove through the middle of the horrendous multiple accident in which our veteran new French team-mate Pierre 'Levegh' — his real name was Bouillon — rammed Lance Macklin's Austin-Healey in front of the pits and hurtled into a packed spectator enclosure opposite.

The organizers made the right decision in allowing the race to continue in order to keep the majority of the vast crowd at the circuit, so freeing the access

7 August 1955 — Swedish GP, Kristianstad — two stages of 300SLR air-braking demonstrated by Fangio and Moss on the Rabelovsbana country road circuit. The air-brake on Fangio's leading car is lowering; this is the position in which Stirling discovered the cornering advantage of aerodynamic download at Le Mans.

roads for ambulances. Since they saw fit to continue, I felt very strongly it was right for us to continue, too. Into the night Fangio and I held nearly three laps lead and no way was the 'SLR going to break. I think it was poor 'Levegh's' co-driver John Fitch who suggested to Mercedes' management they should withdraw in respect for those who had died. But that struck me as a rather empty theatrical gesture which came close to accepting some responsibility for what had happened. It would achieve nothing except hand a very prestigious race on a plate to Jaguar. Time has not altered my view, and I was very frustrated when we were ordered to withdraw at 2 am Sunday morning.

Some years later I was racing in America when I met an Indy car entrant who raised the subject of Le Mans and the 'SLRs. He told me he *knew* why 'Levegh's' car had burned so fiercely after the crash. It was 'obvious' to him that Mercedes had filled the chassis tubes with nitro-methane to be injected into the normal fuel flow to boost power in the dice against Jaguar . . .

I was just astounded that this know-all should believe such stupidity.

Quite apart from the volume within the frame tubes of an 'SLR being utterly inadequate for 24-hour racing, this would have been totally illegal and I was astonished that anybody close to racing of *any* kind should believe that Mercedes

24 September 1955 — Dundrod — the Mercedes-Benz 300SLR in as-delivered condition was a handsome and well-balanced study in how the finest front-engined sports-racing car of the '50s really should look.

could try such a thing when racing as a German team in France's greatest sporting event . . . only ten years after the war. I have been left speechless very few times, but that was one of them.

We reappeared in Sweden for the sports car Grand Prix at Kristianstad, Fangio and I running round to team orders and finishing 1-2, in '0003' and '0004', respectively. I used the air-brake there both for braking and stability, but had a narrow escape when a stone smashed my goggles. My vision seemed unaffected, but I could feel the blood running down my face. Immediately after the finish I went to hospital where a surgeon picked splinters out of my left eye . . .

Five weeks later, on my 26th birthday, 17 September, we competed in the much-longer RAC Tourist race at Dundrod, over 84 laps, 623 miles. Mercedes were anxious to accumulate World Sports Car Championship points. I was paired with John Fitch in '0004', Fangio/Kling drove '0005' and von Trips/Andre Simon '0003'. Mike Hawthorn was a driver who had good days and bad, but that day in Ulster he shone for Jaguar.

I took an early lead, drawing away from Mike and Fangio, which meant driving very hard, and on one lap I was rather lucky to get away with clouting the bank at Quarry Corner. Fangio was involved in a terrific dice behind me with Hawthorn, which only ended with Mike's scheduled pit stop after 25 laps. Fangio then made his stop which allowed Desmond Titterington — the local ace — to retake second place in Mike's Jaguar.

I was nearing my scheduled stop when a terrific bang and flapping from behind me announced my right rear tyre had burst. I was doing about 135 mph uphill when this happened, but fortunately did not hit anything. The petalled edges of the damaged rear wing had to be cut away before John Fitch could rejoin. Titterington took the Jaguar into the lead, while John could not match his local knowledge so lost ground.

Our car had dropped back to third when Neubauer put me back into it to catch the Jaguar, which at that moment led Kling by 3 mins 23 secs.

As rain began to fall, I caught and passed Kling for second place and set off after the Jaguar, closing just a little every lap. At fifty laps Des stopped to hand the leading car back to Hawthorn and that stop enabled me to close to within 25 seconds. As Mike took a while to get into the groove and the Jaguar was still heavy with fuel, I retook the lead from him five laps later, but my routine stop came two laps after that. Before I could rejoin, Mike was past and away into a nine-second lead, but no more than that. At the end of the next lap I was ahead, but Mike had the Jaguar tucked under my car's tail.

Gradually I managed to draw away. The 'SLR was clearly superior to the D-

24 September 1955 — This thrown Continental tyre tread at Dundrod gave Stirling quite a nasty moment and caused major surgery to the 300SLR's originally pristine flanks. Sharing the car with John Fitch, he won his third RAC Tourist Trophy.

Type on this quite rough-surfaced road circuit, and even before Mike's hard-pressed Jaguar blew-up on the penultimate lap I felt quietly confident. So with John Fitch's assistance I won my third RAC TT, heading another Mercedes-Benz 300SLR 1-2-3 finish.

Now Mercedes could steal the Sports Car Championship from Ferrari if they competed in the final round, the Targa Florio in Sicily on 16 October. No decision had yet been taken on whether or not to enter, and I was actually on holiday on the French Riviera when Stuttgart instructed me 'to proceed to Sicily'.

Practice and reconnaissance there were interrupted by a nasty bout of 'flu. Nevertheless, I spent long hours trying to learn the 45-mile mountain circuit in the Mercedes saloons and a 300SL provided. I had recommended Peter Collins as a very capable and quick co-driver. We were to share my usual car, the Mille Miglia and TT winner '0004', Fangio/Kling drove '0005' and Fitch and our other new recruit Des Titterington '0003'. It was to be a thirteen lap race, over 511 miles, and the staggered start would begin at 7am. Thereafter the cars would depart at thirty-second intervals and race positions would be decided on elapsed time.

I hardly slept at all the night before the race and felt pretty awful when I arrived at the start between the sea and the small town of Cerda. I perked up once seated in the car, and felt better still when I found myself in the lead! Castellotti, Ferrari's great hope, lay second, with Fangio on his tail third. I accumulated a minute's lead on my opening lap, and after three laps my cushion was five minutes. Then, far up in the mountains, I was just leaving a right-hand curve and had the car set up nicely through a fast left-hander when I lost control on either mud or loose gravel.

The 'SLR swung its tail out, just as it had that time in the Mille Miglia, bounced off a bank and hurtled straight off the edge of the road into space . . .

I was quite frightened at this point, because for one terrifying moment I hadn't a clue whether we were flying over a drop of three feet, or three hundred!

Fortunately the roadside field sloped downhill just there, and when I crunched down to earth I had fallen only ten or twelve feet. The problem then was to find a way back on to the road, because the car, although battered, was still running. Some locals rushed to my assistance, and after a lot of manoeuvring and pushing and yelling I managed to gun the car back on to the road and tear off towards the pits, but I had lost about twelve minutes and now lay a distant fourth.

Back at the pits, Neubauer, Peter and the crew had virtually given me up for lost until I came hurtling in. They checked the car very quickly and Peter took off with the bit firmly between his teeth to stage a brilliant recovery drive.

Under the regulations, no driver was allowed more than five consecutive laps unrelieved. Our plan now was for Peter to do three, then for me to take over for the final five, and despite hitting a wall along the way — which he said 'wasn't a very good wall, it simply seemed to crumble away before me' — the 'SLR again survived and when Pete brought it back in he was leading from Fangio — who had led briefly — and Castellotti.

Our car was still going unbelievably well considering the way we had both abused it, and I was able to trim the lap record several times in that final stint to win by 4 mins 55 secs from Fangio/Kling, who in turn were over 5 mins ahead of the Castellotti/Manzon Ferrari, whose pit had made a muddle of their stops as well as each drivers' lap allowance. Our other car finished fourth.

This Mercedes 1-2-4 result decided the World Sports Car Championship in our favour by one point, so Mercedes-Benz won both the Formula 1 and sports car titles that season.

That was the last time I ever drove a Mercedes-Benz racing car in anger, which I was sad about, but for me the 300SLR obviously has very special significance as the one car in which I could with some confidence believe that I could give Fangio a race!

16 October 1955 — Targa Florio — Whenever anything happens somewhere, no matter how remote, in Sicily, a crowd instantly gathers. Here after Stirling had careered off the road, he examines the extent of the damage and the problem, the locals give a hand, and he regains the road to win — helped by a superb performance from co-driver Peter Collins. The 'SLRs are Champions of the World.

Mille Miglia, 1955 —
Moss/Jenkinson
300SLR race progress

Mercedes-Benz 300SLR — chassis '0004/55' — race No '722' — start time from Brescia 7.22 am, 1 May 1955.
Brescia to Ravenna — 303 km
1 hr 36 min 20 sec — *2nd*, 1 min 51 sec behind Castellotti's Ferrari.
Ravenna to Pescara — 327 km
1 hr 42 min 53 sec — *3rd*, 56 sec behind Taruffi's leading Ferrari, 42 sec behind Herrmann's second-placed 300SLR.
(Brescia to Pescara aggregate — 630 km — 3 hr 19 min 13 sec — 2nd overall 15 sec behind Taruffi, who had averaged 189.981 km/h — 117.978 mph — to this point).
Pescara to Aquila — 100 km
37 min 42 sec — *1st* ahead of Herrmann, Taruffi, Fangio (300SLR) and Kling (300SLR).
(Brescia to Aquila aggregate — 730 km — 3 hr 56 min 55 sec — 1st overall, 35 sec ahead of Taruffi, average 184.88 km/h — 114.815 mph).
Aquila to Rome — 144 km
1 hr 6 min 7 sec — *1st*, 1 min 17 sec ahead of Taruffi.
(Brescia to Rome aggregate — 874 km — 5 hr 3 min 2 sec — 1st overall, 1 min 52 sec ahead of Taruffi, average 173.050 km/h — 107.464 mph).
Rome to Siena — 227 km
1 hr 48 min 14 sec — *1st*, 1 min 36 sec ahead of Herrmann.
(Brescia to Siena aggregate — 1,101 km — 6 hr 51 min 16 sec — 1st overall, 5 min 40 sec ahead of Herrmann, Taruffi having now retired, average 160.625 km/h — 99.748 mph).
Siena to Florence — 70 km
36 min 4 sec — *1st*, 8 sec (!) ahead of Herrmann.
(Brescia to Florence aggregate — 1,171 km — 7 hr 27 min 20 sec — 1st overall, 5 min 48 sec ahead of Herrmann, average 157.064 km/h — 97.536 mph).
Florence to Bologna — 107 km
I hr 1 min 26 sec — *1st*, 4 min 38 sec ahead of Maglioli (Ferrari).
(Brescia to Bologna aggregate — 1,278 km — 8 hr 28 min 46 sec — 1st overall, 27 min 32 sec ahead of Fangio, Herrmann having now retired, average 150.717 km/h — 93.595 mph).
Bologna to Cremona — 185 km
59 min 8 sec — *1st*, 2 min 50 sec ahead of Fangio.
(Brescia to Cremona aggregate — 1,463 km — 9 hr 27 min 54 sec — 1st overall, 30 min 22 sec ahead of Fangio, average 154.569 km/h — 95.987 mph).
Cremona to Brescia — 134 km
39 min 54 sec — *1st*, 1 min 23 sec ahead of Fangio.
(Brescia to Brescia final aggregate result — 1,597 km — FIRST OVERALL in 10 hr 7 min 48 sec, 31 min 45 sec ahead of Fangio in second place, having averaged 157.650 km/h — 97.900 mph.

Porsche 550/550A *(1955-58)*

'By definition, most racing cars of the 'fifties were unreliable. Porsche's greatest attribute above all else was their incredible, legendary reliability . . .

24 July 1955 — Civil Governor's Cup, Monsanto Park, Lisbon, Portugal — Moss winning in a sports car built by Germany's second-greatest racing car manufacturer, and one with its engine in the back; the Porsche 550 Spyder.

*T*he first time I tried a Porsche, in Portugal the week after I had won the 1955 British Grand Prix for Mercedes-Benz, the first thing I discovered was that its seat was far too big. A little modification had me snug and properly supported, and I soon became acclimatized. The car was powered by a flat-four cylinder air-cooled engine distantly derived from the Volkswagen, mounted behind the cockpit, and it was certainly quite quick for a 1,500, and I saw 7,000 rpm on the straight which was around 118 mph. It was also very well balanced and nimble and, although its brakes tended to lock, I had no problem adjusting to what I had expected to be peculiar rear-engined handling — despite my long experience of air-cooled Coopers with the engine in that end. In fact, the strangest part about it all was merely sitting in a sports car without a long bonnet projecting ahead of me.

*U*nder the terms of my 1955 Mercedes-Benz contract I was free to drive other cars when the race dates did not clash, and so I made my Porsche début in this factory 550 Spyder at Lisbon's Monsanto Park circuit on 24 July. We were competing in the Civil Governor's Cup race, and I was quite impressed by the car in practice but then unfamiliarity spoiled my start as I gave too many revs and merely sat there with the wheels spinning but no traction. I subsequently caught the field and ran through them into the lead, eventually won at 80.98 mph, and set fastest race lap at 83.53.

I could see that this Porsche would be nicely suited to Goodwood, and with the annual 9-hours race coming up — for the last time as it happened — on 20 August, I arranged with Huschke von Hanstein of Porsche to share one of these cars there with him. It was terribly over-geared in practice but we were in pretty good shape come race day. After seven of the nine hours, we were well set to win our class when I took over from Huschke, but I hadn't been out very long when Tony Crook's Cooper-Bristol spun on spilled oil and slewed back into my path. There was nothing I could do to avoid him, and I rammed him fair and square, which thoroughly smashed the Porsche's front end and put us out after 237 laps. Dammit.

*1 January 1958 — Buenos
Aires 1,000Kms — Jean Behra
and Stirling with the quite
incredible Porsche 550A
Spyder which they had taken
over at short notice for the
opening round of the new
season's World Sports Car
Championship. They are
about to give the works
Ferrari drivers a terribly hard
time . . .*

I drove a Porsche 550 only once more, round the other side of the world
from Goodwood the following January, in the sports car race supporting the
1956 New Zealand Grand Prix on Auckland's Ardmore aerodrome circuit. It
was a handicap race but the handicappers were not too unkind, which allowed
me a comfortable ride and an easy win . . . my second for Porsche in my first
three races for them.

Two years passed before I next drove the improved Porsche 550A in the
model's last appearance as the factory team's spearhead. Jean Behra and I really
fell into this drive in the 1958 Buenos Aires 1,000 Kms after the Maserati 300S
originally entered for us just fell apart as practice began. Huschke von Hanstein
offered us one of his works Porsches instead. It proved just a joy to drive and
we were able to go giant-killing amongst the works Ferraris which really were
deeply satisfying. The Porsche felt much the same as the 550-1500RS which
I had driven in 1955-56, but its chassis was now a true spaceframe in place of
the basic 550 platform type. It weighed only some 1,170 lbs against the 550's
1,300 and the latest flat-four air-cooled engine was now a 1600 with around
142 bhp compared to the old 550's 114 or so.

The Buenos Aires 1,000 Kms was quite a kind race to me, especially in 1957
and 1958. In both instances the original Maserati assigned to me failed as some
point, so I took over other cars which gave me a couple of the most sensationally
satisfying drives of my career — see page 141 for the other one . . .

In practice for this 1958 BA 1,000 Kms, I did only two warming-up laps in
our intended Maserati 300S. They were sufficient, because it was so awful I
was quite relieved when its crankshaft broke! It was then that von Hanstein
invited Jean and me to try one of his 1.6 Porsche 550As, and we liked it very
much.

What impressed me most was that rugged-sounding air-cooled engine behind
my shoulders winding up to 7,400 rpm while at the same time feeling utterly
unburstable.

My practice time was sixth fastest overall, and in my diary I enthused '*V.V.G. Fangio 3:29 in 300S, Gendebien 3:30, S.M. 3:39, Behra 3:43 in same car.*' So Jean and I ran the Porsche in the race which was punctuated by numerous crashes, including one which sidelined Fangio . . . as even he made a mistake.

Early in the race, after fifteen laps, I lay second — the silver meat in a Ferrari sandwich. I held that position for 2 hr 20 min before handing over to Jean and he continued to run second and third, to Ferrari's perplexed embarrassment. I then took over for the final stint, back in third place until, with only seven laps of the 5.8-mile circuit to go, Luigi Musso stopped his Ferrari for fuel and tyres. This let me through into second place behind the leading Collins/Phil Hill car, but Gendebien then took over from Musso and with my 1500 Porsche flat-4 I wasn't really in a position to argue with his 3-litre V12, so I settled for third overall, but we still won our class by miles . . . Jean lapped at 3:36 during the race and I ended it lapping in 3:30s, which was only two seconds slower than Phil Hill's pole position time in the Ferrari Testa Rossa.

It had been thoroughly enjoyable as we had forced the Ferraris to run harder than they had really wanted, *all day* long.

Standard 10 *(1955)*

'Nice little car — I had a very special one for the road which was really quick, but it never handled as well as my Minor . . .'

Signing for Mercedes-Benz for 1955 ended my Jaguar career and I quite missed my annual charge round Silverstone in those marvellous Mark VII saloons. Just for fun, I returned to touring car racing with a one-off drive in a Standard Ten at Oulton Park late that year.

I owned a Standard Eight which cried out for more power, so Alf Francis put a Ten engine into it, and tuned it at Barwell Engineering's facilities in Chessington. He fitted a balanced crank, rods and pistons, and two big Solex carburettors and it worked quite well, powerful yet also flexible although it tended to drift off tune. Its suspension was lowered and a Panhard locating rod fitted to the back axle to prevent wandering at speed. I had competition linings fitted in its drum brakes and cooled them by fitting lightweight — and enormously expensive — Borrani wire wheels carrying Dunlop racing tyres. The interior was equipped with a Radiomobile and all kinds of other gadgetry which I have always appreciated and enjoyed.

It really was a little bomb. It could reach 80 mph, which was very good for a small saloon in those days, and it nipped round corners well. It was two-tone cream and green, and I registered it 'SFM 777'.

In August 1955, at the Oulton Park *Daily Herald* meeting in which I drove a Connaught in the main event, I also raced a loaned Standard Ten in a fifteen-lap saloon car race. The entry included Mike Hawthorn's Raymond Mays-modified Ford Zephyr, Ken Wharton's Austin Westminster, Jo Bonnier's Alfa 1900 and Tony Brooks' DKW *Sonderklasse!* You can imagine how hectic it became once the flag dropped.

I made a bad start, then according to *The Autocar* '*revealed just how much the normal production saloon will put up with; frequently daylight could be seen beneath both inside wheels on the corners . . .*' I finished second in class after averaging 62.79 mph. Quite good fun really.

Driving Techniques 2

Following the Master

When I managed to finish third, driving my new Maserati 250F, in the 1954 Belgian Grand Prix it gave me confidence in believing that I could do justice to a competitive car in the best company. But at that time I was still a very straightforward driver. I braked on quite a tightish line into corners but still essentially entered wide, swept into the apex and then accelerated away wide again, relying heavily upon my natural quickness of eye and reaction rather than upon any consciously learned, or developed and applied technique. I firmly believed from my previous experience that the quick way was to keep everything neat and tidy, and the 250F, as a well-balanced, essentially oversteering car, was very nice to drive that way.

Meanwhile, Mercedes' new W196s had been developed for their début that season to replace oversteering tail-happiness with initial understeer which would turn to oversteer. I had learned the advantages of inherent understeer in my under-powered Kieft 500, but Mercedes had possibly gone too far in their W196 — at least in that original 1954 form.

I had a ringside view of this from my Maserati's cockpit at Silverstone when the Mercedes drivers almost despaired of persuading their streamlined cars to turn into the corners at all. Even Fangio was having to let his car understeer heavily on the way in and then yank at the steering wheel and stamp on the throttle to put the tail into a rear-wheel skid. This succeeded but in the hands of anybody other than Fangio it was just too slow to win. Consequently Ferrari beat the Mercedes there, and although the roles were reversed in the Italian GP at Monza, there even Fangio spent much time churning along the verges and certainly knew he had been in a race come the finish.

When I joined Fangio in the Mercedes team for 1955, engineer Uhlenhaut's W196 developments had reduced this inbuilt understeer and brought the car's front-end adhesion into better balance with the rear. Therefore I found the cars far more manageable than I understand they had been through the latter part of 1954.

By that time my driving techniques had become attuned to the Maserati and although I quickly adapted to the shorter-chassis W196, which was more powerful and faster, I always found it much harder to drive. Fangio then taught me a vast amount by allowing me to follow him very closely to see his line and study his technique at close quarters. Our two silver Mercedes actually became known as 'The Train' . . .

For example, at Spa we would run nose to tail going down past the grandstands and pits, but climbing back along that very fast and deceptive back stretch from Stavelot to La Source Hairpin behind the paddock he would draw away at a pace which at that time I simply could not match. I would then close up into the hairpin, we would do our formation bit down past the stands, then he would draw away from me again, but this time along another section, showing me how . . .

Because he was taking me along like this, our average speeds during some of those 1955 Grand Prix races could have been higher had he chosen not to school me in this manner. But all of this was unspoken. He simply, tacitly, chose to play it that way. If I could keep with him he would happily provide the lead. If I had not been quick enough to keep in touch, then I am sure he'd have gone on his happy way regardless.

Neubauer sometimes ticked us off for running so close together — 'If one of you spins, the other will hit him so both of our cars will be out' — but Juan had confidence in himself, and presumably in me, and no way was I going to let him think that I would always be happy just to follow him . . . I liked to press a bit as well, you know.

In the timed practice sessions it was truly free for all between us and neither would hold back at all. At Monaco I was very pleased when I lowered Caracciola's long-standing lap record from 1937 — with a 600 bhp car — from 1:46.5 to 1:42.6, yet Fangio promptly went out and did 1:41.1, which put me thoroughly in my place . . .!

In those days you had to be fairly careful with your brakes, otherwise they simply would not survive race distance. I am not convinced that Mercedes' inboard brakes were as good as has been claimed. They worked smoothly but the cockpit filled with brake dust and acrid smells, and because air was drawn out around the driver through the open cockpit he became ingrained with an inky mixture of oil and that dust. Hence our grimy faces, with clean rings round our eyes where our goggles had been.

Because of the Mercedes drum brakes' exceptional width, we were warned not to warm them up too abruptly or else they would crack. So we always had to take it easy in the opening lap of any race until they had thoroughly warmed through.

On the plus side, I never feared for one moment that anything would break off a Mercedes, as happened to me at other times with HWMs, Maseratis and Lotuses, and even the rugged Coopers, so there was never any inhibition involved on that score. I would never rate the Mercedes amongst the best-handling or most pleasant of Grand Prix cars which I drove, but they felt unbreakable and after Monaco '55 I always felt securely confident that, while one of our rivals' cars might somewhere prove able to outrun us, it would never outlast us.

In effect that enabled me to concentrate totally upon simply driving the car and sharpening my skills by studying Fangio's example at close quarters. In my mind there is no doubt that when I rejoined Maserati for 1956 I was a more complete driver than when I had left them in 1954 . . .

Maserati 250F (Second Phase) *(1955-56)*

'When I rejoined Maserati for 1956 I found their 250F cars had benefited from two full seasons' development — they were far more reliable, and were still lovely cars to drive, but Ferrari's Lancia-based V8s seemed to have the edge on ultimate power.'

After Mercedes' withdrawal at the end of 1955 I took up the Orsis' offer to return to Maserati as number one. I was able to win two World Championship GPs on two of the most taxing circuits in the calendar — Monaco and Monza — and with second place at Nürburgring and a shared third place at Spa I finished the World Championship for the second year in succession as runner–up — to Fangio.

Joining Maserati as team leader for 1956, I made my début for them in the Argentine GP at Buenos Aires on 22 January. My assigned car blew a piston while being warmed up before practice and I qualified the spare on the second row of the grid. My original car was repaired ready for the race but it began a poor day for me by running over my foot!

I managed to take the lead, but Fangio, having blown up his original Lancia-Ferrari V8, had taken over Musso's sister car and closed rapidly. My rebuilt engine began to smoke, then another piston collapsed and Fangio won, to begin his World Championship defence in the Lancia-Ferrari.

My piston trouble may well have been due to running too exotic a fuel, I cannot really recall now, but we certainly used a milder alcohol brew in the Buenos Aires City GP which was run at Mendoza. Although we lost horsepower, at least our Maseratis were reliable, but again Ferrari overpowered us, although I finished second.

Back home, Maserati sent a brand-new car — '2522' — to Easter Monday Goodwood for me, using their own fuel injection system based on a Bosch pump. The car also carried wider drum brakes and the five-speed gearbox. Just like my own old car on SU injection, this one refused to handle and when a piston seized in practice a spare engine was despatched from Modena while my old car was brought down from Tring as a stand-by. I tried both cars on race morning and the works team's was 0.2 sec quicker. Clearly engineer Alfieri preferred us to use it and I managed to win the Glover Trophy after a terrific scrap with Archie Scott-Brown's Connaught, during which I set a new lap record.

The factory concentrated upon sports cars and Formula 1 preparation before the European World Championship series began, so I ran my own car during that period — see page 140 — and won at Silverstone in my Vanwall début.

Monaco marked my return to the factory 250Fs, where I drove '2522' again, now fitted with a four-speed gearbox specially for the street circuit. My team mates were Jean Behra and Cesare Perdisa, the latter's car being rigged with a right-side throttle pedal like mine in case I should need to take it over during the race. Fangio was a fraction quicker in practice, but I made a better start and led by a hundred yards at the end of the first lap and extended it thereafter to win my second *Grande Epreuve*, and my first for Maserati.

Fangio bent his own Lancia-Ferrari and took over his team mate Peter Collins's to finish second, with Behra third. I had a fright when a backmarker suddenly braked in front of me on one of the short straights and I rammed him. Fortunately my car's crumpled nose cowl did not restrict cooling, and nothing vital had been bent so I could breathe again.

Engineer Alfieri had our cars modified for the high-speed Belgian GP at Spa. They now carried long tapering nose cowls *à la* Vanwall, with top ducts to exhaust hot radiator air. The experimental works car — '2501' — had also been fitted with reprofiled bodywork around its cockpit, giving it high sides and a full wrap-round screen. I tried it on both fuel injection and carburettors and, although both engine specs performed similarly, the injected engine was more thirsty so we elected to race on Webers instead.

Despite my making a better start, Fangio's V8 came howling past at the end of the Masta Straight and inexorably drew away. There was nothing I could do about it, and then climbing the long hill after the pits my car's left rear hub shaft snapped, releasing the wheel, hub and brake drum complete, which bounded away into the woods. I managed to bring the car to rest otherwise unscathed and sprinted the half-mile back to the pits to take over my Monaco-winning car — '2522' — from Perdisa. I broke the lap record in it, but really could do very little about the Lancia-Ferraris, and finally finished third after Fangio's engine had failed and his new team mate Peter Collins won his first *Grande Epreuve*.

Our cars were clearly too slow along the straights, so for the French GP at Reims Alfieri produced his streamlined car — '2518'. It was rigged with Dunlop disc brakes and a fuel-injected engine but it was a dead loss. I used my first Spa car but got left behind before my gear lever snapped off at its base. I retired in the pits and they flagged-in Perdisa's fuel-injected car for me, but when he stopped its cockpit was awash with oil. I rejoined pessimistically in it, but finished fifth, considering myself rather fortunate.

Reims had been an appalling outing for Maserati but the Orsis insisted things would improve for the British GP. The fuel injection experiments were shelved, and they concentrated on setting-up the carburettor engines properly and I was able to qualify on pole position at Silverstone. I took the lead on lap sixteen with Fangio on my tail before an ignition fault sent me into the pits. I rejoined in second place but my gearbox broke just eight laps from the end — a typical closing-stages 250F-type failure — and I retired with just a solitary Championship

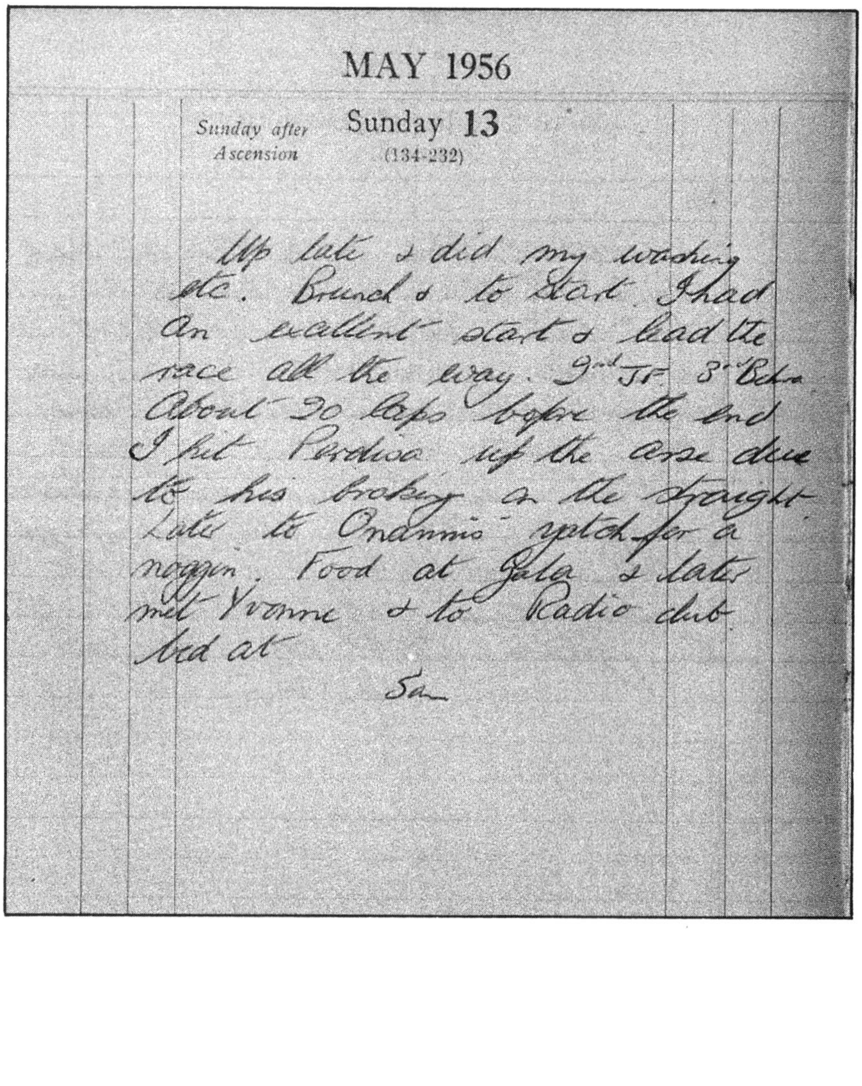

MAY 1956

Sunday after Ascension

Sunday 13

(134-232)

Up late & did my washing etc. Brunch & to Start I had an excellent start & lead the race all the way. 9nd J. 3 Before about 30 laps before the end I hit Perdisa up the arse due to his braking on the straight. Late to Ondrinis — watch for a noggin. Food at Gala & late met Yvonne & to Radio club bed at

5a—

1 July 1956 — Maserati's appalling outing in the French GP at Reims caused Ing. *Giulio Alfieri a major design rethink in preparation for the Italian race at Monza in September. Here the team's experimental car '2501' shows off its latest high-sided cockpit body mods as Stirling in visor negotiates Thillois Corner.*

point for fastest lap.

At Nurburgring, Fangio was again quite unbeatable in his Lancia-Ferrari and I just could not find a way past him, although we swopped the fastest lap to and fro between us. The Maestro finally won, with me second.

Only the Italian GP remained to complete the 1956 World Championship series. I was out of the running for the Drivers' title, but Peter Collins could still beat Fangio if he could win at Monza and set fastest lap without Fangio scoring another point.

Maserati appreciated they had to produce some kind of trump card to stand a chance in their home Grand Prix, and Alfieri did just that by building two brand new 250Fs, one for me and the other for Jean Behra. His idea was twofold; to reduce frontal area and to lower the cars' centre of gravity. To achieve these aims he had a wider spaceframe chassis designed, with the engine mounted at an angle across it.

This directed the prop shaft across the floor at an angle from right-front towards left-rear into a normal five-speed gearbox modified to accept a new offset input, which coupled the angled prop shaft to the normal gearbox and permitted the driver's seat to be dropped down in the frame beside the prop shaft instead of sitting above it. The seat was now on the undertray with the prop shaft angling beneath the driver's left knee. This lowered us some eight inches within the car, which was a terrific advance, while the steering column was lowererd and the bodywork was completely reprofiled to become very handsome indeed. The radiator was fully ducted, hot air exiting beneath the engine this time. These two cars were numbered '2525' and '2526' and I drove the former.

The race began with a fearful scrap between Musso and Castellotti which ruined their Ferraris' tyres. I sat back and watched behind them until they stopped, whereupon I inherited the lead under pressure from Harry Schell in the fast-developing Vanwall and the inevitable Fangio. Harry led before the

Vanwall's gearbox failed and I moved ahead again. Fangio's car was failing but Peter Collins stopped and handed over his car, a terrific gesture typical of Pete, who was surrendering his own chance for the Championship. I set a new lap record at 135.5 mph on lap 47 but suddenly the Maserati faltered and died beneath me . . .

No fuel!

I spotted Piotti, the Italian Maserati privateer, coming up behind and gestured frantically for him to use his car to push me to the pits. He understood, and offered up the nose of his car to the tail of mine and punted me gently round to the pit lane.

Musso had taken the lead but his Ferrari failed and after taking on a few vital gallons of fuel I had rejoined and managed to hold off Fangio to win by just six seconds, a victory which delighted everybody at Maserati and perhaps compensated for our disappointment in this race in 1954. Winning at Monza meant the world to them, for the Autodrome really was the spiritual home of Italian racing. Much like Indy to American enthusiasts.

I would drive a Formula 1 Maserati only once more that season, 12,000 miles away at Albert Park, Melbourne, in the Australian GP on 2 December. I managed to win and set the lap record, and then drove 250Fs again in the 1957 Argentine Grand Prix at Buenos Aires on 13 January. By that time I had signed with Vanwall but they were not entering the *Temporada* races and gave me *carte blanche* to drive anything else I could get. Maserati made me the offer so I accepted, to team up again (if only temporarily) with Fangio and Behra.

Maserati fielded three new lightweight 250Fs for us and I set fastest practice lap on both days, emerging 1.1 secs quicker than Juan, but in the race my car's throttle linkage parted at the start and I lost nine laps having it repaired. That gave me terrific stimulus to fight back and I recovered a lap on Fangio, set fastest lap . . . yet finished only eighth.

The *Formule Libre* Buenos Aires City GP was run as usual, in two thirty-lap heats, in fantastically hot weather; 156°F on the track surface with eighty per cent humidity.

I was equal fastest with Fangio in practice but Castellotti's Lancia-Ferrari led heat one from Fangio and me. I was second by lap two but regretting my decision to use sixteen-inch wheels as my car was sliding all over the place. I took the lead from Castellotti on lap thirteen, but could not maintain it and Fangio went whistling by. I was suffering in the heat. My engine lacked low-down torque, and then the brakes began locking. I just had to stop, while the imperturbable Fangio won comfortably.

For the final laps of heat two I took over Carlos Menditéguy's car, but I could only hold on steadily to sixth place. I would drive Maserati's factory sports cars for the rest of the season, but never again would I handle a 250F in a significant international event. For me, another chapter had ended.

Maserati 300S (1956-58)

'No doubt about it, apart from the 'Birdcage' this was my favourite front-engined sports Maserati . . . one of the easiest, nicest, best-balanced sports-racing cars ever made . . .'

*F*rom 1956 to 1958 I started thirteen races in 300S Maseratis, and I took them over after having started in a different type of Maserati on three more occasions. From that total of sixteen events, the 300S gave me nine wins, three second places, a third and a fifth and only two retirements. With a record like that, can you see why I have such fond memories of these beautiful cars? It defies Maserati's long-standing reputation for grace, pace and unreliability, but that's what the 300S was all about.

It was strong and dependable, also quite like an Aston Martin DB3S in its general feel and responsiveness, but it was even better balanced and, in my experience, almost unburstable. Today, people rave about Ferrari's fantastic reliability. True, they used to spread it wider across the board amongst all their customers, but a decently-prepared 300S had a chassis which was infinitely superior to any front-engined sports Ferrari and although it lacked their wonderfully smooth and powerful V12 engine, its 6-cylinder was always man enough for the job.

*W*hen I joined Maserati in 1956 my programme for them included a busy a busy series of sports car races which I dovetailed into my Aston Martin commitments. I drove the smooth and powerful 300S in eight races, from Buenos Aires to the Bahamas, and won seven times. In 1957 while I drove Rob Walker's Cooper and the Vanwall against Maserati in Formula 1, I still drove their sports cars, including the 300S, and into 1958, despite Maserati being in deep financial trouble and having retired from Formula 1, I had three final 300S races, and managed two wins and another second place.

These 3-litre 6-cylinder cars produced about 250 horsepower at 6,500 rpm against the 2½-litre Formula 1 engine's 240 at 7,200. The chassis used Maserati's usual coil-and-wishbone front suspension and had a de Dion axle and transverse leaf spring at the rear. On the Mulsanne Straight at Le Mans in 1955 the organizers sited a speed trap at a point where the cars had not quite wound up to maximum speed. They clocked a D-Type Jaguar at 175.27 mph, my 300SLR Mercedes at 168.09, Castellotti's rip-roaring 6-cylinder 4.4 Ferrari at 181.15 (!) and the best 300S Maserati at only 153.85. Even that was nearly 8 mph quicker than Peter Collins' quickest Aston Martin DB3S, the best British 3-litre car.

1 January 1956 — Buenos Aires 1,000 Kms — Moss in the Maserati 300S which he shared with the great Argentinian all-round sportsman Carlos Menditéguy to score Maserati's first victory in a World Sports Car Championship qualifying race. The 'YPF' decals proclaim the state Argentine oil company's sponsorship of the Temporada race series, comprising Grand Prix, City GP at Mendoza and 1,000 Kms.

In that original form the Maserati clearly lacked the speed to succeed at top level. But by the time I joined them for 1956 things had improved, and I won the Buenos Aires 1,000 kms sharing a 300S with local all-round sportsman Carlos Menditéguy. It was Maserati's first-ever win in a Sports Car World Championship round. Fangio chased us so furiously in a Ferrari that it blew up, which was one in the eye for Maranello; our mechanics' jubilation was lovely to share.

I drove a works Aston Martin at Sebring, then the 'special' 350S Maserati in the Mille Miglia, before returning to a 300S for the Nürburgring 1,000 kms. Jean Behra, who always used to go well, co-drove with me, but during his stint our car's rear spring broke away from the chassis and put us out. Our team manager, Nello Ugolini, then switched us to the sister Taruffi/Schell 300S which lay third and Jean worked it up into second place behind Fangio's leading Ferrari. I took over when we were 66 seconds behind and in that kind of situation I always used to benefit from an enormous adrenalin charge.

I really loved the challenge of coming from behind. It pumped me up, and by going on the brakes later, coming off them early and getting back on the power absolutely as soon as possible, I could lower my lap times without really compromising the car too much. In this case I took six seconds a lap out of Fangio's lead, and when he stopped to refuel I went by and was able to win by 26 seconds. It was Maserati's second win in a Championship round.

In the British GP meeting at Silverstone I was able to beat Roy Salvadori in his Aston Martin by some margin. Then came a street race at Bari the following weekend where the opposition was weak but I had some fun winning in the 300S on a circuit really better-suited to the 200Ss — in which Jean and Cesare Perdisa finished second and third. Piero Taruffi's sister Maserati 300S finished fourth, which in a way compensated for him having taken my Ferrari ride there at Bari five years earlier.

27 May 1956 Nürburgring 1,000Kms — Moss always had a reputation for eagle-eyed reading of the regulations. Here he saves seconds at a 300S refuelling stop by using the hoses from both the Maserati pits' gravity refuelling towers. Nowhere did it say you shouldn't. It took two cars to do it but he and Behra won!

14 July 1956 — British GP
supporting sports car race,
Silverstone — Diving in
towards Copse Corner's apex,
Stirling on his way to winning
in his handsome factory 300S
— pole position, fastest lap
and first place.

Final round of the Sports Car World Championship was at Kristianstad, in Sweden, where we tried the prototype 450S V8 in practice but thankfully ran 300Ss in the race. For me, it was a dead duck. I led before handing over to Jean, but during his stint the drum brakes gave trouble. Maserati's drums used very deeply sculptured cast cooling fins and were normally very good by drum-brake standards — but not that day.

We fell to sixth, with our team mates Villoresi and Schell fifth. Ugolini then put me into their car, and after I'm afraid a typically chaotic Maserati pit stop I shot off to regain lost time. But they managed to set fire to Jean's car during his next refuelling stop, and when my borrowed car's brakes eventually failed completely I ended my day far up an escape road . . . and happy to have found it.

I ended 1956 with one of my most successful and longest-distance tours ever, winning every race I started in the 300S; beating Fangio's Ferrari at Caracas, Venezuela, then adding the Australian TT in Melbourne and finally the Nassau Trophy in the Bahamas Speed Week. We sold the cars I drove in Venezuela and Australia to local owner-drivers, so I borrowed the Nassau 300S from my old Sebring-winning OSCA co-driver Bill Lloyd.

There really was something about the 300S and me. We seemed to be made for each other.

The big 450S V8 then became Maserati's main weapon for the 1957 Championship, which Adolfo and Omer Orsi, who ran the company, were determined to win along with the Formula 1 title. Fangio was leading their F1 attack, and while I was doing my damndest to beat them in the Vanwall in Formula 1 we were all on the same side in the war against Ferrari for the Sports Car title.

The Buenos Aires 1,000 kms was run on a rather alarming new dual-carriageway circuit at Costanera, which was bumpy, unmarked and dangerous. At one point cars were passing in opposite directions on the dual carriageway, only feet apart at 160 mph — a closing speed of 320! They introduced a new chicane after first practice, and in the race the 450S I shared with Fangio packed

9 December 1956 — Nassau Trophy, Bahamas — Stirling has the front wheel of Bill Lloyd's venerable 300S airborne over the Windsor Field aerodrome circuit's notorious 'Bump' on the way to another win. The Maserati's nose is held together by 'racer-tape' since Lloyd had a collision earlier in the meeting.

up after 57 laps, so I took over the Behra/Menditéguy 300S and really went after the leading Ferrari. Although the 300S was not as quick as the 3.5 Ferraris it was much easier to handle and suited the circuit very well. I set fastest lap and by lap 88 had taken second place and was closing on the leader, Musso. His brakes wilted under the strain, but I was just unable to catch him as the flag fell after six hours, 98 laps, with the gap still 80 seconds.

It had been a wonderful race for me which I enjoyed enormously despite the 450S's failure, and I wrote in my diary '*This was my greatest drive. Car fabulous — 6,400 rpm and I braked at 250-metres, in 450S braking at 500-metres . . .*' Some difference!

I retired Harry Schell's borrowed 300S from the Cuban GP with engine failure after starting the race in a 200S, and then after a stay in Nassau, where I was having a house built, I shared a 300S in preference to a V8 at Sebring. Harry was my co-driver, and I took the start, reckoning to drive the first five hours before handing over. But I had to come in for new tyres after 4 hrs 10 mins. Harry did twenty laps, just over an hour, then I took over for a further three hours, the car going well with something in reserve in case the leading 450S should break, which it did not. I used only 5,900 rpm. Harry did another hour, and I then took the final stint, recovering 167 secs from the Hawthorn/Bueb D-Type to take second place behind Fangio and Behra in the V8, a good Maserati 1-2.

I drove the big V8 for the rest of the season, but at Nürburgring when they had all kinds of trouble I took over Giorgio Scarlatti's 3-litre and found it handled so atrociously I soon handed it back! Ugolini then brought in the Godia-Sales/Horace Gould car from eleventh place, which proved much better and I managed to climb into sixth place before handing it to Fangio. We finally finished fifth.

At Kristianstad I ended the day sharing the third-place 3-litre with Bonnier, Scarlatti and Schell and then at Caracas I drove the V8 as our race — which could have clinched the Championship for us — turned into that celebrated nightmare of accidents and fires which partly precipitated Maserati's collapse.

Although Maserati were in receivership into 1958 they quietly continued development, and combined a modified 300S chassis with a 3-litre development of the V12 Formula 1 engine. I tested it at Nurburgring on Monday 16 June. I didn't think much of it. I noted '*No power high up, NBG, oversteer and difficult . . .*' We never raced it.

On 13 July Jean and I ran a pair of 300S works cars at Vila Real in Portugal — a difficult but nice road and street circuit where we never got into fifth, peaking instead at 6,500 rpm in fourth. We put on a show of passing and repassing for the crowd and finished 1-2, with the Spanish privateer Francesco Godia-Sales' sister 300S third. It was a 1-2-3 swansong for the factory.

I needed a car for a Scandinavian tour that August, and Alfieri at Maserati's obliged with a 300S. I won at Karlskoga without much problem, but at Roskilde, in Denmark, the Copenhagen GP was run in six heats over two days, on the most Mickey Mouse circuit in a former gravel pit. In heat one on the first day the car's engine failed so I borrowed Brian Naylor's 200S-engined JBW for the other heats that afternoon and won them both.

A replacement engine went into the Maserati overnight, and I used it in all three heats next day, ending up second overall, less than a second behind Gunnar Carlsson's Monza Ferrari who baulked me so badly I actually punted him deliberately in the tail — the only time I can ever recall having been moved to do such a thing.

That was the last time I raced any 300S. It really was one of the nicest of all Maseratis. I remember them and the team, the Orsis, Alfieri, Bertocchi and the other mechanics, with affection. Despite all the frustrations and occasional frights they caused me, I had found my feet at top level driving their cars and for three seasons enjoyed a lot of success with them. As the company slid down the tubes during 1958, I didn't realize it, but I hadn't yet finished with them, for the best of all their cars was still to come . . .

13 July 1958 — Vila Real, Portugal — Maserati's famous chief mechanic 'Guerrino' Bertocchi directs his charges' line-up with Stirling's factory-loaned 300S alongside Jean Behra's and Francesco Godia-Sales'. That's a pontoon-fendered Ferrari Testa Rossa *humbled on the row behind . . .*

Aston Martin DB3S (1956)

'One of the most pretty sports-racing cars but lacking the simple elegance of some of the Jaguars; a really good road-racing car, nimble and quick but liable to lift its inside rear wheel too easily . . .'

2 April 1956 — Easter Monday Goodwood — Looking a little high-built here as it rolls through St Mary's, but oh so shapely, the works DB3S on its way to winning the sports car race in Stirling's hands.

When I raced against the early DB3Ss in the works C-Type Jaguar I was impressed by their agile handling, and after driving for Mercedes-Benz in 1955, I tested a works DB3S at Goodwood in February 1956 and signed on with the team for that season. Their team manager, John Wyer, talked me into accepting a signing-on fee of £50, I remember.

I drove those cars six times that season, winning twice and finishing second three times. They always handled nicely, and felt small and easy to drive but their engines were very pernickety about rev limits and the rev band always seemed very restricted. You could run it up to the red line in an intermediate gear, change up . . . and the power would just seem to have faded. It was a characteristic one quickly became used to, and above all it was a very pleasant team to be a part of. For one thing John Wyer certainly knew all the best restaurants and hotels.

Aston Martin had developed their DB3S as a lightweight 3-litre sports-racing car in 1953 and it went through a long evolution which meant it should have been pretty well sorted-out and well-understood by the time I joined the team for its fourth season. Unfortunately, this was not always so.

My first DB3S race was the Sebring 12-Hours, for which I was teamed with Peter Collins. Mike Hawthorn did 3:28 in his D-Type in practice, Fangio 3:33 in the Ferrari and my best with the '3S was only 3:34.1. Its brakes were only going to survive eight hours and the tyres only two, so we were not in good shape. Fuel consumption was 9 mpg.

I made a super start. Those Le Mans-type run-and-jump starts were something of a forté of mine. I enjoyed them and practised them quite a lot. I ran second, between Hawthorn and Fangio, managing to lap 3 secs quicker than I had in practice, but an hour and a half after Pete took over, our car's engine broke.

Back home, after winning the sports car race at Easter Goodwood, we prepared for the May Silverstone meeting, where Roy Salvadori's car was 2 secs quicker than mine in practice. Being number one driver I asked John if I could try Roy's car, but he rather sheepishly explained that Roy's wasn't a works car at all, he actually owned it. Roy was a very bright chap, and he'd obviously spotted a very good car and made Aston's an offer they couldn't refuse! I remember thinking it's not very bright for a works team to sell its quickest car . . . but believe it or not these things do sometimes happen.

I must confess I was not very happy about that, and I started the race knowing that my car should have been better. I made a terrific start and led to Hanger Straight, where I moved to the right and waved Roy past on the left with his quicker car. Unfortunately, we both needed the same piece of road at Stowe Corner and I came off second-best. While I was sorting that out the Jaguars driven by Desmond Titterington and Mike both went by me and then at the next corner, Club, my diary records, '*Roy drove Des off the road and Mike retired with seized steering*'. In fact, the shunt at Club Corner not only put out two D-Types but also two of our Astons. Roy won with me second, not terribly impressed about it all.

We took four cars to Rouen where we found an interesting characteristic concerning the '3S's disc brakes versus drums. Peter Collins had not liked his car's handling on discs at Nürburgring a few weeks earlier, and for Rouen had asked to have drums refitted which I think might have been marginally lighter and therefore seemed to allow the wheels to follow the road surface more consistently. My car had discs and with 40 psi tyre pressures it was pattering badly and oversteering too much. I lapped in 2:35, but then when I tried Pete's drum-braked car it was much nicer to drive and my times tumbled to 2:32.8. Since Pete did 2:37 in each car, he suggested I should have the choice and I took the one on drums. That was quite typical of him, but I'm not sure he really liked the idea too much.

When the race began he made a great start and rushed into the lead in what had been my car, and then it blew up. I started slowly and the car didn't feel right, but I profited from retirements and got into a big dice for the lead with Castellotti's Ferrari, which he won by 3.9 secs. For some reason my car had not handled as well as I'd hoped and I felt very tired afterwards.

Le Mans followed, where Pete and I would share a car. My best practice time was 4:24, Pete's 4:27 while Mike Hawthorn's fuel-injected D-Type got down to 4:17, which was very depressing for us! I led from the start so the accident which eliminated two of the Jaguars occurred behind me, while I settled into a dice with Ron Flockhart's Ecurie Ecosse D-Type. Our Aston had neither the power nor the straight-line speed and then in the night Pete came in to report he'd lost second gear and we dropped 1½ laps, which effectively cost us the race. The car kept going like a train and we finished second, matching my 1953 result in the works C-Type.

It was at this race that I was passing time in the Aston pit, talent-spotting in the crowd opposite. I'd spotted this cute-looking girl and went up on top of the pits with a pair of binoculars to make sure! Eventually she noticed me, so I beckoned her over. She shook her head and tapped her arm, indicating she didn't have a pass. I waved one at her, pointed to her side of the track and went over and met her and we had dinner that Sunday night. She was Canadian. Her name was Katie Molson, and she would become my first wife.

The *Daily Herald* Trophy race was run at Oulton Park, and there my '3S proved just too much for the opposition. Rain fell in torrents but I always enjoyed racing in the wet and I led from start to finish for an easy win. It was my last race in a DB3S.

It was always a forgiving car which one could throw around, rather like my favourite Maserati 300S but with rather less power. The Aston was too prone to lifting its inside rear wheel under really hard cornering, which would permit it to spin, and sometimes one had to ease off to prevent this happening in corners in which other cars might sustain full throttle all the way. On a winding road circuit the DB3S would out-handle a D-Type any time at all, and by coming to it direct from the Mercedes 300SLRs I found it so much smaller and lighter, and easier to drive. For a circuit like Nürburgring I would have loved to combine the nimbleness of the '3S with the sheer speed and reliability of the 'SLR. But of course, nothing is ever perfect.

Cooper T39 Mark II 'Bob-tail' (1956)

'It seemed like a good idea at the time, but my brief ownership of what should have been a very competitive new sports car was not very happy at all . . .'

When the 1,100 cc Coventry-Climax FWA four-cylinder 'fire pump' power unit emerged in 1954 it had all the ingredients of a superb racing engine. It was very light and compact and offered very good power. It was not expensive and it would become available off the shelf. When John Cooper built a central-seat sports-racing car around it for 1955, based on his contemporary 500s with outriggers attached each side of the chassis and the new Climax engine in the back, driving through a modified Citroen *Traction Avant* gearbox, it performed very well. Into 1956 Climax made 1,500 cc FWB engines available and the central-seat Cooper sports cars were uprated as Mark IIs to match. After driving one of the works cars successfully, I bought a new Mark II which Alf Francis prepared, fitting the engine with Weber twin-choke carburettors in place of Cooper's usual SUs, and it was a disaster.

These cars were unusual at the time in several ways. The centreline driving seat was one, the rear-mounted water-cooled engine was another, but perhaps most comment was attracted by their sharply cut-off tails. There was quite a bit of lofty technical explanation about the aerodynamic theories of cut-off car tails as propounded by Professor Kamm in Germany. Others claimed that somebody had cut off the original tapering tail of a similar car and found it instantly went faster along the straight. John Cooper, however, was a very practical guy, and he said that they had cut off the first of these 'Manx-tail' or 'Bob-tail' Cooper bodies simply 'to make it fit in our truck!'

Certainly, in the old 500 days, an early Cooper tweak was to cut a hole or slot in the tip of the tail. Some claimed this was simply to let hot air escape easily from the engine bay, but others insisted that this relieved the pressure inside the bodywork and so made the cars go faster. John would grin and tell you confidentially that the reason they cut off the end of their early 500s' tail was simply so that it would not scrape on the ground when it was hinged open.

My first experience of these little Bob-tail cars, and of the Coventry-Climax four-cylinder engine, was in the British Empire Trophy race at Oulton Park in April 1956. I drove a works car formerly raced by Ivor Bueb's protégé Mike MacDowel, and finished fourth in the small-car heat. We were then mixed in with the large-capacity cars in the final, which was run on handicap, and in which I took the lead with Colin Chapman breathing down my neck in his Lotus Eleven. He passed me but spun, which left me to win with the Lotus second.

I bought my own Bob-tail Cooper with BP backing, and had it registered 'BPB 777'. Alf Francis prepared it and fitted its Climax engine with his favourite Weber twin-choke carburettors, and it was ready in time for the Aintree '200' meeting. It proved dreadful, handling like a pig. I could only salvage fifth place. Alf checked it carefully at Cooper's afterwards but it seemed OK and then, when I again complained of its diabolical handling at Crystal Palace, old Charlie Cooper blamed the carburettor conversion. He said 'They've altered the engine's characteristics and upset the handling . . .' I got Alf to fit SUs, against his will, and I won there but only by overdriving the car desperately hard to hold off Les Leston's better-handling Bob-tail.

When Alf asked me after that race what he should do with the car next, I simply said 'Sell it'.

In my absence, he then got Jack Brabham to test it a week later at Brands Hatch. They found its chassis had been misaligned in the building jig and the front transverse leaf-spring had been bottoming out against the damper brackets. That had made the front end go solid so it would wash out into an understeer. As the tyres slid so they relieved the load, which allowed the spring to free again, whereupon the front tyres would grip, and the tail would flick round before the spring bottomed and made the front let go again. It felt as horrible as it sounds.

A Reims 12-hour race for small-capacity cars was coming up so we hastily entered the Bob-tail for it, and I arranged for Phil Hill to share the driving. It was vastly improved, and very quick for its size along the straights. I led for the first half-hour, at least five seconds a lap quicker than the opposition, but then the engine began running rough. Phil took over, but soon retired with overheating caused by running lean at such sustained high speeds.

The following weekend I was driving the works Aston Martin DB3S at Rouen, so we entered Peter Jopp in the Cooper. Possibly due to brand-new unscrubbed tyres being fitted just before the start, he rolled it spectacularly on the opening lap. It took some time to repair the damage, and we then sold the car to Robin Mackenzie-Low.

At Oulton Park in August I drove John Willment's gaudy red-and-white striped Bob-tail in place of its usual driver Les Leston, who had spiked his foot on a nail. I started back on the third row but that was a very well sorted car and I was quickly amongst the leaders, with Mike Hawthorn right on my tail in Ivor Bueb's Lotus Eleven. Then he slid off, rode up a bank and overturned, flying back across the track upside-down, clean over Roy Salvadori's head in the works Cooper. The Lotus actually scraped Roy's helmet, and hit a tree after throwing Mike out. Fortunately he wasn't badly hurt but it was certainly a spectacular way to leave a motor race . . .

This presented me with another easy win; a pleasing end to a rather unfortunate relationship with Cooper's first proper rear-engined sports car.

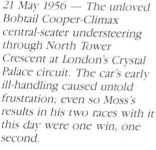

21 May 1956 — The unloved Bobtail Cooper-Climax central-seater understeering through North Tower Crescent at London's Crystal Palace circuit. The car's early ill-handling caused untold frustration; even so Moss's results in his two races with it this day were one win, one second.

Maserati 350S (1956)

'It was one of the most unpleasant drives I ever had. At high speed the car wandered on the straights and understeered badly in the corners, its rear-end grip completely overwhelmed the front, and I finally drove it off a mountain . . .'

4 April 1956 — The hastily-finished new Maserati 350S still in primer on test at Modena's Aerautodromo; *the concerned-looking group beyond include Giulio Alfieri (fourth from left), Bertocchi in helmet and goggles having just driven the car, chassis/transmission designer Valerio Colotti, SM about to take over and Denis Jenkinson — intrepid navigator.*

*T*he 300S Maserati never really had the power to tackle Jaguar and Ferrari on equal terms, so Alfieri and his people in Modena set out on the 450S V8 project. While that was under development they tried to fill the gap by adapting their forthcoming 3500GT road car engine to a more or less 450S-type sports-racing chassis. The deeper they got into it the less like a production engine the 3500 six-cylinder became. Eventually they went to full dry-sump lubrication, and found 290 bhp, and then they installed it in a chassis with the new Colotti-designed five-speed transaxle and de Dion rear end intended for the V8. Two of these cars were completed in a great rush for the Mille Miglia, one for myself navigated again by Jenks, and the other for Piero Taruffi, who was a wise old fox . . . and he opted to race the proven 300S instead.

*O*ur Mille Miglia car was completed so late I only managed the briefest tests just before the great race. Jenks and I had been out on a recce in an old 1954 car, rigged with right-hand drive and a detuned Formula 1 engine, in which we covered 2,000 miles in 2½ days. The new car still wasn't ready but the Maserati people looked really crestfallen when we suggested we should race a 300S instead. Then it became clear that Taruffi also preferred the 300S, so Alfieri agreed to prepare a spare one for us as well, just in case.

Two days before the race the new car had still only progressed as far as the bodyshop with 22 mechanics swarming all over it. We kicked our heels around the works all that Friday, poised to try the car, until finally night fell and it still wasn't finished. Eventually we were told to get some sleep, and return at 5.30 next morning.

When we arrived, the 350S was finished at last, and Bertocchi had already tested it at Modena *Aerautodromo* two hours earlier! A protruding spoiler had been added under the radiator intake and there were mutterings about the nose lifting above 130 mph, but this would cure it . . .

I wanted to try the car back-to-back against our spare 300S, so with Bertocchi driving the spare car we went up to the Raticosa Pass where we chose a 10 Km stretch for timed runs both up and downhill. After three runs each way, the new 350S was clearly quicker, but I can tell you it was a whole lot harder to drive.

On the way there from Modena I had wound it up to 5,200 rpm in fifth, which was about 145 mph, but at that speed the nose really did wander most disturbingly. I also found on the Raticosa that should I enter a corner too fast and induce understeer to help slow and steady the car, there was then no way I could convert that initial understeer into oversteer to bring the tail round and point the nose back into the corner. This was most disconcerting — quite unlike 300S behaviour — and although the new car was clearly much quicker than the 300S it left terribly little margin for error. It was most unforgiving, and if there was one thing necessary for the Mille Miglia, it could be forgiveness.

But there was no time at all to improve matters. The whole team set off immediately on the two-hour drive to Brescia for the start, the mechanics driving the 350S, and when we arrived they told us that our new car was 'making a funny smell at over 120 mph'.

So at 6 pm — when we had originally planned to be going to bed — we took it out on to the Autostrada, and sure enough at high speed it did smell of burning rubber, but nobody could find the reason. It was not easy to sleep that night, with the thought of unexplained burning smells at 120 mph in a car capable

29 April 1956 — Mille Miglia — The 350S is painted, numbered, badged and polished but still far from raceworthy — and its crew know it. They are about to leave the Brescia ramp.

of 165! There was also its wandering and understeer to ponder. Then Jenks remarked that the protruding lip spoiler had miraculously disappeared without anybody telling us why . . . sweet dreams.

Up early on race day, and we were waved down the starting ramp at 5.54 am. It was immediately obvious that I had a real battle on my hands. The way the car wandered on the straights and washed-out at the front dictated considerable caution. Jenks sensed I was far from happy as I was lifting off before bumps on 150 mph straights which the previous year we had simply ignored in the Mercedes 300SLR. Then near Padua we encountered an extra problem. It began to rain.

When a car has been completed so hastily, and tested so briefly, minor items like sealing and water deflection are inevitably overlooked. Now as the rain beat down and we began hitting deeper and deeper puddles at high speed, water fountained up between the seats. It was cascading in behind us, and coming in like rolling surf above the screen. I was more used to this than Jenks, who wrote subsequently how uncomfortable it became, but even though I liked racing in the wet this was something different. Rain had always bothered me less than most other drivers, but soon several inches of water were washing around beneath my seat. It was coming in quicker than it was draining out. Jenks was drying spare goggles for me as mine became opaque, and on a 130 mph straight near Ferrara we were groping our way along when Luigi Musso went flailing by in his Ferrari. I wasn't having that, so I caught up with him again on a winding section and embarrassed him into giving way as I cut by in a village.

We were then baulked for miles behind a little 2-litre Ferrari whose driver hadn't a clue we were behind in his spray, then we overtook John Heath driving carefully in his HWM-Jaguar and waved . . . goodbye as it proved, for he crashed soon after, and was fatally injured.

Just before Fano, Musso went by again and I couldn't hold him, but after Senigallia we saw his car stopped by the roadside with Luigi standing beside it relieving himself! I sympathized . . .

Nearing Pescara the rain stopped and we closed on Perdisa's 300S, but our car was so unwieldy it took a long time to get by, though I finally managed it just before the Maserati depot in the town. They told us we were sixth overall, but as we climbed out of Pescara into the Abruzzi the rain came pelting down again. Perdisa closed up and we passed and repassed. It was obvious he was having a far easier time in the 300S. I began to push the 350S harder and managed to shake him off, but it was obvious my favourite 300S was far superior. At Aquila the rain abated, but then fell even harder on the descent towards Rieti.

Along this section the car picked up its wheels in one really big slide which nearly took us off the road with me working overtime, then — soon after — we entered a gentle downhill right-left ess leading into a tight right-hander above a village named Antrodoco. I started to brake in a straight line through the ess, setting up the Maserati for the right-hander, but the front brakes locked and the nose washed-out instantly into a wild understeering slide, which there was not enough room or time to correct.

We crashed through a small stone wall on the right, and the Maserati shot up the hillside beyond, tipping up on its ear and almost rolling over. It then bounded over the crest and down to leap off the top of a three-foot high retaining wall where the road looped round through that right-hand corner. We then flew clean across the roadway, burst through the concrete barrier on the opposite side and crashed down a steep grassy slope into a small tree, some fifteen feet from the roadside.

We baled out quickly and waved to Musso and Perdisa driving by, then studied what had happened. Somewhere *en route* we had burst through a barbed wire fence, and I found I had in fact been very lucky. The barbed wire had left only the tiniest nick just below my right eye, but the car's windscreen, my goggles and helmet were deeply scratched, and so was the glass on my wrist watch.

The 'ole. Apart from that missing section of cast-concrete barrier, this is more or less the view which Moss and Jenkinson had as the 350S launched them into the far blue yonder . . . high above Antrodoco.

OK, so the 350's flight down the mountainside was not arrested by the only tree around, but certainly it was the only one of much substance and it really did prevent the car cartwheeling 300-feet or more down into that rock-strewn river bed below.

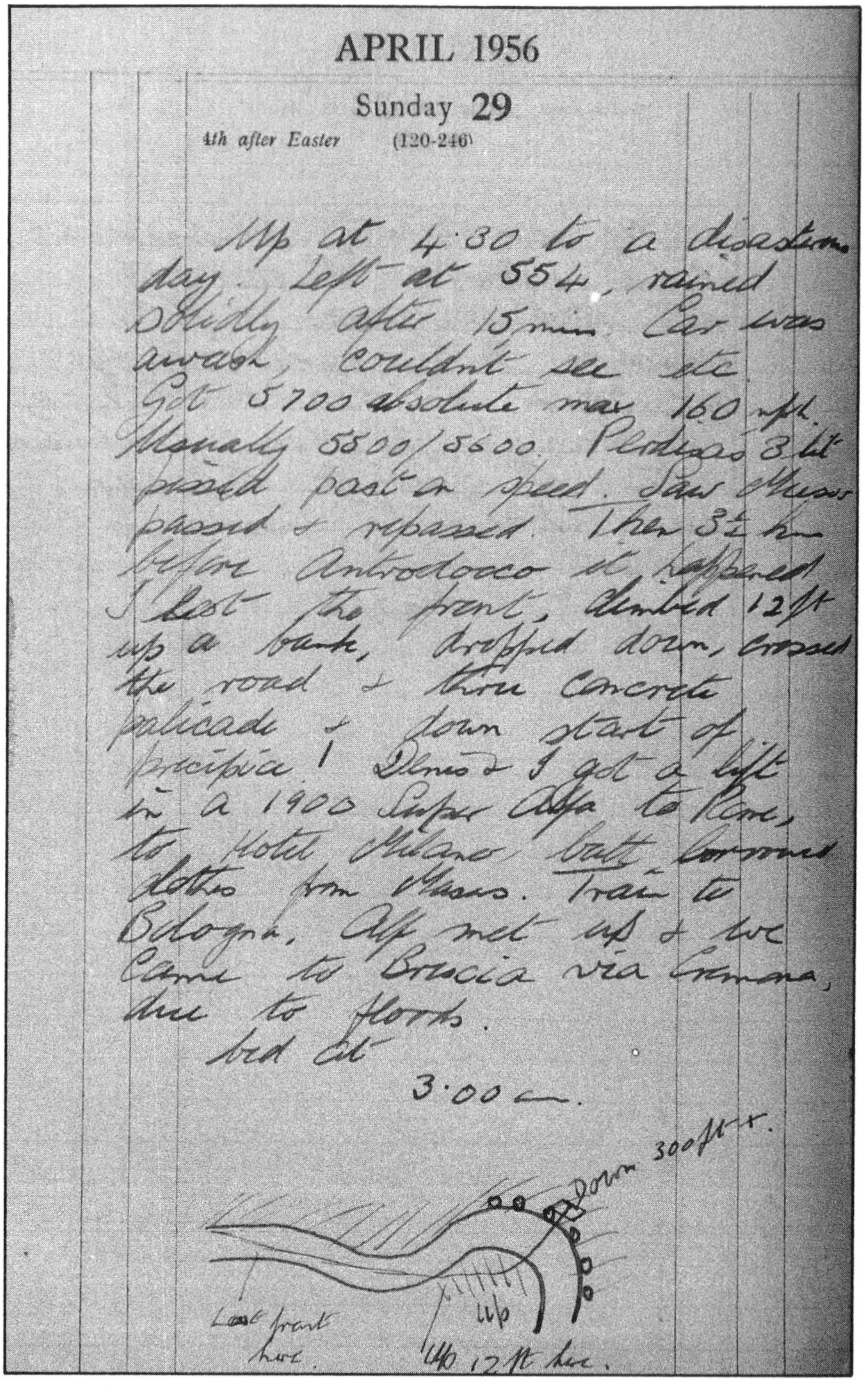

APRIL 1956

Sunday 29

4th after Easter   (120-246)

Up at 4.30 to a disastrous day. Left at 5.54, rained shortly after 15 min. Car was awash, couldn't see etc. Got 5700 absolute max 160 mph. Usually 5500/5600. Pedroza 3 lit passed past on speed. Saw Musso passed & repassed. Then 3½ km before Antrodoco it happened I lost the front, climbed 12ft up a bank, dropped down, crossed the road & thro concrete palicade & down start of precipice! [illegible] & I got a lift in a 1900 Super Alfa to Rome, to Hotel Milano, bath borrowed clothes from Musso. Train to Bologna. Alf met us & we came to Brescia via Cremona, here to floods.

bed at

3.00 a.m.

We also realized that the Maserati had hit the only tree for yards around, and beyond it the slope steepened and plunged away, 300 feet or more into a river bed strewn with very big, hard, ugly boulders.

I understand Alfieri eventually extracted 325 horsepower from that 350S engine, but the car's chassis was far heavier than the standard 300S and, although this kind of hybrid half 300S/half 450S car was undoubtedly quick, it was never really raceworthy. Failing like that in defence of our Mille Miglia title was quite a disappointment, but Maserati had an even bigger one up their sleeves for us the following year . . .

Racewear

'One simply did not consider the risks'

When I started racing I wore a normal pair of white garage mechanic's overalls, simply to look racey and to save my everyday clothes from the inevitable smears of oil or grease. I chose white because it looked smarter than the alternatives, blue, black or khaki!

I had grown up avidly reading the motoring magazines, which were full of photographs of heroes like Farina, Wimille, Nuvolari and Caracciola wearing similar-looking overalls. None of them wore crash helmets, preferring soft linen or leather wind caps instead.

Imagine my intense chagrin when my father said 'If you are going racing you are going to wear a crash helmet'. I said 'Don't make me wear a crash helmet, Dad. It's cissy'. After all, none of the aces did, so why should I? But he insisted and I had to do as I was told. He rigged me out with an enormous motor cyclist's black leather crash hat. I quickly realized it was far too big and heavy and then discovered the neat Herbert Johnson helmet for £5 12s 6d, quite a lot of money, but worth it . . .

Herbert Johnson (of Bond Street in London), made very nice lightweight protective helmets essentially for polo players. The Johnson helmet was largely made of laminated canvas and gum, with canvas side pieces over one's ears, but later I talked them into making mine with thin and supple white leather instead. It looked nicer and was more comfortable, even though there was a small extra charge. I bought a white one late in 1948, a great improvement over that enormous black original.

I wore ordinary goggles at that time, then later adopted ski-ing goggles or a visor, which was best in the wet as it would not mist up. RAF fighter pilot's goggles with the break in their lenses were good, but I eventually went to goggles with very light aluminium frames and sponge rubber padding. They had the all-important ventilation holes around them to prevent misting. But, of course, they were still not good in the wet.

In my early wet-weather races I wore a semi-waterproof jerkin or jacket outside my overalls. Early on, my Cooper carried a sign-painted lucky horseshoe emblem, with seven studs in it for luck. Subsequently, of course, I adopted the race number '7' whenever I could as my lucky number. I am quite superstitious,

The original motor-cycle despatch rider's crash helmet was big, black and heavy. Here are Moss pere et fils in happy mood in the paddock at Prescott with their first Cooper-JAP Mark II.

something inherited from my mother who was very much inclined that way. Seven she claimed was her lucky number, everybody in our family was born on the 7th, 17th or 27th. She had been born on 7 July, the seventh day of the seventh month — my birthday was 17 September, my sister Pat's 27 December. As for poor old Dad, he had no lucky 7s in his birthdate at all, having been born on 30 May — don't know how he made it really . . .

In my first season the horseshoe on the Cooper surrounded a red heart emblem, terribly twee in retrospect, but then I was a romantic-minded fellow. Later the heart was replaced within the horseshoe by a Mobil prancing horse for much more practical — and rather more lucrative — reasons . . .

Once I began racing with HWM in hot and sunny climes like San Remo, Naples or Rome, I began wearing just lightweight cotton overall trousers with a short-sleeved sports shirt on top. In later years we used to soak our cotton overalls in a recommended flame-retardant solution — which I seem to recall was based upon some kind of baking powder — but really we paid hardly any attention to safety in general, and to fire risks in particular. The idea was that if your car caught fire you would jump out of it and get away. Simple as that.

You must remember that many of the people in racing had just survived six years of bloody war, so racing was a piece of cake in comparison. One simply did not consider the risks.

In the very early days, Pirelli provided some comfortable pale-blue Italian overalls which became quite popular, a sensible design with cross-over front, which were given to us at the start of each season. But with HWM we had our overalls made in Monte Carlo by a company named Bienfait who I believe made Lance Macklin's shirts for him. Lance introduced me to them, after they had made him a pair of lightweight, comfortable trousers. We then had some nice, light, cool and washable silk-poplin overall trousers made by them.

Subsequently, Suixtil sports shirts came along, introduced by Fangio, Gonzalez and the other South Americans, coming from a clothing company in Argentina who would give us the shirts on a promotional basis, rather like Boss today except Suixtil's range was, of course, much smaller, not nearly as fashionable, and the company was not nearly as generous.

So far as footwear is concerned, I started off with ordinary shoes or plimsolls, then found they slipped on oily pedals so tried thin-soled high-ankled boxing boots. But the HWM footwell was enormously hot; we could burn our feet on the gearbox and the pedals, which conducted heat from the engine and exhaust. Consequently, I got a company to make me some white asbestos boots with leather soles, which I wore in the HWMs to ward off the heat a bit. Then I returned to boxing boots and ultimately specially made driving shoes, both with supple, chrome leather soles so they would not slip. The soles, of course, were very thin to provide maximum feel, and had no welt due to the danger of it catching under a pedal as we danced from one to another.

We were not conscious at all of fire protection, we would just wear whatever socks we had. Fire occurred in something like forty per cent of all accidents but for some dumb reason each of us was confident we'd get away with it. There were no directives from the racing authorities, and even crash hats were not made mandatory until 1952 . . .

I doubt I ever raced bare-headed, even early on. It was The Thing to use driving gloves, and later when somebody asked me to endorse Stirling Moss driving gloves — 'available in all handy sizes' — I naturally did so. Oil was very common, so gloves helped a lot.

I preferred thin open-backed gloves, not the shiny type. In the HWM, I always used to tuck a rag between my legs to wipe my goggles, and of course we often carried a spare pair of goggles round our necks just in case. I learned so many of the basics with that team it was incredible.

One thing I recall was in-race refreshment. I had not needed it in the Cooper, when the cockpit was too small and generally the races too short. We would

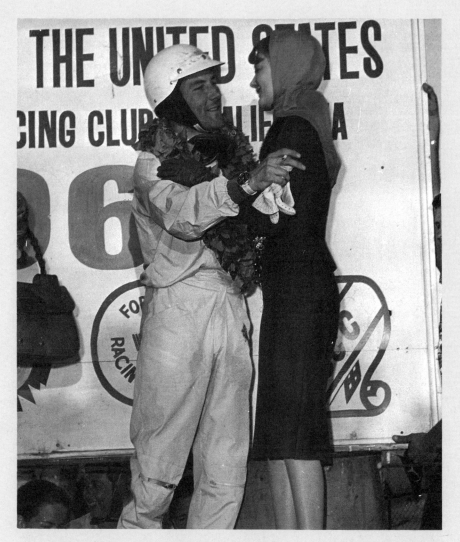

To the victor — the spoils; Stirling with film star Shirley Knight after winning the 1960 United States GP at Riverside, wearing his flame-proofed two-piece Dunlop overalls, thin-soled driving shoes and carrying his string-backed gloves. The rather modern-looking Bell crash helmet was worn only this late-season — his old-faithful Herbert Johnson type returning to favour for 1961–62.

use something like lemon juice or lemon barley, dependent on what was available and not too expensive, and never fizzy. I would carry it in a thermos flask, with a tube, usually kept between my legs or down beside the seat, dependent upon the layout of the car.

The idea then was to reach down amongst all the oil and general gunge lying about on the floor, pick up this dreadful dirty old tube and stuff it in your mouth for a drink. It worked fine, but there was a trick to it. You had to blow the fluid back down the tube a bit when you had finished, otherwise it would siphon out when you dropped the tube back on to the floor, so next time you wanted a drink there'd be none left.

All this experience accumulated over the years. Eventually, around 1957, I approached Dunlop about overalls for they were increasingly interested in all kinds of sporting goods. I pointed out how Pirelli had got all that free advertising by supplying well-known drivers with their lettered overalls and I designed some driving overalls for them which they produced.

I had reckoned they would be better with a gusset in the back for freedom of movement, and with pockets with a rounded bottom down near your ankle where earplugs for example had no sharp corner in which to become lodged. They were made in lightweight blue cotton poplin, both two-piece and one-piece designs, and became the overalls I wore until the end of my professional career.

The Vanwalls *(1956-58)*

'The Vanwall was a terribly important car for me. At last a British-built Grand Prix car capable of winning against anybody. But it did not do its winning easily . . . bad flat-spots, bad gearbox and a car which demanded delicate handling, but very fast, with good brakes, and acceptably reliable . . .'

'ThinWall' bearing manufacturer Tony Vandervell was a rugged — and dogged — industrialist who had grown impatient with BRM in their early days after being initially one of their most active backers. He stamped off to build a racing team of his own, initially using Ferrari cars which his people developed into the imposing series of *'ThinWall Special'* racing cars. Then in 1953 he launched development of a 2-litre Formula 2 car largely of his own company's design and manufacture, apart from using a Cooper-designed chassis. After its début as the *'Vanwall Special'* in 1954 in under-sized Formula 1 form, it reached maturity in 1955 as the 2½-litre Vanwall.

Its four-cylinder engine combined Norton motor cycle cylinder head technology with a Rolls-Royce industrial engine bottom end, plus Bosch fuel-injection. The car also carried Goodyear-derived disc brakes, which were very advanced and powerful at that time. It showed great potential. For 1956 Vandervell engaged Colin Chapman of Lotus and Frank Costin, the aerodynamicist, to design a new car to carry this engine and together they produced the British-green cars which would topple Italian domination of Grand Prix racing.

I was proud to contribute to Vanwall's effort as one of their drivers.

After my Mercedes-Benz season, Maserati had made me a very tempting offer for 1956. Ferrari had also been making noises, but first I wanted to check the current level of the British teams. I first drove a Vanwall on 12 November 1955, at Oulton Park. It was the Cooper-designed car 'VW2' and I was quite impressed by its handling but not by its engine, which was dreadfully flat below 4,700 rpm and misfired at 6,800-7,000. I tried a BRM that same day, which lapped 2.7 secs quicker on a damp track.

On 22 November, Vanwall, Connaught and BRM each provided a car for me to test at Silverstone. I lapped in 1:53 with the Connaught on Dunlops, then

4 May 1956 — Practice for the BRDC International Trophy race at Silverstone, Moss about to put Tony Vandervell's new teardrop Vanwall on pole position. He looks happy enough climbing into the high-sided cockpit. 'The Guv'nor' (left) perhaps offers typically gruff advice . . .

1:50.3 on Pirellis. The BRM was quicker, 1:50.5, but the Vanwall — 'VW1' — was quicker still; 1:46.9 and only a second slower on full tanks.

That was quite impressive, but I emphasized I would make no hasty decisions, and on the last day of November we announced that I was joining Maserati. Results would show this was the right decision at that time, but I told Mr Vandervell I would certainly like to drive for him when other commitments allowed, if he would like me to.

Through that winter, Chapman and Costin redesigned the Vanwall and, when Maserati opted out of the early-season British F1 races, it was arranged for me to drive one of the new teardrop-shaped Vanwalls on their début — at May Silverstone.

The new car was not only sensational-looking and really exquisitely well built but also 100 lb lighter than the rival Lancia-Ferrari V8s. Its fuel-injected engine could produce a great deal of power — up to 290 bhp at 7,500 rpm on alcohol by the end of '57 — but its long stroke and separated valve gear made it very tall. Only 12 inches behind its front-axle centres the cambox already stood 26 inches above ground, and the driver's seat was perched above the bulky gearbox so its underside was 12½ inches above the road surface. This meant that the driver's head when seated was four feet high so the Vanwall had an inherent frontal-area disadvantage, and the only way to minimize it was to adopt an exceptionally low-drag body — which Frank Costin had now provided.

I drove new teardrop car 'VW2' while Harry Schell had the prototype 'VW1'. Our new British-green cars lined-up 1-2 on the grid ahead of the Fangio and Collins Ferraris — a terrific sight. I felt quite proud to be driving that car, and I won comfortably and broke the lap record. It was only a 180-mile race, not a full 312-mile GP distance, but this was very encouraging.

However, there was obviously still work to be done before the Vanwall team and its car became real World Championship contenders. Even so, Maserati's engineers asked me some penetrating questions when we next met . . .

During that season the Vanwall increasingly impressed, especially when Harry Schell left my Maserati for dead on straight-line speed at Spa, Reims and Monza! Clearly, despite its flat-spots, the Vanwall engine was very competitive. I still doubted its reliability, but when Vandervell invited me to sign for 1957 I readily tried his car again. I wanted to drive it really hard for a full Grand Prix distance, to prove it could survive.

I first tried it briefly at Silverstone on 10 October, my diary assessing it simply as '*Bloody quick.*' They took two cars to Oulton on 22 October for the GP-distance test. I drove one for 1 hr 50 mins until its suspension broke, having lapped in 1:48.5, and the other for 2 hrs 30 mins, until an injector pipe broke.

I had many reservations, but this was clearly the first green Grand Prix car I had ever driven which showed such winning potential. We prepared a press statement on 29 October which was released on Wednesday 31 October. I was to drive for Vanwall in 1957.

I was always keen to help improve our cars if I possibly could, so I immediately made a long list of suggestions; improved dampers, larger rear brake discs, improved drive-shaft pot-joints to allow greater wheel movement, and research into improved fuel economy.

Mr Vandervell's team manager, David Yorke, then signed-up Tony Brooks — a very quiet character, who I rate as the greatest 'little known' driver of all time.

In 1957 Vanwalls were modified with tall rear coil-spring/damper struts replacing the original transverse leaf spring. Colin Chapman designed this system to encourage inherent understeer through the combination of a high roll-centre with relatively small weight transfer between the wheels at the rear, and large weight transfer at the front. To enhance rear-end grip still more, he gave the rear wheels three degrees' negative camber, leaning inwards at the top. This also, if anything, made them even more convenient as footsteps to help us climb into that high, deeply screened cockpit!

20 July 1957 — The Great Day when the British first won their own Grand Prix — Stirling hustles his originally assigned Vanwall 'VW1' through Aintree's Melling Crossing showing off its exquisite tool-room finish. When this car developed problems early in the race he took over Tony Brooks' sister 'VW4' to win.'

Like Maserati, Vanwall had been running Pirelli tyres, but Pirelli wanted to withdraw and only reluctantly continued to supply. Meanwhile, Dunlop had made great progress with a new R4 design using nylon cord casing which proved superior to contemporary Pirellis in the wet, and only marginally slower in the dry.

Our first race came on 7 April at Syracuse, Sicily. I qualified my car — 'VW1' — on the front row once we geared it properly, and I took the lead and was able to extend it by a second a lap as the car was running beautifully. After 32 laps my lead was 35 secs, but then the four-cylinder engine's vibration cracked a fuel injector pipe. I lost four laps before rejoining seventh. Tony's car had a water pipe split; it overheated and cracked the cylinder head. I managed to regain two laps on Collins' leading Ferrari and set a new lap record, but could only finish third.

This had been a frustrating début, but the Vanwall's potential was clear. Then Easter Monday Goodwood saw more frustration. My car felt great in practice, pulling 7,700 rpm on 6.50 section tyres and holding 7,000 rpm out of the long curve at Fordwater. I led for 13 of the 32 laps until its throttle linkage broke on Lavant Straight, while Tony's had already parted after just four laps — though he subsequently rejoined.

Everybody in the Vanwall racing shop, from The Old Man down, displayed enormous determination to succeed, and there was no doubting *his* dissatisfaction after Syracuse and Goodwood . . . For Monaco, on our recommendation, they adopted more steering lock, more torque low down for the tight corners and cut-back 'Monaco noses' to avoid damage to the normal long beak. To resist vibration new Palmer Silvoflex injector pipes were used, and the same material was adapted to form a flexible joint in the throttle shaft.

Unfortunately, early in Monaco practice, I rammed the chicane, bending 'VW5's' chassis, steering and suspension. I took over Tony's car, 'VW3', with my engine installed and managed a good start from the outside of the front row and led for three laps with Fangio and Collins in my mirrors, then Tony fourth. Approaching the chicane I hit the brake pedal as normal, and I swear there was a system failure. The team said they could find no problem later, but I am adamant the front brakes had gone when I hit that pedal.

The now over-braked rears instantly locked, and my only course was to go straight on, smashing through a pole-and-sandbag barrier, crushing 'VW3's' nose and breaking mine against its steering wheel. Collins and Hawthorn crashed their Ferraris in the general confusion, Fangio — of course — dodged through completely unscathed and went on to win for Maserati, while Tony turned his right hand into something resembling a plate of raw meat on the Vanwall's agricultural gear-change as he drove home into a secure second place, scoring Vanwall's first points of the year.

Unfortunately, Tony then crashed his Aston Martin at Le Mans and was unfit to drive the Vanwall at Rouen and Reims . . . and so was I.

After Le Mans I had gone down to La Napoule near Cannes for a few days' holiday with my fiancée, Katie Molson. I had been water-skiing which I very much enjoyed. I was trying to monoski backwards, but as I turned, the plume of water ripping off the ski blasted straight up my nose. It was very painful, and when we arrived at Rouen next day for the French GP, I went straight to hospital instead, with a terrible sinus infection.

Roy Salvadori and Stuart Lewis-Evans took our places at Rouen and Reims, and Stuart performed so brilliantly he secured a permanent number three position in our team.

I was discharged from the London Clinic just a couple of days before travelling to Aintree for the British GP. Tony was still battered and sore, and in Thursday practice I tried all three cars but Fangio and Behra's Maseratis were faster. Next day both Tony and I qualified on the front row, with Stuart just a second slower.

I managed to lead at the end of the opening lap in 'VW1', and settled down to draw away. Stuart and Tony ran 5-6 by the twenty-lap mark, at which time I had 9 secs lead from Behra. But a lap later my engine fluffed and misfired. I stopped to have an earth wire ripped out and rejoined seventh, but the car was still sick so I stopped again. We had arranged for Tony to hand over his car — 'VW4' — to me if necessary, because he was not fit enough to drive the whole ninety laps. He came straight in and was helped from the cockpit so I could take over. The stop cost 13 secs. Tony took over my original car and soon retired it with magneto trouble, while I had resumed ninth.

By lap thirty, I was seventh. Behra led by over a minute. Four laps later I passed Fangio, and Stuart meanwhile passed Collins into third place. I closed on Musso and passed him on lap forty for fifth place, six laps later taking Collins for fourth. David Yorke signalled me '– 55 secs' from Behra. On lap 51 Jean lowered the lap record to 2:00.4, but two laps later I managed 1:59.2 — the first 90 mph lap at Aintree. With 22 laps to go I was 28 secs behind.

On lap 69 I caught and passed Stuart for third, and at that moment Behra's clutch disintegrated and Mike Hawthorn, in second place, ran over some of the pieces and punctured a tyre. This was a fantastic stroke of luck for our team, and it left myself and Stuart running 1-2 in the British Grand Prix in our green Vanwalls, with twenty laps to go.

That was a marvellous moment; one I had dreamed about for years. But it did not last. Two laps later Stuart stopped with his throttle linkage adrift, and now I was leading Musso's Ferrari by over a minute, but feeling terribly alone.

With ten laps to go I stopped for some fuel as a precaution and rejoined with 41 secs still in hand over Musso. I took no chances at all in those final laps, and eventually took the flag to win at a record 86.8 mph — Tony and I thus becoming jointly the first British drivers to win a *Grande Epreuve* in a British car since Segrave for Sunbeam at Tours in 1923 . . . and also the first all-British winners of a British Grand Prix.

Stuart finished seventh but was disqualified for leaving his car's bonnet out on the course after reconnecting his throttles, which we thought was rather harsh.

Tony Vandervell was delighted and we were absolutely thrilled. It meant an awful lot to me, particularly after having missed two races through my own fault by larking about on a water-ski. That evening I made a brief TV broadcast, then drove off with Ken Gregory and his fiancée to dinner in Chester and bed at 1 am in the Kenilworth Motel, ending one of the most satisfying days of my entire career.

But yet again, a high note was followed by a flop.

The Vanwalls' taut suspension was totally unsuitable for the Nurburgring, where they took a fearful hammering, Stuart crashed, I finished a distant fifth and Tony was ninth, having been sick in the cockpit. We were both stiff, sore and worn out but my engine never missed a beat and on the last lap along the hump-back straight in a battle with Behra which I won by one second I saw 7,600 rpm in top.

These basically stable understeering cars had to be driven between very precise limits and were never as forgiving, indeed delightful, in their handling characteristics as the essentially oversteering Maserati 250Fs. Sometimes one could lift an inside front wheel and I rarely found another car so sensitive to damper settings and fine tyre differences, but the change from transverse leaf spring to coil spring rear suspension had undoubtedly been a great leap forwards.

Those Goodyear disc brakes were as good as any I had tried to that time, while the problematic flat-spots in the engine power curve would diminish as development progressed. We would be better prepared for Nurburgring the following year, but what never improved was the agricultural nature of that hefty gearchange.

Since the Belgian and Dutch GPs' cancellation, the Italians were allowed to

20 July 1957 — British GP, Aintree — Moss in Brooks's original Vanwall takes the chequered flag. John Morgan of the BARC (left) looks on as SM and that superb driver Tony Brooks share the spoils . . .

18 August 1957 — Pescara GP, Italy — Beating 'Those bloody red cars' had been Tony Vandervell's great ambition. His Vanwall team had just done that at Aintree; here at Pescara Stirling rubbed it in on their home soil.

add the Pescara GP to the Championship. Ferrari sent only a single car for Musso because of the hoo-ha following de Portago's Mille Miglia crash, but Maserati fielded four works 250Fs.

In practice there my Vanwall — 'VW5's' — high back-axle ratio and 17-inch rear tyres gave only 6,900 rpm instead of the normal 7,200-plus. I started from the front row alongside Musso and Fangio.

There were still mechanics on the grid when the flag dropped and Musso made the best start but I was on his tail with Fangio some way behind. Tony had the wretched luck to have his engine fail on the opening lap. Meanwhile, I found a way past Musso on lap two and then held the lead relatively easily to the end. Apart from fluctuating oil pressure, which made me stop to add oil, the Vanwall never missed a beat. Fangio could not make contact and I beat him by over three minutes. Stuart was fifth after tyre problems, but now we had proved that the Vanwall could win on a classical road circuit, and we had at last beaten what Tony Vandervell called 'Those bloody red cars' on their own soil. Another deeply satisfying moment.

The Italian GP itself followed at Monza, where practice went sensationally well for us, with Stuart on pole from myself and Tony so our three British-green Vanwalls lined-up 1-2-3, with Fangio adding just a dash of Italian red on the outside of the front row. Our cars completely outclassed the Ferraris, and the race became a straight fight — Vanwall versus Maserati.

As far as I was concerned, the terrific early slipstreaming battle between ourselves and the Maseratis seemed to be resolved on lap thirteen.

My gearbox began to hang-up between gears and I lost ground, but after four laps of worry it somehow cleared. Tony's throttle had begun to stick and he made a pit stop. I led again from Stuart, until his steering tightened and he stopped to investigate, so I was left with five seconds' lead over Fangio and Behra, but again worried about Vanwall reliability.

There was no need. By lap forty I was nearly 18 secs clear of Fangio, and when he changed tyres I moved nearly a full lap ahead. I began to relax, able now to ease off and conserve my car.

With ten laps to go, as at Aintree and Pescara, I made a precautionary pit stop

— this time to add some oil and fit fresh rear tyres — and then there was the chequered flag. I had just won Vanwall's third Grand Prix of the season, and at the heart of Italian motor racing. Fangio finished second, Tony seventh. Fangio and I between us had won every World Championship round, and I was thus second to him in the Drivers' table for the third successive year.

If only I had not tried to water-ski backwards at La Napoule I could have run in the French Grand Prix, and who knows what might have been the outcome then?

I demonstrated 'VW5' briefly at the September Goodwood meeting, but its engine blew out a spark plug after only five laps, not having been touched since Monza, which rather left me with egg on my face since the demo had been more my idea than Vanwall's!

Only the non-Championship Moroccan GP remained, at Casablanca, but I developed Asian 'flu during practice and flew home before the race.

For 1958, Formula 1 regulations were changed, banning alcohol fuels and substituting maximum-130-octane AvGas petroleum instead. In addition minimum GP distance was slashed from 500 km to 300. Vanwall were anxious to re-tune and redevelop their engines before the season began seriously in Europe, so when an Argentine GP was hastily organized as a season-opener The Old Man refused to enter, but gave me permission to handle Rob Walker's little Cooper-Climax there instead. We won! — see page 186.

Vandervell was only interested in Championship races, so I drove Rob's Cooper in minor events before Vanwall reappeared at Monaco. I had tested one of our new AvGas-burning cars at Silverstone, lapping in 1:39.2 against the lap record of 1:43, and now on Dunlop tyres I ran eight consecutive 1:40 laps. The AvGas-tuned engines produced around 262 bhp at 7,500 rpm, about 30 bhp down on 1957, but the flat spot had diminished.

However, Monaco practice was bitterly disappointing. My engine popped and banged and the car's front end pattered wildly. I tried Tony's, which was better, and since as number one I had choice of equipment I asked for my engine to be fitted in his car. David Yorke told me to wait 'til next day when my own car should be running better. It was not, so I asked again but David and Mr Vandervell refused. I was not feeling well in any case, which didn't help, but in the final session I managed 1:42.3 on a track smeared with spilled oil which left me on row three, beside Stuart. Tony was up there at the front.

I managed a fair start in third place but was soon demoted to fourth by Mike Hawthorn's Ferrari. We caught and passed Tony's Vanwall which had lost a spark plug, but Stuart went out when his header tank burst, leaving me as Vanwall's last hope. Mike inherited the lead with me second until lap 32 when I eased by to lead for nearly seven laps, but on the 38th what had been a growing smell of oil announced real trouble as my engine's valve gear failed.

No Vanwall finishers — a bad start to our season.

Just eight days later, at Zandvoort for the Dutch GP, fortunes changed. My 'VW10' was still quite tricky on the high-speed swerves but Stuart finally took pole at 1:37.1, with me on 1:38 and Tony completing an all-Vanwall front row at 1:38.1.

For the race I ran wire wheels on the front, the latest cast-alloy type at the rear. The wires gave better front end 'feel', and promised to cool the brakes more adequately.

I made a terrific start from Stuart while Harry Schell's BRM charged through to third place from row three. Tony lay fourth but his car was handling poorly after being nudged at the start. Mine felt fine, apart from weaving on the straight in the strong wind. After twenty laps I had 15 secs lead over Schell, and at 39 laps I was signalled ' +29 secs'. My only problem now, apart from the weaving, was oil pressure sagging on right-hand corners to only 20 lb. Tony had retired, and Stuart lost third place on lap 46 with valve trouble. I was again Vanwall's sole survivor, but drew away from the BRM despite limiting the revs to 7,200

17 May 1958 — Stirling practising for the Monaco Grand Prix aims his short-nosed, alloy-wheeled Vanwall for the apex at the Tabac. After a hectic practice period, he led briefly next day before retiring.

and won our first GP of the season quite comfortably.

Since I had won in Argentina and Maurice Trintignant had won at Monaco, both in Rob's Coopers, this was the third consecutive British win against the previously unbeatable Italian cars. The British green — and Rob's Scots blue — really had arrived at last.

For the Belgian GP at Spa-Francorchamps I experimented with tyres and finally decided on 16-inch wheels, which made the car feel more stable, instead of the normal high-speed circuit 17s. I was easing back at 7,300-7,400 rpm along the straights, and seeing 7,000 rpm uphill as well as holding it in fifth round most of the Stavelot curve, eventually scrubbing down to 5,700 rpm at the exit there.

Race day was really hot and the starter kept us waiting far too long with our engines overheating. I got away first and hurtled through Stavelot with a 200-yard lead. I wound my engine up to 7,200 rpm in fourth, and then grabbed the change to fifth. I thought it had engaged, so lifted the clutch and floored the throttle, but the 'box was actually still in neutral, the revs shrieked sky-high and my engine disintegrated.

I was appalled by what I had done. It was entirely my own fault and I watched the rest of the race. Fortunately Tony won, but Mike Hawthorn was second and took another extra Championship point for fastest lap.

At Reims my Vanwall dropped a valve in practice. The mechanics repaired it but had to fit a higher-than-optimum back-axle ratio to restrict the revs for the race. Tony's engine was our only good one.

I started from row three and ran fourth on the opening lap but found my engine misfiring between 6,400 and 6,800 rpm. I began changing up early to miss this flat spot, and then my left-front brake began locking. I could also see in my mirrors that I was trailing smoke. I could smell the oil haze, and then the first-gear lock-out guard on my gearchange slipped and partially baulked second and third. Mike Hawthorn ran away to win with ease. When poor Musso crashed — fatally as it transpired — I inherited third place, dicing with Behra's

BRM and Fangio's *Piccolo* Maserati in what was to be Juan's farewell race. Tony retired with gearbox trouble, but rejoined in Stuart's car. Fangio dropped back leaving the second-place battle to Behra and me, but Jean's engine failed which left me in a safe, but to me very unsatisfactory, second place behind Mike's Ferrari. This was to be his only Grand Prix win of the season, but again he took that important extra point for fastest lap.

I took pole position — at last! — at Silverstone, but Pete Collins simply rocketed past me on acceleration out of the first corner and steamed away into the middle-distance in his Ferrari . . . and there was nothing I could do about it. After ten laps I was minus 7 secs from Pete, but by twenty laps had recovered two of them. Then at 25 laps my engine threw a rod as I came through Woodcote Corner towards the finish line and I coasted down round the far end of the pits, straight into the paddock to retire.

At that moment I felt my World Championship chances were finally gone. The Ferraris won easily, Pete and Mike 1-2, and Mike again setting fastest lap.

After our débâcle at Nürburgring the previous season, Vanwall was much better prepared for this year's German GP. Mike took pole position, but Tony and I joined him on the front row, with Pete's second Ferrari on the outside. I led away in my regular car 'VW10', broke the lap record at 9:16 on the second lap and led the Ferraris with Tony fourth. Third time round I lowered the record again to 9:09.2 and my lead was a healthy eighteen seconds. My Vanwall was still full of fuel but was going like a rocket and I felt sure I could crack the nine-minute barrier as it lightened.

I was using only 7,000-7,100 rpm, I felt good and the car was simply splendid, handling beautifully. Then it seemed as if somebody had switched off the ignition. It was as sudden as that. The engine just cut, dead.

A tiny screw inside the magneto had vibrated loose and fallen into the works, shorting it out. This was one of the most agonizing retirements of my entire career.

David signalled Tony forward to get amongst the Ferraris. He did so and won after poor Pete Collins crashed fatally, and Mike retired.

We were all very sad about Pete's death, but in motor racing life always has to go on. The inaugural Formula 1 Portuguese GP was run in Oporto, and there I eventually set fastest time in my car using wide-spaced gear ratios, running up to between 7,300 and 7,400 rpm, water registering 70 degs C and oil 90 degs, with a constant 45-50 lb pressure. I had a cold next day but retained pole from Mike Hawthorn — who was embittered and grieving over Pete's death but still very hard to beat — and Stuart, with Tony's Vanwall on the second row.

The circuit was damp as the race began. I made quite a good start, but Mike caught me on the straight next time round and at five laps led by a second. I repassed him on lap eight and by twenty laps held a 38-second lead. By half-distance, 25 laps, I was a minute ahead and had set fastest lap. Mike stopped for attention to his car's drum brakes, so Behra inherited second place for BRM. I eased back and gave Stuart a tow. Tony spun and stalled, out of the race. On lap 42, with just eight remaining, Mike suddenly repassed Behra's ailing BRM and during this fight back bettered my fastest lap. David Yorke signalled me 'HAW-REC' which unfortunately I misread as 'HAW-REG' meaning 'Hawthorn — Regular', and since I knew he had made a pit stop it never occurred to me his car could have been going so fast. This misunderstanding ultimately cost me the Drivers' Championship.

I lapped Mike just before the end, but the sight of his face as I did so softened my hard old heart so I backed off and let him unlap himself. As we came up to the chequered flag he crossed the timing line to start his last lap just before I crossed it to win. To qualify for his second place he still had to complete that final lap, but he promptly spun his car and stalled. I came upon his stalled car on my slowing-down lap and saw him struggling to push-start it in the direction of the race, uphill. I slowed beside him and bawled 'Push it downhill; you'll never start the bloody thing that way!'. Which he did, ensuring his second place, with Stuart third.

Under the regulations one could be disqualified for proceeding against the race direction, and Mike was hauled before the stewards for having done just that to restart downhill. But I appeared on his behalf. I testified that he had not proceeded against the race direction because he was on the pavement at the time, not on the race circuit. Consequently his second place was confirmed, along with his extra point for fastest lap. Having misread that signal really irritated me! I am sure I could have taken that record back if only I had realized.

For the Italian GP at Monza Ferrari then fitted disc brakes to Mike's Ferrari while we experimented unsuccessfully with a streamlined perspex bubble canopy. It gave only an extra 50 rpm, but I could not live with the possibility of it popping off and doing some damage, despite the cockpit being neither too hot nor too fumey beneath it.

I was entering the *Curva Grande* at 7,200 rpm in fifth, and exiting at 6,700 rpm, having scrubbed off speed through the Vanwall's inherent understeer all the way through, but my practice ended when I missed fifth — again — right in front of the pits, and bent a valve.

On the Saturday I tried a lower final-drive ratio, and was quickest using 7,000 rpm in fourth through the *Curva Grande,* and our three Vanwalls occupied the front row again, but instead of Fangio's Maserati it was now Mike's Ferrari which provided the Italian interest . . . How times had changed.

The opening laps saw another enormous slipstreaming battle which raged until lap thirteen when Tony stopped to investigate an oil leak, restarting ninth. Unfortunately my gearbox began to tighten, then broke with a crunch and I coasted into the pits to retire. Despite his early delay, Tony — incredibly — came right back to win, while Mike's Ferrari was crippled by the loss of its clutch and he limped home second thanks to his new team-mate Phil Hill backing off to preserve his number one's Championship lead.

I still had an outside chance of the title. I had to win the final GP at Casablanca and set fastest lap, with Mike finishing lower than second.

It was a nerve-wracking five weeks before the Moroccan trip, and I must confess the tension got to me. I really coveted that Championship title. After Fangio's retirement I felt I was his natural heir. Only his presence had kept it from me for the previous three seasons. Does this sound like arrogance? I don't believe it was — I was still a young man, a very competitive young man, and it was a natural, almost instinctive attitude which developed within my mind.

Mike sat his Ferrari on pole position after my engine blew in practice, with my Vanwall — 'VW5' this time — and then Stuart's alongside him.

I made the best start, with Stuart in my wheel-tracks and Phil Hill leading Mike, driving very hard, wheel-to-wheel with me past the pits. On lap three I brake-tested him, leaving my braking point very late just to emphasize my discs' advantage over his Ferrari drums. He shot up the escape road, while I consolidated my lead. After ten laps I was 9 secs ahead, with Phil back into second place and Tony third ahead of Mike. But at thirty laps Tony's Vanwall broke and Mike was third with his team-mate second and sure to give that position to my great rival near the finish, should they survive that long.

All that Mike had to do was to adjust his pace to match mine to preserve that certain second place. I was leading, I had set fastest lap, I had done everything possible, but while I might win the Grand Prix I was going to *lose* the World Championship, and I knew it. My Vanwall felt as if it was going to survive the distance — but even so only luck could now rob Mike of the title and give it to me.

Twelve laps from the end I saw a car burning furiously beside the track. It was poor Stuart's Vanwall. Its engine had broken, sending him spinning off the road. He had been fatally burned.

The last lap came round, I won and 38 secs later Mike Hawthorn passed by in the Ferrari to become the first British World Champion Driver. He deserved

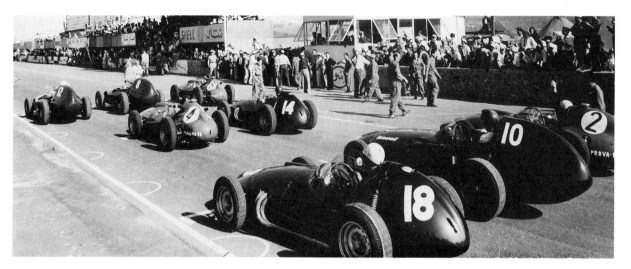

19 October 1958 — Moroccan GP, Ain-Diab circuit, Casablanca — Start line-up for 'The Showdown' Championship decider between Moss and Hawthorn. Mike's Ferrari Dino ('6') is on pole, the Vanwalls of Moss and the ill-fated Stuart Lewis-Evans alongside him. Jean Behra's BRM ('14') and Phil Hill's Ferrari are on row two, Gendebien (hand up in Ferrari '2'), Tony Brooks and Jo Bonnier (BRM) on row three.

19 October 1958 — Despite having just won the Moroccan GP and set fastest lap, bitter disappointment is etched into Stirling's face as Mike Hawthorn has just beaten him regardless to that coveted Driver's World Championship title . . . and team-mate Stuart Lewis-Evans has been severely burned.

it. My congratulations were genuine, but I could not hide my deep depression because of poor Stuart's crash as well as my own disappointment. It really did hurt and I cursed the luck which had confined me to runner-up for the fourth consecutive season. But within days the knot in my stomach relaxed, and I realized it didn't really matter . . . not *that* much. I became far more philosophical and, perhaps, more mature.

Although Mike had won the Drivers' title in his Ferrari, Vanwall won the new Formula 1 Constructors' Championship by a giant margin. Tough, uncompromising old Tony Vandervell had realized his dearest ambition. He had always been very decent to me — as to all his drivers — but the strain of running his racing team had taken too much out of him. He was not in the best of health, and poor Stuart's death in that last race had been a terrible blow.

On 12 January 1959 he announced Vanwall's withdrawal from serious Formula 1 competition. Casablanca, 1958, had seen my last drive in one of those spectacular green cars. From now on, with one minor exception, all my Grand Prix cars would have the engine in the back . . . and they would all be British.

Maserati 150S *(1956)*

'Overbodied and gutless, but in many ways typical of the front-engined Maserati sports car series, nice-handling and predictable . . .'

I n 1956 I raced the little 1½-litre 4-cylinder Maserati only twice and the first time it didn't even survive the opening lap. All the production Maserati sports-racing cars of this period used more or less similar chassis and bodies, which meant that, while the 300S 3-litre 6-cylinder version was a lovely car, the 200S 4-cylinder was rather under-powered, and its 150S little sister really was struggling. However, against the right opposition in a Continental 1,500 cc class, one could still make it perform by trying hard enough . . .

M y first race with the 150S was the Supercortemaggiore at Monza, where Ugolini teamed Piero Taruffi and me. But on the opening lap its prop shaft broke and thrashed around in the cockpit, smashing its way through the reserve fuel tank which was over on the passenger's side. I exited smartly, and they subsequently put me into a works 200S in which Perdisa and I finished second, not a bad end to a day which began so badly.

Maserati then entered a pair of 150Ss in the sports car race supporting the German GP at Nürburgring in August, largely to give Porsche a fight on their home soil!

Jean Behra and I drove, and in practice I put mine on pole position. But then Maserati under-geared the cars for race day, so we were pulling 7,900 rpm along the switchback straight, with less powerful centre-seat Cooper-Climaxes pulling away from us. There was no way I could hold on to Hans Herrmann's works Porsche in such circumstances and he won quite easily with me second again. Jean was thoroughly cheesed off by the whole affair and finished sixth.

Essentially the little 150S engine gave around 145 horsepower, and the car was good for the best part of 140 mph . . . when it was geared properly.

24 June 1956 — Supercortemaggiore GP, Monza — Stirling hammering on after his early delay and the enforced car-change from Maserati 150S to this 200S, seen here at high speed in the difficult Ascari Curve on Monza's backstretch.

Maserati 200S *(1956)*

'The 2-litre Maserati was as quick on a twisty circuit as the 3-litre and really could handle very nicely . . .'

I raced this larger of the two 4-cylinder-engined sports Maseratis only twice — the first time due to *force majeur* in the 1956 Supercortemaggiore race at Monza. There, Maserati's team manager Nello Ugolini had teamed Piero Taruffi and me in a little 150S — see page 168 — but its prop shaft broke and thrashed around in the cockpit on the opening lap! Ugolini subsequently put me into Cesare Perdisa's works 200S in place of his listed co-driver Bellucci and we came home second.

My other race in a 200S came early in 1957 in the Cuban GP at Havana. I had been scheduled to share one of the works team's big 450S V8s with Fangio, but they had been held up by a dock strike in New York. Maserati managed to borrow a privately owned 200S for me, Harry Schell had a Brazilian-owned 300S and Fangio had the solitary works 300S which had been delivered safely. We were still, however, meant to be 'The Maserati Team'.

This was the Cubans' first big race and they ran it on a three-mile circuit arranged mainly on Havana's Malecon highway. It was very slippery and bumpy and, of course, Fangio was fastest in practice, but my 2-litre was 15 secs faster than anything else in its class. We went to a boxing match that evening, in which the local favourite was beaten and the proceedings ended in a full-scale riot, including gunfire!

My race lasted only five laps before the 200S's engine seized. 'Fon' de Portago led Fangio convincingly in his Ferrari, and around the fifty-lap mark I took over Harry Schell's 300S in an attempt to deprive Carroll Shelby of third place. The 300S lapped in 2:02.4 against the 200S's 2:05 before its engine dropped a valve. De Portago had his throttle break and lost two laps, leaving Fangio to a rather lucky win.

Was Moss a car-breaker, or was this fairly typical of privately-owned Maseratis? I'm inclined towards the latter belief . . .

Lotus Eleven Series I *(1956)*

'The Costin-styled Lotus Elevens were gorgeous-looking little sports cars and the bubble-canopied Monza record car was the most beautiful of them all. Pity it simply fell to bits, but that was typical Lotus at that time . . .'

I first experienced the work of Colin Chapman on chassis design and Frank Costin on aerodynamic body shapes when I won the 1956 May Silverstone race in their new teardrop Vanwall. That had been a freelance job for them, but essentially they were the brains behind the Lotus sports cars. Colin asked me to drive a record-breaking Lotus Eleven for him at Monza later that year, and I accepted. I thought it would be interesting. It was . . .

T he objective was to attack International Class G 1,100 cc records. We had planned originally to run in October, but the track would not be available so we had to bring our date forward, ending up at only eight days' notice on 3 September 1956, the day after I won my first Italian GP in the Maserati.

Monza's banked high-speed track was very rough and bumpy, and the lightweight Lotus Eleven would inevitably take a battering. It had a bubble canopy, a special highly polished paint finish, and all its body panels were carefully matched and the undertray joints masked over. The bubble was fixed, so I had to worm my way underneath through the little hinge-down door. Oversize rear tyres were fitted and on the bumpy bankings they hammered on the tail section until it finally blew off, a rear frame member snapped and the tail-mounted battery dropped down to hammer along the track behind, all at 130 mph-plus. So the attempt was called off, but not before we had taken the 50 km record at 135.54 mph and 50 miles at 132.77.

Frank Costin's canopy design was most impressive, as air entered through a slit below the front of the screen and exited through slots in the perspex above my head. It worked brilliantly well, because although I had plenty of fresh, cool air I was never troubled by draughts blustering round me. In the next few years I would experience a lot more of Frank Costin's work.

3? September 1956 — The Lotus 11 streamliner record attempt at Monza came the day after Stirling had won the Italian GP there in the 'offset' Maserati. With Denis Jenkinson, Noele MacDonald Hobley, 'Dunlop Mac' and Colin Chapman in attendance, Stirling insinuates himself beneath the Frank Costin-designed 'bubble' canopy.
Above right *Out on the Speedbowl this pretty car's tail broke away, spoiling the attempt . . .*

Mercedes-Benz 300SL *(1956-57)*

'I tried twice to beat the GT Ferraris in the Tour de France with the Gullwing Merc, but it wasn't quite up to it — it was a fast and exciting road car but one which demanded respect . . . and in the wet it could bite you — hard.'

17/23 September 1956 — Tour de France — Stirling and Georges Houel on their way to a hard-fought second place in the 'Gullwing' Mercedes 300SL, seen here at Nouveau Monde hairpin during the Rouen circuit race — one of the Tour's numerous épreuves.

The *Tour de France Automobile* was a very special event in which pure racing driver skills were very important. While the road sections took us all round France like a rally, the competitive element actually involved several circuit races and speed hill-climbs. The prize money was exceptionally, irresistibly, good and I arranged to compete in a specially prepared 300SL Gullwing, the first time in 1956 partnered by the experienced French rallyman Georges Houel, and then in 1957 by Peter Garnier, Sports Editor of *The Autocar*.

The 3-litre 6-cylinder Gullwing Mercedes had a terrific following at that time as it basked in the charisma of the 300SLRs' World Championship win of 1955.

The 1956 Tour followed the Italian GP in September, and started from Nice. Our main rival was 'Fon' de Portago with his friend Ed Nelson in a beautiful Ferrari 250GT Europa, and the Tour became quite an exciting battle between us, Oliver Gendebien's Ferrari and other Gullwings driven by Rene Cotton, Jacky Pollet and Willy Mairesse. We were dogged by a severe misfire due to an ignition fault and it was not cured until the final ten-lap test at Montlhéry where I finally set FTD. De Portago and Nelson won from Georges and me in second place. I felt confident we could win next time.

The 1957 Tour was again run in September and the prize fund that year totalled £23,000. After scrutineering at Nice before the start Peter and I drove out to La Turbie hill-climb for some private practice. But the local gendarmerie disapproved and fined me 2,700 Francs on the spot, which I thought was rather unsporting of them . . .

But this time the Ferrari GTs proved much too fast for our heavy and demanding Mercedes, though we ran seventh. Halfway through the event the Mercedes began losing a gallon of water every 100 km. After the St Etienne test we lay fourth and in the final 200 km night race at Reims I managed to secure that place overall. We finished despite that persistent water leak, a jamming starter, broken bumper and only second and top gears left in the gearbox. It could have been a different story if the old 300SLR had been eligible, and available, but it was too much to expect the production 300SL to match the latest Ferrari GTs.

Maserati 450S *(1957)*

'Really a case of brute force and ignorance, lacking any of the delicacy essential in most road races . . .'

*T*his big 4½-litre V8-engined Maserati was a monster. In some respects, certainly in terms of sheer power and speed, it marked the high-tide of front-engined sports car development. Its performance, together with that of Ferrari's rival four-cam V12, really persuaded the rule-makers to ban them both by applying a blanket 3-litre limit to the Sports Car World Championship for 1958-59.

The 450S, therefore, survived only one full season, but on the right day, on the right circuit, it could simply steamroller all opposition. Sadly, that day seldom dawned and there were very few circuits which suited it.

The one day it truly looked sure-fire favourite was 12 May 1957 when Jenks and I seemed poised to win the Mille Miglia for the second time. But the traditional Maserati luck turned things round and bit us well and truly in the backside . . .

*M*aserati under the Orsi regime began toying with a large-capacity V8 to combat Ferrari in 1954. Then the American millionaire Tony Parravano asked them for a 4.2-litre racing engine for Indianapolis. With him paying the bills, Giulio Alfieri and his engineers dusted-off the V8 drawings and built it for him. By the middle of 1956 the prototype engine had been wound up to 400 horsepower, which was very exciting, and a 4.5-litre version was then planned for the works team.

Maserati's chassis specialist Valerio Colotti designed a beefed-up 300S-type sports chassis and suspension to accept this power and torque.

Because engine development lagged behind his new chassis, they took the first frame and fitted it instead with a 3500GT-derived six-cylinder engine to form the 350S which we came to know and loathe in the Mille Miglia.

After our accident, the six-cylinder engine was taken out and replaced by the prototype 450S V8. It was tested briefly at Monza, and then in August we took it to Kristianstad in Sweden for the next Championship race. Predictably, it was even quicker than the 350S in a straight line but it was almost as uncontrollable and its brakes were totally inadequate. We couldn't approach 300S times with it around the *Rabelovsbana* road circuit, so Maserati scrapped that chassis and went back to the drawing board.

I shared my first brand-new 450S with Fangio in the 1957 Buenos Aires 1,000 km season-opener. It would reach 181 mph on Mille Miglia gearing and accelerated from 0-100 mph in about 11 seconds. It was quite an experience, and I could simply streak away at the start to build a minute's lead from Masten Gregory's Ferrari after the first ten laps. By thirty laps my lead was more than doubled. Even so I was handling the car with great discretion because it really was a handful. There's little doubt I *could* have gone quicker still if I'd been pressed, but I was happy not to be . . .

I handed over to Fangio on lap 33, and fifteen laps into his stint he'd lapped the entire field but for Castellotti in Masten's car. Then the inevitable happened. The Maserati's clutch linkage broke, Juan had to change gear without it and eventually this broke the gearbox.

The 4.5 had given notice of its strength but we had also realized its weaknesses — and the 300S was still a better car.

The 4.5 then behaved itself at Sebring — which suited it — where Fangio and Behra won while Harry Schell and I finished second in a 300S. Then came the Mille Miglia.

Jean Behra crashed his 4.5 on the road during pre-race testing and hurt himself, but Jenks and I went to the start in this great rumbling beast as clear favourites. Maserati had spent time to prepare it far better than our ill-fated 350S the previous

The office of the big Maserati quattro e mezzo 450S V8 as prepared for Moss/Jenkinson in the 1957 Mille Miglia. The pull-handle protruding through the centre 'console' to the left of the gear-lever is the selector for the additional two-speed gearbox. Designer Colotti intended it only to be used with the car at rest in the Pescara and Bologna controls, but Stirling found it would change perfectly on the move and planned to exploit it throughout the 1,000 miles. In fact the car survived only seven of them . . .

year. We had tested it on parts of the course, and on the Raticosa timed its acceleration from 20-150 kmh — which is from 12 to 93 mph — at just six seconds . . .

Its brakes were not good, but on race morning Jenks and I felt really quite confident. The car had an extra two-speed gearbox just behind the clutch, the 405's standard gearbox of course being mounted at the rear. The idea was that using this device we could run with an extra-high set of ratios to Pescara, then I could select 'low' for the mountain section to Bologna, and then 'high' again back to Brescia, changing normally on the main gearbox all the time. But I had discovered that this intermediate two-speed box would change beautifully on the move, so we intended to swop around as necessary all the way. The car was clearly the most powerful and fastest car in the entire entry. I drove it gently down the starting ramp, and we were hardly out of Brescia itself before we were up into high-ratio fifth and the rev counter needle was hovering on 6,700 rpm, which was near as dammit 180 mph, and we couldn't help grinning at each other. It was a fantastic experience . . .

I notched it down into normal fifth as we entered a series of fast swerves, and then about three and a half minutes into the race, as we approached a tighter left-hander at something like 145 mph, I hit the brakes to take off more speed.

Everything seemed fine; early in the race, not trying anything really heroic. The car began to slow.

Then my foot suddenly banged down to the floorboards and the car seemed to leap forward as the brakes were released.

The brake pedal had just snapped off.

My brain momentarily just couldn't take it in.

Had my foot slipped off the pedal?

I searched frantically for the pedal with my foot.

It just wasn't there.

Jenks sensed this was no longer normal cornering and curled-up in his seat. I was trying simultaneously to see where the car was going and look down at the pedals, and I changed down through the gearbox as quick as I could — all this far quicker than it takes to read these words.

I managed to scratch round at about 120 mph and then Jenks was wagging his finger at me, indicating it was a bit early to start dicing. I just pointed numbly down at the floor; he glanced down, and his jaw dropped . . .

We coasted almost to a halt, then jumped out and brought the car finally to rest by hand. There was no way we could repair it. The pedal had sheared off just above the pivot and there wasn't even a usable stump left. So our Mille Miglia was over before it had really begun.

We could only wait until the last starters had gone by, then limp back to the Maserati garage in Brescia. Our people were just packing up and ready to go when they heard the V8 grumbling back up the road towards them at walking pace. They had lavished so much effort and love on that car, the sure favourite which would at last win the Mille Miglia for Maserati, that they were struck dumb. Some just burst into tears. Our anger evaporated. We couldn't take it out on them . . . just one look at their grey faces was enough. They felt as sick as we did.

So that was the premature end of my last Mille Miglia, because 'Fon' de Portago crashed his Ferrari into a group of spectators near the finish, and that great Italian race would never be run again.

The following weekend saw me crash my Vanwall at Monaco when its brakes failed, and seven days after that I was at Nürburgring to drive the 4.5 again with Fangio in the ADAC 1,000 kms. I took the start but the engine wouldn't fire, losing me about a minute. Tony Brooks was leading in his Aston Martin, but I managed to get by him after eight laps and drew out about thirty seconds before a hub-shaft broke near the *Schwalbenschwanz*, my 4.5's left-rear wheel fell off and went bounding by . . .

I hitched a ride back to the pits where Fangio took over the other 4.5 from Harry Schell. But its oil tank broke loose. It was lashed up for me to take over but after only two more laps we had finally to retire.

Maserati produced a 4.5 Coupé for Le Mans — see page 177 — and then for Kristianstad we had one last chance — it seemed — to take the Sports Car Championship from Ferrari. Maserati had to win with Ferrari placing no higher than fifth, but that hardly seemed likely.

It was a six-hour race. Jean Behra and I took the start in our two 4.5s, and were able to run first and second until I came in and handed over to Harry Schell. I then took over Jean's car when he stopped, and rejoined without losing his lead. Light rain began to fall and Ferrari encountered brake trouble. I handed back to Jean for the final two hours, and took over our best-placed 300S but it immediately developed gearbox trouble. We plugged on, profiting from

26 May 1957 — Nürburgring 1,000Kms — an alert bystander snapped the 450S's left-rear wheel bounding away after Stirling had its hub-shaft snap near Schwalbenschwanz. During that season, what with errant wheels, brake pedals which snapped off and throttles jammed-open by spanners left lying in the works, Moss did wonder occasionally if somebody was perhaps trying to spoil his day . . .

11 August 1957 — Swedish GP, Kristianstad — imagine the ground vibrating to the rumble of these two mighty V8s as Stirling leads Jean Behra in the sister 450S around the Rabelovsbana. Stirling shared both the first and third-placed cars on this occasion.

retirements, and eventually I shared both first place in the 4.5 with Jean and third in the 300S with Harry, Jo Bonnier and Scarlatti. But Ferraris placed second and fourth, so the Championship seemed to be theirs.

However, this disappointment was short-lived, because the previously cancelled Venezuelan Grand Prix at Caracas was then reinstated, which gave us another chance to take the title.

Everybody in the Modena works got stuck into the job and they sent 4.5s for Jean and myself with a third for the private Temple Buell team to be driven by Masten Gregory and Dale Duncan, plus a 300S. In Caracas it seemed as if my recent Formula 1 victories for Vanwall had made me unpopular at Maserati, because Orsi gave Jean first choice of the two 4.5s and I had to drive 'No 4', the worst-handling one.

I made one of my worst-ever starts, losing a minute which it took me an hour to recover, while Masten rolled his 4.5 in the opening stages. Already one 4.5 down, two to go. I began to progress and after two and a quarter hours I led by nearly two minutes. The circuit included a section of dual-carriageway, and I was hammering along there at around 170 mph when I came up behind a American amateur, Max Dressel, in an AC Ace-Bristol. I aimed to pass him on the outside into the braking area for the next corner and he was well over to the right side so I made my move. Then to my horror he pulled across right into my path, taking his own line for the approaching corner, obviously without a clue that I was there.

I could do nothing to avoid a collision and hit him a tremendous wallop, somersaulting him into a lamp-post which broke his AC completely in two. My 4.5 went on up the road spinning like a top before coming to rest, wrecked but right side up. My only injury was a black third toe. I returned to the pits, where as Harry brought in Behra's car for refuelling it burst into flames! Jean's hands were burned, so I took over but soon discovered its seat cushion was still smouldering as it burned clean through the seat of my overalls and my underpants, and then started on me!

I handed over to Harry Schell, while my flesh wound was attended to, and then out on the circuit — just to make Maserati's day complete — Jo Bonnier's 300S lost a wheel at precisely the moment Harry came tearing by in the 4.5. The two works Maseratis collided and our hopes for the Championship ended in another almighty bonfire.

Fortunately neither driver was badly hurt, but it had been an almost unbelievable catalogue of accidents, and it was the end of Maserati as a serious factory team, which was tragic.

I have to say, however, that I wasn't particularly sorry to say goodbye to the big, brutal 4.5 . . .

Maserati 450S Berlinetta (1957)

'But for the BRM V16, this could be the most horrible car I ever raced . . .'

In 1957 I suggested that Maserati should build an aerodynamic-bodied Coupé version of the 450S V8, primarily for Le Mans. I recommended Frank Costin to design it since he had done such good work on those beautiful Lotus Elevens and on my Vanwall which was beginning to worry Maserati in Formula 1. I think there was very little wrong with the design Frank produced for Maserati, but it just was diabolically badly made in a typically Italian last-minute panic. It was cramped, visibility was dreadful, it was unbearably hot, stuffy and noisy, and we had to suffer all this on top of the normal 4.5 problems found in the open cars. I disliked Le Mans in any case, so all things considered that was not one of my favourite weekends.

Maserati car bodies were normally made by roly-poly Medardo Fantuzzi and his panel-bashers in Modena, but they were flooded with work when the Coupé project came up so Maserati asked Zagato in Milan to bridge the gap. They were briefed primarily to finish the thing in two weeks flat, and only secondly to follow Costin's precise design. They met their target date, but cut so many corners to do so that when the car arrived at Le Mans I could not believe the number of vital features omitted or fouled-up. One omission, for example, was the full-length undertray which Frank had specified in his original design!

In practice at Le Mans it was slower than the normal open 4.5. The French press nicknamed it *Le Monstre*. Fangio opted for an open car so I was teamed with Harry Schell in this thing. We worked hard to cool its cockpit. We fitted windscreen wipers — it had been completed without any — but the airflow blew them clear of the screen. They would just make contact sufficient to smear the screen as we braked, and then lift clear again to quiver in the airstream as

22 June 1957 — Le Mans 24-Hours — Unloved and unlovely, the Maserati 450S Berlinetta had seemed like a good idea at the time . . . !

we built up speed, leaving us peering through the smeared screen. The lights were poor and the throttle jammed.

I was not happy.

The Coupé was difficult to start, a common problem with all 4.5s, so I made a slow start, but I won back some of the deficit along the Mulsanne Straight and lay third behind Peter Collins' Ferrari and Tony Brooks' Aston Martin as we came back past the pits. Peter's engine broke, amazingly, and Mike Hawthorn led for Ferrari with me second, but I was having to drive desperately hard just to keep in touch, and not enjoying life at all. Mike pulled out thirty seconds' lead in ten laps, and after an hour Jean passed me in the open 4.5. By this time that diabolical Coupé was vibrating badly and trailing smoke, its cockpit filling with heat and fumes. I handed over to Harry, but it only survived three more laps before an oil pipe let go. It was repaired and I rejoined, pessimistically, which was justified when a rear universal joint seized. The same fault had afflicted one of the open cars, and that was curtains.

In the final reckoning, the 4.5 Coupé was more Zagato than Costin, and the poor quality of Zagato's work against the clock, combined with the Maserati 4.5's usual shortcomings, was more than we could stand . . . I have no regrets about never having driven that car again.

MG EX.181 *(1957)*

'An almost unreal experience, a fascinating, daunting thing . . .'

*I*n 1957 John Thornley of MG invited me to attack International Class F — 1,101 to 1,500 cc — world records in their new EX.181 record-breaker. I was fascinated by this strange challenge. I had grown up reading about Goldie Gardner's record-breaking exploits for MG before and after the war. Now they were aiming to raise his mark of 203.9 mph, set on the Dessau record stretch in Germany in 1939. The new target was 240 mph and MG's brilliant chief engineer Sydney Enever built EX.181 with a mid-mounted engine and superbly streamlined teardrop body to achieve it. The attempt was made on Bonneville Salt Flats in Utah, USA, and it went quite well.

My top speed was only 70 mph more than I had been pulling in the Vanwall on the long seaside straight at Pescara, or for that matter in the 4.5 Maserati on the outskirts of Brescia before its brake pedal snapped off. But it felt two or three times quicker, I think because the whole environment was so unreal. Knowing that if anything went wrong the car would still take two or three miles to stop, and with so few visual cues outside with which to orientate myself, I felt very exposed, isolated and helpless; not fully in command of my own destiny, and for me that was a most unaccustomed feeling which I did not really enjoy.

*M*G ran two record cars at Bonneville late that August. While I was winning in the Vanwall at Pescara, my one-time benefactor Tommy Wisdom was co-driving their 1-litre push-rod EX.179 with David Ash to raise the Class G 12-hour record to 118.13 mph. The car averaged 49.8 mpg, and then — running supercharged — Phil Hill clocked 143.4 mph over the flying-start mile.

EX.181 used a twin-ohc Shorrock-supercharged 1½-litre engine based on the BMC B-Series. It ran 32 psi boost to produce 290 bhp at 7,300 rpm. The car's rear track was only 2 ft 6¼ in, the front 3 ft 6 in, and the wheelbase 8 ft. To enable it to be built so low it was on 15-inch wheels with special slick tread thin-carcass Dunlop record tyres, and everything was made and calculated to minimal tolerances. The driver lay on his back, with the steering wheel horizontal above his lap and the engine behind his shoulders. They had tailored the cockpit to me in the Abingdon factory, but before I could drive the car we had a problem with the Salt Flats course.

George Eyston, former World Land Speed Record-holder at Bonneville, was our adviser and he looked grave because unseasonal rain had soaked the Flats. We waited two days for the salt to dry, until on Friday 23 August it was just about 'on' come 4 pm.

They levelled the course with a chunk of rail on a vee-shaped tow drag, then stained a centreline on it. I wedged myself into EX.181's cockpit and the mechanics Dzus-fastened the canopy hatch above me.

I did not enjoy that feeling very much. There was no way I could get out unaided.

They had briefed me to set off very gently, easy on the throttle, then to build up to around 200 mph before I really stood on it in top gear, otherwise I could set the driven wheels spinning with their slick tyres.

I took it up through the gears to 6,900 rpm on that first exploratory run, fascinated by the mirages shimmering on that bright white salt. It was incredibly noisy with that methanol-burning engine bellowing away behind my head. On the second run I lost third gear, and when I finally changed direct from second to top I fouled the plugs and it stammered and spat before clearing.

There was only a single inboard disc brake acting on the rear wheels, and as it was applied a flap opened up in the tail for cooling. But it was all rather marginal, and I had to brake very delicately indeed or risk locking the wheels.

*23 August 1957 — Bonneville
Salt Flats, Utah, USA —
Stirling takes stock of a whole
new world of competition
motoring as he cleans his
shoes on a mat laid upon the
salt before entering the
horizontal-wheeled cockpit of
MG EX.181.*

I was also advised not to go down through the gearbox to slow the car. Once clear of the timed section I had to cut the ignition, select neutral and floor the throttle to prevent a blow-back. Phil Hill had warned me that, when you did this, methanol fumes entered the cockpit through its ventilation slots, so I should take a breath first and hold it as I switched off.

Straight line record attempts of that kind are timed as the average of two runs made within one hour in opposing directions over the same measured strip. In my inexperience, the first time I approached the turn-around depot at one end of the run I saw a guy standing there waving his arms above his head, showing me where to stop. I stroked the brake pedal, but despite the crew all leaping up and down waving their arms I was already far too late to stop and they could only drop their arms, whip their heads round and watch open-mouthed while I went sailing right on by. Distance is deceptive on featureless salt . . .

I made two more runs, regardless of the loss of third gear, and eventually entered the mile at 6,500 rpm and saw 7,000 by the 5 km post. The timekeepers confirmed we had taken five world records; 1 km at 245.64 mph, 1 mile at 245.11 mph, 5 km at 243.08 mph, 5 miles at 235.69 mph and 10 km at 224.70 mph. I then headed for home, where I was due to be best man at Ken Gregory's wedding on 2 September, and where Katie Molson and I would marry on 7 October.

In retrospect, driving EX.181 was more like lying in the cockpit of a fighter 'plane than in a car. There was an incredible din, everything about the driving position, the steering and that engine behind my shoulders was weird, while having that cockpit hatch with its little canopy clamped shut like a coffin lid above me was not at all pleasant. I had driven racing cars at around 180 mph, but here beyond 240, it really was a journey into the unknown. The car weaved slightly all the way, as if it was tram-lining, and with nearly 300 horsepower hurling me along that blurry black line on otherwise totally featureless salt, it all seemed unreal. I was quite thrilled to see the occasional marker post whizz by, because that at least was something familiar.

So it was quite a daunting experience, but also a fascinating challenge, and I returned to Bonneville with Phil Hill and EX.181 in September 1959, following my win in the Italian Grand Prix. MG had now enlarged the supercharged engine to 1,506 cc to enter 2-litre International Class E.

On the way there, recalling how it had felt the first time, I began to wonder why I had agreed to do it. As it happened, our scheduled attempt was weathered-out, and I had to return home for the Oulton Park Gold Cup, leaving Phil to drive the car alone. He averaged 254.91 mph to set MG's fastest-ever world record, just as I expected. . .

Aston Martin DBR2 *(1957-59)*

*'The big-engined
Aston Martin sports
car, a lot of power
but in my experience
never enough!*

*T*he DBR2 was developed to combine the big 3.7-litre DB4 engine with the chassis of a 1955 Aston Martin project which they entitled the Lagonda Project 166. The chassis was a multi-tubular backbone type, with the driver in effect sitting alongside its main central structural element. When the Le Mans club waived capacity restrictions for their 1957 24-Hours race, Aston Martin entered a new 3.7-litre DBR2 to accompany a pair of normal DBR1s. It was shared by the Whiteheads and was potentially very fast. I got to drive a works DBR2 for the first time, briefly and unsuccessfully, at Nassau in December 1957, and then raced it sporadically to the end of 1959.

*M*y DBR2 début was made in the car in the Nassau TT where an ignition problem lost me 17 minutes and I finished 24th! I was up against Shelby, Gregory and Phil Hill in Ferraris and Maseratis, all over 4-litres. We managed fourth place in the Governor's Trophy, but then loaned the car to Ruth Levy for the Ladies' races. Unfortunately she crashed it in the second of them, after a good drive in the first.

Back home, I reappeared in the DBR2 at Easter Monday Goodwood, where I won the sports car event in it. The circuit seemed very slow that day, and I could not put down all the DBR2's power — 284 bhp at 5,500 rpm they claimed. Archie Scott-Brown led me for the first eight laps in his much lighter Lister-Jaguar, and there wasn't much I could do about it . . . Eventually his steering failed and he retired, so I inherited a fortunate and not very satisfactory first place.

*3 December 1957 — Tourist
Trophy, Oakes Field, Nassau,
Bahamas — the big Aston
DBR2 is in ignition trouble, as
here Rex Woodgate (cap) and
Reg Parnell attempt —
successfully — to revive it
under Moss's anxious gaze.*

I drove the DBR2 once more for the works team that season, alongside Tony Brooks' sister car in the British Empire Trophy at Oulton Park. The race was run in its usual format of three class heats of twenty laps each, then a 25-lap final involving the first three in each heat, plus the nine next-quickest qualifiers irrespective of capacity.

In practice Tony's car was quicker and had better brakes than mine, and I managed to lap a second quicker in it than I could manage in my own original car. Archie Scott-Brown set FTD in the Lister, and John Wyer then gave me Tony's DBR2 for our heat, in which we ran 2-3 behind Archie until the Lister snapped a steering arm. This enabled me to inherit the lead as at Goodwood, but the DBR2 was vibrating and was spinning its wheels too easily. Still Tony and I managed to finish in line astern for an Aston Martin 1-2.

Our mechanics changed the brakes before the final, which I managed to lead from Tony before Cliff Allison inserted his Lotus between us. Eventually its engine packed up and, despite losing third gear quite early on, I retained the lead to the end, to win my third British Empire Trophy from Tony and share a new Oulton Park lap record with Graham Hill and his Lotus.

Two DBR2 events, two wins; not bad considering in both cases a Lister-Jaguar had shown the Aston Martins a clean pair of heels — while it lasted.

In the autumn of 1959 I arranged to drive a DBR2, now fitted with an enlarged 4.2-litre engine, in the *Los Angeles Times* Grand Prix race for sports cars at Riverside, California. The car was being cared for over there by Rex Woodgate, a former HWM mechanic, and the bills were being paid by an entrant named Elisha Walker. The Riverside race was the jewel in the crown of the developing US West Coast professional series of sports car races run each autumn, forerunner of the CanAm Championship of the late '60s-early '70s.

The poor old DBR2, despite its enlarged engine, was completely outclassed. It pulled 149 mph on a 3.25:1 back axle in practice, against Richie Ginther's older 4.1 Ferrari pulling 165! The Aston's tyre wear was high, I found it handled better with fifteen gallons-plus in the tank, but I needed either a higher third or lower fourth. Race day was chaos, starting with twenty minutes' mass practice for all events and all classes, then one timed flying lap each!

The car felt dead, pulling 5,700 max, 143 mph, to Richie's 161. I still managed to lead out of Turn 1 but then six cars passed on the straight. I weaved through them back up to second place round some twists then saw the red flag. The race had been stopped due to a shunt at the start. It was restarted thirty minutes later. I ran second, Phil Hill's 3-litre Ferrari yowled past, I spun and lost time then retired with overheating and the oil pressure gone . . .

Not one of my better outings.

We ran the DBR2 again in the Bahamas Speed Week that December, where in practice it felt better than at Riverside — perhaps it could hardly have felt worse! It pulled an honest 5,500 rpm on the straight and set fastest time during practice on 3 December. Next day I won a minor five-lapper and the important twelve-lap Governor's Trophy in the DBR2, which pulled 5,700 rpm on a slippery track.

Two days later before the Nassau Trophy, the fuel tank sprang a leak and Rex sealed it with a plug. The starter jammed and I lost forty seconds, but managed to take the lead after seven laps only for the battery to break and splash acid on to me. I zoomed into the pits calling for water, and got petrol — splashed all over my face! That cost me two minutes; I rejoined and lapped 0.8 sec faster than in practice and then the right-front disc sheared . . . ending a hectic farewell appearance in the big-engined Aston.

Ferrari 290S 3.5 V12 *(1957)*

'This was the first time I ever raced a sports Ferrari, and it brought my first two wins in one . . .'

Superbly smooth if rather top-endy V12 engine in a chassis which wasn't a patch on the Aston Martin DBR1s and 2s to which I was accustomed. Its steering was heavy and the driving position bad and Ferrari's drum brakes were also pretty pathetic compared to the DBR's excellent all-disc system. Where this Italian car really scored over the green one was in its marvellously direct and precise gear-change whereas Aston's had always been absolutely hopeless.

The annual Bahamas Speed Week was first and foremost a great social event, which attracted enormous American support, and only secondarily was it a compact series of international road races. The circuit used was laid out around the perimeter of Nassau's Oakes Field aerodrome, which was flat and strangely featureless with low brush making most of the bumpy concrete-surfaced corners virtually blind.

In the 1957 Speed Week I was entered to drive an Aston Martin DBR2. I had trouble with it in the Nassau TT, and then loaned it to an American lady driver named Ruth Levy for the ladies' race. She was only just beaten, by one foot, in the first heat, but in the second she unfortunately rolled the car. She escaped with nothing worse than cuts and shock but the Aston was too badly bent to be repaired in time for the Nassau Trophy race in which I was meant to drive it.

The Americans were a very friendly and sporting bunch, and Temple Buell did a deal with an owner-driver delightfully named Jan de Vroom for me to drive his 3.5 Ferrari. Unfortunately it had a central throttle pedal, which was a layout I had vowed never to use again ever since my Bari experience in David Murray's car, and my 250F shunt at Barcelona, years before.

De Vroom most obligingly had the car converted overnight to what for me was the conventional right-side throttle layout, and although his car had rather heavy steering, I had a fairly easy 100-mile race in it. I wrote, '. . . *led from first*

8 December 1957 — Nassau Trophy, Oakes Field, Bahamas — Katie Moss looks on around the raised boot-lid of Jan de Vroom's Ferrari as Stirling digests his first racing experience of a V12 Ferrari.

8 December 1957 — Nassau Trophy, Oakes Field, Bahamas — Stirling making the most of de Vroom's 3.5 V12 290S.

lap to end, including two stops to ask if I should continue!'. I beat Carroll Shelby's private Maserati 450S by a minute.

In the accompanying 250-mile race I noted '. . . *bad start, got lead after 3 laps, changed tyres, made up and won. Car OK but bad brakes . . .'*

Since I had not got as far as the start at Bari over seven years earlier, these had been my first-ever races in a Ferrari of any description, and after the drama beforehand it was nice to enjoy two easy victories.

The Cooper-Climax 'F1' Cars (1958-59)

'Unsophisticated but so easy to drive, a car which cast me as the underdog — a role I always relished . . .

For 1958, two very significant changes were made to Formula 1 which played into the hands of the smaller specialist manufacturers like Cooper. Alcohol fuel was banned and AvGas aviation spirit substituted. Engines produced less power on AvGas, but burned it more economically, so fuel tankage could be reduced, permitting smaller cars. Secondly, minimum race distance to qualify for Championship status was slashed from 500 km, or a minimum three hours, to only 300 km or two hours' duration. This reduced the required fuel capacity even further, minimized pit stops and tyre changes and enabled the whole car to be smaller, lighter and simpler.

When an early-season Argentine Grand Prix was then confirmed at short notice, Vanwall and BRM both opted out, saying they were busy perfecting their engines to run on AvGas fuel. Vandervell released me to drive another car, and private owner Rob Walker offered me his little rear-engined F2-based 1.96-litre Cooper-Climax, prepared by Alf Francis.

I jumped at the chance, and found the car just as easy to drive as my previous line of rear-engined 500s. It really could be thrown around very confidently and, although it obviously felt very small and at first a little strange to be sitting so close to the front wheels, I was never bothered by suddenly finding myself seated some eight inches closer to the road than in my lofty Vanwall.

That trip paid off handsomely . . . as the Cooper showed us the future . . .

During that winter of 1957-58, Rob Walker and I had reached a verbal agreement — we never ever had a written contract — for me to drive his F1 and F2 Coopers in any race which did not clash with my Vanwall commitments. This situation arose sooner than expected when the Argentine GP was announced for 19 January and, although I never really dreamed that the 1.96 Cooper would be competitive there against the new V6 Ferraris, at least I had a drive.

It was powered by a 1,960 cc version of the normal 1.5-litre Formula 2 twin-cam Climax four-cylinder engine, which produced about 165 horsepower at 6,500 rpm. This was, in fact, less than I had the last time I had driven a Cooper in a Grand Prix, at Monza nearly five years earlier! There, you will recall, my front-engined nitro-burning Cooper-Alta had raised many eyebrows . . . mine included.

Rob had under-written Cooper development of these 'stretched' F2 cars to enable them to run in a few Formula 1 races during 1957. Jack Brabham and my former chief mechanic, Alf Francis — who now worked for Rob — had both built enlarged versions of the twin-cam Climax FPF engine before the factory agreed to supply 1,960 cc and later 2.2-litre versions of their own.

Jack had just driven Rob's car in the Boxing Day Brands Hatch meeting, burning alcohol fuel as usual, and then back at Rob's Dorking workshop Alf Francis changed its Weber carburettor chokes and jets to re-tune it on to AvGas for Buenos Aires. There was no further track-test of any kind. It was simply put on an aeroplane and Alf and Australian mechanic Tim Wall flew down to look after it in BA, where Katie and I met them. Rob did not make the trip, which as it turned out was unfortunate.

After first practice my diary reads '*Cooper feels fast but road-holding only fair, particularly on fast corners.*' After second practice and some work by Alf and Tim; '*Car better-handling when full of fuel, tyre wear seems excellent! Fangio 1:43, SM 1:44, Musso 1:46 . . .*' Fuel economy was good. We quietly planned to run non-stop.

My practice ended when the gearbox drain plug fell out. This caused some anxiety, for Cooper's Citroën-based gearbox was already the car's Achilles heel, without running it dry.

Later that day I was horsing around with Katie when she accidentally stuck her finger in my eye and scraped 4 mm off my cornea. It hurt like hell. A doctor gave me some drops and pain-killers but I had to drive with an eye-patch, which was possibly unique!

Rob's team had found the latest Continental racing tyres to be very good, so we were using them on the Cooper. We put 4.50 section tyres on the front instead of 5.00s, which improved the handling, but we were told our tyres would not last more than thirty to forty laps, while the race was over eighty. The Cooper wheels were retained by four studs instead of centre-lock knock-offs, so any tyre change would have been a fatal handicap, possibly taking two minutes or more.

On the Saturday I did only three laps' practice, because my vision was still blurred and to conserve my tyres. I was seventh fastest. On race morning I saw the doctor again. He did what he could, but said it would be five days before my eye healed.

The race began late that afternoon once the midday heat had passed, and the eye felt better. I started quite well, fourth behind the Maseratis of Fangio and Behra and Hawthorn's V6 Ferrari, and then took third. But on lap four I struck trouble.

The gearbox was rigged with a clutch-interlock mechanism which had been introduced to stop it jumping out of gear. Far from jumping out of gear I now had the thing jam in second! I did almost a complete lap like that. I tried to change gear all the way round, running the engine up to about 6,000, putting out the clutch and trying to move the lever, but still it was jammed solid.

I was just about to pull into the pits when suddenly it freed. It was, in fact, one of the luckiest breaks I ever experienced, a virtual miracle. I thought that the gearbox had jammed, but what in fact had happened was that the clutch had broken . . . the clutch interlock mechanism was only released by putting out the clutch, which meant that this was a car on which you could not make clutchless gear changes. When the clutch broke, the car was locked into second gear, and as the clutch would not withdraw the locking device would not unlock.

Well, somehow, by sheer providence, a stone had flown up and jammed under this mechanism and opened it for me. It was *incredibly* lucky.

This problem cost about fifteen seconds and allowed Musso to get by. I came back at him and repassed, and began to close on Behra in third place, with Hawthorn ahead of him and Fangio in the lead, of course. I was going as fast as I could along the straights, then easing the car into the corners to conserve my precious tyres. I accelerated very gently, trying to find optimum traction and avoid wheelspin.

At eighteen laps I took third place and began closing on Mike, and took his second place. On lap 35 Fangio made his refuelling stop so I inherited the lead. Half-distance — forty laps — and my Walker-blue car led Behra by 22 secs, but he had yet to make his scheduled stop. I had a minute's lead over Fangio, whose car was now slowing. That was another lucky break because if he'd been on a charge I would not have been able to respond and still conserve my tyres. To lull the opposition, Alf made a great display of preparing fresh tyres for me in the pits. But of course to stop would have killed any chance we might have had of winning.

When Behra made his stop around lap 54, Musso was second and Mike third, and Musso then began to attack my lead.

Ever since half-distance I had been watching my front tyres closely, and also studying my rears in the mirrors and occasionally craning round for a proper look when I had the chance. I knew what I was watching for, and with about fourteen laps to go I saw it.

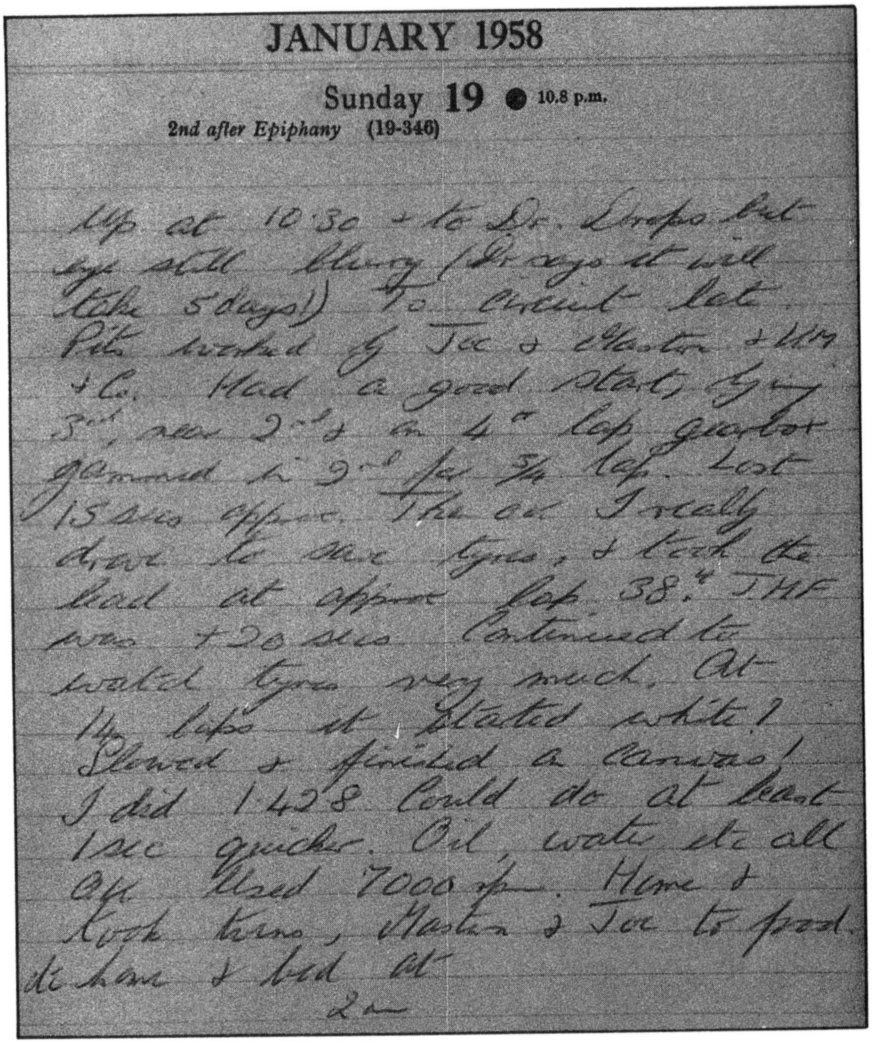

JANUARY 1958

Sunday **19** ● 10.8 p.m.

2nd after Epiphany (19-346)

[Handwritten diary entry:]

Up at 10.30 + to Dr. Drops but eye still blurry (Dr says it will take 5 days) to Circuit late. Pits worked by Joe + Masten + Alf + Co. Had a good start, trying 3rd row 2nd on 4th lap gearbox jammed in 3rd for 3/4 lap. Lost 15 secs approx. Then on I really drove to save tyres, + took the lead at approx lap 38. JHF was +20 secs. Continued to watch tyres very much. At 14 laps it started white! Slowed + finished on canvas! I did 1.42.8 Could do at least 1 sec quicker. Oil, water etc all OK. Used 7000 rpm. Home + took turns, Masten + Joe to food. At home + bed at 2 am

A little white spot began flicking round the left-rear tyre. It showed where the tread had worn through, and the white breaker-strip between tread and carcass had been exposed. The other tyres were soon going, too. These spots became longer, and longer, they became a continuous line and then began to broaden into an undulating band which now darkened as the casing proper was exposed. Then the bands became indistinct, looking fuzzy as the tortured carcass began the first stage of shredding, by growing tiny 'hairs' . . .

Alf and Tim in the pits signalled me that Musso was closing fast. I slowed and slowed, balancing my lead against my tyres' increasingly desperate state. Oil and water gauges were reading OK, I was still pulling 7,000 rpm along the straights, tensed for a tyre burst all the time, and I lapped in 1:42.8 which I knew I could have lowered by another second if only I had some rubber on my tyres!

Now I was actively seeking out the oily, slippery bits of road to molly-coddle my tyres. I kept off anything abrasive where adhesion — and wear — might be high. I got it just about right, whereas Musso had begun his charge just too late, and I won by 2.7 seconds from Luigi, with Mike third.

This was quite staggering. I could scarcely believe it. We had beaten those powerful 2.4-litre Ferrari V6s with a little 1.96 special which had survived eighty laps without a tyre change, with its clutch inoperative, and after hardly any special preparation. Alf had merely changed its chokes and jets for AvGas and I could not have had a happier introduction to Rob Walker's superb little team.

Top *19 January 1958 —
Argentine GP, Buenos Aires
Autodrome — Stirling in Rob
Walker's tiny little 1.96
Cooper closes up on Mike
Hawthorn's new 2.4 Ferrari
Dino V6.* **Above** *Bristolian
Maserati privateer Horace
Gould has his mirrors full of
Moss signalling for room to
duck by as Harry Schell's
250F forms the sandwich
between the Walker Cooper
and Hawthorn's pursuing
Ferrari.* **Right** *Possibly the
most sensational, certainly the
most unexpected Grand Prix
win of Moss's entire career —
Cooper's first World
Championship GP victory,
and the first ever for a rear-
engined Formula 1 car.*

It was a wonderful result for my reunion with Alf Francis. It was also Cooper's first-ever Formula 1 victory, and only the fourth-ever in World Championship GPs by a British car. Vanwall had just won the previous three the season before, and each time I had been the lucky chap behind the wheel.

There was still some question over whether or not this race would actually count towards the World Championship. When the CSI had said yes to the Argentine club, neither Vanwall nor BRM had been ready to run their newly modified AvGas cars. Consequently they protested the race's inclusion in the series. Their protests were to be heard by the next CSI meeting in Monte Carlo. But now that I had won in the Cooper perhaps they would figure it had all been a fluke. Or perhaps it would do my Vanwall chances for the world title no harm, and it was most unlikely that the small-engined Cooper-Climax would win anywhere else in my hands, so their protests were quietly dropped, and the Argentine race remained in the series . . .

I drove Rob's hybrid Coopers seven times more. In the *Formule Libre* Buenos Aires GP, held in pouring rain two weeks after the Grand Prix, alcohol fuel was allowed, so Alf rejetted the carburettors and I qualified second fastest to Fangio, 2:17.2 to his 2:15.6.

I made a good start but then the gearbox jammed in second again. I managed to wrestle it out but by that time I'd lost a lot of speed. I stuffed it back into first, then straight up into third, not risking second again. I lay third into the first corner behind Hawthorn and Fangio when suddenly there was a tremendous impact from behind which tossed the Cooper bodily into the air, spun me round and away backwards across the wet grass verge. A local driver named Iglesias had braked far too late behind me and skated straight into my tail in his heavy Chevrolet special. I was unhurt but livid, for Rob's unique Grand Prix-winning Cooper was quite badly bent around the tail. That time we ran it on Pirelli Stelvio tyres.

It was subsequently rebuilt with a new frame back at Dorking, and I next drove it at Easter Goodwood, but came on to the grid late and stalled just before the flag fell. Alf and Rob's foreman Don Christmas push-started me while the rest got away, and I came back through the field to run second behind Hawthorn's Ferrari until the hybrid engine threw a rod at half-distance. Still, I shared a new lap record with Mike at 1:28.8, 97.30 mph, and the Cooper had gone through Fordwater virtually flat, pulling 6,200-6,300 rpm on the exit.

Alf then built up a further-enlarged 2015 cc Climax engine for the car in time for the Aintree '200'. I found the engine a little stiff but the car was handling better during practice, and then in the race I built up a useful lead, eventually a clear minute from the works hybrid Coopers of Brabham and Salvadori. But I was in trouble, because the Cooper was overheating, with the water at 115 degrees C and oil pressure down to 30 psi. With 27 laps to go my clutch began slipping, but Roy had encountered the same trouble and was falling back. Jack closed to within thirteen seconds while I could do nothing but nurse Rob's car along.

Into the last lap I thought I was safe with a six-second lead but down the straight Jack came hammering past. I nipped into his slipstream as he went by and just managed to hold on. We then came into the difficult kink at Melling Crossing, just two corners from the finish, and Jack backed off. I believe that once he passed me he had relaxed. He learned his lesson that day and would never do it again!

I exited Melling right under his tail, pulled wide to the left — the outside — for the last right-hander at Tatts Corner, and still he didn't know I was there because he'd last seen me as he whizzed by, 15 mph faster on the straight.

I cut back across his tail, took the inside line into Tatts and left my braking desperately late. I shot out right under his nose, with my Cooper all crossed-up, but my impetus held the advantage to the line and I won by about two feet, a fifth of a second. It must have given Jack a terrible shock, and frankly I felt a little bit quivery afterwards as well . . .

Tony Brooks was third overall and won the Formula 2 class in Rob's second car; this was a very satisfying win for me — my hat-trick of Aintree '200's.

I drove a new 2,015 cc car for Rob at May Silverstone but it boiled in practice, while Maurice Trintignant drove the older car which I tried later and found faster than mine but less stable. I stalled at the start, just like Goodwood, because the clutch in those cars was very marginal. Once I got going I found I was 300 rpm down and the engine was misfiring low down in third gear. The gearbox finally broke after nineteen laps.

My calendar was then full of Aston Martin and Vanwall commitments until the Reims Formula 2 race accompanying the French Grand Prix. At Monaco my Vanwall broke, and who should win but Maurice in my Aintree car! The first two World Championship races of 1958 had thus both gone to Rob's private Cooper specials.

At Reims he entered two Formula 2 cars for Maurice and me then the day after the British Grand Prix there was the minor F1 Caen GP in Normandy. By this time Rob had a 2.2-litre Climax engine and I won easily in his Cooper after Begra's BRM retired from second place. I set a new lap record at 1:20.8 and Maurice finished fourth in Rob's other entry to win the F2 class. It was a good day for us privateers.

I drove Rob's F2 Cooper at Brands Hatch, and then returned with a new 2.01 car in that winter's Tasman races in Australia and New Zealand. The Melbourne Grand Prix in Albert Park was run in two heats and a final. The Cooper was over-geared and had a dragging clutch and locking brakes, but I took pole position 1.2 secs quicker than Brabham in a similar car. We each won our respective heats, but my car was overheating badly. It lost all its water in an eight-lap heat so I wasn't optimistic for our chances in the 32-lap final. I managed to build a big lead before the gauge went off the clock, and for the last dozen or so laps the water had gone entirely and reports said that the car was glowing visibly! But we won again, and set fastest lap, with Jack second. It was my nineteenth and last win of the season. For the fourth time I was runner-up in the Drivers' World Championship — dammit! — and for the eighth time in nine years I had won the BRDC Gold Star.

Coventry Climax had a full-sized new 2 ½ -litre engine on the stocks for 1959, and Rob ordered two for me.

My last outings with the hybrid Cooper were in the January 1959 New Zealand Grand Prix at Ardmore aerodrome, where I led until the last half-mile of the preliminary heat when a half-shaft broke. Jack very sportingly loaned me a spare from his second Cooper, which we fitted in a rush. I rolled out on to the back of the grid just in time for the start, and I lay second into the first corner thanks to everybody else getting away slowly. I managed to pass Jack and drove away until my engine began boiling again and its oil pressure slumped. I eased off, but I had almost a complete lap's lead by this time and came home first.

In eight races in Rob's 1.96, 2.01 and 2.2 Coopers I had won five times, including one Championship-qualifying Grand Prix. The next time I raced a Cooper-Climax, it would have a fully-fledged 2 ½ -litre engine installed, and that made it a match for any contemporary Formula 1 car, bar none.

Ferrari 335S 4.1 V12 *(1958)*

'For much of my career I relished beating the Ferrari team perhaps above all, but whenever I drove one of their V12 cars I really enjoyed those beautifully smooth, powerful and reliable engines . . .'

I very rarely got to drive the open sports Ferraris. My first opportunity to do so came as late as December 1957, with Jan de Vroom's 3.5 at Nassau, but it was only two months later that this second chance arose with a big 4.1 in Cuba. It was entered by Luigi Chinetti's North American Racing Team, and I found it had a lot of power and, despite being rather heavy to handle, it was well-suited to the Havana street circuit. But I remember more vividly what happened during and around that race than anything about the Ferrari I drove.

*T*his Cuban meeting was organized in typical style, practice due to start at 1.15 pm finally beginning at 5.20! It simply did not pay to be impatient by nature. I set best time at 2:0.7 but then Masten Gregory equalled it in his Ferrari. Fangio was running a 300S Maserati and his best was 3.3 secs slower than ours. I was also fastest in second practice the following day, before a bridge collapsed on to the circuit, hurting a lot of people, and that evening Fangio was kidnapped by Castro's rebels.

This caused immense excitement, but Juan's kidnappers treated him very well and explained they merely wanted to protest about Battista's government spending more money on motor racing than on Cuba's poor. They took Fangio at gunpoint from the lobby of the Lincoln Hotel and apparently wanted me as well, but the old boy told them 'No, leave Moss out of it. He is here with his wife and it will upset her. After all, you have me, so why don't you leave it at that?' Can you understand my total respect for this man?

From then on we were given bodyguards, but they seemed far more threatening than the rebels. During the night before the race its organizer, Azua, woke us up at 5 am by knocking on the door just to see if I had been kidnapped yet, his husky voice saying, 'Moss, Moss, are you all right?'. I was quite unable to get off to sleep again.

but we eventually started without him and I led for five laps before waving Masten through because the course was slick with oil, there was a long way to go and early dicing was stupid. He had been sitting right on my tail so I decided he might as well go in front and find where the oil was for me.

I followed him round until we came upon a dreadful scene, because a driver named Cifuentes had drifted off on the oil, straight into some unprotected spectators, five of whom had been killed. This was the final straw for Azua, who had the race red-flagged and stopped.

Now international regulations stipulate that the red flag only applies when given by the Clerk of the Course, who would be at the start and finish line, so that any other red flags around the course are advisory but not mandatory. We threaded through the debris, with red flags waving like Moscow on May Day, but I knew they were only advising us that the race was going to be stopped when we reached the finish line. So it was not yet over. But Masten was looking round at all the confusion and was probably still in third or fourth gear, so I saw my chance approaching the finish line, snatched second and booted my Ferrari past his. I crossed the finish line first and stopped immediately, having won, but Masten was pretty upset and reckoned I had cheated him out of victory.

I explained that sometimes it pays to know the regulations. I reckoned it was fair, but suggested we should pool our prize money then split it fifty-fifty. Masten was happy with that so we parted as friends. Katie and I caught a plane to Miami that evening and the rebels released Fangio to the Argentine Embassy next day. It was not a great race, nor a great win, but now I had driven my first two Ferraris within a three-month span and had won my first three races in them. No wonder the works cars were so hard to beat . . .

Above *14 May 1949 — British GP meeting 500cc race, Silverstone — Stirling's first important race win. Despite the extra cockpit padding, Stirling has to steady himself against cornering load in the long-wheelbase 'two-way' Cooper-JAP Mark III. Note the lucky horseshoe.*

Right *17 September 1949 — Autumnal scene at Goodwood's end-of-season meeting, recorded in this rare colour shot by Guy Griffiths who had known the Moss family well since the mid-1930s. Stirling — in overalls, left — has won the Madgwick Cup on this his 20th birthday but there is a problem with the Cooper-JAP 1,000 and he will (briefly) drive John Cooper's in the Formula 1 Goodwood Trophy. To the right here are Aileen, Alfred (kneeling) and their former German PoW mechanic Don Muller.*

Right *26 August 1950 — BRDC International Trophy, Silverstone — After the new BRM broke on the startline, Moss's 2-litre Formula 2 HWM captured here in colour by Tom March gave the crowds something to cheer, finishing sixth in the Final amongst the supercharged F1s. Autosport reported 'without a doubt . . . Moss definitely achieved stardom . . .' In fact Continental crowds had been watching him and the HWM perform this well all season.*

Below *20 October 1951 — Half-Litre Car Club open challenge races, Brands Hatch — Stirling in his superb one-off Kieft-Norton climbing Paddock Hill on the short Brands circuit, which in those days was used anti-clockwise. He won two heats and a final this day — lucky '7' paying off, of course . . .*

Right *19 July 1952 — British Grand Prix Silverstone — Another offset single-seater, this time the very sophisticated but highly unsuccessful G-Type ERA, with Stirling heading for retirement as its dry-sump Bristol engine overheats. The car could corner very well but woefully lacked power, straightline speed and reliability . . .*

Below *9 May 1953 — BRDC International Trophy, Silverstone — Deceptive beauty; the Cooper-Alta built largely by jazz musician-cum-demon welder Ray Martin, flattered only to deceive, its best performance being here under number '7', as in Heat One of the Trophy race Stirling finished second to De Graffenried's Maserati. It was a different story in the final . . .*

Above *9 May 1953 — BRDC Trophy, Silverstone meeting — The C-Type Jaguar etched itself into Stirling's memory as one of his favourite all-purpose sports-racing cars but this was not one of his happier outings. 'XKC 037' here has been hastily rebodied after overturning in practice and its bruised and sore driver struggled against fading brakes to finish seventh.*

Right *22 May 1955 — Monaco GP, Monte Carlo — Photographer Yves Debraine proving that by this time Moss could lead a Grand Prix with his eyes shut . . . Balancing power against steering, Stirling accelerates his factory Mercedes-Benz W196 hard out of the Gasworks Hairpin. Much to everybody's surprise its supposedly unbreakable desmodromic-valved engine will break during the race.*

Right *'The Train' formed by Fangio and Moss running 1-2 in their Mercedes-Benz W196s became the abiding memory of the 1955 Formula 1 World Championship season for all who witnessed it. Here at Aintree — on 16 July 1955 — Tom March froze this moment as Moss set up his car to take first place in the British GP from the Argentinian double World Champion.*

Below *13 May 1956 — Monaco GP, Monte Carlo — Moss and the factory-entered Maserati 250F hurtle along the harbour front on their way to Stirling's second Grande Epreuve victory and the first of his three in the Principality. With its intimate atmosphere and the proximity of the crowds, Monte Carlo became one of Moss's best-loved circuits. Of course with race number '28' Stirling felt confident — four times '7' you see . . .*

Left *22 June 1957 — Le Mans 24-Hours — Rare* Motor Sport *magazine shot of what Moss considers to have been — bar the BRM V16 — the worst car he ever drove; Maserati's Zagato-bodied 450S V8 Berlinetta in the paddock before the start of the 24-Hour Grand Prix d'Endurance. The number on its tail is a Bologna test-plate enabling the car to be driven on the public road . . .*

Below left *20 July 1957 — British Grand Prix, Aintree — The great day's action begins as Stirling's Vanwall and Behra's Maserati 250F surge away at flagfall, with Tony Brooks's Vanwall hidden this side. Moss will take over the Brooks car to score the first all-British Grande Epreuve victory since 1923 — at last he has found a green car capable of winning Grand Prix races . . .*

Right *18 May 1958 — Monaco Grand Prix, Monte Carlo — Locked in what became their season-long battle for the World Championship title, Moss and Mike Hawthorn race towards the Gasworks Hairpin in Vanwall and Ferrari Dino 246 respectively. The Vanwall's normally graceful, streamlined nose has been cut back and fitted with a bumper bar for slow-speed street racing such as this. But this time four times '7' let Moss down.*

Above *26 May 1958 — Dutch Grand Prix, Zandvoort — Edward Eves captures all the elegance, power and speed of the exquisite tool-room built British Vanwall in this magnificent study of Stirling on the way to winning his second Grand Prix from three starts thus far that season.*

Right *1 June 1958 — Nürburgring 1,000 Kms — Drivers' circuit; between the thick, springy hedgerows which lined the magnificent 14.2-mile Eifel circuit, Moss's victorious Aston Martin DBR1/300 rips away from Adenau Bridge to begin the long climb to the Karussel and on to the highest point at Höhe Acht. Sharing the drive with Jack Brabham, this was the first of Moss's three consecutive wins in the German sports car classic.*

Above *6 July 1958 — F2 Coupe de Vitesse, Reims-Gueux — Stirling's first season driving Rob Walker's private Coopers concentrated upon non-Championship Formula 1 races which Vanwall ignored and upon Formula 2, as here at Reims where he set fastest lap before his car's Climax engine lost its oil pressure. Rob was born to the Johnny Walker Scotch whisky family.*

Right *19 October 1958 — Moroccan Grand Prix, Casablanca — Vanwall swansong; 5pm with an autumnal North African sun low in the sky and Stirling about to win his fourth Grand Prix of the season, set fastest race lap, yet still lose the world title to Mike Hawthorn. The Vanwall's nose has been crushed against Wolfgang Seidel's Maserati while lapping it, the Vanwall crew signalled 'WATCH TEMP' — but all was well.*

Left *12 July 1959 — Coupe Delamere-Deboutteville, Rouen-les-Essarts — Debut of the brand new Maserati Tipo 60 'Birdcage', in Stirling's view the greatest front-engined sports-racing car ever built. Edward Eves's shot here shows him entering Nouveau Monde hairpin, leading handsomely after starting from pole position, and all set to win and set fastest lap — the perfect motor racing performance.*

Above right *13 September 1959 — Italian Grand Prix, Monza — Moss directing matters as Alf Francis, John Chisman (with the moustache) and the other Walker boys roll their Cooper on to pole position at Monza — Ferrari well and truly in the background on their home soil.* **Right** *The Boss; Stirling's long-time friend and entrant Rob Walker relaxes upon their Cooper on pole position, before the start of a race which will bring Stirling his third Italian Grand Prix victory and will clinch for Cooper Cars the Formula 1 Manufacturers' World Championship title.*

*19 March 1960 — Formula 2
Syracuse Grand Prix, Sicily —
The Mediterranean island's
road circuit was fast with a
lap average above 100mph
and was lined much of the
way with these unyielding
stone walls. Here Edward
Eves has joined the locals to
enjoy a close-up view of
Stirling practising typical
precision in the Porsche . . .*

Right *24 September 1960 —
Oulton Park Gold Cup —
Lucky number '7' and
'Golden Boy' near his peak;
Moss in the 2½-litre Walker
Racing Lotus 18 about to win
the Cheshire race for the
fourth time. Note how the
2½-litre Lotus had no roll-
over bar behind its driver's
head. Such protection then
became mandatory for the
new 1½-litre Formula of 1961.*
Below *14 May 1961 —
Monaco Grand Prix, Monte
Carlo — He might have been
driving his hardest yet the
artist in Moss still made it
look so relaxed and easy in
this Geoff Goddard photo.
The Walker Lotus 18's side
panels had been removed to
keep Stirling cool that close
and muggy day. Just before
the start he had spotted a
cracked chassis member by
the gearchange bracket — Alf
Francis wrapped the
brimming fuel tanks with wet
towels and calmly welded a
repair on the starting grid . . .*

Left *14 may 1961 — Monaco Grand Prix, Monte Carlo — Rounding the Station Hairpin in Rob Walker's now obsolescent 1½-litre Lotus 18, Moss the Maestro is leading the race and the three much more powerful but less agile factory Ferraris, and is driving at his inspired best 'flat out all race . . .'*

Right *6 August 1961 — German Grand Prix, Nürburgring — On Dunlop D12 green-spot 'rain tyres' Moss made a mockery of Ferrari's horsepower advantage to score his final Grande Epreuve victory in classic style behind the wheel of Rob Walker's now updated but still really outmoded old Lotus 18/21.*

Above *19 August 1961 — RAC Tourist Trophy, Goodwood — Lucky '7' on the Rob Walker/Dick Wilkins Ferrari 250GT short-wheelbase Berlinetta at St Mary's Corner, as Stirling powers towards his seventh TT victory, and his fourth in successive years. Eight months later his career will end just short of this point on the Sussex circuit . . .*

Right *23 April 1962 — Glover Trophy, Easter Monday Goodwood — Moss the Maestro, making up time as only he could, flat-out in the V8 Lotus special on loan to UDT from Rob Walker. With its inside front wheel virtually airborne he hammers through Madgwick Corner on the way to Fordwater and St Mary's . .*

The Aston Martin DBR1/300s *(1958-59)*

'These handsome cars revealed the DB3S breeding in their heritage by being very good on proper road circuits, like Nürburgring; solid, strong and dependable, with really good brakes but a ghastly gear-change . . .'

After driving sports cars for Maserati in 1957, I returned to Aston Martin for 1958-59. They were making a serious attempt on the World Championship with their spaceframe 3-litre DBR1 cars, and I drove them twelve times in those two seasons, winning two consecutive Nürburgring 1,000 Kms, of which I am very proud, and in that second year we won the Championship as well.

While we had been struggling with our big 4.5 and 300S Maseratis in the 1957 Nürburgring 1,000 Kms, Tony Brooks and Noel Cunningham-Reid had a great day and won in Aston Martin's new 3-litre six-cylinder DBR1/300. In the Maserati team we were pretty shaken by its performance and I decided that a return to Aston Martin for 1958 would be no bad thing. They felt likewise so I made my return début for them in a DBR1 at Sebring to start that new season.

Sebring was very rough and bumpy by this time, but the DBR1 immediately impressed with its ability to soak up such punishment. I clocked 3:23.6 in practice, with Shelby, Brooks and Salvadori in the 3:27-3:28 bracket in the sister cars, all faster than the Ferraris. Next day I tried Roy's car, which braked better than mine but steered worse. That terrible gearbox was common to all the cars. Its gear-change was heavy, stiff and vague and we could never be sure if we had engaged the next gear or not. Still, when practice ended I had clipped a second off Behra's Maserati 450S lap record.

I took the lead from the start and had a lap in hand over Roy and Mike Hawthorn's Ferrari approaching the two-hour mark. Then a tyre blew which lost us three minutes in the pits. Tony Brooks re-joined and, when he handed back to me after four hours, we were a lap and ten seconds behind the Ferrari. I had managed to pull back all but fourteen seconds, when the gearbox broke. I had lapped in 3:20.2 which trimmed three seconds off Jean's old record so the DBR1 certainly had great potential, spoiled by that awful gearbox.

It occurred to me that a car which behaved as well as this one over rough roads must surely stand a chance in the Targa Florio, so I talked John Wyer into entering the Sicilian classic. Reg Parnell was managing the team by this time and he took out a DBR1 for Tony and myself, plus a DBR2 for practice. I flew out via Modena where I tried Maserati's new 3-litre V12 briefly, which felt fantastic. Katie met me in Palermo and next day I did three laps of the 45-mile mountain circuit in a hired Fiat 1100. The poor thing probably cried itself to sleep that night, because it lapped in 1 hr 13 min, then 1 hr 2 min and finally 59 min 15 sec. Having reminded myself of which way the road went, I then took Katie round in the DBR2, doing 47:34 and 46:26 in amongst the traffic . . .

Next day I tackled official practice in the DBR1 but its engine was missing badly and I had to stop twice. Despite these delays, my time was 46:14 so its potential was clear.

I started the race at 7 am next morning, but after only 20 kms I was stupid enough to hit a rock. I had to change the nearside rear wheel, cursing my foolishness. I lost just over a minute. After 40 kms the crankshaft damper then came adrift and a weird vibration affected the whole car. I thought it was something loose at the rear, and stopped to have a look but I could see nothing wrong so continued to the pits. They rightly diagnosed the problem and spent about half an hour trying to fix it. I was then sent off to do five more laps before handing over to Tony. The car seemed hot but otherwise fine, and then on the fourth lap that gearbox packed up again and deprived Tony of his drive.

Still, my best lap was 42:17.5 which beat my existing 300SLR lap record of 43:07, despite the fact that I had spun the Aston on that very lap! After our delays the adrenalin had been pumping hard, and I was probably trying harder than I had been in the big Mercedes.

Jack Brabham made his works Aston début as my co-driver at Nürburgring. I lapped at 12:37.5 in pouring rain in our DB2/4 practice car. The DBR1 then felt very skippy at the back and very over-geared; it would not pull more than 5,900 rpm anywhere. I asked Reg Parnell to have a lower back axle installed for next day.

Now Reg knew how critical those Aston engines were on revs. If the limit was set at 6,5 then it meant 6,5; 6,600 and things would come unstitched. I assured him that, despite a lower final-drive ratio, I would stick religiously to the rev limit by lifting off along the straight and down the *Fucksröhe* descent. Reg looked dubious. I doubt if he believed me, but he said he would have it changed.

Next morning I realized he had dropped the ratio only part-way towards what I wanted, without telling me as much. So when I returned to the pits I said, 'I'm sorry Reg, but we're going to have to change the engine'.

He asked why and I explained, 'I know you dropped the ratio but as I'm only getting 6,300 rpm where I should be getting 6,5, it's obvious that the engine's gone off-tune . . .' Then he finally owned-up, and gave me the back axle ratio I wanted for the race.

By the end of the first lap I held a twelve-second lead, and on every one of my first ten laps I broke my previous year's Maserati 450S lap record. My best was 9:43 on my third lap. When Jack Brabham took over he did not maintain the pace, and next time round Mike Hawthorn's Ferrari was right behind and then drew out thirty seconds on him. Jack did three laps before stopping for tyres and fuel, and I rejoined third behind Mike and von Trips. I passed Taffy, and then Mike when he had a tyre burst. After eleven laps I handed back to Jack and he did another five, holding our lead this time though Collins closed up on to his tail in the Hawthorn Ferrari.

I took over the Aston and Mike the Ferrari for our final stints, but I left the pits first and by lap 33 held a 33-second lead. The Aston just ran perfectly to the finish, and we won handsomely, but I had not appreciated how much that drive was taking

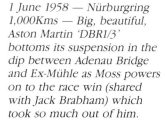

1 June 1958 — Nürburgring 1,000Kms — Big, beautiful, Aston Martin 'DBR1/3' bottoms its suspension in the dip between Adenau Bridge and Ex-Mühle as Moss powers on to the race win (shared with Jack Brabham) which took so much out of him.

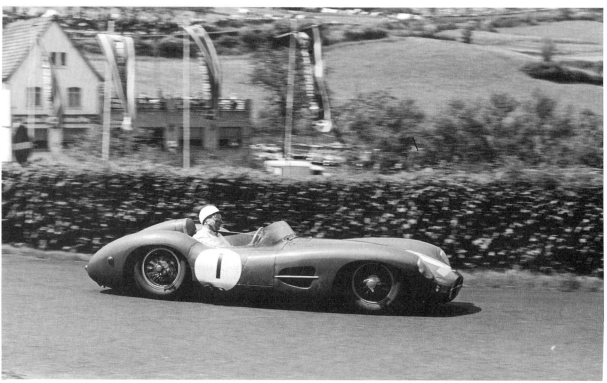

out of me. I had driven 36 of the 44 14-mile laps, and I felt absolutely shattered afterwards. I really was very fit in those days, but my pulse rate was sky-high at 130 against my normal 70-75 and it took a week for me really to feel OK again. I had driven terribly hard, and it took me longer to recover from winning that 1,000 Kms than it had from winning the 1955 Mille Miglia.

At Le Mans the DBR1s pulled 5,900 rpm down the straight and their disc brakes were so good I was braking at 300 yards into Mulsanne Corner. On every lap we could leave the drum-braked Ferraris for dead at that point. I found I could go through the Dunlop Curve after the pits almost flat. I lapped in 4:07.3, Tony 4:08.4, Shelby 4:13 and Brabham 4:18 on the first day. Next day I tried a 3.19 back axle instead of the 3.09 and saw 5,990 rpm but the lap time fell to only 4:10 and a 2-litre Lotus did 4:12 which made me blink.

I led the early stages quite easily, leading Mike by 1:24 after two hours, but then my engine broke and I stopped at Mulsanne. I hung around to watch and by 6 am the rest of our team had also retired and we returned to our hotel in La Châtre and had the most tremendous party.

My last race for Aston that season was the TT, just revived at Goodwood after the fateful 1955 race at Dundrod. But since Ferrari did not enter we had a walk-over and finished 1-2-3. I did a 1:32 in practice, going through Fordwater curve flat. Our only problem seemed to be tyre wear. Avon estimated a set would only last forty laps. They were wrong, because Tony Brooks and I were not pressed in the winning car and it needed only two tyre changes throughout.

David Brown's main ambition was to win Le Mans, not necessarily the World Sports Car Championship, and after the failures of 1958 the works team concentrated solely on the 24-Hours classic for 1959. I thought this was unfortunate and I knew that the DBR1 was just perfect for the Nürburgring so I pestered John Wyer to let me use the spare car — which was not being prepared for Le Mans — in the 1,000 Kms. I was so convinced it could win again that I offered to pay all expenses including transport in return for use of the car. John softened, and despatched it with two works mechanics on Aston's tab, but all other expenses would be mine, as would be any prize money we might win.

I wanted a steady, reliable and trustworthy co-driver and invited Jack Fairman to do the job. He was prepared to do just a couple of laps if necessary and then hand back to me. This time we began practice with the 3.62 back axle and I was immediately pulling 5,800-5,900 rpm. It still seemed a touch too high, so I got them to put in a 3.74 ratio which gave us the perfect 6,000 rpm. I clocked 9:43.1, just 0.1 sec outside my lap record. Jack's best was 10:16.7. Next day the Behra and Brooks Ferraris lapped 4-6 secs quicker than my time but I was confident we could go quicker if necessary.

On the opening lap I was able to build an eleven-second lead, and maintained the pressure for seventeen laps before handing over to Jack. I had broken my old lap record on sixteen of those laps, leaving it at 9:32, eleven seconds inside the old mark.

As Jack drove away it began to rain, and on his sixth lap he was baulked by a slower car which pulled across him and he spun into a ditch. To his enormous credit he did not give up even though the Aston's tail was down in the ditch and its nose cocked high, with one front wheel clear of the road. He crouched down behind and beneath the car, gave it several almighty heaves and manhandled it back on to the circuit, jumped in, restarted and came straight back into the pits where I was despondently packing my bag, ready to go home.

Gendebien's Ferrari had come by in the lead, then Behra followed him and no sign of the Aston. I had just put my crash helmet and goggles and shoes away and was about to leave when somebody yelled 'He's coming in!'

I pulled my gear on, poor mud-stained Jack was dragged from the cockpit and after a quick check on the car I took off with a seventy-second deficit in place of the six-minute lead which we had held.

It was the kind of challenge I relished. People had been saying I was a car-

7 June 1959 — Nürburgring 1,000Kms — Yer putcher left leg in . . . Moss in, Fairman out, as Stirling hurdles into dented 'DBR1/1's cockpit, Jack having just manhandled the car bodily from the ditch into which it had slithered out in the country. The stage is set for one of Moss' most majestic come-back drives . . . a drive which set up Aston Martin to win the 1959 World Sports Car Championship!

breaker. Well if the car broke now, at least they would have to say 'Oh boy, did he go'.

I went after those Ferraris as fast as I had ever driven at the 'Ring. I retook the lead on lap 29, and by lap 33 I had built a two-minute cushion. Jack took over for two laps and was extremely careful not to end up in the ditch again, so the Ferraris came back at him, Phil Hill going by to lead by 22 seconds as I took over for the final nine laps.

It took four laps for us to regain the lead and I eventually finished 41 seconds ahead of Hill/Gendebien. This was Aston's third successive Nürburgring 1,000 Kms victory. They were alone amongst British cars in having won this German road-racing classic and it was the kind of motor race which I enjoyed most — one green Aston alone against the entire team of red factory Ferraris . . . a great day for me, and paradoxically one made largely by poor Jack's early misfortune and marvellous work in retrieving the car.

Aston's cars were painstakingly well-prepared for Le Mans, where Jack Fairman was again my co-driver. A Ferrari was marginally quicker in practice but I made another good start and led for the first hour. Behra finally caught me in his very fast Ferrari and I slipstreamed him along Mulsanne to see 6,050 rpm at the 4 km post, where unassisted I had been reaching only 5,700! After 38 laps I handed over to Jack, and he did another 35 laps before handing back to me, but one lap later a valve broke so yet another Moss Le Mans bit the dust.

As it happened, Aston's careful preparation paid off for the others. Ferrari reliability collapsed and Roy Salvadori and Carroll Shelby at last achieved David Brown's ambition of winning the *Grand Prix d'Endurance*, and what's more Maurice Trintignant and Paul Frère in second place completed a memorable Aston Martin 1-2. I was really delighted for the team.

Now Aston Martin suddenly found themselves leading Ferrari in the World Championship with the final outcome all down to the Goodwood TT. Consequently, we fielded a full works team of three cars there, facing strong opposition from Ferrari and Porsche.

Throughout the DBR1's career we had roundly criticized its dreadful gearbox and in TT practice I drove one fitted for the first time with a Maserati transaxle, which was superb. At last the DBR1 really had become a fabulous car, and I was pulling 6,300 rpm in top and 6,500 through the gears, and still — just — taking Fordwater flat.

I led for the first 1¼ hours but then had to change tyres as the canvas was showing through! The car had built-in hydraulic jacks which worked brilliantly well, and Roy Salvadori took over and quite comfortably maintained our lead. But when he made his stop some fuel was spilled on to the hot exhaust and

5 September 1959 — The Moss Le Mans start technique was world-renowned; the art is demonstrated here, RAC Tourist Trophy, Goodwood. Some others haven't even begun to move, but then neither — apparently — has the flag.

197

exploded. The whole place seemed to catch alight, but thank goodness nobody was too badly burned although it was desperately spectacular. Our leading car was wheeled sadly away, blanketed in foam, and I was then put into the Shelby/Fairman car which was lying second.

Now it was like Nurburgring all over again and I ripped into the situation with gusto and shortly after half-distance I caught the leading Porsche. But our big Aston was much heavier on tyres than the little German car, and as I stopped for my last set of Avons the Porsche retook the lead. I rejoined and managed to catch it again, and finally came home to win by 32.4 secs from the Porsche, which just beat Tony Brooks' Ferrari by two seconds.

I had driven 4 hr 36 min of this six-hour race, and Aston Martin had won the World Championship title in dramatic style on our home soil . . . not a bad outcome to a season in which they had planned solely to race at Le Mans.

For me it was the end of a generally very happy and successful association with the Aston Martin DBR1, which today is regarded quite justifiably as a really great classic British sports car.

5 September 1959 — RAC Tourist Trophy, Goodwood — Stirling's fifth win in the event also saw Aston Martin clinch the World Championship, but the original car — 'DBR1/3 — which he shared with Roy Salvadori and which is seen cornering here at Fordwater **above** *was burned in a refuelling fire so he finished in the sister Shelby/Fairman 'DBR1/2' instead* **right**.

Aston Martin DBR3/300 (1958)

'I had the dubious pleasure of driving this car in its only race . . . and we didn't finish . . .'

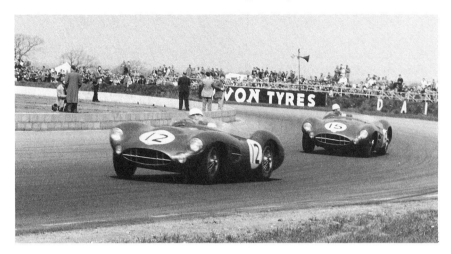

3 May 1958 — May Silverstone sports car race — Stirling in the big-engined Aston Martin DBR3 — see its distinctive bonnet bulge — leading Roy Salvadori's DBR2.

The Aston Martin DBR3 emerged during the first season of my second period with Aston Martin in 1958. It resembled the other DBRs externally, but it used a short-stroke, reduced-capacity version of the DB4 production 6-cylinder engine. Its chassis also differed in using a new type of wishbone and torsion-bar front suspension under development for Aston's forthcoming F1 car. The 3-litre engine was meant to give 300 horsepower at 7,500 rpm but when I drove it at May Silverstone it had only 260-262 at 7,400. I described it as being *'rather flabby'* and it had poor brakes. I had a pretty undistinguished outing, as it was way over-geared — something of an Aston Martin habit — and my race ended when it ran its bearings and seized after fourteen laps. They subsequently converted it into a conventional DBR1/300, which seemed a better idea.

Maserati 'Eldorado Special' *(1958)*

'The nearest I ever came to Indianapolis racing, a lot more powerful than a Formula 1 car but not necessarily any faster along the straights . . .

The Monza authorities seemed to be virtually at a loss to know what to do with their banked high-speed oval track once they had built it in 1955 until, in 1957, they organized their first 'Two Worlds Trophy' speedway race on it. They brought over from America a powerful group of Indianapolis cars and drivers to face European opposition — which did not materialize. They tried again in 1958 and this time the financial inducements were too good to be ignored, so when Signor Zanetti of the 'Eldorado' ice cream company asked Maserati to build him a track-racing car, based on 250F-type bits and powered by the 4.2-litre V8 engine, I was asked to drive it.

Zanetti's *Eldorado Special* was quite an imposing-looking car, sprayed white and plastered with 'Eldorado' logos and advertising stickers, which all looked most outlandish in Europe at that time. Its 4.2-litre V8 engine was topped by four massive twin-choke Weber carburettors tuned to run on alcohol fuel, and its multi-tubular chassis was rather like a 250F's, but used the heavy-duty front suspension of the big 4.5 sports car and a Formula 1-style de Dion layout and two-speed transaxle at the rear. It rode on cast-alloy wheels as favoured by the Americans, who had again made the long journey to Italy confident of carrying off all the prize money.

We were to lap the speedbowl anti-clockwise, left-handed as at Indianapolis, the opposite to what we were used to.

My first practice in the car certainly proved its power, but it skipped and bounded over the bumpy bankings and I cannot say I liked it very much. I lapped in 57.9 secs, an average of 164 mph, and next day when I arrived the skies were heavily overcast and rain was drizzling down.

All the Americans were standing around looking bored. Nobody was running, simply because in American USAC racing nobody ran in the rain. Naturally I told Bertocchi to warm-up our car. Some of the Indy people asked what on earth we were doing.

I said, 'I'm going out,' and they gasped, 'But you can't! It's raining!'. This was too good an opportunity to miss, so I said that in Europe we didn't mind whether it was raining or sunny, we raced in all weathers. It might yet rain on Sunday, race day, so what would they do then? 'We won't race,' they said flatly. 'OK,' I said, 'That's great. There are a few European drivers here and we'll go racing quite happily . . .' That set them all ticking and clucking and worrying about the prize money . . .

I took off in the *Eldorado* and felt my way round the bankings. Then when I came down on to the straight past the pits I wiggled the steering just enough to make the car snake under full power. It must have looked quite dramatic from the trackside but it wasn't really, because the rear wheels were not breaking traction and wagging the tail, it was me intentionally inducing a weave because I knew it would make some of these Indy boys, who clearly did not think much of us road-racers, stand back and blink.

Actually I lapped in 64.3 secs in the drizzle and then on one lap, while doing my snaking trick past the pits, I very nearly came unstuck and the moment I was out of sight on to the banking I backed right off to catch my breath! Meanwhile somebody had leaned on the organizers, and they flagged me in next time round.

I noticed that some of the Indy people regarded the road racers with a little more respect after that. In fact they understood and respected anyone who was prepared to 'stand on it', which most of us at that level were.

Qualifying was run Indy-style, the average achieved in three consecutive flying laps deciding one's place on the grid. But the *Eldorado* was still not right. I was seeing 6,700 rpm entering the banking and then speed was scrubbing away to only 6,200 rpm leaving it. The car felt bad with its front suspension set too high.

Next day I tried lower gearing which felt better and improved my times. Real hero of the day was Luigi Musso who was out in a special 4.1-litre single-seat Ferrari, which he drove with enormous courage because it was obviously another difficult and demanding car. He qualified on pole before his own crowd, which really made the Indy contingent stand back and think.

The race was arranged in three heats, the result to be decided on aggregate,

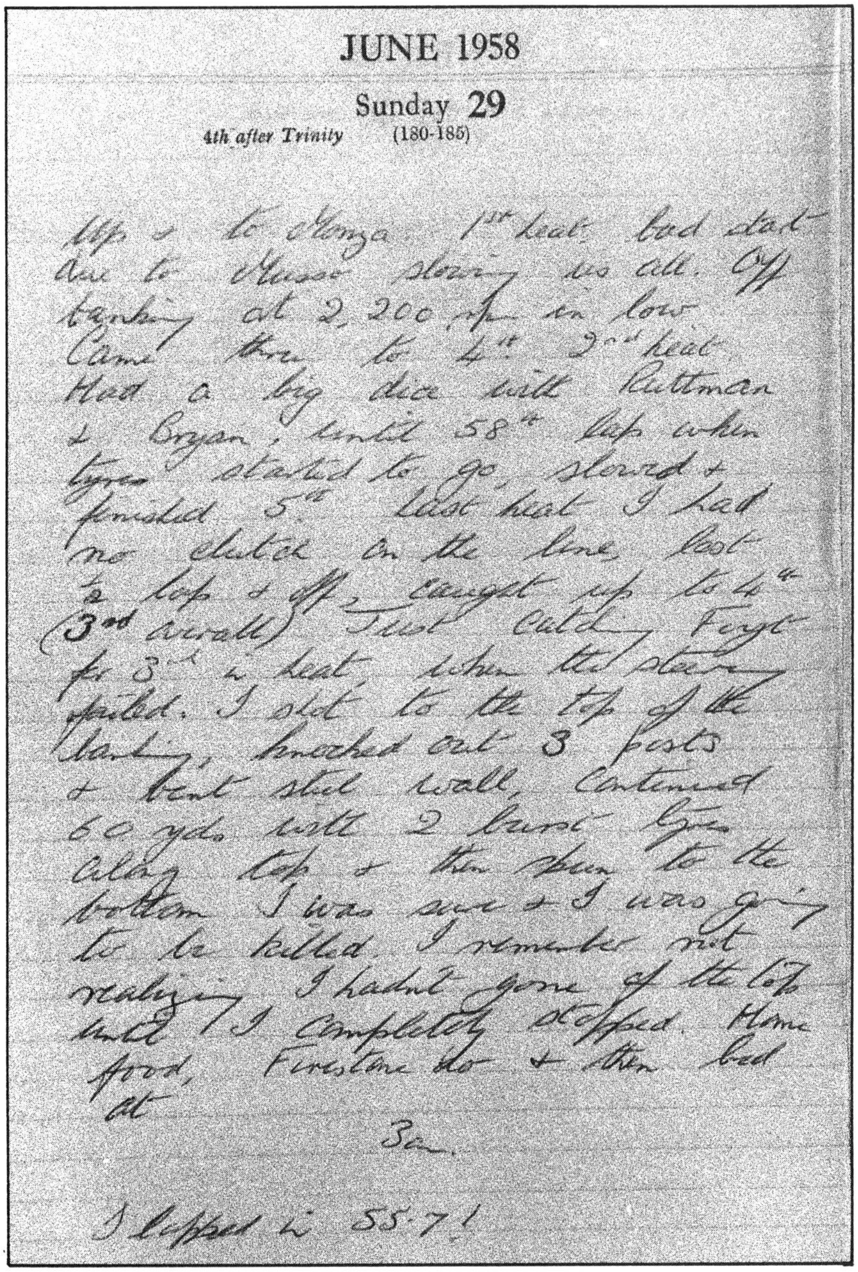

JUNE 1958

Sunday 29

4th after Trinity   (180-185)

[handwritten diary entry]

29 June 1958 — Two Worlds
Trophy, Monza — Stirling
opening-up the big 4.2-litre
Eldorado Maserati along the
Autodrome's Pista de Alta
Velocita main straight shortly
before its steering broke,
precipitating one of the most
alarming accidents of his long
career . . . Note the cast
Halibrand wheels replacing
Maserati's traditional Borrani
wire-spoked type.

and while Musso held everybody back on the pace lap and then used his road-racing gearbox to make a super start to heat one, mine was dreadful back in the middle of the grid. It was so bad, in fact, that when I came off the banking I was pulling only 2,200 rpm in low gear!

I managed to recover from ninth to fourth, then third, but after about 52 of the 63 laps I fell back to fourth again. Those Indy cars had lots of power and, although they were not noticeably quicker along the straight, they seemed more manageable round the bankings.

In heat two I was beginning to get the hang of this type of racing, and had a tremendous dice with Troy Ruttman and Jimmy Bryan, who would eventually win overall. We three were lapping at around 168 mph, battling for third place, but with five laps to go my tyres started to lose grip so I had to ease down and finished fifth.

By the time we formed up for the third and final heat my clutch had gone and I lost half a lap on the line, which I could not recover, although I climbed back into fourth place. I was behind a young American named A. J. Foyt, aiming to deprive him of third place, but the Maserati was feeling strange, wanting to drift high on the bankings and I was having to use increasing effort on the steering to hold it down to six to eight feet below the lip of the banking, running tight and fast. I was doing this, at over 160 mph, when suddenly my arms crossed as the steering sheared!

The car was fitted with tiny little 150S sports-car brakes — because normally they would hardly be needed in this kind of racing — which proved utterly ineffective as I hit them hard in the effort to save my life. It really was a very frightening moment, probably my worst ever, because there was no evasive action whatsoever that I could take.

The *Eldorado* swooped up towards the lip because I'd been running faster than the natural 'hands-off' speed for the section of banking I was on. It cannoned heavily along the steel barrier, which was all that remained between me and the drop beyond. It was a heavy car, travelling enormously fast, and it flattened two or three of the heavy barrier posts and bent the railing back for some distance. I was tensed there with my right foot jammed on its brake pedal and the other braced against the clutch-rest, pushing myself back into the seat.

The impact burst both tyres and plucked off a wheel and then the car slithered back down the track, losing speed all the way, until it finally subsided in a cloud of dust by the ditch at the bottom of the banking.

I stepped out and walked back, and that was the end of my speedway racing. I never let my mind brood on the possible consequences of such a frightening incident as that. They were an ever-present risk of my profession and as a professional I had trained myself not to think of the consequences. It had happened, I had survived, and I was able very successfully to close my mind to it. This showed neither courage, nor fearlessness, and certainly not foolhardiness on my part. Race-driving was for me a carefully considered business, and I have no doubt that I would have been ready mentally to drive that car just as hard round that same banking the following day had the need arisen, because I knew the risks, I was comfortable with them and through experience they did not unduly bother me.

Signor Zanetti subsequently had his car repaired and ran it — most unsuccessfully — at Indianapolis the following year, but because the American 500-Mile classic clashed with important World Championship races in Europe, it never made sense for me to tackle it; an enforced omission which I now regret.

Cooper-Climax T45 Formula 2 *(1958)*

'Formula 2 didn't mean much to me until I got into the Borgward-engined Cooper for 1959, but the previous year's Climax version was quite good, gutless compared to Ferrari and Porsche, but quite good fun . . .'

A new 1,500 cc unsupercharged Formula 2 class was instituted to run through 1957-1960. Cooper quickly produced a single-seat open-wheeled version of their central-seat Bob-tail sports car, using a similar water-cooled four-cylinder Climax engine in the rear. It drove through an ERSA-modified four-speed Citroën gearbox, which had been turned about-face as it was now in the rear end of a racing car instead of in the front end of a Light 15 saloon. The result was a very quick and nimble little car in which some had seen the beginnings of a potential Grand Prix winner.

I started late in Formula 2, halfway through 1958 in fact, its second full season. My début in the class came at Reims where the French GP was preceded by the 12-Hours and then the new Formula 2 *Coupe de Vitesse*. Rob Walker entered Maurice Trintignant and myself in his two Formula 2 Coopers which used bolt-on streamlined body farings for this very fast circuit. This was an Alf Francis mod, and in first practice it seemed to work well. I set fastest time of 2:37.6, 2.1 seconds faster than Peter Collins's much more powerful but conventional front-engined V6 Ferrari.

However, next evening I ran the Cooper unstreamlined, and although that cost 200 rpm along the straights my lap time improved to 2:35.6! So I raced it like this, and after a fair start I ran second behind Behra's sports-bodied Porsche, but only for eleven laps as my engine lost oil pressure and I retired.

Formula 2 did not enter my programme again until the Kentish '100' meeting at Brands Hatch on 30 August. I had tested both of Rob's cars, one leaf-sprung and the other on coils, which seemed better. The lap record in those pre-Grand Prix circuit days was 58.2 seconds, and my best in Rob's coil-sprung Cooper was 56.2. Prospects looked fine for what would be my first race at Brands in four years.

Main opposition came from the family! My father and my business manager Ken Gregory had founded their own team, the British Racing Partnership, running a Cooper for Stuart Lewis-Evans. I started from pole position, but my engine had a flat spot around 5,500 rpm and it hesitated as I left the line, enabling Stuart to take the lead. Brabham displaced him in the works car, and it took me ten laps to pass Stuart. That wretched flat spot lost twenty yards a lap to Jack, and my car did not handle as well as it had in testing. I equalled his new 57.8 seconds record but could only finish second. It was the first time Jack Brabham had ever beaten me, but unfortunately it would not be the last . . . Before heat two, Alf found a broken rear wishbone and cracked damper on my car, and blamed excessive fuel pressure flooding the carburettors for the flat-spot. I then made a bad start, but by lap three I was up into third place behind Stuart and Jack, and the car was going quite well. We set a new 57.4-second lap record. I passed Jack and attacked Stuart's lead, eventually taking it on lap sixteen. By lap 29 I was far enough ahead of Jack to lead overall on aggregate and so the Walker F2 Cooper notched another win, its first with me in charge.

My Formula 2 Cooper-Climax career thus involved only two events, but at least I won half of them! When I next sat in a Formula 2 Cooper it would have a fuel-injected 16-valve German engine, and my starts/wins ratio would improve.

'Knobbly' Lister-Jaguar *(1958)*

'A good car, lots of power from a 3.8 Jaguar engine, superior to the D-Types and hefty works Astons facing it . . .'

19 July 1958 — British GP supporting race, Silverstone — on the way to another victory, this time in the works-entered 'Knobbly' Lister-Jaguar.

*B*rian Lister's Cambridge company built a fine series of Jaguar-engined sports-racing cars in 1958, which were based on a 1957 prototype in which the brilliant little Archie Scott-Brown had been virtually unbeatable in English international meetings. However, poor Archie had been killed in his '58 works car at Spa, soon after having been beaten by the Ecurie Ecosse team's customer Lister-Jaguar, driven by Masten Gregory, at May Silverstone.

Brian wanted to put Ecosse in their place. We were both contracted to BP, so he asked me to drive for him in the British GP supporting race. In practice there at Silverstone I clocked 1:44.4 against Masten's 1:46.8, but while trying to improve his time he crashed heavily, doing his famous trick of stepping out *before* his car hit the bank! He broke his arm and shoulder, which left the tough American Walt Hansgen as my main rival, in our second works Lister. I liked my car, with its pugnacious 'knobbly' body, and I was able to lead from start to finish, averaging 97.2 mph, which was quicker than my fastest lap with the Formula 1 Maserati, four years earlier. Such is progress.

JBW-Maserati *(1958)*

'A car I never expected to drive at all, but one which did me a good turn . . .'

The JBW Formula 1 and sports cars were private-owner specials built for Brian Naylor by his mechanic Fred Wilkinson. The sports car which I drove used a Maserati 200S four-cylinder engine and its bodywork looked reminiscent of the contemporary pontoon-fendered Ferrari *Testa Rossa*. It was lighter than the Maserati and had potential, even though it remained very much a one-off and there never seemed to be any intention of selling replicas to anyone else.

I first tried this interesting special in practice at Karlskoga, Sweden, in August 1958, partly because I was interested and partly as a friendly gesture to Brian Naylor. I was quite impressed, because it was a second quicker there than my own more powerful, but much heavier, works-entered Maserati 300S.

The following weekend we met again at Roskilde in Denmark for the Copenhagen Grand Prix, a strange six-heat, two-day affair on a quite extraordinary circuit laid around an old gravel pit, and about the size of a football stadium. It had seven corners, and was most unsuitable for my 300S whose engine broke in the first heat. I did not finish, but the organizers gave me the time of the slowest finisher so that I could continue.

Naylor then lent me his JBW-Maserati, which was much more at home on this circuit than the 300S, and I was able to win the second heat with it by 11.8 secs and then the third by 19 secs. That night a spare engine was fitted to my Maserati for the following day's heats, so I returned the JBW with thanks. It was another type in my 'log-book' — and two more wins in two more races, albeit in this case only a third of the heats making up the event proper. Still, thanks to Brian Naylor's generosity and sportsmanship I had been able to maintain and improve my average . . .

'Costin' Lister-Jaguar (1959)

'A quick but rather ugly and over-bodied car which lost the advantage its predecessors had enjoyed in 1958 . . .'

I raced the 1959 Lister-Jaguar only once, under Briggs Cunningham's colours at Sebring. It was virtually the same as the 'knobbly' model beneath the skin, but now Brian Lister had adopted an almost banana-shaped Frank Costin-designed aerodynamic body which made the car both look and feel vast. Even so, it still felt good in testing so I was looking forward to sharing it at Sebring with the dependable Ivor Bueb.

In late-February 1959 we tested the new car at Silverstone. I was quite pleased with it. I found it handled better with 40 lb in the rear tyres than with the original 35 all-round, and with a 3.7 axle I saw 6,000 rpm on the straight and 6,100 after Abbey Curve.

Sebring was in March, and Ivor and I immediately found the Lister was over-geared. We corrected that and assessed the opposition — Ferrari, Porsche and a lone Aston Martin for Salvadori. We felt Ferrari would not go too hard early on if not pressed, so Ivor took the start. After 2½ hours we lay fifth, two laps down, with Ferraris 1-2-3. I took over and made up those lost laps to lead just into the fifth hour. It began to rain and in those conditions my lead increased, until I simply ran out of fuel.

We had obviously omitted the final churn-full at the preceding stop. Walt Hansgen brought his sister Cunningham-team Lister up behind to push, but there was too far to go to the pits so I waved him on. I hitched a lift on a marshal's motor cycle to fetch some petrol, but after sixteen laps in the rain I was disqualified for *not walking* to and from my car . . .

I later took over Lake Underwood's Cunningham Lister, but it was sixteen laps behind the leading Ferrari at that point and there was little I could do about it.

I did not drive the Costin-bodied Lister again. During the British season it became clear that Lister's day was over, for the new rear-engined Cooper Monacos and lightweight Lotus 15s ran rings round them. Poor Ivor died following a Formula 2 accident, and Lister closed down their racing interests soon after.

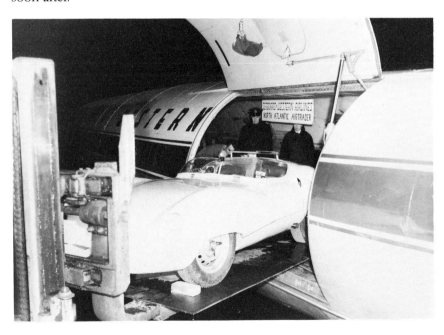

March 1959 — One of the Briggs Cunningham team's brand-new Costin-bodied Lister-Jaguars arrives in America courtesy Seaboard & Western airfreight, in time for the frustrating race at Sebring.

The Cooper-Climax Formula 1 Cars (1959)

'The 1959 Cooper really did corner at astonishingly high speed and was extremely responsive to the helm. I could dictate to it and throw it around, aim it and dice it as I wished . . .'

The interim-engined Formula 1 Coopers' successes during 1958 persuaded Leonard Lee, head of Coventry Climax, to authorize development of a full 2½-litre version of their four-cylinder Type FPF engine for 1959. It would produce around 240 bhp with a great deal of eminently usable mid-range torque and Climax would supply it to the Cooper and Lotus works teams, and to my entrant Rob Walker, for me.

These engines at last made the rear-engined Coopers truly competitive against the front-engined opposition. They became capable of winning anywhere. They could out-accelerate and out-corner most front-engined cars and could match them on straight-line speed.

The 260-horsepower Ferraris or BRMs could show their power advantage only rarely, because we could usually get back on to our 240 horsepower long before their drivers could exploit theirs.

There were some circuits, like Reims, where I might have preferred my Vanwall, but the Cooper was just as quick and its all-round performance much greater. The engine had so much torque it actually felt as if it had more outright power, which it did not. But it escaped the dreadful flat-spot of the Vanwall, and that enabled me to balance this already nimble car far more easily and consistently. It was easier to drive than the front-engined cars I was accustomed to. There was less motor car to control, it had adequate disc brakes, adequate performance and really very few problems.

Following Vanwall's withdrawal after the end of the 1958 season I arranged to drive Rob Walker's latest Coopers in the new year. Cooper actually sold him what were virtually kits of parts from which our mechanics, under Alf Francis, could build complete cars incorporating all our own tweaks. But Cooper could not help on a gearbox, which of course would be crucial.

Their old ERSA-modified Citroën-based gearboxes had hardly been man enough to cope with 2.2-litre power, and Cooper were not very confident about how they could improve them sufficiently to survive the new full-sized engine's power and torque over Grand Prix distances.

We thus had to make our own arrangements, and we turned to Valerio Colotti — who had been Maserati's chassis and transmission specialist — and who was now running his own *Studio Tecnica Meccanica* — TecMec for short — in Modena. Alf visited him and he agreed to design and manufacture a suitable transmission for us. This Colotti gearbox would shoot us in the foot during that Championship season — and we took a lot of cricitism for using it — but the truth of the matter is that we had no other choice.

Our first 2½-litre engine arrived in time for Easter Goodwood, on 30 March 1959. Our new car was what Cooper called the Mark IV although none of us used type numbers at that time, it was just 'the new car' or 'the 1959 Cooper' and that was it. That way we knew what we were talking about, even if today the historians want to put us right. The chassis had coil-and-wishbone front suspension and a transverse leaf spring at the rear which, as delivered from the factory, also provided upper lateral location for the rear wheels. There was a single lower wishbone, but during the winter Jack Brabham had experimented with additional upper wishbones to relieve the leaf spring of its wheel location duties. He found that they provided better control of rear wheel camber-change, which reduced the car's inherent tendency to oversteer. So double rear wishbones became standard on the works cars.

Mine, however, retained a single-wishbone rear end with leaf spring top location, and initially a normal Cooper gearbox. At Goodwood I encountered some most untypical problems. A steering bracket bolt was loose, which allowed the steering column to come adrift, and I clattered into the wattle fencing at Fordwater. The brakes were good but the car was difficult to handle.

I started from the second row and tailed Harry Schell's leading BRM. On lap ten I squeezed ahead at St Mary's, and finally won by about twelve seconds from Brabham. But the throttle had been sticking, the clutch was adrift and the gearbox packed up on the last lap! The car had been sliding about badly and I was working untypically hard to maintain control, though the new engine seemed quite good.

Our bet-hedging Cooper-BRM was being completed at this time and Alf took it to Modena to have the first Colotti gearbox fitted — see page 208.

I raced the BRM-engined car at Aintree and then the four-cylinder BRM itself at Silverstone, but at Monaco I chose the 2½-litre Cooper-Climax for my first Grand Prix of the season. It proved infinitely preferable to the unfortunate Cooper-BRM there.

How times had changed. The Monte Carlo grid saw eleven British cars facing four Italian and one German; the green (and Scots' blue) was dominant. I lay second behind Behra's Ferrari from the start, with Jack Brabham right behind me in his works Cooper. The order remained unchanged for the first 22 laps. I tried very hard to find a way past Behra, and finally did so by using the Cooper's basic cornering power to go faster through Ste Devote, which was slick with oil, and that enabled me to pass Jean up the hill towards the Casino.

Jack followed me through and the race settled with me easing up, some forty seconds in the lead. This wonderful state of affairs continued until lap 81, when my new Colotti gearbox broke. The bolts attaching its crown wheel to the diff cage had been threaded right down to the bearing surface instead of including

10 May 1959 — Monaco GP, Monte Carlo — winner and loser; Stirling leads the race here at Mirabeau Inférieur in Rob Walker's latest 2½-litre Cooper-Climax from Jack Brabham in the matching works car. Stirling's new Colotti gearbox will fail, Jack's Citroen-ERSA works 'box will survive. And he will win.

a smooth shank, and had sheared off due to this manufacturing oversight. The amputated bolt heads had picked up in the gear teeth, and — crunch — I was out.

That was the first Grand Prix I lost to the Colotti gearbox.

My car was fitted with double rear wishbones in time for the Dutch GP at Zandvoort. There I was pulling 6,750 rpm down the long straight into a head wind, over 150 mph, and although tyre wear was high the car felt good. I made a bad start — again — which in retrospect I believe was due to over-caution on my part, trying so hard to conserve those suspect transmissions. I was up into sixth place on lap 12, fourth on lap 24, and second by lap 40, and I was then able to close the gap on Jo Bonnier's leading BRM until I found a way past it on lap 60. I was leading my second consecutive Grand Prix, with only fifteen laps to go, but I only survived three of them before a ball race supporting the clutch shaft inside Colotti's bell housing broke up.

That was the second Grand Prix I lost to the Colotti gearbox.

The media made a lot of fuss about '*Moss Jinx Strikes Again*', and my old — in my view totally unjustified — reputation as a car breaker resurfaced. Jack's Cooper had won at Monaco with its gearbox internals still operating, but fit only for scrap; the gearbox environment in a 2½-litre Cooper really was murderous.

Otherwise, I had really taken to the car. It certainly could be thrown around, any time, any place, in an almost entirely carefree and certainly instinctive manner, and doing this never frightened me. Its low weight, carried low, also had a profound effect upon cornering speeds, and therefore on lap times. The Coopers weighed around 1,250 lb ready to run and their quite wide 6.50-section rear tyres and 5.00 fronts could generate cornering loads around 0.8G. Despite Cooper's massive-looking frame tubes, I could feel the chassis flexing, and in tighter corners the car would regularly lift its inside front wheel. In one way this was an advantage, because it reduced overall front-end adhesion and thereby balanced the car's natural inclination towards oversteer. But I also had to take this wheel-waving tendency into consideration when braking up towards the apex of a corner, because the lightly loaded wheel would easily lock.

After Zandvoort Rob suggested it might be better if I did not drive his cars until the gearbox problems were ironed out. This is why I drove the BRP BRM in the French and British GPs, and then returned to Rob's new Cooper for the German race at AVUS, Berlin.

During Friday practice there my car was geared for 188 mph at 7,000 rpm and I saw 6,600 on the straight. Even so, these little cars never gave the impression of going as fast as they actually were. Jack Brabham was timed at 181 mph at Reims, and I must have gone nearly as fast at AVUS, but it never felt like it. A car must be good if it gives that impression . . .

I was entering the tall North Turn banking at 140 mph but the suspension was bottoming there on the brick setts. The Ferraris were quicker, and then poor Jean Behra was killed in the sports car race. The Grand Prix was to be run in two sixty-lap heats, but I only lasted into the second lap of the first heat as a gearbox ball race again disintegrated, and fragments jammed the step-up gears which stripped.

I doubt if I had a chance of winning at AVUS in the face of Ferrari's power and speed, but that was the third Grand Prix . . . etc, etc.

The Portuguese race followed on Lisbon's Monsanto circuit. I took pole position but made another slow start, although I was able to recover and pass both works Coopers, driven by Jack and Masten Gregory, on the first lap. I pulled away without over-straining my car, and when I saw that Jack had crashed while chasing me I slowed right down by the pits to shout to John Cooper that he had gone off but seemed OK. I eased down and down, treating my car — and especially its gearbox — like Dresden china, and it held together. I lapped the entire field, finally 'doubling' Masten in second place with five laps remaining. The Colotti gearbox was right at last, this was my first Grand Prix win of the season and I was so pumped-up with delight I couldn't sleep a wink that night . . .

The Colotti gearbox had won its first Grand Prix!

For Monza Alf fitted knock-off rear wheels in case a tyre change should be needed. But we found it was left-front tyre wear which caused anxiety, not the rears'. There was no knock-off front hub available so we had a real problem. At Zandvoort, wily Jack had compensated for excessive left-front tyre wear by fitting a sports-car Dunlop, which had a full 8 mm-deep tread, so he had more rubber to wear away. Now he borrowed a similar tyre from Scuderia Centro-Sud, while we eventually found one on a very fast Lotus Elite which had been running in a supporting race before being shunted.

The Championship lay between myself, Tony Brooks of Ferrari and Jack Brabham, and we qualified in that order. Tony's clutch burned out at the start to wreck his chances, while I lay second early on between two Ferraris, Phil Hill's leading. I was content to sit there, while behind us Jack was intent on saving his tyres. When the heavier Ferraris inevitably stopped for fresh tyres I inherited the lead — as I had planned — and I won comfortably from Phil, with Jack third on tyres worn dangerously thin. I had started with 7 mm of rubber and finished with 1½-2 mm left. Denis Jenkinson wrote in *Motor Sport* '. . . *it is the ability to go fast and conserve his tyres, and to plan strategy while he is racing, that makes Moss the great artist that he is . . .*'

More to the point, Cooper-Climax clinched the Constructors' Championship with that result, so it had fallen to a British marque for the second successive year.

And the Colotti gearbox had won its second successive Grand Prix!

At this stage Jack, Tony and I had each won two Championship rounds and the Drivers' title would be decided by the inaugural United States GP, at Sebring on 12 December.

Meanwhile I drove Rob's car in the minor Oulton Park Gold Cup. I was on pole, Jack jumped the start — perhaps first-place money of £2,000 had something to do with that? — and unknown to me until I saw a signal on my eighth lap he was penalized sixty seconds for it. We ran in very close order: I was happy to hold a tight lead of only two or three seconds with that minute cushion, but meantime the stewards were reconsidering and when Rob signalled me the lead as being two seconds, not 62, I sprinted and won eventually by 5.2 seconds.

Now our much-maligned Colotti-gearboxed Cooper had won three F1 races in a row.

I was anxious to have as much going for me as possible in the Championship decider. Remembering how effective the Vanwall's coil-spring rear suspension had been, I thought a similar system could improve the Cooper, so we fitted

26 September 1959 — Oulton Park Gold Cup — Spirit of the age; Moss at speed in the Italian GP-winning Walker Cooper, about to add another Gold Cup to his tally.

18 October 1959 — Watkins Glen Libre *GP, upper New York State — Moss is push-started in the pristine Yeoman Credit 2 ½ -litre Cooper. Facilities were primitive up on the plateau in those days.*

a double-wishbone and coil-spring rear suspension to what had been my new regular car since AVUS. When I tested it, and told the press it felt better than the old leaf spring rear end, Rob told them 'It was Stirling's idea, so it had to work . . .'

I had two engagements in America followed by the Bahamas Speed Week prior to the US GP, driving an Aston Martin at Riverside, California, and then one of the Yeoman Credit-sponsored 2 ½ -litre Coopers operated by my father and Ken Gregory in the *Formule Libre* GP at Watkins Glen. This was the F1 Cooper's American début and we made the most of it.

I missed first practice watching TV, and the second was wet so I lined up seventeenth for the rolling start amongst a poor field. I lay second first time round and won by seven laps. The *Road & Track* report observed '. . . *Moss, while extremely affable, seemed to be a bit of a disappointment to the spectators. From their conversations, it appeared they had expected at least a Cary Grant in Mercury's winged helmet and sandals . . .*'

To beat Jack for the Championship I had to win at Sebring and set fastest lap. If I won but Jack set fastest lap he would take the title. Tony had to win and set fastest lap with both Jack and myself finishing lower than second place, so he was on the longest odds.

Both of Rob's cars, mine with its new rear suspension and Borrani wire wheels, and Maurice Trintignant's, had the latest FPF engines with the Mark II big-valve heads, which the works had been using since Aintree. I started from pole ahead of Jack and led, while poor Tony's chances evaporated as he was rammed on that opening lap by his team-mate von Trips. I felt confident, fairly sure that I could pull out an extra two seconds a lap if necessary. I had the measure of Jack and Bruce McLaren in their works cars behind me.

My confidence survived six laps, until the transmission broke abruptly, and I had lost the race and the Championship, again.

I was still not finished with the 2 ½ -litre Cooper. I drove it in the 1960 New Zealand Grand Prix, winning the heat but retiring from the main event with clutch failure; the Glover Trophy at Goodwood where I was well beaten into second place by Innes Ireland's new works Lotus 18; and the International Trophy at May Silverstone where Innes beat me again in the 18. By that time I was convinced that what we needed was one of these boxy-bodied new Lotuses, and although I would drive and enjoy my big InterContinental Formula Cooper through 1961 and on into the 1962 Tasman series — and would also race a standby 1.5-litre car very briefly at Aintree in '61 — my Formula 1 career in these marvellously uncomplicated and somehow friendly cars was over.

Cooper-BRM *(1959)*

'Another car I seem to have blotted from my memory . . . certainly not one of our greatest ideas!'

I had always admired BRM's 2½-litre four-cylinder engine and when I joined Rob Walker for 1959 we planned to evaluate alternative Climax and BRM engines in the latest Cooper chassis. We had no way of knowing if the new full-sized Climax engine would be competitive, whereas the BRM had a proven record as long as it kept running in their team's unreliable cars. It seemed a good idea to combine this proven engine with a Cooper chassis whose enormous potential was already clear . . .

S everal options had been open to me for 1959. Vanwall had withdrawn. I was very happy driving for Rob's well-run little team. I did not want to go with Tony Brooks to Ferrari and I still basically mistrusted BRM disorganization and unreliability.

I must also admit that I loved being cast as the underdog, and the prospect of driving for a little private team against the big factory battalions had terrific appeal. If I'm honest I should qualify that observation by adding that perhaps this was because the 'big factory battalions' in 1959 were not exactly up to Mercedes-Benz standards . . .

Ken Gregory set our Cooper-BRM project in motion by approaching Sir Alfred Owen, head of the Owen Organisation which owned BRM, and a loan engine was quickly arranged and delivered to Rob's Pippbrook Garage at Dorking.

Alf Francis would build the engine into a specially adapted rear-engined Cooper chassis, but we had the problem of finding a suitable gearbox. Cooper's could not or would not supply one, BRM had nothing suitable, so Alf approached our old Maserati chum Valerio Colotti who accepted the job.

Alf converted a standard production chassis with help from Rob's other mechanics, John Chisman and Mike Roach. Cooper's standard curved tubes were replaced with straight ones in the rear, and the major tube junctions were

18 April 1959 — Aintree '200' — Leading in Rob Walker's hybrid special Cooper-BRM before the first of what would become an agonising series of Colotti gearbox failures. It was difficult to merge BRM's ideal tuned-length exhaust manifolding into the Cooper package! The bulges on the nose make room for the large radiator which the powerful 4-cyl engine demanded.

all boxed and gusseted. The driving position went forward slightly because the new engine was longer than a Climax.

The car was completed with wider-than-standard front track, non-standard bodywork and Alf's own brand of rear suspension with a single top radius rod providing rather better-than-normal location for the leaf spring system.

In April it went to Modena for its new Colotti Type 10 gearbox and I tested it there at the Autodrome. We entered it for the Aintree '200' which I would have liked to win for the fourth consecutive time. But the car shuddered violently at the front under heavy braking, and was really difficult to drive. I was slower in practice than the works' front-engined BRMs, but in the race I made a good start from the third row and managed to run second behind Masten Gregory's quicker works Cooper-Climax until its clutch broke, so I inherited the lead. I was able to build a 27-second cushion and set a new lap record at 1:58.8 on lap 29, but it was very hard work.

Meanwhile, behind me in the gearbox a tab washer, which was intended to locate a nut on one end of a gearbox shaft, had broken. The nut worked loose, allowing the shaft to slide axially, which put the gear wheels out of mesh, and me out of the race. This was the first of many disappointments that season centred on Colotti's gearbox. His sidekick Giorgio Neri — who had been a race mechanic at Maserati's when I was with them — was in our pit that day, and he was heartbroken . . .

So was I.

Two weeks later I tried a front-engined BRM at Silverstone, but we took the Cooper-BRM to Monaco to back up our new Climax-powered car. It proved unstable and under-powered in practice, before its gear-change went awry so it was discarded and eventually sold, *sans* engine — a very low-mileage race car but one we did not miss.

Micromill *(1959)*

'To me all my racing was fun, but some of it was 'just for fun' which is a different thing. The Parisian Micromill circus provided a bundle of laughs, and an enormous shunt . . .

8 April 1959 — The indoor Grand Prix d'Europe des Micromills, in Paris, was a load of laughs — Harry Schell is leading here, but looking less than fully confident.

*T*he Micromills were tiny little French dirt-track cars run amongst stock car programmes, and sometimes indoors. This particular invitation event took place at the Paris *Palais des Sports* on 8 April 1959, and left me wondering just what I had been talked into doing . . .

*M*y diary entry records more or less — expletives deleted — the following: *'My car had duff clutch, last but came through to win first two Heats, in third Heat back axle snapped and fell on the ground — tried other cars but no good. In Final 'Harry'* [Schell] *'Nano'* [da Silva Ramos] *and SM charged round and Harry hit bale head-on, grand incident, my car turned over — ran and got second car, finished second. I was first overall, Nano second and Jean'* [Behra] *last. Food & bed at 2.30am . . .'*

Cooper-Borgward
Formula 2 *(1959-60)*

*'A very fine little
Championship-
winning Formula 2
car with a
particularly good
fuel-injected German
engine which was
more powerful than
the usual Coventry
Climax . . .'*

Both the British Racing Partnership and Rob Walker opted to use Borgward power in their 1959 F2 Coopers. This not only introduced much-needed variety but also offset the handicap which all 'independent' teams obviously suffered when racing against the factories who built our cars. Otherwise, they were always one jump ahead with latest developments. I was to drive Rob's Cooper-Borgward in Formula 2, and for the same season we were developing a new Cooper-BRM for Formula 1. We had thus fired two shots; the first would score a bull's-eye, but the second missed its mark completely.

We had heard a lot about this racing engine, designed for Carl Borgward by his chief engineer Carl Ludwig Brandt, which had been introduced in the Bremen company's 1500RS sports-racing cars. It was a 16-valve four-cylinder using Bosch fuel injection, and Ken Gregory had approached Borgward on our behalf through their London concessionaire. Carl Borgward was in his seventies but he was a shrewd old bird and made it clear he would supply engines, but only if I would drive one of the cars.

We agreed, and Rob was to run one car for me, while BRP ran two cars, initially for Ivor Bueb and George Wicken. George, however, was soon replaced by an incredibly quick newcomer named Chris Bristow.

Our prototype car was assembled in Bremen by Rob's mechanic John Chisman, using Rob's 1958 Monaco Grand Prix-winning chassis. In initial testing at Goodwood I was disappointed. This much-vaunted Borgward engine seemed down on power compared to a Climax, but Maurice Trintignant drove it at Easter Goodwood where I concentrated upon Formula 1 and then my turn came at Syracuse, five days later.

I had a new Cooper chassis — which Doug tells me was actually the Mark IV, although at the time I must say none of us bothered much with Mark and Type numbers. All I know is that it felt pretty good there, and certainly accelerated crisply. I beat Behra's front-engined Ferrari V6 by 0.3 second for pole position, and for twenty laps or so we had a wonderful dice. I got away from him while lapping back-markers but then he came back at me until I managed to gain five seconds as he was held up in traffic. I took the Borgward up to 7,900 rpm to consolidate my lead, and then in trying to regain contact Jean spun and so I found myself over a minute ahead with 21 laps to go. He closed to 23 seconds but I was watching the gap carefully and paced it to the end, thus winning on my Cooper-Borgward début, which pleased the old boy in Bremen very much. This was the first-ever British F2 victory over Ferrari — which was nice — and the new car had really excelled.

I did not drive the Cooper-Borgward again until Reims in July, commencing a busy series of French F2 events known as *Les Grands Prix de France*. The car was again very quick, screaming down the Soissons Straight at 7,800 rpm in top and achieving 7,300 rpm out of the fast curve just past the pits. I qualified on pole ahead of Cliff Allison's Ferrari — the car we had beaten in Sicily — and Hans Herrmann's streamlined works Porsche.

The F2 race followed the roastingly hot Grand Prix, in which I had exhausted myself trying to push-start my BRP BRM after a spin. Fortunately the afternoon had cooled, and I had recovered sufficiently to lead the F2 field with a Porsche on each side. Herrmann and I had a terrific dice, his Porsche having a higher top speed and better brakes than my Cooper-Borgward but eventually I managed to confuse him into taking the escape road at Thillois Hairpin so I emerged in a clear lead. Cliff Allison had made a poor start but ripped through the field to compensate, only for his engine to break with two laps to go.

That took the pressure off me, and I was able to cruise home to my second successive F2 win. Just for once I was delighted my day's racing was over. I was very tired, and very thirsty . . .

At Rouen the following weekend I was to drive the Reims car in Formula 2 and début the prototype Maserati Birdcage in the accompanying sports car race. I led both races throughout. Three Cooper-Borgward races, three wins.

After the British Grand Prix at Aintree it was back to France for the Clermont-Ferrand Formula 2 round in which, tragically, Ivor Bueb was fatally injured in his BRP Cooper-Borgward. This was my first visit to the new circuit, high in the hills, and the good-handling Cooper with that powerful and torquey German engine really suited it well. Borgward's fuel injection gave very crisp response and pick-up. The car was geared to 124 mph, and achieved it. Again we started on pole but the starter 'Toto' Roche — whose amazing antics had fascinated us for years at Reims — this time surpassed himself by stepping in front of me as he dropped the flag! I was boxed in as the rest shot off and Chris Bristow led initially in the BRP car with me in his wheel tracks. He drove very rapidly and very well. As I told Ken afterwards, he never put a wheel wrong, until I pulled ahead after four laps and held my advantage to the end. The news of poor Ivor's injuries robbed us of all enjoyment in this fourth victory in four outings, and Ivor finally died in hospital the following Saturday. Within a few hours Jean Behra's death had also been announced, killed instantly on the precipitous banking at AVUS in Berlin as he crashed his Porsche.

My first Cooper-Borgward race in Britain followed at Brands Hatch in August, but there we got it wrong. These 1959 Coopers used double-wishbone rear suspension as standard. The extra wishbone at the top relieved the high-mounted transverse leaf spring of its original secondary duty of securing the top of the hub-carrier laterally. In the earlier August Monday F2 meeting, most runners had found that the older Mark I to Mark III lower-wishbone-only set-

5 July 1959 — Coupe de Vitesse, Reims-Gueux — Shading his eyes from the evening sun while in hot pursuit of Hans Herrmann's Behra-Porsche at Thillois, Moss will win in Rob's fuel-injected F2 Cooper-Borgward. This was another engine which demanded an unusual tuned-length exhaust.

up gave more controllable oversteer for Brands' tight circuit. Most drivers found it useful to hang the tail out in a stable and predictable attitude. I didn't really drive my cars that way, but in the event the single-wishbone cars simply did a better job.

In the race I couldn't really compete. My car felt awful. Jack Brabham won from a Lotus with me third. It was my first defeat with Borgward power, in our last F2 race of the season.

Carl Borgward decided not to continue for 1960, but not before we had one swansong outing in the non-Championship South African Grand Prix at East London on New Year's Day. I drove one of the BRP cars there, qualified on pole and made a good start. Despite exceptional heat, the race progressed uneventfully and I led for fifty laps until one of the Borgward's fuel injection pipes broke. The engine spat and banged, Paul Frère caught me in his Belgian team Cooper-Climax, and he went on to win while my car stammered home second.

Ah well, you can't win them all — but certainly that Cooper-Borgward came remarkably close . . .

Aston Martin DB4GT *(1959-60)*

'All the closed road-going Astons seemed muscular and strong and a little agricultural, but the DB4GT was also quite well-balanced, it had bags of power and when I drove it against Jaguar saloons it was no contest . . .'

2 May 1959 — May meeting, Silverstone of course — Pole position, fastest lap and first place with the new Aston Martin DB4GT.

*T*he DB4GT had a handsomely chunky Touring *Superleggera* body and was powered by a 3.7-litre six-cylinder engine which gave around 300 horsepower at 6,000 rpm. I drove the prototype for the factory in the 1959 May meeting at Silverstone — four months before the model was officially launched at the London Motor Show. I also drove an open DBR1 in the sports car race and Rob Walker's Cooper in the International Trophy that day, but was out of luck in both those races. The new Aston then gave me the small consolation prize of winning the twelve-lap GT race, by beating Roy Salvadori in John Coombs' 3.4 Jaguar saloon.

I raced DB4GTs three times more, at Nassau on 29 November when I drove a car owned by Frank de Arellano of San Juan, Puerto Rico, and then the following year, at Easter Goodwood. In the Bahamas I won a five-lap GT race heat from Salvadori, but had the car break when leading the final, and then at Goodwood I beat Roy — in a 3.8 Jaguar — for the third time. It was odd that each of my DB4GT wins should be at Roy's expense, but none of them was in a very significant race. Even so, they still helped maintain my batting average . . . four more races on the total, and three more wins.

BRM P25 *(1959)*

'I must admit this was potentially a bloody good car! Probably the only Formula 1 car which I felt handled better than the Maserati 250F, very good engine, excellent steering — and not bad brakes when they were working . . .'

In 1959 I was torn between driving the new 2½-litre Cooper-Climax cars for Rob Walker and this now well-developed and very powerful four-cylinder BRM. We tried combining the best features of both in the Cooper-BRM, which didn't work, but I had already had one race in the P25 — unfortunately cut short by a stupid brake failure — and when Rob's Coopers encountered Colotti gearbox problems I was to turn again to the front-engined BRM. My friends in the BRP team were to run it for me, because I still doubted BRM's own ability to prepare Grand Prix cars adequately, but we never achieved the success which this great little car's enormous potential deserved.

Having tested the four-cylinder BRM P25s late in 1955, and then again in 1956 — and both times deciding to drive something else — I appreciated their gradual rise to competitive form in 1958. Two of the cars followed my Vanwall home second and third in the Dutch GP and in preparation for 1959 we began the joint Cooper-BRM project — see page 213.

The day after Easter Monday, 1959, I test-drove Harry Schell's works BRM at Goodwood. I considered the chassis and its general handling quite excellent, but the engine only fair. I lapped in 1:27 before the oil pressure sagged, and then did a 1:26.2 in Jo Bonnier's car, which had a better engine but a less effective chassis. I still managed to take Fordwater flat — hence my time, which was the first-ever 100 mph Goodwood lap.

BRM agreed to loan me one of their P25s for the International Trophy at Silverstone on 2 May. I enjoyed the car enormously there pre-race. Its engine gave 278 bhp at 7,800 rpm, its seat was comfortable and, although the chassis wasn't quite right — it felt a little bit too twitchy — I lapped in 1:40.2, a second quicker than Ron Flockhart's works car.

Jack Brabham beat me off the line in his 2½-litre works Cooper, ahead of the two new factory Aston Martins. I managed to pass Jack — which was never easy — on lap three with the BRM feeling just superb, easily one of the finest front-engined cars that I had ever driven by quite some way. Then something very strange happened.

As I entered Woodcote Corner on the fifth lap something felt weird as I lifted off the brakes and went back on to the power. I could neither specify precisely what it was then, nor can I now, but I was sure something was far from right. Consequently, after accelerating along the short straight past the pits, I decided to brake about 100 yards early for Copse Corner. It was just as well I did, because the front brakes had failed completely . . .

I was doing about 130 mph, and had I braked at my normal point I would have been going even faster and would surely have rammed the bank very hard indeed. As it was I decided by reflex to spin it, pirouetting to rest on the verge, about a yard short of the bank.

My doubts about BRM preparation unfortunately had been confirmed.

Subsequently, following my Dutch GP Colotti gearbox failure in Rob's Cooper, he advised me to find an alternative drive while the problems were sorted out. Before the British GP I tried the new, lightened and lowered Vanwall at Silverstone but its roadholding was poor and it was not competitive.

Meanwhile Ken Gregory and my father had arranged to borrow a works P25 BRM — chassis '2510' — and for their British Racing Partnership mechanics to prepare it at Highgate. It was painted in their colours of pale green with white wheels and I was to drive it in the French GP at Reims.

It felt superb in practice there. I lapped in 2:22.5 which was a new circuit lap record, but it wasn't fast enough, for Tony Brooks' latest V6 Ferrari took pole position at 2:19.4 which put me in my place!

*5 July 1959 — French GP,
Reims-Gueux — Stirling spins
the BRP BRM on melting tar
at Thillois, its clutch has
already broken and he is
unable to keep the engine
running. The temperature is
around 110° in the shade and
the attempt to push-start
unaided and with a broken
clutch utterly exhausts
him . . .*

My BRM ran rather hot, and I tried the works' team's spare before at last managing 2:19.9 in BRP's. On the Thursday we did not bring the car out for practice, so I could only sit and watch as Jack Brabham's Cooper and Phil Hill's second Ferrari bumped me off the front row of the grid. In final Friday practice conditions had changed and the circuit was slower. I tried 15-inch wheels to find some extra revs but saw only 7,900 rpm, while on 16s we had 7,500 which produced better lap times.

Race day was fantastically hot, as is usual at Reims in early July, and Tony went straight into the lead he would hold throughout to win for Ferrari. I diced for second place with the Coopers of Brabham, Gregory and Trintignant, but while the BRM clocked over 178 mph down the straight Tony's Ferrari was uncatchable at 186.

I ran second early on, then fell back to fifth, and despite setting a new race-lap record of 2:23.6 I was driving my heart out, and making no impression.

The BRM's clutch broke, leaving me crunching to and fro between second gear for the hairpins and top for the straights. At last around lap 36 I began to close a little, and two laps later caught Jack for third place. Phil Hill was my next target. On lap forty I set another record of 2:22.8 and Phil seemed within my grasp. Next time round . . . I spun on melted tar at Thillois.

Since the clutch was broken I could not prevent the engine from stalling. We had no onboard starters so I could only restart by pushing the car in gear. Any outside assistance would have disqualified me. I was already drained by the heat, and the hopeless exertion of trying to push-start the clutchless car finished me.

I raced the car again in the British GP at Aintree. I made a good start and lay third into the first corner at Waterways, but the clutch was slipping — as it had in practice — and I was rapidly demoted to sixth. Then the slip cured itself and by lap ten I was clear of the major bunch and running second 10 secs behind Jack Brabham's leading Cooper.

He pulled away, extending his lead to 15 secs by 20 laps and there was nothing I could do about it. On lap 24 I lowered the lap record to 1:58.6, and subsequently in two stages to 1:58.0 but still made little progress against the Cooper. With 40 of the 75 laps gone Jack was 12 secs ahead, by 50 laps just 10 secs but was I closing the gap or was Jack playing me like a fish on a line?

Ken then signalled me in to change tyres. It was a slow change which cost me 31 seconds. Towards the end fuel began siphoning from one tank to another instead of to the engine, causing it to pop and cut out, so I made a second precautionary stop to top up.

I rejoined in contact with Jack's young number two, Bruce McLaren, who drove by into second place. We had a good battle as I caught him a lap later, and although I could pass him I could not shake him off and we had a terrific dice to the line, which I won for second place by 1/5th sec.

I returned to Rob's Cooper in time for the next Grand Prix, at AVUS, Berlin, in which the BRP-BRM was totally destroyed due to another brake failure while being driven by my former Mercedes-Benz team-mate Hans Herrmann, who thankfully was not badly hurt. This was a sad end to a car which was actually vastly better than its results might suggest, and a regrettable finale to the brief BRP-BRM P25 story.

Maserati Tipo 60/61 'Birdcages' *(1959-61)*

'A fabulous car — light, very nimble, fantastic brakes, super steering, enormous torque and good power. Unusually for a Maserati it didn't leak much oil and you could drive it pretty hard and still it stayed together . . .'

7 June 1959 — Testing the new Maserati 'Birdcage' at Nurburgring during the 1,000Kms meeting — 'Guerrino' Bertocchi offering advice, as always, most of it good, for he had immense mechanical experience and was also a quick test driver in his own right.

Despite Maserati being on its beam-ends in 1959, Alfieri and Bertocchi and the boys were as keen as ever, and they produced this extraordinary sports-racing car using as its chassis the most bewildering-looking web of lightweight tubes that we had ever seen. After trying the prototype at Modena I knew it was a winner, and with one or two organizational hiccups that's the way it proved right into 1961.

I drove the 'Birdcage' Maseratis in only five races during my full-time professional career, one in 1959, three in 1960 and one final time early in 1961. My experience of the cars began the day after the 1959 Monaco GP when I reported to Modena to try this strange new Maserati. It had a 2-litre four-cylinder engine, developed from the old 200SI, which was canted at 45 degrees to lower the bonnet line. It produced 200 horsepower at 7,800 rpm, and drove through a five-speed gearbox. That amazingly complex spaceframe chassis carried a de Dion rear axle, and they fitted Dunlop disc brakes all round. The skimpiest aluminium body clothed it all, and the driver sat tall behind a very low bonnet which rose into enormous wheel-arches each side. The car weighed only 1,280 lbs — ridiculously light — and they named it the *Tipo 60*.

I first drove it at Modena Autodrome on Tuesday 12 May. I clocked 61.3 seconds and thought it was fantastic — so easy to drive. Its steering was exceptionally light and the brakes superb.

I asked them to take it to the Nürburgring for me to test again during practice for the 1,000 Kms where I was driving an Aston Martin. Unfortunately it seized on me before I completed a lap. Mmm, Maserati . . . but it felt great before it broke.

I was scheduled to drive in the F2 main event at Rouen in July, where the supporting event would be a 35-lap 2-litre sports car race, the *Coupe Delamere Deboutteville*. I persuaded Maserati to let me run the new car there, and we led throughout, keeping the revs down to 7,6, and so the 'Birdcage' Maserati had arrived.

For 1960 Maserati enlarged the engine to 2.8 litres, producing 250 bhp at 6,500 rpm, and they called this version the *Tipo* 61. They were in receivership, so could not run a works team, but would support any customer willing to pay the bills.

Enter Lucky Casner, an affable, smooth-talking American enthusiast from Miami. He talked Goodyear — who were nobody in international road racing at that time — into sponsoring a Sports Car Championship team of *Tipo* 61 Maseratis, which he bought, Maserati prepared and Goodyear largely paid for. He would provide the drivers, and he called his team Camoradi — CAsner MOtor RAcing DIvision.

Upon their début in Buenos Aires in 1960 the team ran a lone 'Birdcage' for Masten Gregory and Dan Gurney, who dominated the race until its chassis cracked.

Lucky then recruited me for the Cuban GP in Havana, on 28 February. This was now Castro's Cuba, and the Communists certainly ran things more efficiently . . . I learned the new part-aerodrome circuit in a borrowed Porsche Carrera and an RSK 1600 before the Maserati was ready, and when I finally took it out it felt very nice, but not exceptionally fast. For some reason the organizers then decided to cut the GP from 63 laps to fifty, but only told us about it on the start line. I led the opening lap, but without telling me Camoradi had fitted new and harder rear tyres and the car felt peculiar. I used only 1 mm of tread for the entire distance . . . and had negligible grip to match. I won, despite my seat also breaking lose and the exhaust system falling apart. Despite that start line briefing, the flag was finally waved at 51 laps instead of fifty. You can imagine how bad Cuban organization had been in Battista's day!

I was to drive for Camoradi again at Sebring, so I made it clear what I expected in preparation and that I preferred information to inspiration.

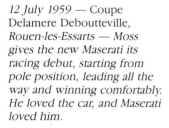

12 July 1959 — Coupe Delamere Deboutteville, Rouen-les-Essarts — Moss gives the new Maserati its racing debut, starting from pole position, leading all the way and winning comfortably. He loved the car, and Maserati loved him.

28 February 1960 — Cuban GP, Havana — The big-engined Tipo 61 'Birdcage' entered by Lucky Casner's Camoradi team, hence its white and dark-blue American racing colours. Those primitive Goodyear racing tyres were far too hard and gripless at the time, but once the company entered road racing seriously from 1964 they would come to dominate.

The 'Birdcage' was very fast there, and I was able to take the lead by lap three. After two hours I handed a fifty-second lead to my co-driver, Dan Gurney, but nobody had warned him I was due in so he wasn't ready when I stopped. That lost us time, but Dan was a superb driver — the best co-driver, along with Fangio, I think I ever had — and he soon pulled it back. By half distance we held a comfortable two-lap lead. We were lapping so easily at 3:23s that we had 5-10 secs in reserve should we ever need it.

But then, with four hours to go, Dan came in to refuel and announced that the transmission was playing up. It was terminal. Three more laps and the final-drive pinion shaft sheared . . . leaving the race on a plate to Porsche. *Road & Track*'s reporter understood Maseratis, as he wrote '. . . *it is to the credit of Moss and Gurney that the car lasted as long as it did . . . Moss drove the Maser with the delicacy of a surgeon . . .*'

In fact, I shouldn't have had to, for a really well-prepared 'Birdcage' would have been as rugged as it was rapid.

Camoradi and Maserati had a big sort-out before the Nürburgring 1,000 Kms where I next drove for them, but I was appalled when I first tried the car there in Friday practice. Its handling and even its normally magnificent brakes were awful. It was also at least 500 rpm over-geared. Next day Dan managed only two laps before an oil pipe broke so I didn't run at all; he reported the car felt better with its suspension lowered, but it was still over-geared. We were very despondent, but at least Camoradi had Piero Taruffi running the pits so our stops should be more efficient.

The 1,000 Kms was run in rain and mist, which made our day. The car had come good and I handed Dan a 2½-minute lead over Phil Hill's Ferrari after my first fifteen-lap spell. Dan then lost half a lap with another broken oil pipe but rejoined with a dazzling recovery drive through the mist and drizzle.

This was the kind of driving the 'Birdcage' allowed. On lap 24 he was 1 min 35 secs behind Phil's Ferrari. Next lap the gap had shrunk to 47 secs, the lap after that 15 secs and on lap 28 he came hammering past the pits in the lead. We dropped to third in our next pit stop, so it became my turn to attack and with 36 of the 44 laps gone I regained the lead to win my third consecutive 1,000 Kms on that magnificent Nürburgring circuit. It felt rather strange not to be in an Aston Martin, but this time I believed I could not have done so well without such a superb co-driver, because Dan was quite brilliant that day.

My Spa accident in the Lotus 18 then interrupted my season, and I would not drive a 'Birdcage' again until the following March in the Sebring 12-Hours. Camoradi's second season really was run on a shoestring, but they had a new rear-engined V12 *Tipo* 63 car for me to share with Graham Hill. It was dreadful in practice, handling twitchily, while the bumpy Sebring concrete hammered its frail rear suspension. Consequently Graham and I took over the team's second-string *Tipo* 61, but I was dubious about its preparation by race day. The field was lined up ready for the Le Mans-type start when, just to be certain, I asked 'Is that battery charged right up?'

'Yep,' they said, 'No problem, she's all ready to go'. The flag dropped and I sprinted across to the car, jumped in, hit the starter and . . . absolutely dead as a dodo. Not a spark. Yet I had specifically asked about it only a minute before! Unbelievable . . .

I lost six minutes before they persuaded the engine to fire. In two hours I hurled that car round to rise from dead last to second overall, and set a new lap record at 3:13.2. But after three hours we had to retire with the exhaust system all to pieces and the car threatening to catch fire. I then took over the *Tipo* 63 from Gregory and Casner and pushed it up from ninth to seventh before its rear suspension finally collapsed.

I did not drive for them again and, although I had no way of knowing at the time, that was actually the end of my long professional association with Maserati cars, almost seven years since that day at Modena when I had first sat in my original 250F . . .

22 May 1960 — Nürburgring 1,000Kms — Dan Gurney drove superbly with Moss in Camoradi's Tipo 61 to help Stirling clinch his third consecutive victory in the ADAC's sports car classic.

Cooper Monaco *(1959)*

'The two-seat Cooper-Climax for 1959 was one of the first large-capacity rear-engined sports cars but I always felt that, although it cornered very well, its wide aerodynamic body was not altogether advantageous . . .'

9 August 1959 — Karlskoga Kannonloppet, Sweden — The Keele Engineering-entered Cooper Monaco used a full 2½-litre Coventry-Climax F1-style engine. Moss won, of course . . .

The 1959 Monaco which I drove was my own. It was virtually a Formula 1 car clothed in a two-seat body, and I had it fitted with one of the first 2½-litre Climax four-cylinder engines to become available outside Formula 1. It was prepared and entered for me by a friend named Mike Keele who ran a light engineering business which built, amongst other things, Keele karts. I raced the Monaco only three times. It was very quick and 'chuckable' but at high speed it all became rather vague, and floated; probably due — I now realize — to aerodynamic lift with that enveloping body.

My début with this white-striped bright-green Cooper was in the British GP meeting sports car race at Aintree, and it was not very auspicious . . .

As the flag dropped it jumped out of gear, and the Hon Edward Greenall's Lotus promptly rammed me from behind. I got going, but stopped at the end of the lap to check damage. There was nothing serious, so I began one of my recovery drives, setting a new sports car lap record at 2:03.2. Then on lap thirteen at Anchor Crossing the cockpit filled with warm, stinking clouds of blue oil smoke. A pipe had broken and sprayed oil on to the exhaust which started a fire, so I retired.

That August I used the Monaco for my usual appearances at Karlskoga in Sweden and Roskilde in Denmark. At Karlskoga I wrote in my diary '*Bad brakes, jumping 2nd gear, duff clutch, broken roll-bar connector etc. F.T.D. 1:35.7 . . . Good start & led to finish. Car goes well, left-front brake locks and I was v. careful with the gearbox . . .*'

The Monaco touched 136 mph on the straight, and then at Roskilde I played around with its suspension, shifting the wishbone pivots to the lower of the holes provided, but that merely induced flick oversteer. Then I had to return to Jack Brabham the only pair of 6.00 tyres available after he had loaned them to me, and my car had proved quicker on them!

That Copenhagen GP was always a peculiar affair, run in three heats on the Saturday and then three more on Sunday, but this time I won four of them and put on a show with Jack's Monaco and David Piper's Lotus. I then sold the car, so my brief Cooper Monaco career involved only three events, yielding two more overall wins to sustain my batting average.

Porsche F2—718 *(1960)*

'Really, the only bad things about that car were its gear-change and the way it looked!'

Porsche initially entered 1,500 cc Formula 2 with their sports *Spyders* stripped of lights and other unnecessary gear. Jean Behra then had an open-wheeled single-seater developed for him from RSK-1500 sports car parts by my old associate Valerio Colotti. The Behra-Porsche ran well, and the Porsche factory quickly followed his lead. They dabbled with the class through 1959, before entering it seriously with a proper works team in 1960, and they loaned Rob Walker one of their new purpose-built cars for me to drive in his colours. It was quick, strong, quite reliable and another winner.

Huschke von Hanstein, of course, was the moving force behind our arrangement, and since these F2 cars would be eligible for 1½-litre Formula 1 racing the following year it would give us all valuable experience, with possible long-term potential. Having the full weight of the factory behind us was an enormous plus as it put us on a more even footing with the Cooper and Lotus works.

I made my Walker-Porsche F2 début at Syracuse, in Sicily, on 19 March 1960. The Porsche had been delivered direct from Stuttgart, resplendent in Rob's Scots-blue and white colours but with two factory mechanics in attendance. It had that little air-cooled engine in the tail, the most enormous drum brakes and stove-enamelled suspension parts. It was not much quicker than our familiar Coopers, but initially it was over-geared so I tried 5.50 rear tyres instead of 6.00s and we soon got into the groove, with quickest time at 1:58.2 against von Trips' 1:59 in the Ferrari. Suddenly Innes Ireland popped out in his ugly new Lotus 18 and knocked a tenth off my time. I had to make quite certain of pole with 1:57.6; Innes next up, then Gendebien's Cooper.

Innes led briefly before I got by, my engine revving its heart out yet feeling unburstable in that remarkable Porsche way. I had to drive quite hard to build a gap, but my lead over the Ferrari was eventually 10 secs. We had twice broken the lap record when rain began to fall. In the wet the Porsche proved quite tricky, and Taffy closed with the Ferrari, but as I completed my 26th lap the Porsche puffed blue smoke — a valve had dropped — and my race was over, Taffy winning for the home team.

OK, so Porsche's flat-four was not as unburstable as it felt . . .

The first Brussels GP on the Heysel circuit saw Jo Bonnier's works Porsche

10 April 1960 — Brussels GP, Heysel, Belgium — Wet weather racing was a Moss forté but Rob Walker's latest F2 Porsche did not offer great confidence in these conditions on the new part-Autoroute circuit.

18 April 1960 — Lavant Cup, Goodwood — Hot pursuit. Stirling trying hard in the Walker Porsche in pursuit of Innes Ireland's staggeringly fast new Lotus 18. The German car will finish second . . . Moss will take note.

pip my best time for pole, but our cars were clearly superior to all the Coopers. This was a two-heat race with the aggregate results decided by one point for a win, two for second place, etc, so the driver with the lowest total at the end of the day would win overall. I passed Jo after the first three laps and pulled away to win. His clutch failed, allowing Brabham's Cooper to finish second.

There were only eleven starters in heat two, mine the lone Porsche facing eight Coopers and two Lotuses. All I had to do was to finish second within 51 secs of Jack, but the Porsche jumped out of gear at the start and I finally staggered away in third gear, last. Jack was gone, right away. It was raining and again the Porsche handled dicily in the wet. I lay fourth until the rain stopped. The wind began to dry the track rapidly and I was able to take second place on lap 25. With two laps to go Jack was only fourteen seconds ahead, but as I left the hairpin my Porsche jumped out of second gear and I spun. Both first and second gears had gone, so again I staggered away in third, but Trintignant had just gone by and my third place finish left me with only second place overall, despite my aggregate time for the two heats being quicker than the winner's.

I feel I was entitled to regard that as a curious way to run a motor race.

At Goodwood on Easter Monday, Innes beat me fair and square in his Lotus 18, which was clearly faster than the Porsche, despite my car going well and having the edge under braking. I drove very hard, but there was nothing I could do about that darned green car. He beat me again in the F1 event, which really persuaded me that a Lotus 18 was the car to have . . .

The Aintree '200' was run to Formula 2, and we all believed the Lotus would probably shine again. However, I was determined to beat it and I put our Porsche on pole, with Jack second quickest and Alan Stacey third in the best of the Lotuses. I made a hash of my start, missing the upchange into third gear, and finding first instead; this punched the engine up to 9,000 rpm, which didn't seem to bother it! This left me down in mid-field, but I began to recover and got into third place behind Brabham and Salvadori, until suddenly they both retired and I led home a Porsche 1-2-3 from Jo Bonnier and Graham Hill, which rather put both Cooper and the new Lotus in the shade.

I did not like the Porsche's gear-change, which lacked a proper cockpit gate and was rather rubbery and vague, so Alf Francis fitted an old 250F gear-change instead. The Germans looked down their noses at us modifying their car, but it was a great improvement.

My Spa accident in Rob's Lotus 18 then knocked a hole in my season, and I did not race the Porsche again until Brands Hatch in August, where it suffered terrible carburation problems in the Kentish '100'. I went into the pits at the end of the opening lap and finished a very poor eleventh. At Roskilde in Denmark the car was again off form with gear-selection problems and I finished a poor fourth, after a young New Zealander named George Lawton had been killed in his Cooper right in front of me during one of the heats, a tragedy which marred the whole weekend.

Since the Porsche had run so poorly in my last two outings, my confidence in it had been considerably dented. The works assured us of their best possible preparation for the Austrian GP, which followed at Zeltweg aerodrome. Hans Herrmann and Edgar Barth drove the works cars there, while I returned in Rob's blue one, and we finished 1-2-3 with my car ahead after Jack Brabham had retired his Cooper with fuel-pump trouble. The race was stopped three laps early because the crowds broke through to the track. Thus my European Formula 2 Porsche career ended on a winning note.

I drove a Lotus with a 1,500 cc Formula 2 engine installed in the Modena Grand Prix but broke a valve tappet and retired, and then returned to the Porsche that December for two of the South African Springbok series 1½-litre races, the Cape GP at Killarney and the non-Championship South African GP at East London. I was able to win them both after a scrap with Jo Bonnier's works car. The East London race was run on 27 December and it felt very strange to be out in a racing car practising on Christmas Eve, and then stranger still to spend Christmas Day sprawled on a sun-soaked beach beside the Indian Ocean. Perhaps just to make it feel like home, I promptly caught a terrible cold!

My programme with that podgy flat-four Porsche had included nine races, of which I had won four and had been classified second in another which I would have won had its aggregate result been decided in a more conventional manner. So shall we compromise, and claim fifty per cent success?

18 September 1960 — Austrian GP, round the straw-bales on the Zeltweg Flugplatz — The final European appearance for Moss in the Walker Porsche, here leading Hans Herrmann's factory-entered car, Jack Brabham's Cooper and Tony Marsh's Lotus 18 special.

Austin-Healey Sprite (1960-62)

'Mention Austin-Healey to me and I instinctively think of Sebring — I had some good races there in those cars, both large and small . . .'

24 March 1961 — Sebring 4-Hours, Florida, USA — Moss leading the sister Sprites of Bruce McLaren and Walt Hansgen out of The Hairpin in pursuit of the far more specialised and potent Fiat-Abarths.

*A*t Sebring in 1960 the World Championship 12-Hour race was preceded by a 1,000 cc GT 4-Hours. BMC promoted their little Austin-Healey Sprite in this event and engaged me to drive for them in an effort to see off the far more potent Italian Fiat-Abarths.

*T*he Abarths were virtually tailor-made racers, against which my modified production Sprite really had no chance. The car understeered badly until I fitted herringbone-pattern Goodyear tyres at the front, when it improved but was still simply too slow. Although I led for the first half-lap after another good Le Mans-type start, there was nothing much I could do. My efforts to keep in touch used up all four tyres and I eventually finished second behind Paul Richards' winning Fiat-Abarth, having averaged 71.5 mph for 56 laps.

In 1961 BMC tried harder to beat the Abarths in the Sebring 4-Hours, running cars for me, Bruce McLaren, Walt Hansgen and my sister Pat — who shared hers with Paul Hawkins. I lapped at 3:55.3 in practice, which left my car needing three new tyres. It was doing only 103 mph with valve bounce at 6,700 rpm, and we were using 7,100! My clutch began slipping after an enormous dice with Walt and Bruce pursuing Bob Leiss' Abarth. He ran wide out of the final corner, Walt cut inside and won by a second after four hectic hours. Bruce and I finished 3-4.

Sebring's 1-litre GT event was only a 3-Hours in 1962. I was teamed with Innes Ireland, Pedro Rodriguez and Steve McQueen — the film star. It rained and I had a terrific time. I fitted Dunlop SP tyres and was able to leave the Abarths for dead even though they were driven by good people, Bruce McLaren and Walt Hansgen. I led by 7 secs at the end of the opening lap and pulled out 3 secs a lap until the rain stopped and the circuit began to dry. Walt and Bruce's cars were 15 mph quicker than my Sprite along the straight! They began to cut into my minute's lead. I felt I could hold on, but into the last half-hour my engine began to misfire with fuel starvation. I stopped to top up and could only finish third.

Jaguar 3.8 *(1960)*

'I raced the 'compact' Jaguar saloon only once, at Silverstone in the 1960 May meeting, and it was nowhere near as much fun as the old Mark VII had been . . .'

14 May 1960 — May Silverstone touring car race — A far cry from the old Mark VII, Stirling was not as impressed by Tommy Sopwith's Equipe Endeavour Jaguar 3.8. He started from pole position, and finished second.

I had been out of touring car racing for a long time, but following Mike Hawthorn's retirement and subsequent tragic death, and poor Ivor Bueb also being killed, there was a dearth of name drivers in the class come 1960. I accepted Tommy Sopwith's offer of a one-off drive in his dark-blue Equipe Endeavour 3.8 saloon at Silverstone. It was quite competitive, but it seemed much more nervous than the old Mark VII and nowhere near as forgiving. I lapped at 2:05 in practice $\frac{3}{5}$ quicker than Roy Salvadori — before that embarrassing accident when I spun my Cooper in a puddle while accelerating out of the pits and crashed into a parked Formula 1 Aston Martin! That was one time I saw Reg Parnell struck speechless . . .

Roy made the better race start. Second time round I cut past him at Stowe Corner and led until I was baulked along Hangar Straight. Roy took his chance to pull alongside, forcing me over to the right; that enabled him to take Stowe ahead of me and he subsequently held his advantage to the finish. I would never seriously race a Jaguar again.

Lotus-Climax 18s *(1960-61)*

'The car I drove during what I suppose was the peak of my career — typically Lotus, neither easy nor forgiving to drive in the Cooper sense but extremely competitive if driven with considerable care . . . a curious mixture of simplicity and sophistication which brought me quite a lot of success; when it wasn't trying to kill me!'

During 1954 in my own Maserati, I had still been learning. In 1955 in the Mercedes, I followed in Fangio's wheel-tracks, and then I made my own mark leading Maserati in 1956 and Vanwall in 1957-58. By the time I drove Rob Walker's private Coopers in 1959 I was confident enough positively to enjoy the role of under-dog by driving a private car against the factory teams. I was turning thirty, I guess I was regarded then as 'fully mature'. I was the driver by whom others measured their performances, and then came 1960 and the introduction of Colin Chapman's first rear-engined Lotus . . . a car which I would drive through most of that season, and far into 1961, and with which I was able to enjoy some great times, and survive a few bad ones.

I believe I first saw the new rear-engined Lotus 18 in the dusty paddock at Buenos Aires before the Argentine GP in February 1960. Team Lotus had previously been struggling with their Vanwall-shaped front-engined Type 16s. Colin Chapman's theories had persuaded him that those cars would be quicker than our comparatively primitive rear-engined Coopers, but they were not. Nothing like . . .

They had a complicated zig-zag prop shaft involving several universal joints as it snaked from the front-mounted engine, alongside the driver's seat, into an offset gearbox at the back. Each change of direction absorbed some power which they could not afford, since they used the same Climax FPF engines as ours. The Lotus 16s also understeered terribly, whereas our agile rear-engined Coopers loved nothing better than to wag their tails and oversteer round tight turns. We could run rings round the Lotuses virtually everywhere.

Even so, I knew from my Vanwall experience just how good Colin's chassis-design skills could be. His sports cars were very advanced and effective, and it was obvious that once he perfected a Grand Prix design then Cooper's practical approach would be outdated.

This finally happened in 1960, but Team Lotus could not build the GP-distance reliability into their works cars which would have been necessary to prevent Jack Brabham winning five consecutive GPs for Cooper to clinch their second consecutive World Championship titles.

The Lotus 18 was nothing to look at — just a biscuit box on wheels with a funny rear suspension in which the half shafts positioned the wheels laterally at the top, assisted by a reversed lower wishbone down below, where the foot of an exceptionally tall cast hub-carrier extended almost to the ground. Two long trailing radius rods each side provided fore-and-aft location.

The 2½-litre Climax FPF engine sat behind the cockpit, mated direct to the latest development of Lotus's own five-speed gearbox-cum-final-drive unit which had a motor-cycle style positive-stop gear-change instead of a conventional gate.

When this gearbox had been introduced in the front-engined Lotus 16s, the driver just jerked the gear-lever back to change up and forward to change down, the lever itself always springing back to the same position between changes in a similar way to the early Cooper 500S. Now in the 18s a migratory lever was used, clocking fore and aft against two ratchets. It took some getting used to, and Colin's right-hand man Mike Costin aptly christened it the Lotus 'queerbox', and it stuck . . . in gear usually. It was typically Lotus, very quick, but very fragile.

We would only use this gearbox three times — at Monaco, Zandvoort and during my brief practice outing at Spa — before fitting the more conventional Colotti 'box when our Lotus 18 unfortunately had to be rebuilt.

In Buenos Aires, Team Lotus driver Innes Ireland left us all virtually for dead in his peculiar-looking new car until it began to fall apart around him, which made us feel a little better!

Back home the 18s then began winning in 1,500 cc Formula 2. At Easter Monday Goodwood, Innes drove two new works 18s, one 1,500 cc Formula 2 the other the 2½-litre for Formula 1, and he beat me in both races which I regarded as exaggerating a bit.

He beat me first in Rob's F2 Porsche and then gave me a close-up view of his F1 car's tail-end for 37 laps in the main race while I drove Rob's Cooper. The 18's traction was undoubtedly superior to my car's, and it was also faster through the corners.

I was being beaten, badly, and then the same thing happened at Silverstone. Same car, same driver, same situation and same result — except that at Silverstone Innes broke the lap record while I broke one of the Cooper's suspension members, something I had never done before.

Rob had already decided we needed a Lotus 18 to combat these works cars, and had placed his order for one after Goodwood. It was a straightforward customer deal — we asked for no special concessions, and got none. Later in the season, when Team Lotus fitted new wide-rim wheels, it was only when I spotted this improvement in the pit-lane that we were able to order some.

Rob's 18 was completed only seven days before the Monaco GP and I tested it very briefly at Goodwood. I lapped at 1:23.7 and found the car staggeringly fast and responsive . . . so responsive it became a pure extension of its driver.

That's not to say it was easier to drive than the Cooper, because it was not. It was never as forgiving nor as 'chuckable'. The Cooper really allowed one to take enormous liberties and get away with them, whereas the Lotus was a far more delicate instrument demanding precision. You had to keep it operating within a very tight envelope and if you could maintain it within those limits its ultimate braking, cornering and traction were all superior to the Cooper's.

With experience I quickly found that if it wasn't doing just what I wanted it to, then there were a host of adjustments which could be made. Once we started racing the car I found there were perhaps too many.

In some ways it was curiously insensitive. For example, we could change the camber on the rear wheels, or their toe-in, without me noticing very much difference on the road. It was all too easy to make a change and find an improvement and so do something else which made it worse, and so on, until time ran out and I had merely worn out the engine trying different things.

So eventually I tended to limit work on the Lotus so that starting with the same tyre pressures front and rear I could get a little more oversteer or understeer by changing pressures and then we refined this by altering the damper settings. I seldom changed the anti-roll bars.

I practised both the Cooper and Lotus at Monaco, and when I clocked 1:36.3 in the 18, 4 secs inside the existing lap record and a second faster than Brabham, I decided to race it.

I moved into second place behind Jo Bonnier's new rear-engined BRM on lap five of the race, and as the rest of the field closed up behind me I was able to ease ahead on lap seventeen. It began to rain and I eased back, which allowed Jack Brabham to take the lead from me in his Cooper. But the circuit was viciously slippery in places and on lap 41 he hit the wall at Ste Devote. When the rain stopped around half-distance I held a fourteen-second lead over Bonnier, and then my engine stammered on to three cylinders. I stopped at the pits expecting the worst, but it was only a plug lead adrift. Jo had inherited the lead, but on lap 68 I won it back and held it to the finish. In the closing stages the normal vibration from the big four-cylinder Climax engine behind my shoulders felt a wee bit harsher, but fortunately I did not appreciate why. In fact, the front engine mounts had snapped and the unit was left hanging on a water pipe. Significantly, the Lotus 'queerbox' survived the entire distance. Just as in 1958 when Rob's team had given Cooper their maiden *Grande Epreuve* win, we had now done the honours for Lotus. It was quite a landmark victory; another for myself and for Rob, to whom nothing was too much trouble. It was always a pleasure to drive for him.

I managed to qualify on pole position for the Dutch GP at Zandvoort one week later, lapping in 1:33.2 but troubled by heavy vibration and the Lotus understeering on empty tanks but oversteering when they were full.

Once again I started slowly, pacing myself into the race to run second behind Brabham. This was a conscious effort on my part, as previously I had told Rob that I was sick of contemporary talk in the media about my being a car-breaker — based on the evidence of our Colotti gearbox problems the previous season. I told Rob I intended to sit behind whoever led, probably Jack we thought, and try to win from behind instead of what had become my usual style of going hard from the start and really racing all the way, which is how I felt sincerely that a proper racing driver should drive. This was the only point upon which my philosophy ever differed significantly from Fangio. He sometimes advocated winning at the slowest possible speed. That was anathema to me. I believed that if you could win and break all records along the way then go for it Boy . . .

As it was, I sat religiously on Jack's tail that day at Zandvoort until on lap seventeen, tearing through the little woodland curve on the far side of the circuit, Jack's Cooper clipped a concrete kerb. To my horror, his wheel flicked up a great chunk of loose kerbing — I believe it weighed 12 kg — which smashed into my Lotus's left-front wheel, bursting the tyre and denting the rim. I slewed wide, missed a tree by a tiny margin and then bumped round into the pits, losing three minutes while Alf Francis and the mechanics fitted a fresh wheel and tyre — which they had to borrow hurriedly from Team Lotus! — and checked the suspension.

I rejoined twelfth — second to last — and ripped into the field. It was another of those come-back drives I relished so much, despite always raging inwardly at whatever misfortune had triggered them. By lap 32 I lay tenth, lap 41 ninth, lap 45 seventh and by lap 60 I was back up to fourth. Graham Hill in the BRM just saved his third place by 1.1 secs on the line.

After that, I was convinced that the only safe way to race was to lead right from the start . . .

The Belgian GP followed at Spa. We knew the front-engined Ferraris should be quick there but in first practice Jack's 'Lowline' Cooper tore round 7 secs quicker than the existing — albeit two-year-old — record, 2.5 secs quicker than Phil Hill's Ferrari and 2.6 quicker than my best in Rob's Lotus.

Early in the Saturday morning session I was travelling through the long downhill sweep of Burnenville Corner at around 140 mph in fifth gear when I struck the hump in the middle of the curve and my car's left-rear wheel came off as the axle shaft broke.

All I knew at that instant was that the car had suddenly developed the most violent oversteer I had ever experienced. I hadn't a clue what had happened. I piled on full opposite lock and jammed on the brakes to scrub off speed — fast!

The car spun like a top, at which moment I saw the wheel bounding away on its own. I realized I was going to hit the steep left-side bank backwards, at around 90 mph. I braced myself between wheel and seat-back — which fortunately spread the load as we did hit backwards — and then I can just remember my head being violently jerked back . . .

I next remember coming round, realizing I was out of the car, crouching on my hands and knees, gasping for breath. The car was lying right-side up at the end of a long smear of tuffets and debris laid across the road. I felt terribly alone. I simply could not breathe. I remembered passing Bruce McLaren earlier on that lap and I couldn't think why he was taking so long to arrive. In fact, he stopped immediately and ran to me. I begged him to give me artificial respiration but he rightly refused in case I had broken ribs. Other drivers arrived, parked their cars, switched off and came to help. Then eventually marshals and an ambulance appeared.

18 June 1960 — Belgian GP practice, Spa-Francorchamps — American gentleman-photographer Jesse Alexander froze these frightful moments as Stirling's Walker Lotus 18 lost its left-rear wheel when set-up at high speed through the Burnenville Curve. The car has already completed one pirouette in the first shot, and it has long since thrown Stirling out onto the far verge as it somersaults back off the embankment in picture two.

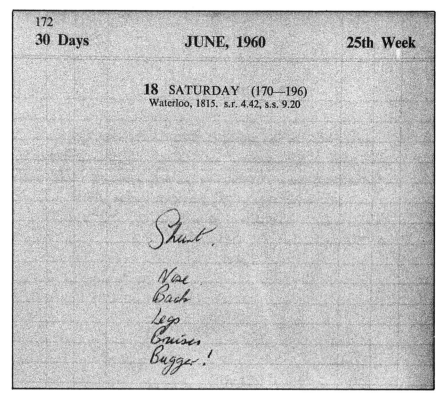

172
30 Days   **JUNE, 1960**   **25th Week**

18 SATURDAY   (170—196)
Waterloo, 1815. s.r. 4.42, s.s. 9.20

Shunt.

Nose.
Back
Legs
Bruises
Bugger !

18 June 1960 — Burnenville Corner, Spa-Francorchamps — Aftermath of the accident with the Monaco-winning Walker Lotus. **Above right** *Belgian driver/journalist Paul Frere examines the cockpit.*

The sun was blazing down so they held a blanket over me for shade. I had to fight for every breath. My nose was crushed. I knew my legs had suffered too. Somebody cut the elastic cuffs of my overalls and removed my watch. I could hear them speaking but my sight had gone — everything was blurred and dark. I was terrified I was going blind, and that a broken rib might puncture a lung — if it had not already. Then came some relief as I remembered that wheel bounding away. At least the accident had not been my fault . . .

They took me to Malmédy Hospital, and two days later I was flown to St Thomas's in London. Jack Brabham had won the race, but in the same practice session in which I had crashed, Mike Taylor was badly hurt when his Lotus 18's steering broke, and in the Grand Prix itself both Alan Stacey and my former Cooper-Borgward protégé Chris Bristow had been killed . . .

As described elsewhere — see page 247 — I was actually back in business within two months, when Rob had a shiny replacement Lotus 18 assembled ready for my World Championship come-back at Oporto in the Portuguese GP. The car now had a Colotti gearbox in place of the Lotus one.

I was already happy that my skills were unaffected, but I could only qualify on row two. As the race developed I ran second behind new boy John Surtees — the multiple motor cycle World Champion who had just turned to cars — driving a Team Lotus works 18. His car control was phenomenal, but boy did he take some chances . . .

My engine then ran rough and I had to make two stops for plugs, falling back to tenth. Surtees spun off and Jack Brabham notched his fifth consecutive GP win and clinched his back-to-back Championship titles. I had a front brake lock on lap 51, just four from the end, hit the bales and stalled. I restarted by pushing my car downhill against the race direction, just as I had advised Mike Hawthorn to do on the pavement two years before, when I inadvertently deprived myself of the world title. Times had changed. This time they disqualified me!

The British teams boycotted the Italian GP at Monza where the entirely unsuitable high-speed track was being incorporated into the GP circuit. I won an F2 race in Austria driving Rob's Porsche, and then returned to the Lotus for the minor Oulton Park Gold Cup. My pole time of 1:40.4 was just short of the 100 mph mark. I made a bad start, but after a terrific dice with Brabham and Innes Ireland's works 18 I inherited the lead when Innes' gearbox broke, and pulled away from Jack to win comfortably by 23 seconds.

I drove a Parnell team F2 Lotus 18 at Medena but its valve gear packed up on me.

We took two 18s to America, where I won the *Formule Libre* GP at Watkins Glen by 7 secs from Jack's Cooper, and then at Riverside, California, for the second United States GP I took a commanding lead after Jack's Cooper caught fire briefly and, despite fluctuating oil pressure for the last fifteen laps, I enjoyed another comfortable win.

Above *14 August 1960 — Portuguese GP, Oporto — Stirling's come-back to Formula 1 in a freshly-built Walker 18. Here Rob's long-faithful racing mechanics John Chisman and Tony Cleverley, and Stan Sparks, prepare to push-start the 2½ -litre engined Lotus. Note how F1 cars built to those regulations had neither roll-over protection behind the driver's head, nor onboard starter motors.*

Above right *Fruitful partnership — Stirling with 'Alf Francis', the master racing mechanic whose skill and application over so many years helped bring out the best in Moss the driver. Theirs was a sometimes stormy but friendly relationship based on mutual respect . . .*

That was the last race of the 2½ -litre Formula, as for 1961 a new ceiling of 1½ -litres would be applied, and the cars would be heavier, with onboard starters and mandatory roll-over protection behind the driver's head.

Because of my Spa accident, I had run the Lotuses in only six races, winning four, starting from pole position five times, and setting one fastest lap. Not a bad success rate . . .

Laurence Pomeroy, the eminent technical journalist, wrote: *'In 1960, driving the Type 18 Lotus, Stirling Moss developed driving technique to a level never before realized and proved himself indisputably the World Master of his time . . .'*

Yes, well . . . nice of him to think so.

At the start of 1961 we raced the 2½ -litre Lotus 18 down under, where I won the preliminary heat before the New Zealand GP at Ardmore, only for a half-shaft to break at the weld in the big race itself, which put me out. Jack Brabham beat me into second place at Christchurch in the Lady Wigram Trophy, but there I was shunted twice, the carburettors were all but knocked clean off my engine, and the race was shortened by fifty miles due to rain. In Australia, at Sydney's Warwick Farm race course, I managed to win again at record speed. The air temperature there was 110 degrees, on the track surface it was 148! That is Hot.

For the new 1961 Formula, Colin Chapman produced an all-new streamline-bodied Lotus 21 to be used by his works drivers. But Team Lotus was backed by Esso while Rob and I were contracted to BP. Thus far Lotus's only World Championship race wins had been achieved courtesy of Walker Racing, BP thus sharing the glory. Esso, quite understandably perhaps, disliked being beaten by the enemy armed with a car whose development they had financed.

So Colin was not allowed to sell us a Lotus 21. There was no alternative chassis on the market which could possibly compete. Therefore we had to make do with the old 18. What's more, the promised new 1½ -litre Climax V8 engine would not be available to anybody until late-season, so we would have to rely on their humble F2-derived 1,500 four-cylinder.

Faced now by Team Lotus with equal engines but a superior chassis, and by the factory Ferrari and Porsche teams with what promised to be superior engine power, I was clearly going to be the underdog with a vengeance that season.

By this stage in my career I regarded this quite confidently as a nice challenge to be positively enjoyed. Our obsolescent Lotus 18, like many other private owners', was to be progressively updated with 21-style ideas that year, replacing the half-shaft lateral rear-wheel location by upper links, and adopting sleeker, more slippery body panelling resembling the Type 21's.

The old car was still in box-body form when we began our new Formula 1 programme at Goodwood on Easter Monday. Old F1 machinery was being perpetuated in the new InterContinental Formula, and I won that race on the Goodwood programme in Rob's Cooper, then fielded the Lotus 18 for the

1½-litre F1 feature race. My engine was off-song throughout so I could do nothing about John Surtees's Cooper, which won easily. I trailed him closely until lap 32 when the misfire began and I fell away through the field to finish fourth.

At Brussels we still could not persuade our engine to run cleanly. I drove our spare car there which had a Lotus gearbox instead of the Colotti in our usual 'Walker Special'.

I was despairing of getting the cars to run properly and it was not until some time later that Alf identified the problem. It appeared mainly at high speed. Weber had recently introduced mass-production in their Bologna factory, changing from what had formerly been a virtually hand-made carburettor. Minor flaws in the mass-produced instruments now caused the floats to stick intermittently, and dependent upon where they stuck the inlet tract would either flood with too much petrol, or starve without enough. Alf cured it by carefully hand-finishing the inside of the float chamber castings. Later, at Monaco trouble persisted in first practice. That night Alf and the Weber rep stripped and matched our carburettors against a new one. One of ours had one tiny drilling omitted!

I was eventually placed seventh in that Brussels GP but then took in a very minor Austrian F1 race, the *Vienna Preis*, on Aspern aerodrome, and won against negligible opposition. But later that April we had a terrible outing at Syracuse, finishing eighth and still suffering that mysterious carburation problem. A

239

```
              XIXme GRAND PRIX AUTOMOBILE DE MONACO

                     CLASSEMENT AU 100me TOUR


                     CLASSEMENT PROVISOIRE

   1er    20    MOSS         LOTUS              2h45'50 1/10    113;787

   2me    36    GINTHER      FERRARI            2h45'53 7/10

   3me    38    HILL   Phil  FERRARI            2h46'31 4/10

   4me    40    VON TRIPS    FERRARI       A DEUX TOURS

   5me     4    GURNEY       PORSCHE       A DEUX TOURS

   6me    26    McLAREN      COOPER CLIMAX A CINQ TOURS

   7me    42    TRINTIGNANT  COOPER        A CINQ TOURS

   8me    32    ALLISON      LOTUS CLIMAX  A SEPT TOURS

   9me     6    HEREMANN     PORSCHE       A NEUF TOURS

  10me    28    CLARK        LOTUS         A ONZE TOURS

  11me    22    SURTEES      COOPER        A 32  TOURS

  12me     2    BONNIER      PORSCHE       A 41  TOURS

  13me    16    BROOKS       B.R.M.        A 46  TOURS



        Meilleur tour N° 20  MOSS     LOTUS     1'36 3/10   Moyenne   117;697 KM

                    N° 36  GINTHER  FERRARI   1'36 3/10   Moyenne   117;697
```

14 May 1961 — AC de Monaco bulletin tells the story.

newcomer named Giancarlo Baghetti dominated in Ferrari's prototype 1½-litre V6 'shark nose' car. Now our chances for the World Championship races really did look ominous . . . At least the InterContinental Cooper was being kind to me during this period, winning again at Silverstone.

The Monaco GP opened the new World Championship on 14 May. We had one of the new Mark II Climax FPF engines there, using a strengthened bottom end developed from the big 2½-litre version which allowed higher revs and a wider torque band. I was able to qualify on pole. We had a panic before the start as a chassis tube was found to be cracked, but Alf calmly welded it on the starting grid, despite thirty-gallons of fuel still in the tanks within inches of his torch-flame because there was no time to empty them!

Jimmy Clark qualified his new Lotus 21 on the front row but it was the works Ferraris of Richie Ginther, Phil Hill and Taffy von Trips which worried me. I resolved that if they wanted to win this race they would have to fight hard for it. I might be in a year-old car, with an inferior engine, but it suited the tight Monaco street circuit, and I would make them go — go all the way.

I won, by 1.2 secs, at the end of 100 laps. It was, I believe, my greatest drive.

I will never forget when *God Save the Queen* was played. I had been wound-up tight for nearly three hours, I had eventually won from Richie Ginther's Ferrari. He and his team-mates had never allowed me to relax for one moment, and then came the chequered flag and that release of pressure and the National Anthem made the old eyes prickle, I can tell you. It really was a very emotional moment, and I don't think I'm a very emotional man.

Beating those more powerful Ferraris with what was essentially an obsolescent car meant a lot to me. Our 150 bhp had beaten Ferrari's 180 bhp.

We had no chance at Zandvoort where the Ferraris could fully exploit their power advantage and I both qualified and finished fourth.

14 May 1961 — The greatest race, Monaco GP, Monte Carlo — Having just toured in from a tumultuous reception on his cooling-off lap, Stirling is hugged by his obviously ecstatic Dad, Jacques Taffe of the AC de Monaco looks on (left), while on right car constructor Colin Chapman shares a quiet word with Dean Delamont of the RAC.

Middle right *Monaco's great former Champion driver Louis Chiron gives SM a Gallic greeting; what was 'Chunky' Chapman thinking behind that enigmatic smile? "Bloody Moss . . . He's magic"?*

Bottom right *The Anthem; a highly emotional moment, for normally unemotional Moss . . .*

I then drove for my father's UDT-Laystall team at Brands Hatch in the minor Silver City Trophy F1 race, using one of their pale-green Lotus 18/21 specials. Surtees and Clark diced for the lead until John crashed and Jimmy buzzed his engine, which enabled me to sail by for another handy win.

Meanwhile, my Walker car had been in the workshop being modified to 18/21 spec with the more streamlined body and modernized rear suspension ready for the high-speed Belgian GP at Spa. Despite the effort it was utterly outclassed for straight-line speed — pulling only 146 mph — and after a bad start I finished eighth. I wrote in my diary '*Car fair, SM fair.*' I cannot remember that race at all but by the look of that comment I must have been pretty unhappy, having clearly driven less well than I would consider acceptable. Certainly Spa was no place to take chances in a potentially fragile car and I presume memories of 1960 had urged caution in what was probably already a lost cause against Ferrari's power.

I was back in the groove at Reims where in practice for the French GP I irritated von Trips into inadvertently 'towing' me round for fourth fastest time to line up behind the Ferrari-filled front row. I ran third, trying really hard until my brakes began to fade. The bridge pipe connecting the two sides of the right-rear disc caliper had fractured, leaking the fluid away. While the car was stationary having a new pipe fitted, molten tar, which had centrifuged around the inside of the wheel rim, dripped to the bottom and solidified. As I rejoined, the wheel was wildly out of balance and I was convinced they had not tightened the wheel nuts properly. I stopped at the end of a very slow lap to have them tightened, but the vibration obviously persisted — nobody had noticed the blob of tar hidden away within the rim. I stopped a third time for attention, and they finally spotted it.

Now I was racing again but Phil Hill spun his Ferrari right in front of me on the melting tar at Thillois and I rammed him, creeping in to retire with bent suspension . . . and 'waving' to Ferrari team manager Tavoni as I passed his pit.

Heavy rain at Aintree was a great leveller. I ran second amongst the Ferraris until lap 24 when I struck an enormous puddle at Melling Crossing and spun twice. I managed to catch the car as its nose whipped around the right way, the engine was still running so I charged off after Trips with only ten seconds lost. As the road dried the Ferraris asserted themselves and then my left-rear caliper bridge pipe broke. I retired the Lotus, and took over the four-wheel drive Ferguson which Rob was also running for Jack Fairman — see page 264.

I drove a UDT-Laystall 18/21 in the Solitude GP outside Stuttgart until its

15 July 1961 — British GP, Aintree — Ideal Moss weather! But once the circuit began to dry Ferrari horsepower would tell . . .

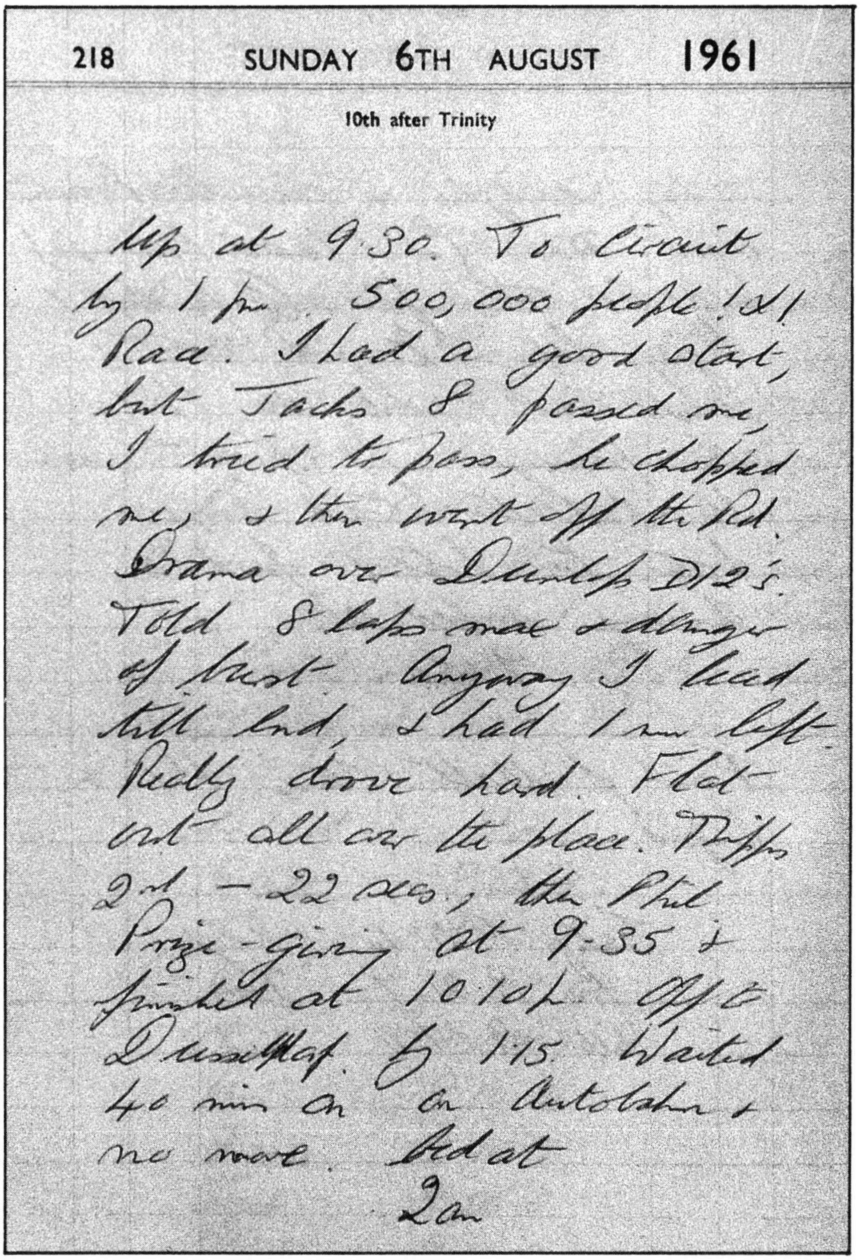
218 SUNDAY 6TH AUGUST 1961

10th after Trinity

Up at 9.30. To circuit by 1 pm. 500,000 people!!! Race. I had a good start, but Jack B passed me, I tried to pass, he chopped me, & then went off the Rd. Drama over Dunlop D12's. Told 8 laps max & danger of burst. Anyway I lead till end, & had 1 min left. Really drove hard. Flat out all over the place. Tripps 2nd – 22 secs, then Phil. Prize-giving at 9.35 & finished at 10.10 pm. Off to Dusseldorf by 1.15. Waited 40 min on on Autobahn & no more. Bed at 2am

transmission failed and then came the serious business of the German GP at Nürburgring.

Like Monaco, this was another driver's circuit quite suited to our ancient Lotus, and in practice we were impressed by Dunlop's high-hysteresis D12 rain tyres on the damp track, but found they wore excessively and broke up in chunks of flying tread as the sun emerged and the track both dried-up and warmed-up. Innes Ireland had just won at Solitude using these 'green spot' tyres on a fast circuit in hot weather, and he reckoned they gave such a grip advantage they were worth the risk. I finally decided to gamble upon their extra grip because race day forecast was showery. Vic Barlow of Dunlop had kittens and would take no responsibility when I insisted on racing them. At one stage we had actually painted the green spots on the tyre side wall black, so nobody would realize what we were up to.

It was a calculated risk which I felt was our only chance against Ferrari — Phil Hill having just clocked the first sub-nine minute lap of the magnificent North Circuit.

In the race I set a fastest lap of 9:13.2 on the damp second lap, and after three laps held ten seconds lead. On lap 8 I went round in 9:2.8, but Taffy von Trips in second place responded with 9:1.6. Next time round he had closed to within ten seconds, and after another lap he and Phil were below nine minutes and within nine seconds of me.

6 August 1961 — German GP, Nürburgring — Glancing anxiously in his mirrors to catch a glimpse of any pursuing Ferrari shark-nose, Stirling is nursing his D12 'green-spot' Dunlop tyres as the circuit dries. Showers during the closing stages were fine by Moss as he wins his 16th and last Grande Epreuve — yet again in an obsolescent car, on "a driver's circuit", at Ferrari's expense.

Two laps later my prayers were answered. It began to rain.

My marginal D12s cooled and I had a marked advantage over the Ferraris. I won by 20.4 seconds — not bad I thought for Rob's old, old car.

The light relief of the Scandinavian tour to Karlskoga and Roskilde followed. I drove the UDT 18/21 to win the Swedish race and also took all three heats to win on aggregate in Denmark. After the long trip to Italy I reappeared in Rob's car at Modena, and scored my fourth consecutive Formula 1 win of the year . . . my seventh overall.

By this time our first Climax V8 engine had been delivered and was being shoe-horned into the rear of Rob's spare Lotus 18 chassis. I would only use my old, but so faithful, four-cylinder car again in practice at Monza and then finally in the US GP at Watkins Glen. There I drove it in preference to Rob's V8, which had been faster in practice but which misfired after every four or five consecutive laps.

In the race Jack Brabham and I led away, swopping the lead between us until he pulled out seven seconds in three laps with his V8 Cooper. But then its water temperature soared and as the V8 boiled it gushed water on to his back wheels which sent him into a huge slide, grazing along the trackside barrer ahead of me. He managed to hold it without damage but shot into the pits, which left me comfortably leading what — as it happened — would be my last World Championship Grand Prix . . .

I was holding a 58 seconds lead on lap 59 when my four-cylinder engine lost its oil pressure. All the gauge readings had been perfect until that moment, and the car had been pulling 7,700 rpm on its own — not slipstreaming — along the straight.

I would have two final outings in four-cylinder 18/21s, both in South Africa that December, driving the meadow green BRP-managed UDT-Laystall cars.

Main opposition there came from the Team Lotus works 21s driven by young Jimmy Clark and Trevor Taylor. I had watched Jimmy's progress with interest during the European season, as he clearly had enormous potential. He was perhaps the strongest threat to whatever position I had enjoyed since Fangio's retirement, but I felt confident I could handle him, although without an equal car I might have to go some . . .

At Durban's Westmead circuit for the Natal GP my engine wouldn't rev above 7,400 without '*a feeling of valve-float*'. I started from the back of the grid and pulled through to second behind Jimmy, but according to my diary '. . . *couldn't make any way on him. I had D9s, he had D12s, got 7,450 rpm with 4.4* [back-axle ratio] *Jimmy 7,500 with 4.2. Track slippery . . .*'

The non-Championship South African GP was then run at East London on Boxing Day. My team-mate Masten Gregory offered me his car for the race after mine was troubled by locking brakes, having smaller calipers, during practice and I had set a quicker time in his. On Christmas Eve I taught Jimmy how to water-ski, but after celebrating Christmas Day I was up all night, sick.

I still felt lousy next morning — when my diary tells the story of the race like this: '*Had good start, Trev & Jim out-accelerated me, Jimmy spun & I had 14 sec lead. Couldn't keep him off. Too quick. My car OK but too slow. Other drivers really bad at getting out of the way. Feel lousy still . . .*'

I finished second behind Jimmy again and it was obvious to me that if I wanted to keep ahead of the Lotus number one during the coming World Championship season we would need an equal car, a Lotus 24 with a Climax V8 engine or perhaps a Ferrari V6 run for me by Rob. Jimmy was good.

Meanwhile I had driven my last proper race in a Lotus 18. No racing driver worth his salt gets too sentimental about his cars. If they are fast and competitive they are marvellous. Once they are old and uncompetitive we are only interested in the new car which replaces them. But looking back on Rob's 18s, which carried me to such success, especially at Monaco and Nürburgring in 1961, I must admit a surge of pride . . . after all, we had beaten the old enemy — Ferrari.

Lotus 19 Monte Carlo *(1960-61)*

'This very potent rear-engined sports car was exactly what you would expect from a two-seater with the heritage of the Lotus 18 behind it. Not a car for amateurs, but a very competitive proposition in the right hands . . .'

23 October 1960 — Pacific GP, Laguna Seca, California, USA — Stirling (far side in the BRP-owned Lotus 19) won both heats and overall and set a new lap record in just the kind of demonstration race promoters and spectators worldwide had come to expect.

Colin Chapman's design genius created in the Lotus 19 one of the finest sports-racing cars I ever drove. It appeared soon after I had scored Lotus's first Grand Prix win in the 1960 Monaco GP. Cooper had called their rear-engined sports car the Monaco after Jack Brabham had won the GP in 1959. Now the new Type 19 was nicknamed the Lotus Monte Carlo.

It was essentially a widened, sports-bodied Lotus 18 which could be powered by the full 2 ½ -litre Climax FPF engine, but which would also accept 2.0- and 2.7-litre variants, or even a little 1,500 if an entrant was sufficiently misguided. One car sold to America was fitted with a big Ferrari engine, and another with a Ford V8

But when the prototype Lotus 19 emerged in mid-season 1960 it was entrusted to what would become the UDT-Laystall Racing Team, which was run by Ken Gregory and my father in what had in previous years been their BRP meadow-green colours. In 1961-62 they fielded a full team of three of these cars, and provided one for me whenever I was available.

On Saturday 18 June 1960 I had broken both legs, and my nose, and crushed three spinal vertebrae when Rob's Lotus 18 had crashed during practice for the Belgian GP. My orthopaedic surgeon, Mr Urquhart, quickly removed my plaster casts and encouraged me to walk again without sticks by 11 July. He was actually fantastic. Within days of the crash he made me put my feet on his instep, supporting my weight on my arms, then told me to take my hands off the rails I was holding. I was amazed, but his philosophy was that if the muscle strength could be maintained it was as good as splints. After a month I was cycling round the hospital grounds. He even encouraged me to go dancing, checking

out at 8 pm and back in at 1 am! I was discharged on 19 July and on Monday 25 July I was well enough to test the new Lotus 19 for the first time at Silverstone. I noted '. . . *understeer due to flat springs but new LR for sports cars, 1:41.4'.* It had clear potential, and I was back in the groove. Next day at Brands Hatch I set quickest time in a test session driving Jimmy Clark's works Lotus 18, before returning to hospital for my daily physiotherapy. On 30 July I tested the 19 at Brands, and on 7 August, seven weeks after the Spa crash, I débuted the new sports Lotus in my come-back race at Karlskoga in Sweden.

It was a short fifty-mile event with a Le Mans-type start which tested my legs quite thoroughly . . .

It became a dice between Jo Bonnier's Maserati and my new pale-green Lotus, and I won after passing him on lap thirteen. My diary comments '*3 secs quicker than Monaco s/c. Car fabulous, used only 4th & 5th later on, brakes heavy . . .'*

This was a pleasing come-back and baptism for the new car, which felt every inch a Lotus, taut, highly-strung, very much an extension of the driver fitted into it, never as easy to drive as any contemporary Cooper, but potentially superior.

I did four more events in it that year, in the American West Coast professional races at Riverside and Laguna Seca, and finally at Nassau in the Bahamas Speed Week. Its crown wheel stripped at Riverside after a fuel line had parted in practice, causing a brief cheery bonfire. At Laguna Seca, the $20,000 Pacific GP was run in two heats, and I won them both comparatively easily. But at Nassau I retired from both races, ending the season on a low but not very consequential note.

In 1961 I drove UDT-Laystall's 19s nine times and won five; at Easter Goodwood, Aintree and Silverstone early-season, then the Players '200' at Mosport Park, Toronto, in Canada that June, and my second consecutive Pacific GP at Laguna Seca, California, in October. Unfortunately the car's preparation seemed to decline — Ken reminds me the car had been sold into private American hands by that time, and it was no longer being prepared by our own mechanics — and niggling problems knocked me down to third place at Mosport in September, while at Riverside I led until a brake seal failed and I finished sixteenth. In Nassau that December I was entered in two races and again retired from them both. Dan Gurney won there in his 19 . . .

I did not race the cars again, as on Easter Monday 1962 my professional career ended in the Goodwood accident. Fourteen months later, I felt well enough to drive a racing car again at Goodwood, to test my surviving abilities . . . whatever they might be. The UDT Lotus 19 was available, and I drove it at Goodwood on May Day 1963 to prove to myself whether or not I still had what it takes . . .

Ferrari 250GT SWB
Berlinetta *(1960-61)*

*'Quite surprising
how good it was — a
really comfortable
Grand Touring car,
with good brakes, a
super engine and
crisp gearbox, and
unusual in that it
would not lift its
inside rear wheel
despite that old-
fashioned live
axle . . . quite
difficult to fault, in
fact . . .'*

*20 August 1960 — the sixth
win in the RAC Tourist
Trophy, this time again at
Goodwood but for the first
time beneath a roof. Stirling
really enjoyed the Rob
Walker/Dick Wilkins-owned
Ferrari 250GT SWBs, this first
one is '2119 GT'. Note the
radio aerial.*

*H*aving had to follow them with my Gullwing Mercedes in the *Tour de
France*, I had considerable respect for the GT Ferraris' power, speed and
reliability, which was confirmed in later years when I won two consecutive
Goodwood TTs in them, and competed in six other races, including Le Mans.
They were very well-mannered, well-balanced cars, especially good for Le Mans
or any other circuit where one could give them their head, although at
Goodwood for example they also impressed me by their ability to change
direction very quickly for they were very quick there through the chicane as
well as round more conventional corners.

The 3-litre V12 engine was a superb example of Italian engineering flair. It
made a lovely crackle and was almost totally reliable. I won seven of my eight
races in these 250GTs, and even when we retired at Le Mans when leading our
category by miles it was not due to any real fault of the car. By any standards
this is quite an impressive record — as impressive as the cars themselves.

*M*y first opportunity to race a 250GT came in the 1960 TT at Goodwood.
It had been reduced in duration from six hours to only three, and was
run to the new Grand Touring car regulations which effectively superseded
the traditional open-sports category. Rob Walker ran Dick Wilkins' 250GT for
me, sprayed in Rob's famous colours, and this would be only my third race since
my Lotus accident at Spa, run the weekend after the Portuguese GP. I needed
an important win, and this TT provided it.

Our greatest problem was tyre wear, for the Ferrari's rears were surviving
only 24 laps. Roy Salvadori's Aston Martin DB4GT matched my practice time,
and although I led the opening stages I could not build an adequate time-cushion
before my first tyre change. I had only six seconds in hand, so Roy inherited
my lead, only to stop a couple of laps later to change all four tyres. That put
me back ahead, and I managed a fairly comfortable win from Roy with Innes
Ireland's DB4GT third.

It was my fourth consecutive TT victory, 1955, then 1958-59-60 — the race
not having been run in 1956-57 — and with my earlier wins in 1950-51 it was
my sixth TT overall. If I am honest it was also perhaps the least exciting. I enjoyed

it because at only three hours' duration co-drivers were no longer necessary, but these GT cars were never as exhilarating to drive as a powerful open sports-racer.

One rather extraordinary GT advantage, however, was that I had a radio receiver, and for further enjoyment as I raced round Goodwood I listened to the BBC race commentary and music in between . . . believe me, it felt strange to hear my own driving being referred to while actually being still in full flight!

The following weekend I won the ten-lap RedeX Trophy race, supporting the F2 Kentish '100' at Brands Hatch, driving the blue Ferrari. It was also an ideal entry for the Bahamas Speed Week that November, where I notched my hat-trick of wins in it. Rob and Dick Wilkins then sold the car to the new Equipe Endeavour/Maranello Concessionaires team, which combined Tommy Sopwith's outfit with Colonel Ronnie Hoare's new British Ferrari company for 1961. It would be driven for them by Michael Parkes. However, Rob and Dick ordered one of the very fast new 1961/*Competizione* models to replace it, which was fine by me.

The new car's engine had bigger valves, paired exhausts and big 46mm Weber carburettors in place of the earlier model's 40s, and it weighed-in at only 1,017 kg. It was delivered to us at Le Mans, where it was entered under the banner of the North American Racing Team. By this stage in my career only a sizeable fee could induce me to drive in the 24-Hours, but the new Ferrari was undeniably an added attraction. My co-driver was Graham Hill, and we averaged over 118 mph for the first 1½-hours, howling along the Mulsanne Straight at 7,700 rpm. It felt fabulous. After 21 laps my best time was 4:08.0 and that night we lay third overall, leading the GT category by miles.

Suddenly, in the tenth hour, the car lost all its water and boiled dry. Unbelievably, NART had not removed its standard road-going fan, and since

10 June 1961 — Le Mans 24-Hours — the replacement Walker-liveried 250GT SWB '2735 GT' was running like an express train at the Sarthe, shared by Stirling and Graham Hill, until an extraordinary oversight in preparation stopped it.

we had been holding high revs for so long one of the fan blades had flown off and slashed clean through a radiator hose. Earlier, we had led Willy Mairesse's prototype Ferrari which eventually finished second. This stupid retirement was enormously frustrating, because it was so unnecessary and unprofessional. Coincidentally, it was also the last time I would ever drive in the *Grand Prix d'Endurance* . . .

Back home, I drove the new car to two minor wins in the big meetings at Silverstone and Brands Hatch, before the Goodwood TT, in which I was aiming for my fifth consecutive win, my seventh TT overall. Mike Parkes was driving another new 250GT *61/Competizione* model for Endeavour/ Maranello and I was very impressed by him. He was certainly one of the finest and fastest non-professional drivers around.

I was the full-time professional racing driver, with a lot of experience and plenty of practice, racing all kinds of cars, somewhere, every weekend so I was well in the groove and would expect to match his times in a similar car fairly quickly. Mike Parkes was not at that kind of pitch, yet those 250GTs were such pleasant cars to drive really fast that his best practice time was only 0.4 second slower than mine. I then flew off to switch on the Morecambe illuminations, and he promptly cut 0.4 sec off my best time for pole position! The race developed into a battle between us.

He set a new GT lap record without taking my lead, but wore out his tyres in the process. As he stopped more frequently than I, my lead grew, and I was able to win quite comfortably. He later told a journalist 'I learned more about race driving from following Moss that afternoon that on any other occasion . . .', which was nice. It did not seem long ago that I had been the young newcomer, learning my trade by following Fangio in a similar car. Now I was the bald-headed old schoolmaster with the talented newcomer following in my wheel-tracks . . . how time had flown.

I had one more race in the 250GT, and one more win, in the Nassau Tourist Trophy that December. I knew a very much more potent version of the 250GT was coming in the new year, and I was very much looking forward to driving it. Little did I suspect fate would deny me the opportunity . . .

8 September 1961 — This extremely rare photo shows Ferrari's left-hand drive GTO test hack on test at Monza where Stirling drove it long enough prior to the Italian GP to recognize that the finished article would have immense potential for '62. The Ferrari deal followed, and what should have been Moss's UDT-Laystall GTO was delivered to Goodwood the following Easter, but the F1 accident there meant he would never race it . . .

Go-karts *(1960)*

'Another circus trick outing, in effect, but it was an interesting first experience of the kind of racing which would replace my form of 500 cc Formula 3 as the basic kindergarten class for racing drivers of the future . . .'

25 November 1960 — Bahamas Speed Week Go-Kart Grand Prix, Oakes Field — the rapidly balding Maestro, by this time very much at the peak of his profession, tries a new kind of motor sport.

*T*he Bahamas Speed Week was always more fun and frivolity and socializing than serious motor racing, and the 1960 Week was no exception. I drove the Ferrari 250GT and Lotus 19 in reasonable earnest after beginning the meeting on 24-25 November involved in an invitation go-kart event. The organizers provided me with a choice of Ariel or Bultaco-powered karts but the Bultacos were late arriving so I handled the Ariel in initial practice. It was over-geared and understeered violently but its brakes and roadholding were fabulous. In contrast the Bultaco was under-geared, but next day in the race I thought it was just fantastic, much more powerful than the Ariel. They condemned me to start from the back of the grid, and I managed to find my way up from 34th to 13th by the end of the five laps. No big deal, but an interesting experience of what at that time was a brand-new branch of motor sport. I could see its potential . . .

Driving Techniques 3

*I*had driven Rob Walker's rear-engined Coopers several times during the 1958 season before running them in the full World Championship season in 1959. By this time I was very much the target at which every other team and driver aimed. I was comfortable with that, but believe me it didn't make life any easier. Having once achieved that kind of level you can't just sit back and expect to maintain it by some kind of divine right. You have to work at it. I had always naturally been quite fit, but I didn't get involved in gymnasium work-outs and jogging to keep fit while I was racing. Oh no. So far as I was concerned the best exercise to keep a racing driver fit was simply to drive racing cars, and I did that three or four days virtually every week. I didn't drink, and only rarely smoked, and my generally rather hectic lifestyle kept me in shape.

Today when you look at the visual differences between a lofty front-engined Vanwall and a low-slung rear-engined Cooper you might think there was a world of difference between them. Of course there was, but it is a driver's job to adapt, as far as possible.

I found it made little difference whether the engine was mounted ahead of me or behind, what mattered was whether or not the car was in balance overall. The Cooper gave enormous peace of mind in this respect — far more than the Vanwall — and instilled confidence that if I did misjudge something I might resolve the situation reasonably simply by an extra tweak on the steering, scrub off a little more speed, then back on the power.

With the Cooper there was no question of waiting for it to signal what it was about to do, because far before the corner I would already have decided what I *wanted* it to do and would have set about ensuring that it obeyed.

Its tendency to lift its inside front wheel when turning into corners could be disturbing, because if this happened while I was braking the lifted wheel would obviously lock. But one had to balance this against the other advantages of braking that late into a corner and of cornering that hard. Once accustomed to such behaviour these minor Cooper foibles did not bother me.

Around that time I told Laurence Pomeroy I had become virtually oblivious to which end of the car the engine was in, and the entire process of driving felt as natural as walking or running or doing cartwheels. The point was that this natural process was much easier to apply to the rear-engined Cooper than it had been to the front-engined Vanwall. A major factor was that there was so much less car to control. It had very adequate brakes, adequate performance and very few problems, although one could actually feel even that massive-looking frame twisting over quite slight bumps, which allowed the wheels to assume very peculiar angles relative to one another. But none of that seemed to slow the car any!

For 1960, Colin Chapman produced his rear-engined Lotus 18. After bad experiences with the power-absorbing understeer designed into his preceding front-engined Lotus 16s, he now moved towards Cooper-style agility with a car offering a small inherent degree of oversteer which could be increased at will by a skilful driver either backing off or by applying power to the rear wheels in precise increments, as either action would enlarge their tyre slip angle.

The new Lotus was much more sophisticated than the Coopers, its chassis lighter and stiffer, and it kept both front wheels on the road as one turned-in hard to corners. This was really a crucial advance of which, by this time, I was sufficiently experienced and equipped to take full advantage. It offered the possibility of using the brakes right into the corner, deep towards the apex.

Few people outside racing can appreciate that race driving is not like driving on the road at all. A racing car is always in an attitude at corners, never pointing as directly fore-and-aft in its line of travel as a road car would be in normal motoring. The racing car is sliding, to some degree, nearly all the time, but to be quick the best drivers try to do the slides and drifts with the least drag possible at moments when drag doesn't matter. One can put the car into a Kristie — a broadside as in ski-ing — to slow it into the corners. But once one has presented the car to a very high-speed corner it's rather like throwing a dart — when it has left your hand you can't do a thing about its path. If you present a car accurately to such a corner it will track through in a long drift on virtually a predestined trajectory. You can make tiny adjustments, but once you have presented it to the corner you can only adjust the trim not make major changes of direction — not if you are on the limit.

Steering is used to present the car, then to compensate for the throttle, because as one opens the throttle, and the car starts to slide you may have to use the steering wheel to compensate — to balance the power. I would describe the steering wheel as the presenter and the balancer really.

Now most between-wars drivers had driven essentially oversteering cart-sprung GP cars in the conventional road-going manner, braking in a straight line, changing down to assist, and to select the right gear for acceleration out. They would then play the throttle on the way through, open it fully as early as felt comfortable or prudent, and finally perhaps apply opposite-lock steering on the exit to counter the slide and possible wheelspin this might produce.

In the late '30s the arrival of Mercedes-style understeer chassis theory made it possible for drivers to slow the car on the straight, twitch the steering into the corner to start the tail sliding, and they then had sufficient surplus horsepower to maintain that attitude on the throttle by degrading rear-tyre adhesion, short of provoking actual wheelspin. As this technique developed, cornering speeds soared.

Obviously, the longer you can lengthen time on the power, and the more you shorten time on the brakes into a corner the quicker the lap time you can achieve. But later in my career I was asking if it was necessary to confine braking to the latest possible point on the straight? By trial and error I concluded otherwise. If one reason for applying power in a corner was to diminish the rear tyres' ability to take side-load then why not achieve the same effect by applying braking torque instead of engine torque?

I found I could brake much later than had formerly seemed prudent, and keep them on pretty hard right in to the apex of the corner. Then I had to get back on to the throttle as quickly as I possibly could, so that one moment the rear tyres were absorbing braking drag followed almost instantaneously — at the right moment on the road — by a similar degree of power thrust.

Obviously, one had to balance the two torques about equally to stand any chance of maintaining car control, and one had to be steering along the right line throughout, so all this was very much an acquired skill, demanding a lot of practice to hone it effectively.

Previously, whatever advantage I had in 'driving skill' over my rivals was natural quickness of eye and muscular reaction, coupled with good visual distance perception into corners, by which I judged my braking points, and a growing fund of experience. Now, I was evolving a technique which few others seemed to use — and one which I was not particularly inclined to explain to them . . .

The point is that the Lotus was probably the first Formula 1 chassis in which such techniques could be applied consistently and with confidence, and it proved itself totally a natural extension of its driver.

In the early days I never went into a corner thinking 'well in order to save seconds I'll have to do this or that,' I just approached the corner, braked, steered, accelerated and drove on round. Right at the end of my career, when I did know technically quite a bit about the process, if I wanted to go faster, say, round Silverstone, to go for the lap record, I would brake absolutely as late as I could but also get back on the power as early as I could. But the sensation of getting round the corner faster was never the thing. The aim was to shorten the braking

Concentrating hard in the Walker Porsche at Syracuse, 1960. Stirling has exited the corner leaving more room than he really likes between his outside wheels and the trackside wall. Next time into the turn he will force himself to watch his gauges until it is too late to back-off . . .

period and lengthen the acceleration, and I always took a tighter line, going less wide on the entry to the corners, than most others.

Sometimes something more than cool calculation came into it. Once, practising at Syracuse with Rob's F2 Porsche, I knew very well that my instinctive confidence lift on the way into a 140 mph corner was unnecessary. Every time I came round I would think to myself 'All right now Moss, keep your foot hard on it this time,' but I would find myself lifting just fractionally every time. I just could not steel myself not to do this and it irritated me madly.

I just *knew* it was unnecessary because I was coming out of that corner every time with six inches to spare between my wheels and the outer wall on the exit. That should have been 1 inch, or less, but my throttle foot just kept lifting. Finally, I remember thinking consciously 'Well you have got to sort this out,' and next time I approached that corner I remember making myself glance down at the instruments, and by the time I looked back up it was too late to back off . . .

I had to keep my foot down or get into an oversteer, and at that instant the greater fear was backing off so I kept my foot hard on the floor, and it was OK, I came out just fractions off the outer barrier and saved another little package of time. Having then done that once, I could repeat it every lap without having to glance at the instruments each time.

In that kind of situation, at very high speeds, it's very difficult to draw the line between bravery and stupidity. Very often they are virtually the same thing. What I had to do that day in Syracuse, glancing down at such a moment was stupid if considered in isolation. But having said that, I knew what I was doing and it enabled me to keep my foot down. So what is brave and what is stupid? Perhaps one is a means to achieve the other?

So, by the end of 1960 I was driving more responsive and sensitive Grand Prix cars than ever before, with more horsepower than those I would have to put up with once the new Formula started in 1961, and I was using a driving technique which gave me a real advantage. For these reasons I viewed the change from the 2½-litre Formula to 1½-litres with especial regret.

In 1961, although the new cars' lack of power narrowed the gap between better drivers and ordinary drivers, tyre developments enabled me to maintain some advantage through braking terribly late, and then continuing to brake while steering up to the apex of a corner, then opening the throttle to maintain even acceleration right the way round — negative towards the apex, positive beyond it.

Paradoxically, the modest speed of 1½-litre cars enabled one to maintain this level of concentration and effort throughout race distance.

Race driving was an athletic pursuit, and an art, which I loved to pursue. When my natural abilities were impaired by the Goodwood accident in 1962 my sense of loss was very real.

Cooper-Climax T53P 'Intercontinental' (1961-62)

'Possibly the least-known and least-recognized, yet probably the best, of all my Coopers — a very forgiving car, a beaut to drive and one with the power to make it really go . . .'

6 May 1961 — BRDC International Trophy, Silverstone — Stirling in one of his all-time favourite cars, Rob Walker's big InterContinental Formula Cooper T53P. For him, in this car, these conditions were ideal.

J ack Brabham was very quick to recognize the potential of the new rear-engined Lotus 18 upon its debut in the 1960 Argentine GP. On the way home he persuaded John Cooper that an all-new car was required at once to combat it. Thus the 'Lowline' Cooper was conceived, with many straight chassis tubes replacing the curves we had come to know and love, using coil spring suspension all round, and with its driver reclined to reduce frontal area. That summer saw Jack win five consecutive World Championship GPs with this car to clinch his second successive Drivers' Championship, while Cooper took their second successive Constructors' title.

As Formula 1 changed to only 1½-litres for 1961, British interests set-up the 3-litre InterContinental Formula to continue racing existing F1 equipment. A very secondary British ICF series was organized, while Tasman racing also admitted these larger-engined cars. Cooper put what was basically their Championship-winning 'Lowline' into customer production as the 1961 Type 53. It would commonly be fitted with either 1,500 or up to 2.7-litre Climax engines to compete in either Formula, and Rob Walker ran one in InterContinental form for me.

I drove Rob's 2.5-litre ICF car only four times in the 1961 British races; at Easter Goodwood, May Silverstone, the British Empire Trophy at Silverstone in July, and finally the Brands Hatch Guards Trophy. I won the first three but retired with transmission trouble when leading at Brands. John Surtees had been leading me there, until he crashed.

The International Trophy race at Silverstone was run in appallingly wet and oily conditions. Racing in the rain never bothered me as much as it did some other drivers, and the big Cooper felt particularly good there. Early on I found a line round one corner which intersected with a patch of surface which offered a little more adhesion than the rest, so next time round I intentionally entered that corner on a very tight line, on the wet, but heading towards the better patch. On the way in I purposely put the car into a lurid oversteer — which was not at all characteristic of the way I normally drove — as I was fairly confident of correcting it when we would skate on to that drier patch.

Sure enough, the big but beautifully balanced Cooper came back sweetly into line, and as I accelerated away and glanced in my mirrors, the following cars had just fallen away behind me. Perhaps they thought 'Whoa, look at Moss sliding, coo it must be really slippery out here . . .' and they all backed off to avoid being 'caught out as I had been'.

I had planted the seeds of doubt in their minds, which is always a marvellous thing for one racing driver to do to another. The car was so good, I was able to lap the entire field that day. Next time out at Silverstone we lapped all but Surtees' sister car, which finished second in the race but had pipped me for pole position by 0.6 sec in practice.

At the start of 1962 we ran in the Tasman series in New Zealand and Australia with a choice of the Cooper — now fitted with an Indianapolis-sized 2.7-litre Climax engine — and Rob's new 2.5 Lotus 21. For the tight and bumpy little track at Levin, I preferred the Cooper but the race was started in torrential rain and then stopped after only eight of the scheduled 28 laps when I was trailing Jack Brabham's sister car for the lead. That really annoyed me. The organizers had been willing to start the race despite the rain. It had not rained any harder, so if it had been safe to start when they had, why was it suddenly unsafe to continue? I felt quite confident we would have been in good shape had the race run full distance.

I won the important Lady Wigram Trophy at Christchurch in the Lotus, and then at Teretonga I drove the Cooper and Bruce McLaren beat me into second place in his similar car. I tried Lorenzo Bandini's Centro-Sud Cooper-Maserati there, which used a 2.8 *Tipo* 61 sports car engine. It had bags of torque, and this was the very last time I tried Maserati power during my front-line career. On the other hand, a first for me on that trip had been qualifying for my first solo flight in Christchurch the previous week.

We then flew to Australia where everybody seemed to tip my Lotus 21 as being 'the perfect car' for the Warwick Farm '100' in Sydney. I must confess that rather irritated me, so I made a point of running the Cooper instead. I cut four seconds off my existing lap record to qualify on pole, and then Jack Brabham, Bruce and I had a terrific dice in the race which was resolved in my favour, although Bruce took the official lap record. Thus my final appearance in a Rob Walker Cooper brought us another first place.

In that 2.7-litre form it really was a terrific racing car. One could quite easily drive it quickly. But it has to be said that the more highly strung Lotus 21 would lap quicker any time, anywhere, if its driver was prepared to make the effort, and was sufficiently sensitive to cope with that highly tuned chassis. Yet the big Cooper was infinitely more fun, and by that stage in my career this was important and to a large degree — at least in relatively minor events — a luxury I could now afford.

Aston Martin DB4GT Zagato *(1961)*

'The original blunt instrument, short, quite highly strung and twitchy, very much a strong-man's GT car . . .'

*F*ollowing the success of the *Superlegerra*-bodied DB4GTs, Aston Martin put through a very restricted batch of short-chassis very high performance cars wearing bulbous new bodyshells styled and manufactured by Zagato. Their quality was light-years ahead of that hasty and horrible 450S Le Mans Coupé which the same coachworks had rushed through for Maserati in 1957. These new Aston Martins were some 150 lbs lighter than the standard DB4GTs and had higher-compression engines delivering around 315 bhp, and I drove one in the Fordwater Trophy GT race at Goodwood on Easter Monday, 1961. I was faced by Ferrari 250GTs and I finished third, which upon reflection was quite logical — being the new model Aston's proper place in such company.

Porsche RS60 2-litre *(1961)*

'A super car, beautifully well balanced and simply tailor-made for the Targa Florio . . . That was one morning when I woke up and could say to myself, 'For today's race you have got the ideal car . . .'

30 April 1961 — Targa Florio — Stirling blasts off the startline in the Camoradi-entered Porsche RS60 which he shared with Graham Hill and in which they dominated all but the final few miles of the race. Beyond the car, white-haired, hand in pocket, stands Piero Taruffi who acted occasionally as Camoradi team manager.

Porsches won the Targa Florio in 1956, 1959 and 1960, and their rugged, nimble, well-braked and reliable cars were superbly suited to the 45-mile Madonie circuit. In 1961 I shared this 2-litre RS60 *Spyder* there with Graham Hill, ostensibly entered by Camoradi, but very much a works car with works mechanics looking after it. We have since been described as moral winners of the race, which is unfortunate, because moral first places don't pay first-place prize money!

Porsche chose the 2-litre engines for the Targa because their 37 per cent greater mid-range torque than the normal alternative 1700s gave the drivers an easier time on such a gruelling and exceptionally demanding course. We wouldn't have to stir that gear-lever about quite so much.

I always thoroughly enjoyed Sicily's classic race, and in practice I first went round in a 1700 in 43:08, before getting down to 40:28 in the team's 2-litre 'mule'. Our race car was just perfect for the course, we could hardly have wished for a nicer, more competitive car, and I led for the first four laps by 1½ minutes from Jo Bonnier's sister Porsche and 2 minutes from the third-placed Ferrari, before handing over to Graham for his two laps. He handed the car back to me, minus 76 secs on the Ferrari, and I managed to change that deficit into plus 65 secs with one lap to go.

That last lap was going together so well it looked like being a sub-40 minute record until — only 8 kms from the finish — the diff failed and put us out!

Unknown to me the bolts holding the transmission case together had been stretching and that allowed the case to flex and distort, which opened its seams and dumped its oil on the road. The rear-engined Ferrari won; lucky blighters.

Porsche RS61 1.7-litre (1961)

'A tyre gamble which didn't quite come off . . .'

28 May 1961 — Nürburgring 1,000Kms — the 1.7-litre Porsche RS61 set a blistering pace on rain-tyres while the weather suited them . . .

After our terrific but ultimately unlucky run in the 1961 Targa Florio with the 2-litre Porsche RS61, Graham Hill and I were invited to drive for the factory again in that year's Nürburgring 1,000 Kms.

Our RS61 *Spyder* was fitted with what was known as the '1.7' flat-four engine which was, in fact, only 1,605 cc just to raise it from the 1,600 cc class into the 2-litre category. On Dunlop D9 tyres I managed 9:31 in the wet, which suggested 9:25 would be within our grasp if it should dry out. Race day began wet so we started the long race on Dunlop D12 high-hysteresis 'rain' tyres. They enabled me to take the lead on the second lap from an Aston DBR1 driven by a young chap named Jim Clark. Believe me he showed promise! But the circuit dried and as it dried my tyres lost this advantage and I was overwhelmed as the works Ferrari V6s used their power. After twelve laps I handed over to Graham who rejoined fifth. Then it began to snow! Graham handed back to me and I found the little Porsche ideal for the 'Ring in such conditions. We climbed into third, then second and the leading Phil Hill/von Trips Ferrari was in trouble up ahead. My Porsche was timed at 207 km/h — 128 mph — down 'The Foxhole' and was flat-out up the other side in the wet.

I was set to take the lead when the stretched and probably over-stressed little car broke, but it had been exciting while it lasted. We then took over a disc-braked Carrera Coupé from Herbie Linge/Sepp Greger, and ended the day by winning the 2-litre sports car class in that, despite — my diary reminds me — going in the ditch twice. With a roof over our heads it was far more comfortable. At the post-race dinner I was presented with a commemorative gold cup for my previous three consecutive wins in the ADAC 1,000 Kms — a very nice gesture.

Lotus-Climax 18/21 V8 Special *(1961-62)*

'After having to resort to heroics with the four-cylinder Lotus in 1961, I had really been looking forward to the V8 because it held the promise of not having to work so damn hard . . .'

The long-awaited Coventry Climax 1½-litre V8 engine finally made its début in the 1961 German Grand Prix, but at that time only one was available for Jack Brabham's works Cooper. Rob and I obtained our first V8 in time for the Italian GP, and it was mounted in the second of Rob's two Lotus 18 chassis, the conversion of which I was later told had reduced its torsional rigidity by about 75 per cent!

Those original V8s gave only a little more power than the four-cylinder, but revved far higher and offered much more torque. They also suffered head-sealing problems which saw them dogged by overheating and misfiring.

Into 1962, Rob's hybrid Lotus V8 ran in UDT-Laystall colours for the early non-Championship races, pending the Lotus 21's return from Australia when it was destined for V8 conversion. Rob also had a brand-new Lotus 24 V8 on order for me, but I never got the chance to drive either car because, before they could be completed, the V8 special took me head-on into the bank at Goodwood on Easter Monday . . .

There was nothing very clever about our 1960-style Lotus 18 once it had been updated with the Type 21-style rear suspension and aerodynamic bodywork and the wide new Climax V8 had been shoe-horned into its tail. Colin Chapman laughed when he saw it, and told me he reckoned its overall stiffness had come down to around 300 lbs/ft per degree, or *one-tenth* the rigidity I had 'enjoyed' in Leslie Johnson's G-Type ERA ten years earlier . . .

First time out at Monza '61 the engine was still terribly new. In practice, both my four-cylinder and V8 cars were slow. I saw 6,600 rpm on the four-cylinder, which was only 137 mph with 6.50 rear tyres, and then the V8 reached 8,200 rpm with a 4.7 axle, which was barely 138! I was lapping the banked section in 1:06, but the V8 soon overheated — it was clearly not yet raceworthy — while the old four-cylinder was far outclassed by the V6 Ferraris. It was then that Innes Ireland made the terrific gesture of lending me his works Lotus 21 for the race.

I then drove the Ferguson at Oulton Park, and won, before returning to our Lotus 18s at Watkins Glen for the United States GP on 8 October. There, with less emphasis on sustained straight-line high revs — and admittedly in Ferrari's absence — the V8 showed real promise. It took us a while to set up the hybrid car's suspension, but it pulled 134 mph along the straight before beginning to misfire after a few laps. In Saturday practice it handled properly, and was quicker than the '4' even when, after four or five laps, it again misfired.

Jack Brabham did 1:17.1 in his V8 Cooper, a tenth faster than my best V8 time, but it seemed a safer bet to race our 4-cylinder. By doing so I kissed goodbye to my last chance to tackle a Championship Grand Prix with V8 power . . .

Still, the V8's American practice performance had been quite heartening, and Climax worked hard to develop it to true raceworthiness through that winter while we were all away racing down-under and in America. I next raced our 18/21 V8 special in Rob's colours at Brussels early in 1962. It was not very good. In first practice it was over-geared though otherwise felt quite nice, and then we had the right ratios for second practice and it pulled 8,800 rpm, but its left-front brake kept locking.

My best practice time of 2:03.3 was only 0.2 sec slower than Jim Clark's new Lotus 24 V8, and then in the first race heat I finished second to a BRM, but my front brakes were still locking, the rear suspension felt unpleasant and I lost thirty seconds. In the second heat I set a new lap record in two minutes dead before finding second gear instead of fourth on a supposed up-change which buzzed my engine to 9,900 rpm! It held together but had lost power so I had obviously touched a valve. Shortly, a timing gear broke so I was out. Perhaps appropriately, it was April Fools' Day . . .

Rob then loaned the car to UDT-Laystall for my use in the British pre-season non-Championship races at Snetterton and Goodwood, while in return they loaned him one of their 4-cylinder 18/21s for Maurice Trintignant to drive at Pau on Easter Monday (where he would win handsomely). The V8 special ran in the BRP-originated meadow green colours of UDT-Laystall, and at Snetterton I took the lead from Graham Hill's BRM V8 before my car's throttle began to stick. I made three pit stops to clear it and lost five laps. I was determined to regain time and try to set fastest lap — to show that I was still a threat — and this I managed to achieve.

Our next date was Easter Monday Goodwood — 23 April 1962 — and there after qualifying on pole position I made a slowish start and lay third behind Graham's BRM and McLaren's Cooper, but not for long before Surtees went screaming by in his very pretty new V8 Lola. Then began the troubles which were the prelude to the accident which ended my career as a full-time professional racing driver . . . and which totally destroyed that car.

April Fool's Day 1962 — Brussels GP, Heysel — Stirling driving his last race under Rob Walker's hallowed colours in the Lotus 18/21 V8 special, and also facing (and leading) a factory Formula 1 Ferrari for the last time — Willy Mairesse in full flow on his home soil.

Lotus-Climax 21 *(1961-62)*

'This was the car which Esso told Colin Chapman not to sell to us . . . in some ways it was the ultimate 1½-litre four-cylinder Grand Prix car, but I never had the opportunity to find out . . .'

Colin Chapman designed this extraordinarily pretty car for the start of the new 1½-litre Grand Prix Formula in 1961. It replaced the box-bodied Type 18 and was very neat, compact, and streamlined. Its front coil springs and dampers were tucked inside the body out of the airstream, while its Climax four-cylinder engine was canted to one side to reduce its height, and drove through a jewel-like ZF five-speed transaxle.

Rob and I were backed by BP. We had won two GPs with the Lotus 18 in 1960, but Team Lotus who had built our car were backed by Esso and they had won none. Esso's competitions manager, Reg Tanner, vetoed Colin selling us this new car for 1961.

That meant we would have to go on using our old Lotus 18. I could understand his action, but it did limit us when trying to take on both Ferrari and Porsche, plus Team Lotus and the other British teams. I did not object to being cast in the role of under-dog, and this was a nice challenge, but I thought this was exaggerating a bit — rather loading the dice against me . . .

The Lotus 21s made their bow in practice for the 1961 Monaco GP, driven by Innes Ireland and his precocious young team-mate Jim Clark. Poor Innes lost his way round ZF's gear-change at high speed in Monte Carlo's famous tunnel. He inadvertently changed down instead of up and had an almighty accident which put him out for some time.

The top link-and-wishbone Lotus 21 rear suspension relieved the half-shaft of locating the rear wheel uprights laterally as they did on the Type 18. This was much more advanced, and the half-shaft instead had rubber universal-joint couplings.

As that season progressed Alf built this type of suspension on to Rob's Lotus 18s, and we also replaced their original box-section bodywork with a more rounded and slippery shape like the new 21s; compromises — sure — but every little bit helped.

When Innes recovered, he really drove his works cars with enormous dash and determination and he won the non-Championship Formula 1 races at Solitude and Zeltweg, and ended the season with a Championship-round win — at last — in the US GP at Watkins Glen. Meanwhile, at Monza for the Italian GP, my old 18/21 with the Climax V8 installed refused to cool properly, and my four-cylinder car had no chance, so Innes made the wonderful gesture of offering me his works 21.

He had grown up in racing as a Lotus man, and the marque's success was genuinely important to him. I was the only Lotus driver left with an outside chance of the Championship if I could beat the Ferraris there. Both Colin and Rob agreed so we swopped Innes's 21 for my four-cylinder 18/21 and the body panels were also swopped around so I drove a car wearing Team Lotus green side panels with Walker dark-blue and white on top.

The 21 had a better high-speed shape than the fatter 18/21 with its outboard front springs and dampers. The race was run on the combined Monza road and banked circuit, and my old car broke its chassis under Innes, while I ran sixth in his car. I diced with Gurney's Porsche for fifth place behind the Ferraris, until two of them retired which left us disputing third. Phil Hill was leading with Richie Ginther second and when Richie's Ferrari dropped out Phil must have felt hunted as his was the only Ferrari left and Dan and I were disputing second place and looking quite likely to inherit the lead.

But the Ferrari did not fail, whereas my Lotus did. The extreme loadings on the left-front wheel, caused by sweeping right-handed round the speedbowl bankings, knocked out the wheel bearing, and I had to retire.

Rob had ordered a Type 21 for me, but by agreement it was not delivered until after the season ended. He had it fitted with a 2 ½ -litre Climax four-cylinder engine for Tasman racing and took it out to New Zealand along with our InterContinental Cooper — one of my favourite cars.

The Lotus was very much more highly strung than the forgiving Cooper. It had greater potential, but to realize that potential it had to be driven constantly between narrow and clearly defined limits, and if you ventured beyond those limits you could lose a lot of time . . .

I drove the Lotus in the New Zealand GP at Ardmore aerodrome in torrential rain. The great problem with the 21 was that its cockpit was so confined I could not fit into it comfortably. Once crammed into place, I took the lead at the start to assure myself of a clear view ahead, and I led on tiptoe in terrible conditions. There was a huge puddle lying on one very fast curve, and everybody was slowing down and dodging to avoid it.

The Lotus, while demanding to be driven very precisely, was giving me quite a pleasant ride, so on one lap I experimented and drove straight into the deep water on the ideal racing line. Sure enough, it picked up its tyres and went into an enormous, long, aquaplane, but it was such a well-balanced car I found I could sustain that slide and it would simply track out of the corner on the correct line and regain adhesion as soon as I arrived on a less-flooded section of track. That gained me an awful lot of time and gave me great admiration for the car. The organizers then stopped the race because of the bad conditions, awarding me an easy win.

I drove the Cooper at Levin, then the Lotus in the more important Lady Wigram Trophy race at Christchurch. That race was run in scorching weather and I preferred the 21 there on Dunlop D12 tyres. I led throughout and shared a new lap record with John Surtees in a Cooper, but at the finish my rear tyres were completely bald and there was very little rubber left on the fronts.

I would not drive the 21 again, as it was still on the high seas returning to England when I ended my career in its older sister, against the bank at Goodwood . . .

January 1961 — Tasman racing in New Zealand saw Moss's maiden race (and win) with Rob's Lotus 21 in the flooded NZ GP at Ardmore Aerodrome, and second time out in the car at Christchurch in the sun he added the Lady Wigram Trophy to their tally.

Ferguson-Climax Project 99 *(1961)*

'A truly fascinating car, a tremendously exciting and stimulating project with which to be involved and an intriguing problem when it came to adapting one's driving technique to use four-wheel drive in road racing . . .'

*T*ony Rolt was a former Le Mans-winning Jaguar works driver who became head of Ferguson Research. In 1960-61 they produced this remarkable front-engined four-wheel drive racing car which could accept either a 2½-litre Climax engine for InterContinental Formula or a 1½-litre version for Formula 1. The car was prepared by them to be entered by Rob Walker Racing, for whom it was driven in 1961 by Jack Fairman and me. In my hands it became the first, and thus far the only, four-wheel drive Formula 1 car ever to win a Formula 1 race, and I was quite fascinated by it.

*T*he Ferguson made its debut in 2½-litre form at Silverstone on 8 July 1961, in the InterContinental Formula British Empire Trophy race. Jack Fairman drove and it showed some promise, despite not really being raced seriously. For the following weekend's British Grand Prix at Aintree, an F1 1½-litre FPF engine was fitted, and while I did my best with our Lotus 18 against the Ferraris in pouring rain, Jack traipsed round in the Ferguson. I had been challenging for the lead until conditions began to dry and I encountered brake trouble which soon put me out.

I asked Rob to call in Jack, so I could rejoin in the Ferguson. But in fact it should already have been disqualified because he had been push-started. In those still-damp conditions I found it went like a rocket!

But it also felt most odd. It was nothing like any other car I had ever driven. It made absolutely unique driving demands, but I began to appreciate that, once I could learn how to use its potential, then it really would offer great advantages.

At first acquaintance it felt peculiar as one applied power to accelerate out of the corners, but once it came straight its traction was fantastic and it really did sit up and fly. It also had phenomenally good brakes, possibly because of its more forward weight distribution than rear-engined cars. The much-vaunted aircraft-style Dunlop Maxaret anti-lock brake system which had been designed into it was not, in fact, fitted when we raced it.

Inevitably, with me driving and the car now going so well, somebody protested Jack's original push-start so I was soon black-flagged, but I could already appreciate the sensational possibilities of 4WD in otherwise impossible conditions.

It was completely different to driving a rear-engined car, and obviously the fact that all four wheels were driven, and that there was power as well as cornering load being applied to the front wheels, asked the driver questions which initially perhaps he could not answer very intelligently. Therefore it was up to him to try to analyse it all, and to find the key to unlock that potential.

When I accelerated in a corner, as I would to balance a conventional rear-drive car, the Ferguson would begin to understeer as the demand upon the front tyres to generate both cornering force and tractive effort overwhelmed their ability to provide grip. This meant that I found myself using more road than ever before as I lapped the familiar Aintree circuit. This power-understeer effect meant I was obviously going to have to adapt my technique to make the most of this very different new racing car.

Where in a conventional car one could change its cornering attitude almost instantaneously by momentarily backing-off the throttle, the Ferguson did not react that way. If I backed off the Ferguson did not instantly tighten into the corner. Instead it would simply decelerate. I therefore realized that one had consciously to steer this car, not merely use the steering to set it up before the corner as one would with conventional rear-wheel drive to present the car in a certain attitude upon a certain line. Oh no, the Ferguson demanded to be consciously steered, and one had continuously to balance its power very directly against steering reaction.

The car fascinated me, and we ran it in the non-Championship Oulton Park Gold Cup race that September. It felt fairly good on this quite tight parkland circuit, but I could not find first gear at the start so had to take off in second. It certainly wasn't easy to drive because its behaviour was so different from anything I had experienced before, and its cockpit was very hot; I had forgotten what it was like to sit *behind* the racing engine, with prop shafts and gearboxes against my hip!

But with a little luck we won, which was — in technical terms at least — quite an historic achievement. The Ferguson's great strength was racing in bad conditions, when its four-wheel drive system's inevitable weight penalty was more than compensated for by its enormously good traction and enhanced braking on all four wheels. When racing conventional cars in the wet the driver does not steer on the throttle as much as he does in the dry. Therefore, when wet conditions place restraints upon the driver of a conventional car, such restraints are reduced by the Ferguson system.

To me the advent of four-wheel drive in the Ferguson was as momentous, and as great a change from anything I had been used to, as the famous 'rear-engined revolution' which for me was marked by the move from Vanwall to Cooper-Climax.

It really was an extraordinary, absorbing car, and one which I would dearly love to handle again in modern historic car racing, should the opportunity arise.

23 September 1961 — Oulton Park Gold Cup — A new shape on the circuits; Ferguson's four-wheel drive P99. Learning a whole new style of driving by adapting to its specialized requirements, Moss the Maestro scored the system's first and thus far only F1 win.

Sunbeam Alpine *(1961)*

'Just a publicity stunt really but very counter-productive because this car as 'prepared' was the biggest bunch of old junk you could imagine . . .'

*I*n October 1961 the big Riverside sports car meeting in California included a three-hour production car race, and my old friends in the Rootes Group asked me to share an Alpine in it with Jack Brabham.

After two laps practice its big ends fell out, after we had found we only needed third and fourth gears and it would pull 6,000 rpm along the straight. On race day the temperature was 115 degrees F, a rear brake seal failed which caused a sixteen-minute pit stop and finally the gearbox broke. Still the history books say we won our class and placed third overall.

The Alpine was quite a nice if rather effeminate-looking car but it was never a sports car in a real performance sense, although this outing made it feel a lot worse than it really was!

Ferrari 250GT Berlinetta Speciale *(1962)*

'A most superior car, forerunner of the GTO, in a race which I remember most for its amusing start . . .'

*T*his was a very elegant and shapely GT prototype, forerunner of the 250GTO, which used a short-chassis 250GT frame fitted with a *Testa Rossa* V12 sports-racing engine, clothed in very elegant almost Superfast II bodywork by Pininfarina. It had run at Le Mans '61 driven by Tavano and Baghetti, where it was obviously very fast until it retired. Ferrari had then ceded it to Luigi Chinetti's North American Racing Team, Chinetti being their influential American importer, and I drove it for him in the 3-Hour Daytona Continental in February 1962.

*M*y formerly very distant relationship with Ferrari had improved, either in spite of — or perhaps because of — my beating his cars at Monaco and Nürburgring in 1961, and the fact that I had also won two consecutive Goodwood TTs in his GT cars.

Anyway, in the winter of 1961-62 Mr Ferrari and I effectively buried the hatchet. I went to see him at Maranello and we had a meal together in the restaurant across the road. He asked me to drive for him but I wanted to continue driving for Rob, whose company and whose manner of going racing I really enjoyed. I told Mr Ferrari 'I would love to drive for you if the car is painted Walker blue and you let Rob run it, while you — Ferrari — supply and maintain it . . .' We agreed in principle, and I was also to drive a new 250GTO which was to be entered by the UDT-Laystall-sponsored team which had been BRP, and which

11 February 1962 — Daytona Continental — Taking NART's very special GT class-winning 250 GT Speciale or Sperimentale '2643 GT' round the Floridan Superspeedway's high bankings.

267

was still run by my father and Ken Gregory. We also arranged to obtain a rear-engined V6 sports-prototype which we announced would be loaned to UDT for other drivers when I was otherwise engaged.

I had been invited to try a new GT prototype — forerunner of the GTO — before the 1961 Italian GP, and it had really impressed me. Then in February '62 I went to Daytona to drive Chinetti's '61 Le Mans *Berlinetta*.

The Daytona road circuit was being used, which combines a long section of the high-banked Speedway with a flat infield loop in front of the main grandstands. It's not really the kind of place where road racing legends are written. Sports-prototype cars had been accepted to make the entry look more exciting, and Dan Gurney would win in a Lotus 19 from Phil Hill and Ricardo Rodriguez in a rear-engined Ferrari. Innes Ireland drove my old TT-winning ex-Walker/Wilkins 250GT which UDT had now bought pending delivery of the GTO. There was also a great fuss about a chap driving an old 3-litre Maserati, whose name was Guido Lollobrigida, brother of Gina, the Italian film star!

My Ferrari was overgeared in practice, pulling only 6,900 rpm down the straight and 6,6 off the banking, but in the race it sang right on up to 7,600 rpm and ran like a train. I finished fourth overall — only two laps behind Dan's winning Lotus, and won the GT category by three clear laps.

A funny thing happened on the way to the start. It was a Le Mans-type run-and-jump, and I was standing on my mark ready to go when Chris Economaki, who is America's best-known motor racing TV commentator, shoved a microphone in front of me and began asking questions on camera. I answered as politely and fully as I could until, out of the corner of my eye, I saw the flag drop! So Chris's in-depth real-time Moss interview ended with me shouting 'Sorry, must go now' and sprinting out of picture . . .

I suspect that may have been the first, and last, live interview with a driver as he actually started a race.

Moss telling TV commentator Chris Economaki what it was like out there. Overall winner Dan Gurney relishes the moment — beyond — in his Arciero Bros' very special Lotus 19.

Ferrari 250
Testa Rossa/61 *(1962)*

'Super car, which felt absolutely unburstable, although it was rather heavy and simply ate front brake pads — but the team who ran it for us was a shambles . . .'

25 March 1962 — Sebring 12-Hours — Stirling rounds the hairpin in NART's Ferrari TR61, '0794' which he shared with Innes Ireland, little suspecting that they have already been disqualified . . .

Into 1962 I was at last on better terms with Ferrari. Innes Ireland and I shared this car, which had won Le Mans the previous year, in the Sebring 12-Hours. It was basically similar to the cars against which I had raced in 1958-59 with the works Aston Martins, but had been updated and developed into this 1961 form with more aerodynamic, high-tailed bodywork evolved by Ferrari's engineer Chiti. It went well, and our North American Racing Team-staffed pit was packed with people. Unfortunately it seemed that only Innes and I knew anything at all about racing, and they didn't even realize the importance of keeping a lap chart, which cost us dear.

In February '62 I had driven for NART in the Daytona Continental 3-Hours, and we subsequently did a deal whereby our Ferrari entries in major long-distance races would be backed jointly by UDT and NART. My first race following this announcement was Sebring in March, where Innes and I were originally intended to share NART's brand-new rear-engined V8 Ferrari, but the car didn't impress in practice. It was fabulous to handle but had no power, despite revving to 7,400. It was unbelievably slow, lapping around 3:26, while the basically three-year-old *Testa Rossa* clocked 3:17 with more in reserve, so we chose it for the race.

It had a lot of power and was nicely balanced and suited to the bumpy circuit. The fact that Innes took the Le Mans-type start instead of me caused a lot of comment, but so had Ivor Bueb when we shared the Costin Lister there in 1959. Innes got away most spectacularly, haring along the grass verge, neck-and-neck with Pedro Rodriguez's Ferrari! He led briefly until Pedro went by and then, at 11.37, the car was refuelled and I took over. NART were hopeless. They had eight cars in the race and didn't keep a lap chart! It seems quite unbelievable but this was so, and in fact Innes came in for fresh brake pads before covering the minimum twenty laps necessary under the rules. The marshal in charge of the filler-cap seals should have refused to cut them, but understandably he didn't have a clue how many laps we had completed since our last stop, and was possibly rather overawed by the whole business anyway.

This meant that while I was blithely racing on, trouble was stirring in the pits, but nobody told us about it. Firstly, the organizers penalized us fifteen seconds for Innes entering the pit area at a dangerous speed. Then somebody protested our early stop, and the stewards conferred and studied the timekeepers' records and eventually decided to disqualify us. Really they had no option, but the way they did it absolutely incensed Innes and me.

Soon after 1 pm I had returned the car to Innes in the lead as the Rodriguez brothers had just made their change-over, and an hour later I took over again. We had lost some time having to change the front brake pads again, but by the five-hour mark we were running happily in second place, one lap down on the Rodriguez car. Around 3.30 their engine predictably broke — they both pushed terribly hard — so I then led by a lap from the Bonnier/Bianchi car. At half-distance we led by two laps, and only then — after over four hours of futile racing since the offence had been committed — were we black-flagged and disqualified!

We were both infuriated. I wrote disgustedly in my diary '*I lapped at 3:12, no flag marshals, officious pit marshals, no food, bed at 8.30pm . . .*' There were hard words about the Sebring organization but really the fault for the original offence lay with NART's joke pit organization. It was a sad end to a race which we should have won. As it was, Sebring '62 marked an unfortunate end to my World Championship endurance racing career . . .

The Goodwood Crash

I have no recollection of racing at Goodwood on Easter Monday, 1962. I recall practising there previously, and driving down to the circuit that morning, and even something of what went on in the paddock before the Glover Trophy race, but the next I am aware of is waking up a month later in hospital — and realizing I had barely survived a pretty massive shunt.

The magazine reports tell me that I ran third behind Graham Hill's BRM and Bruce McLaren's Cooper early in the race, before Surtees went hurtling past me in his new V8 Lola. They then relate how I subsequently '*came past the pits half out of the cockpit and peering round, looking very unhappy.*' After nine laps I came in to have the gear release mechanism attended to, which lost me a lap, and I went to work and lapped in 1:23.0, 104.10 mph, then lowered that mark by another fifth of a second, before Surtees lapped even faster, getting down to 1:22.0. I must have been really pumped-up by that time, because I equalled his record, and by lap thirty I was seventh and '*going really fast,*' they say . . .

Surtees retired, and I negotiated Madgwick Corner closing rapidly on Graham's BRM, though still a lap down. Leaving Fordwater I seem to have gone wide towards the left-hand verge, which was not in essence unusual. But I was closing on Graham, possibly without him realizing it. My usual racing line was very tight, while Graham normally preferred to take a broad sweep into a corner. I understand that a blue flag was shown to him by marshals warning that my car was closing up behind. Just possibly, and this is pure surmise on my part, he acknowledged the flag with a wave of his hand — something I would generally do.

Perhaps I saw that signal and wrongly interpreted it as indicating I should pass on the outside, his left. If he had not appreciated how rapidly I was closing, he might then have swung across to the left after Fordwater as he normally would to take his customary wider line into St Mary's. There is no question there was considerable space between our cars, but perhaps having now committed myself to passing him on the left and still closing fast did I now feel he was moving across into me? I simply cannot tell.

Whatever the cause, the effect was that I simply went straight on, leaving the circuit on the left where it turns right and slightly downhill into St Mary's.

23 April 1962 — Glover Trophy, Goodwood — Moss holding the now UDT-liveried Lotus 18/21's engine cover as team mechanics refit the tail-cowl after tackling his gearbox problems. Back in the race after a long delay he will set about the lap record . . .

Stirling Moss: My cars, my career

23 April 1962 — St Mary's Corner, Goodwood — Moss is on the left-side verge well before the real entry to the corner; braking hard he applies right-lock but there's little reaction on the slippery grass. The car is slithering straight ahead and spears headlong into the earth bank. The enormous impact folds the chassis around its driver — trapping him.

I seem to have tried to brake hard on the slippery grass, before impacting almost at right angles against the solid earth bank there. I stopped in about 18 inches from around, say, 60 mph. My car's spaceframe chassis collapsed upon me, I had been thrown forward by the impact because of course we had no seat belts in those days, and rescuers had to spend forty minutes cutting the crumpled wreckage apart before I could be extricated and removed to hospital.

I survived, but for Stirling Moss, professional racing driver, this was the end . . .

The crash left me with deep facial wounds, my left cheekbone was crushed, my eye socket displaced, my left arm was broken, the leg broken at knee and ankle and badly cut, my nose was broken — again — I was generally battered and muscle-torn, and the right side of my brain had been so severely bruised that I was comatose for a month and paralysed on the left side for six months.

The beauty of this situation was that I knew neither the state I was in, nor anything at all about the accident, its immediate aftermath and the events preceding it.

When I finally regained consciousness and eventually began to mend, I soon realized it was not going to be the same as after the Spa accident . . . no quick recovery this time.

I might exercise again to the point of agony to mend the mechanical parts of my body quickly, but there was nothing I could do to speed recovery of my injured brain. Initially I could only achieve the simplest things, like picking up a pen, by consciously giving myself step-by-step instructions. My doctors advised me that control, co-ordination and even reaction times might recover quickly, but more worrying was their assertion that my vision and concentration would not recover for perhaps two years, maybe longer.

The pressures upon me to return were immense. Press and public alike clamoured insistently 'Will you race again?' I had to know. I wanted to take out a car on a closed, private circuit, and drive in solitude to judge myself, and I decided that, if my reaction time and my vision and concentration were not as they had been before, then I would call it a day.

After being discharged from the Atkinson Morley Hospital I convalesced in Nassau. I drove a Mini-Minor, and for the first time the island's limitations suited me just fine. Back home I drove other cars more quickly. Through the autumn

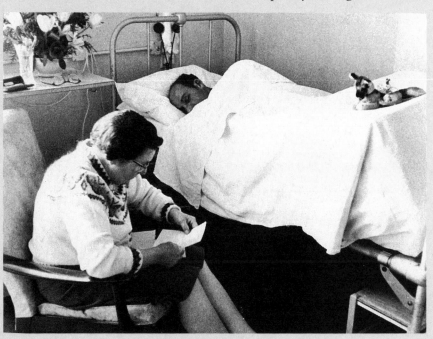

May 1961 — Hospital in London — Mum reads the get-well mail aloud, Stirling remains unconscious . . .

of 1962 I had two spells in St Thomas's for corrective surgery to my left eye platform, the surgeons grafting-in bone taken from my hip to elevate the eye into its proper position. It had actually been displaced in my skull, creating a condition called diploplia, I believe, in which one eye loses focus as it scans.

Into the following winter my vision was sufficiently good for me to drive my Lotus Elite much as I had before. I took up numerous working engagements — the business of living was starting up again.

On 1 May 1963 I drove down to Goodwood, where Ken Gregory and Tony Robinson waited with one of UDT's by this time ageing Lotus 19s. It had rained that morning, and the circuit was still part-wet as I drove out of the pits and up through the gears into the long, never-ending right-hander at Madgwick Corner, then Fordwater. I had first gone this way in September 1948 in my original Cooper 500. I had last gone this way in April '62, having just broken the lap record, heading towards the St Mary's verge and that unyielding outside bank . . .

I wondered if something might come back to me as I approached that spot, out of Fordwater, over the little brow and downhill right-handed through the St Mary's dip. But it didn't. Not a thing. I wasn't bothered at all; no sudden glimpse of buried memory . . . just another piece of road.

I lapped for more than half a hour, trying about eight-tenths I would guess, but very early on I began to realize — or possibly I *thought* that I began to realize — that I really had lost It; the old automatic reflexes, the old instinctive way of doing this, then that, I couldn't find It within me any more.

Afterwards I felt I was no longer doing automatically what I had used to do. I now had to do it all consciously. I lapped in 1:39s on a damp track, three seconds a lap outside what I would have considered a competitive time, yet even at that pace I was using up all my mental capacity to do what I was doing. I told them — 'I had to think. I had to give orders to myself; here I'll brake, here I must change down . . . and another thing, I used to look at the rev counter without taking my eyes off the road, not only that, I could see the rev counter and the road *and* a friend waving to me, all at the same time . . . I've lost that. It's gone . . .'

As I drove back to London to begin my new life as a retired racing driver, Ken called the Press Association, and gave them their quote; 'I've decided to retire. I will not drive again . . .' I was an old man of thirty-two.

Looking back now, I realize my decision was premature. What I then believed to be permanent impairment was to a large extent only temporary. I would still improve, but under intense pressure to return I had not allowed myself the time.

For months everybody, the media, *everybody* had been asking me incessantly 'Are you coming back?', 'Will you drive again?'. Everybody was hammering at me for an answer, not an answer in a month or two or three, or a year, but now, tell us *Now*, our public want to know . . .

I wanted desperately to come back, and against that public background that's why I set myself that Goodwood test so soon.

Subsequently, by the end of 1965, maybe into the high summer of '66, I knew I was nearly mended properly. Certainly, I was desperately out of practice. Sure, it would take time to build up again, but I really felt that I could do it. At 35 I was still young enough. But equally by that time I had so many other business interests, life was so full of so many other things, that without major revolution it simply was not possible to fit in a racing come-back.

I regret how this worked out. I really do feel that for a few more years perhaps I could have continued racing to a properly competitive standard, but to do so would have compromised so much else within my life as 'a professional retired racing driver' that on balance it wasn't worth the gamble. I guess I needed someone to give me that little shove, to have helped me decide to try again. Still, cars, tyres, engines, the whole structure of motor racing had changed enormously since early '62 and perhaps I would not have liked what I found . . .

Postscript

. . . and now a message from the boss . . .

When Stirling asked me if I would write an extra chapter for his book (actually I felt I could have written a whole book on him), I was very honoured, not only because of our long-standing friendship, but also because I hold a great admiration for him, and all he has achieved. Stirling has done a great deal for me. In fact, I suppose our association altered the whole of my life and gave me opportunities I had never dreamt of.

I had intended to write something about Stirling's brilliance and complete mastery of every type of racing car. But when I read Doug's introduction I found he had written everything that I would have said, in virtually the same words.

Our association really started at the September Goodwood meeting in 1957. Stirling was contemplating buying a Formula 2 car for himself to drive the following year. I had both my F2 Cooper-Climax and my under-sized 1,960 cc F1 car at the meeting for Tony Brooks to drive, and Alf Francis, Stirling's ex-mechanic, was now my head mechanic. Stirling asked me if he could try the Cooper as he was not sure whether to buy one of these or a Lotus. Naturally

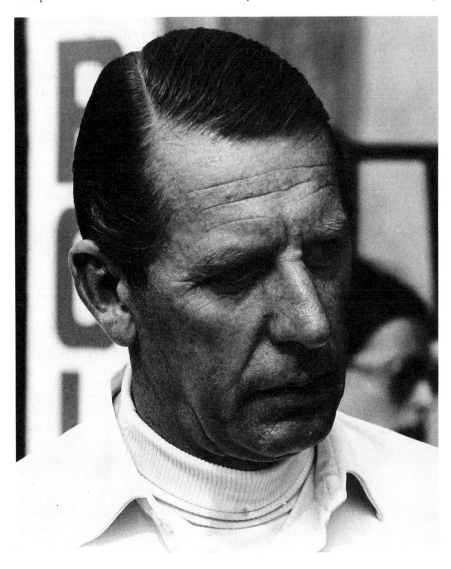

Rob Walker.

I agreed, and Alf very wisely put him in the larger car. He took it out during the last half hour of practice, which was a 'free for all', with small MGs, saloon cars and Heaven knows what. It was not time to go fast. Stirling did one warm-up lap, then a flying one, and the last just slowing down and returning to the pits. During the flying lap, he was weaving in and out of the traffic, and at the same time he broke the lap record! I think he was impressed; I certainly was.

At the last F1 race in Casablanca Stirling had the bedroom next to me, and one evening he asked if he could come and have a talk to me. When he arrived he suggested that he might drive in F2 for me during 1958. He was already committed to Vanwall for F1. Of course I jumped at such good fortune. During 1957 Jack Brabham had been my driver, but on the flight to Casablanca Jack had told me that he wanted to drive for Coopers next year, so I said, 'All right, I will get another driver.' When I told him it was Stirling, he said that when I had told him I would get someone else he had never dreamt it would be Stirling. Nor had I, actually. The next day Stirling caught Asian 'flu and had to go home, so I just hoped it had not all been a brainstorm.

As the book records, in January 1958 the Argentine Grand Prix was held. The Vanwalls were not ready to run on Av-gas, so Stirling asked if he could run my Cooper. In the most incredible David and Goliath act he won, and thus started one of the most wonderful and enjoyable partnerships in my life. I think together we won over 50 Grand Prix and other races.

We never had any contracts; it was all done by a 'gentleman's agreement',

Greatest race — leading at Monaco 1961, in Rob Walker's Lotus 18.

although perhaps I would write a letter to confirm what we had said, in case we might forget later on. Motor racing contracts are stupid anyway, because if someone does not want to drive for you, he just loses interest and does not try.

Stirling and I had only had one disagreement, and even then he did not 'let the sun go down on his wrath', which is true wisdom. It happened at the United States Grand Prix at Riverside in 1960. Our differential was rather worn and anyway was slightly suspect. Lotus managed to get a new one to us on the evening before the race. I gave it to Alf and told him that Stirling wanted it fitted for the race. I went to our garage at about 10.30 pm and Alf told me that it would take him the whole night to fit the new differential and that would give him no time to prepare the car for the race, and anyway our old one was quite good enough for the race. So I said, 'OK, forget the new one and prepare the car with the old one'. Stirling had been to the cinema and came into the garage about midnight to see how the preparation was going. When he found that I had given orders not to fit the new crown wheel, he was furious and asked how I expected him to win the race on the old one. I explained the situation, but he just stormed out of the garage and went back to our motel. About 2 am a note was pusned under the door from Stirling. On it he had written, 'You know whatever happens tomorrow, I shall do my very utmost to win for you.' I think we both went to sleep happy in the knowledge that we were mates again.

Stirling won the race, and as he took the flag and went past the pits, Alf held up a crown wheel to show him. The only thing that upset Stirling was that I had not signalled him to take fastest lap as there was $1,000 for it. I replied that as the differential was dodgy I thought to win the race was enough. Stirling said that if he had to go faster he always took it out of himself, not the car.

The Press loved to slam Stirling as a car breaker, which is entirely unfounded. Obviously he was putting a certain amount of strain on the car as he was going faster than anyone else, but I cannot think of a single instance when the car broke because of his driving. Of course, everything Stirling did was news and I suppose they liked to fix this label on him.

A good example of his care of a car was the Albert Park race at Melbourne in 1958 when he had to run the last eight laps with no water at all (and it wasn't a Porsche), but he still won. Our real problem was gear boxes, because we had to have our own made, and although they were beautifully designed by Colotti, the gears were badly cut and time and time again when Stirling was a long way in the lead, the box would break and Stirling would be blamed for being too hard on it. In fact he lost the World Championship in 1959 for just this reason.

Actually the one disadvantage of having Stirling as a driver was that if he did not win it was always my fault, because he was so good that he would invariably win unless the car let him down, but he would never blame me. The Press of course always said he had inferior machinery, but I would provide him with the best I could get. Tyres and wheels seemed to play a large part in our racing. First there was the tyre wear in the 1958 Argentine Grand Prix, where Alf walked out on to the track and showed Stirling a wheel. Ferrari thought, 'Oh, he is going to come in for a tyre change', but Stirling went right on with his tyres showing the white canvas — and won. You wouldn't believe it, but we did exactly the same trick at Monza in 1959. Ferrari swallowed the bait again, and we won again.

Then there was the chunk of paving thrown up by Jack Brabham at Zandvoort in 1960 which hit Stirling's front wheel, bursting his tyre and bending the wheel. Stirling records Alf took three minutes to change it, but what he doesn't say is that there was only one spare wheel between the whole of the Lotus Team and ourselves, and Alf had to dash to the Lotus pit and borrow it!

The next race was Spa where Stirling had the terrible accident, when his rear wheel came off. That was purely a design fault.

Lastly, at Nurburgring in 1961 we blacked out the green spot on the wet tyres, so that outwardly they appeared to be dry tyres. I don't think even Stirling's skill could have won that race without wet tyres, but we did tell Dunlop about it before we started.

The nice thing about Stirling was that he was not just a driver, but a real friend and fun to be with. We both used to help each other when we were feeling down, and my wife Betty was very fond of him, too. When Stirling split up from his first wife Katie, he felt very low and he was talking of giving up racing completely. So we had him to stay down at my home in Somerset. Betty said that he must take up some hobby that would occupy his mind and she would teach him to paint. He applied himself to it so hard that the still life that she had set him to paint was almost perfect. The *Daily Express* took a photograph of the painting beside the real thing, and we could hardly tell the difference.

Stirling was recognized wherever he went in the world. We could be walking down a main street in Lisbon or Vienna and all the passers-by would turn their heads and say, 'Look — Stirling Moss'. If he went into a restaurant, all the waiters would come up and ask for his autograph. We went into a tiny shop in a small village in Sicily to buy some toothpaste and immediately the girl serving produced a photo of her boyfriend and asked Stirling to sign it. At Zolder in Austria, Stirling was chased by 10,000 fans. We rushed into my transporter, locked the doors, and put it in gear with the handbrake on. They still moved it 100 yards down the runway and we were only rescued by the firemen turning their hoses on the crowd. Once we were driving very fast along some back roads in Italy, when inevitably we were stopped by a policeman. He was in the midst of giving Stirling a hell of a ticking off for dangerous driving, when he suddenly recognized who it was and his eyes nearly popped out of his head and he became speechless.

Stirling had many hobbies, such as designing gadgets for houses, but let's face it, when he was not married the real hobby was girls. They used to come from all over the world to be with him and it was like the play *Boeing Boeing*. I remember in Brussels he went to the airport to see one girl off to Paris, and waited there for half an hour to greet another one coming in from Vienna. When he was injured in hospital, the phone was always ringing with girls calling from everywhere, asking if they should fly there immediately. I just answered, 'It is no good, he is unconscious'. Whenever we were together and he spotted two girls, it was always, 'Mine is all right, but I don't think much of yours, Rob.' Fortunately as I was happily married it did not matter to me that my one wasn't up to much. I think Stirling's feeling for girls was typified by the time he went to visit his father who was very ill in hospital. He asked, 'Do you fancy any of the nurses, Dad?'. His father answered, 'No.' Stirling just remarked, 'My God, you must be ill!'

Stirling has of course become a household name. If someone in the theatre or circus or even on the road goes speeding past, it is always, 'Who do you think you are — Stirling Moss?', not Jimmy Clark or Jackie Stewart, or anyone else. Stirling has some wonderful characteristics. He is very loyal and in the early days when he might drive for three different teams in a week, he was always completely loyal to the team he was with at the time, even to the point of turning down Ferrari's first offer of a drive in 1951.

He was modest, although he obviously knew he was the greatest driver of his time, after Fangio retired. He never exaggerated and you could always trust his word. A good friend indeed.

Rob

RRC Walker
Nunney
Frome
Somerset

. . . Apart from that
they had a lot of fun.

Racing Record

First Steps

*S*ince Stirling Moss's pre-1954 diaries seem sadly — and most untypically — to have been mislaid long ago, his only *clearly recorded* drives in motoring competition before his serious career really began in earnest with the Cooper-JAP 500 in 1948, seem to be as follows:

1947

Date	Race & Venue	Car	Result & Comments
2-3-47	Harrow CC Moss Trophy Trial	BMW 328	**Won** Cullen Cup
6-4-47	NW London MC Inter-Club Trial	BMW 328	Snapped half-shaft
28/29-6-47	JCC Eastbourne Rally	BMW 328	**1st Class Award** — **1st** easy-starting test — **1st** steering test
1-9-47	Brighton Speed Trials	BMW 328	7th in 2-litre standard sports class
6-9-47	Poole Speed Trials	BMW 328	Third in class
20-9-47	Chichester Speed Trials, Merston Aerodrome	BMW 328	Unplaced

For the Record

What now follows has been compiled from the best available information. Several early minor-race best performances, eg fastest lap, best practice time or pole position, may have been omitted in the absence of hard corroborative evidence, the same also applying to a few later events. Otherwise this listing of Stirling Moss's career 1948-1962 is as complete as it has been possible to make it, but full contemporary records are not available in all cases . . . and I am only human. DCN.

Abbreviations used: PP = Pole Position; BPT = Best Practice Time (when grid positions were decided by ballot in early days but also applicable to some later events); FL = Fastest Lap; LR = Lap Record; FTD = Fastest Time of the Day; NCR = New Climb Record; DISQ = Disqualified; UNC = Unclassified, ie finishing too far behind leader to be classed officially as a finisher; o/a = overall result; DNS = Did Not Start; n/a = not available.

1948

Date	Race & Venue	Car	Result & Comments
9-5-48	Prescott Hill-Climb, GB	Cooper-JAP 500 Mk II	4th in class, 51.01"
5-6-48	Stanmer Park Hill-Climb, GB	Cooper-JAP 500 Mk II	**FTD** in class, 58.78"
7-4-48	Brough aerodrome races, GB	Cooper-JAP 500 Mk II	**1st** in heat, **BPT, FL**
		Cooper-JAP 500 Mk II	**1st** in final
		Cooper-JAP 500 Mk II	**1st** in handicap race
15-7-48	Bouley Bay Hill-Climb, CI	Cooper-JAP 500 Mk II	**FTD** in class, 63.80", **NCR**
18-7-48	Prescott Hill-Climb, GB	Cooper-JAP 500 Mk II	**FTD** in class, 49.51"
25-7-48	Great Auclum Hill-Climb, GB	Cooper-JAP 500 Mk II	**FTD** in class, 23.46", 2nd o/a
7-8-48	Boscombe Speed Trials, GB	Cooper-JAP 500 Mk II	**FTD** in class, 31.40", 2nd o/a
5-9-48	Brighton Speed Trials, GB	Cooper-JAP 500 Mk II	4th, sick engine, best time 34.14", beat Stan Coldham in first run, Eric Brandon in second.
12-9-48	Prescott Hill-Climb, GB	Cooper-JAP 500 Mk II	3rd in class, 34.14", heavy rain

18-9-48	Goodwood 500cc race, GB	Cooper-JAP 500 Mk II	**1st, BPT**, 3-laps, 71.92mph. Inaugural Goodwood race meeting.
25-9-48	Shelsley Walsh Hill-Climb, GB	Cooper-JAP 500 Mk II	**FTD** in 750cc racing car class — not 500 — 43.84″. First appearance in white crash helmet
2-10-48	Silverstone 500cc race, GB	Cooper-JAP 500 Mk II	**PP**, 3:17.4, 66.98mph, led but Rtd, gearbox sprocket
9-10-48	Dunholme Lodge aerodrome, GB	Cooper-JAP 500 Mk II	**1st**, 500cc 8-laps, 78.56mph

1949

19-4-49	2nd Easter Handicap, Goodwood, GB	Cooper-JAP 1000 Mk III	**1st**, 79.76mph, **BPT, FL** 82.44mph
	500cc race	Cooper-JAP 500 Mk III	Rtd, piston
14-5-49	British GP 500cc race, Silverstone, GB	Cooper-JAP 500 Mk III	**1st**, 68.81mph, **FL** 70.95mph
26-5-49	Manx Cup, Douglas, IoM	Cooper-JAP 1000 Mk III	Rtd, magneto
28-5-49	Blandford Hill-Climb, GB	Cooper-JAP 500 Mk III	**FTD** in class, 36.62″
11-6-49	Shelsley Walsh Hill-Climb, GB	Cooper-JAP 1000 Mk III	2nd, 1100cc class, 38.57″
25-6-49	Bo'ness Hill-Climb, GB	Cooper-JAP 1000 Mk III	2nd, 1100cc class, 36.1″, 4th o/a
10-7-49	IX Circuito del Garda, I	Cooper-JAP 1000 Mk III	3rd in heat
	IX Circuito del Garda, I	Cooper-JAP 1000 Mk III	3rd in final, *1st* 1100cc class
17-7-49	*Coupes des Petites Cylindrées*, Reims-Gueux	Cooper-JAP 1000 Mk III	'9th', UNC, chain broke!
21-7-49	Bouley Bay Hill-Climb, CI	Cooper-JAP 1000 Mk III	2nd 1100cc class, 3rd FTD o/a
31-7-49	Zandvoort 500cc, NL	Cooper-JAP 500 Mk III	**1st, PP**, ran single cylinder engine on twin-cyl crankcase
20-8-49	BRDC Silverstone, GB	Cooper-JAP 500 Mk III	2nd, ran single cylinder on twin-cyl crankcase
27-8-49	Prix du Leman, Lausanne	Cooper-JAP 1000 Mk III	Rtd, engine, awarded Gold Cup for 'most meritorious performance'
11-9-49	Prescott Hill-Climb, GB	Cooper-JAP 1000 Mk III	**1st**, 44.77″ **NCR** by 0.99″ in 1100cc class
17-9-49	Madgwick Cup, Goodwood, GB	Cooper-JAP 1000 Mk III	**1st, FL**
	Goodwood Trophy	Cooper-JAP 1000 Mk III	Rtd — Driving John Cooper's car in F1 race
24-9-49	Shelsley Walsh Hill-Climb, GB	Cooper-JAP 1000 Mk III	**FTD**, 38.19″
2-10-49	Brough aerodrome races, GB	Cooper-JAP 500 Mk III	3rd in heat 2, engine down on power
	Brough aerodrome races, GB	Cooper-JAP 500 Mk III	3rd in final, behind Coldham and Parker
	Brough aerodrome races, GB	Cooper-JAP 500 Mk III	Rtd in handicap race, ran 3rd, engine finally failed.

1950

10-4-50	Easter event 1, Goodwood, GB	HWM	6th
	Third Easter Handicap	HWM	2nd
16-4-50	500cc races, Brands Hatch, GB	Cooper-JAP 500 Mk IV	Rtd, piston
30-4-50	Paris GP, Montlhéry, F	HWM	Rtd, con-rod

13-5-50	BRDC 500cc. Silverstone, GB	Cooper-JAP 500 Mk IV	**1st, BPT, FL** in heat
	BRDC 500cc, Final	Cooper-JAP 500 Mk IV	2nd after piston failed on approach to final corner when leading
14-5-50	Prix de Mons, B	HWM	6th heat 1
	Prix de Mons, B	HWM	7th in final
20-5-50	Prix de Monte Carlo, MON	Cooper-JAP 500 Mk IV	**1st** in heat, **BPT, FL**
	Prix de Monte Carlo, MON	Cooper-JAP 500 Mk IV	**1st** in final, **FL**
28-5-50	Circuit du Lac, Aix-les-Bains,	HWM	Rtd in heat, both car and driver sick
	500cc race, Aix-les-Bains, F	Cooper-JAP 500 Mk IV	Rtd, engine failure
11-6-50	Rome GP, Caravalla Baths, I	HWM	**FL,** Rtd, stub axle, ran 3rd to Ascari and Villoresi
17-6-50	Goodwood 1500cc sports cars	Cooper-MG	5th, **FL,** 74.5mph
25-6-50	Brands Hatch 500cc races, GB	Cooper-JAP 500 Mk IV	**1st, FL** open challenge heat 1
	Brands Hatch 500cc races, GB	Cooper-JAP 500 Mk IV	**1st,** open challenge final
	Brands Hatch 500cc races, GB	Cooper-JAP 500 Mk IV	**1st,** 500cc production cars heat
	Brands Hatch 500cc races, GB	Cooper-JAP 500 Mk IV	**1st,** 500 cc production cars final
	Brands Hatch 500cc races, GB	Cooper-JAP 500 Mk IV	**1st,** Ten fastest cars race
2-7-50	Coupe des Racers 500, Reims, F	Cooper-JAP 500 Mk IV	6th
2-7-50	Coupe des Petites Cylindrées	HWM	3rd behind Ascari and Simon
9-7-50	Bari GP, I	HWM	3rd behind Farina and Fangio, *Formula 1 race*
22-7-50	Naples GP, Posillipo, I	HWM	**1st** in heat 1, **FL**
22-7-50	Naples GP, Posillipo, I	HWM	*Crashed* in final while leading
7-8-50	500 Trophy, Brands Hatch, GB	Cooper-JAP 500 Mk IV	**1st** in heat 2
	500 Trophy, Brands Hatch, GB	Cooper-JAP 500 Mk IV	2nd final to George Wicken, *LR* 67.54″
	Daily Telegraph Trophy	Cooper-JAP 500 Mk IV	**1st** in heat
	Daily Telegraph Trophy	Cooper-JAP 500 Mk IV	Rtd in final, carburettor
12-8-50	Prix de Berne, CH	HWM	Rtd, gearbox, *FL*
26-8-50	BRDC Silverstone, GB	HWM	9th heat 2
	BRDC Silverstone, GB	HWM	6th in final
	BRDC Silverstone, GB	Cooper-Norton 500 Mk V	**1st PP FL**
10-9-50	Circuit de Mettet, B	HWM	4th heat 1
	Circuit de Mettet, B	HWM	**1st** heat 2 — 2nd o/a on aggregate
16-9-50	RAC Tourist Trophy, Dundrod, NI	Jaguar XK120	**1st**
17-9-50	500cc races, Brands Hatch, GB	Cooper-Norton 500 Mk V	**1st** in heat 2
	500cc races, Brands Hatch, GB	Cooper-Norton 500 Mk V	Rtd in final, gearbox
24-9-50	Circuit de Perigueux, F	HWM	2nd heat 1
	Circuit de Perigueux, F	HWM	3rd in final
30-9-50	BARC Goodwood, GB	HWM	7th
	BARC Goodwood, GB	Cooper-Norton 500 Mk V	2nd **FL** after engine seized in practice, hastily rebored
7-10-50	Castle Combe, GB	HWM	**1st**
	Castle Combe, GB	Cooper-Norton 500 Mk V	**1st** in heat
	Castle Combe, GB	Cooper-Norton 500 Mk V	Rtd in final, carburettor float sank. Brake failure in practice sent SM 300yds across field!
	Castle Combe, GB	Frazer Nash	**1st** 2-litre sports car
	Castle Combe, GB	Frazer Nash	Team handicap

Date	Event	Car	Result
15-10-50	X Circuito del Garda, I	HWM	Rtd, stub axle
24/25-10-50	Montlhéry 24-Hour Jaguar 'demonstration', F	Jaguar XK120	2,579.16 miles in 24-Hours, average speed 107.46mph, averaged 112.4mph in final hour, fastest lap 126.2mph
17-11-50	*Daily Express* Rally, GB	Aston Martin DB2	Finished road course unpenalised, failed final tests
21-11-50	Record Attempts, Montlhery, F	Kieft-Norton dohc '350'	
	International Class J — 50km	126.24km/h — 78.44mph	
	50 miles	126.75km/h — 78.75mph	
	100km	127.28km/h — 79.08mph	
	1 Hour	127.77km/h — 79.37mph	
	100 miles	128.14km/h — 79.62mph	
	200km	124.10km/h — 77.11mph	

In all the above SM shared driving with Ken Gregory

Date	Event	Car	Result
23-11-50	Record Attempts, Montlhéry, F	Kieft-Norton sohc '500'	
	International Class I — 50km	144.94km/h — 90.06mph	
	50 miles	145.85km/h — 90.63mph	
	100km	146.26km/h — 90.87mph	
	1 Hour	146.99km/h — 91.34mph	
	100 miles	147.09km/h — 91.4mph	
	200km	142.50km/h — 88.6mph	
	200 miles	140.00km/h — 86.99mph	

In this set of records SM co-drove with Ken Gregory and Jack Neill

1951

Date	Event	Car	Result
10-2-51	Chiltern Night Trial, GB	Morris Minor	In Tony Woods' car, map-reading errors . . .
26-3-51	Lavant Cup, Goodwood, GB	HWM	1st
	Richmond trophy, Formula 1	HWM	5th
8-4-51	Marseilles GP, F	HWM	3rd
22-4-51	San Remo GP, Ospedaletti, I	HWM	5th in Formula 1 race against works Ferraris.
29-4-51	Mille Miglia, Brescia-Brescia, I	Jaguar XK120	Minor accident on oil — with Frank Rainbow
3-5-51	500cc Luxembourg GP, Findel	Kieft-Norton 500	Rtd in heat 2, 1950-type car, new double-knocker engine
5-5-51	BRDC International Trophy, Silverstone, GB	HWM	6th in heat 1
	Silverstone, GB	HWM	14th in Final, 2-litre F2 car in F1 race
	1 Hour Production sports race	Jaguar XK120	**1st, FL,** Team Prize
13-5-51	Monza Autodrome GP, I	HWM	4th in heat 1
	Monza Autodrome GP, I	HWM	3rd in heat 2, *THIRD* on aggregate, discovered slipstreaming
14-5-51	Whit-Monday Goodwood, GB	Kieft-Norton 500	9th in heat, new car's debut
	Whit-Monday Goodwood, GB	Kieft-Norton 500	**1st** in final, **FL, LR**
20-5-51	Columbus Centenary GP, Genoa, I	HWM	Rtd after leading, transmission
	500cc race	Kieft-Norton 500	Rtd, led from start to 3 laps from finish when suspension cable broke

27-5-51	SWISS GP, Bremgarten, Berne	HWM	8th — *SM's FIRST WORLD CHAMPIONSHIP-QUALIFYING GRANDE EPREUVE*
3-6-51	Circuit du Lac, Aix-les-Bains, F	HWM	**1st, FL,** heat 2
	Circuit du Lac, Aix-les-Bains, F	HWM	2nd in final
10-6-51	Rome GP, Baths of Caracalla, I	HWM	4th
14-6-51	British Empire Trophy, Douglas, IoM	Frazer Nash	**1st, FL,** 3:23, 69.78mph
24-6-51	Le Mans 24-Hours, Sarthe, F	Jaguar C-Type	Rtd, engine after leading, broke **LR** three times, best 4:6.8, 105.85mph
1-7-51	AVUSRennen, Berlin, D	HWM	Rtd, engine (very thoroughly!)
8-7-51	Rouen GP, Les Essarts, F	HWM	Rtd, gearbox
14-7-51	British GP 500cc race, Silverstone, GB	Kieft-Norton 500	**1st, PP, FL, NR** 2:02, pole time 1:59.6, 86.95mph
15-7-51	Circuit de Mettet, B	HWM	4th
22-7-51	Dutch GP, Zandvoort, NL	HWM	3rd, ran 2nd until last-minute engine problem
	Dutch GP 500cc race	Kieft-Norton 500	**1st, PP, FL**
29-7-51	German GP 500cc race, Nürburging	Kieft-Norton 500	Rtd, **PP, FL** steering arm broke on lap 3 of 6-lap race, after lowering 500cc North Circuit lap record by 40secs in practice . . .
5-8-51	Freiburg Mountain Climb, D	HWM	4th Formula 2, 8:24.08, 53.3mph
	500cc class climb	Kieft-Norton 500	**1st** 500cc, 8:18.99, 53.8mph
12-8-51	GP OstSchweiz, Erlen, CH	HWM	Rtd, suspension broke when leading
2-9-51	Bari GP, I	Ferrari 166	DNS in Formula 1 race, the Ferrari 'works drive' débâcle, practised David Murray's old car instead, it broke
8-9-51	Wakefield Trophy, Curragh, EI	HWM	**1st, LR,** 3:31.8, 83.96mph
	O'Boyle Trophy concurrent	HWM	**1st**
15-9-51	RAC Tourist Trophy, Dundrod, NI	Jaguar C-Type	**1st, BPT,** Team Prize
23-9-51*	Modena GP, I	HWM	Rtd
29-9-51	Madgwick Cup, Goodwood, GB	HWM	**1st, FL,** 1:39.0, 86.54mph
	Sports car race	Jaguar C-Type	**1st, PP, FL,** 1:41.0, 84.83mph
	2nd September Handicap	Jaguar C-Type	**1st, FL,** 1:39.6, 86.02mph
	3rd September Handicap	HWM	2nd, behind Farina . . .
	Daily Graphic Trophy	HWM	5th in Formula 1 race
13-10-51	Winfield races, Scotland	HWM	**1st, FL,** 1:27.7, 82.1mph
20-10-51	Brands Hatch 500cc races, GB	Kieft-Norton 500	**1st** Open Challenge event heat 3, DNS in final having broken gearbox replaced

* This weekend Ken Wharton ran the Moss Kieft at Shelsley Walsh and set 500cc class FTD

| 20-10-51 | Brands Hatch Championship | Kieft-Norton 500 | **1st** in heat 2 |
| | Brands Hatch Championship | Kieft-Norton 500 | **1st** in final |

1952

22/29-1-52	Monte Carlo Rally	Sunbeam-Talbot	2nd o/a with Desmond Scannell/John A. Cooper
17-2-52	Kitching Trophy Trial, GB	Harford III	7th in one-off Trials drive, passengered by John A. Cooper
24-3-52	Lyon-Charbonnières Rally	Jaguar XK120 Coupé	2nd in class, 15th overall, navigated by Gregor Grant
12-4-52	Castle Combe 500cc races, GB	Kieft-Norton 500*	**1st, FL** in heat 3, **LR** 77.9mph
	Castle Combe 500cc races, GB	Kieft-Norton 500	**1st FL**
	Team relay race	Frazer Nash	Unplaced, took over Roy Salvadori's car
14-4-52	Earl of March Trophy, Goodwood, GB	Kieft-Norton 500	**1st, PP, LR** 1:48.6″, 79.56mph
	First Easter Handicap	Jaguar C-Type	4th **FL**, 1:44.6, 82.60mph — Jaguar's first race using disc brakes
4-5-52	Mille Miglia, Brescia-Brescia, I	Jaguar C-Type	Rtd, ran 4th — with Norman Dewis, car on disc brakes
10-5-52	BRDC Silverstone, 500cc	Kieft-Norton 500	3rd, **PP, FL**, 2:20.0, 75.27mph, brakes began binding when in lead
	Touring Car race	Jaguar Mk VII	**1st, PP, FL** 2:18.0, 76.36mph
	Production sports cars	Jaguar C-Type	**1st, PP, FL,** 2:01.0, 87.08mph
	'The Race of The Champions'	Jaguar XK120	**1st, FL,** 2:12.0, 79.83mph
11-5-52	Brussels GP, Bois de la Cambre, B	Kieft-Norton 500	Multiple collision, car w/o
18-5-52	SWISS GP, Bremgarten, Berne	HWM	Withdrawn following suspension failures on sister team cars
22-5-52	Luxembourg GP, Findel	Kieft-Norton 500	**1st** in heat 2 in Derek Annable's car
	Luxembourg GP, Findel	Kieft-Norton 500	6th in final, intermittent magneto short
25-5-52	Eifelrennen, Nürburgring, D	HWM	2nd to Rudi Fischer's Ferrari
	500cc race	Kieft-Norton 500	**PP,** Rtd, rear hub sheared off axle shaft when 2nd, driving Annable's car
29-5-52	British Empire Trophy, Douglas, IoM	Frazer Nash	Rtd, ignition
2-6-52	MONACO GP, Monte Carlo	Jaguar C-Type	**PP** DISQ for 'outside assistance' after multiple collision
	Prix de Monte Carlo	Frazer Nash	**PP,** Rtd, wheel fixing damage after leading
7-6-52	Ulster Trophy, Dundrod, NI	BRM V16	Rtd engine, clutch, team etc
14/15-6-52	Le Mans 24-Hours, F	Jaguar C-Type	Rtd, overheating
22-6-52	BELGIAN GP, Spa-Francorchamps	ERA G-Type	Crashed after engine failure on opening lap

* Car modified over winter with more stubby nose, fared suspension etc. latest short-stroke double-knocker Norton engine.

29-6-52	Reims sports car race, F	Jaguar C-Type	**1st** — Tommy Wisdom's car, first major win on Dunlop disc-brakes
	Marne GP	HWM	UNC, '10th', drenched in oil
11-7-52	Alpine Rally	Sunbeam-Talbot	**1st** in class, *Coupe des Alpes* with John Cutts
19-7-52	BRITISH GP, Silverstone	ERA G-Type	Rtd, overheating
19-7-52	500cc race	Kieft-Norton 500	**1st, PP, =FL,** 2:04.0, 84.98mph with Don Parker, whose primary chain broke when leading on second-last corner
20-7-52	Namur GP, B	Kieft-Norton 500	**1st** in heat, Annable's car
	Namur GP, B	Kieft-Norton 500	Rtd from final when leading, front suspension broke
27-7-52	Fairwood Aerodrome, Wales, GB	Kieft-Norton 500	Rtd, new works car smashed in heat 2 collision
	F3 Invitation race	Kieft-Norton 500	3rd in Annable's now tired car
28-7-52	Prescott Hill-Climb	Kieft-Norton 500	2nd in Annable's car
2-8-52	*Daily Mail* Trophy, Boreham, GB	ERA G-Type	3rd
	Sports car race	Jaguar C-Type	**1st, PP, FL,** 90.00mph, in Tommy Wisdom's car
	500cc race	Cooper-Norton Mk VI	3rd in John Cooper's 'works' car
4-8-52	August Sprint, Brands Hatch, GB	Kieft-Norton 500	2nd in heat 4, Annable's car
	August Sprint, Brands Hatch, GB	Kieft-Norton 500	2nd in final, beaten both times by Don Parker's Kieft.
	Daily Telegraph Trophy,	Kieft-Norton 500	**1st** in heat 3 **LR** 71.43mph, Annable's car
	Daily Telegraph Trophy	Kieft-Norton 500	Rtd in final when engine threw rod after leading 15 laps
5/12-8-52	Seven-Day Records, Montlhéry, F	Jaguar XK120 Coupé	Total 16,851.73 miles averaging 100.31mph, teamed with Leslie Johnson, Jack Fairman and Bert Hadley
		10,000kms	107.31mph
		3 days	105.55mph
		15,000kms	101.95mph
		4 days	101.17mph
		10,000 miles	100.66mph
16-8-52	Goodwood 9-Hours, GB	Jaguar C-Type	**PP,** 5th after leading, co-driver Peter Walker
17-8-52	DUTCH GP, Zandvoort	ERA G-Type	Rtd, engine, after running 8th
	500cc race	Cooper-Norton 500 Mk VI	**1st** in John Cooper's car
23-8-52	Turnberry, Scotland	Jaguar C-Type	**1st** in heat 2
	Turnberry, Scotland	Jaguar C-Type	**1st** in final
	500cc race	Cooper-Norton 500 Mk VI	**1st, PP**
31-8-52	Grenzlandring, NL	Cooper-Norton 500 Mk VI	3rd (just) behind Eric Brandon, John Cooper won at 102.59mph in works

			Cooper 500 streamliner
7-9-52	ITALIAN GP, Monza	Connaught A-Type	Rtd, engine, when lying 10th
27-9-52	Goodwood 500cc race, GB	Cooper-Norton 500 Mk VI	**1st,** beat Parker who led most of the way, using a lot of road
	Sports car race	Jaguar C-Type	2nd, **PP, LR,** 1:41.2, 85.37mph
	Madgwick Cup F2	ERA G-Type	Rtd, first corner collision
	Goodwood Trophy *F. Libre*	ERA G-Type	5th
4-10-52	Castle Combe 500cc race, GB	Cooper-Norton 500 Mk VI	**1st** in heat 1
	Castle Combe 500cc race, GB	Cooper-Norton 500 Mk VI	**1st, PP, LR** 1:22.2, 80.58mph in final
4-10-52	Formula 2 race	ERA G-Type	**PP,** Rtd steering broke
11-10-52	Charterhall, Scotland	Jaguar C-Type	2nd
	500cc race	Cooper-Norton 500 Mk VI	2nd **BPT, FL,** 1:33.8, 76.9mph, lost lead to Eric Brandon when forced to avoid Coombs' car as it lost a wheel
11-10-52	Formula 2 race	ERA G-Type	4th
12/15-11-52	*Daily Express* Rally	Jaguar XK120 Coupe	13th overall, class award with John A. Cooper
2-12-52	15-Countries run	Humber Super Snipe	Completed in 3 days 18hrs, with Leslie Johnson, John Cutts, David Humphrey

1953

20/27-1-53	Monte Carlo Rally	Sunbeam-Talbot	6th, with Desmond Scannell and John A. Cooper again
??-3-53	Jabbeke Records, B	Sunbeam-Talbot Alpine	120.459mph
??-3-53	Montlhéry Records, F	Sunbeam-Talbot Alpine	116mph for single lap of speedbowl
6-4-53	Lavant Cup, Goodwood, GB	Cooper-Alta Spl	7th
	Earl of March Trophy 500cc	Cooper-Norton 500 Mk VII	3rd, beaten by Alan Brown's Beart Cooper Mk VIIA which set new lap record
26-4-53	Mille Miglia, Brescia-Brescia, I	Jaguar C-Type	Rtd, back axle — with 'Mort' Morris-Goodall
9-5-53	BRDC International Trophy, Silverstone, GB	Cooper-Alta Spl	2nd in heat 1, **=FL** with 'Toulo' de Graffenried, 1:54.0, 92.43mph
	BRDC International Trophy, Silverstone GB	Cooper-Alta Spl	9th
	Production Touring car race	Jaguar Mk VII	**1st, PP, FL,** 76.36mph
	Sports car race	Jaguar C-Type	7th after rolling this car at Abbey Curve in practice, DNS in 500cc race for this reason.
16-5-53	Ulster Trophy, Dundrod, NI	Connaught A-Type	**PP, FL,** 2nd in heat 1, gearbox failed, not allowed to change cars to start in final
25-5-53	Coronation Trophy, Crystal Palace, GB	Cooper-Alta Spl	4th in heat 1
	Crystal Palace, GB	Cooper-Alta Spl	5th in final
	500cc race	Cooper-Norton 500 Mk VII	**1st FL**

31-5-53	Eifelrennen, Nürburgring, D	Cooper-Alta Spl	6th
	Eifelrennen 500cc	Cooper-Norton 500 Mk VII	**1st**
6-6-53	DUTCH GP, Zandvoort	Connaught A-Type	9th
13/14-6-53	Le Mans 24-Hours, F	Jaguar C-Type	2nd, co-driver Peter Walker
18-6-53	British Empire Trophy, Douglas, IoM	Jaguar C-Type	2nd in heat 3 behind Reg Parnell's new Aston Marton DB3S
	British Empire Trophy, Douglas, IoM	Jaguar C-Type	4th in final
28-6-53	Rouen GP, Les Essarts, F	Cooper-Alta	UNC '10th' in Formula 1 race
5-7-53	FRENCH GP, Reims-Gueux	Cooper-Alta	Rtd, clutch disintegrated
	Reims 12-Hours	Jaguar C-Type	**1st** co-driver Peter Whitehead
10/16-7-53	Alpine Rally	Sunbeam-Talbot Alpine	*Coupe des Alpes*, penalty-free run
18-7-53	British GP 500cc, Silverstone	Cooper-Norton 500 Mk VII	**1st, PP,** =**FL** with Stuart Lewis-Evans, 2:02.0, 83.37mph equalled record
26-7-53	Jubilee GP, Lisbon, P	Jaguar C-Type	2nd
2-8-53	GERMAN GP, Nürburgring	Cooper-Alta Mk II	6th in new car built in only 11 days
9-8-53	Sables d'Olonnes GP, F	Cooper-Alta Mk II	4th in heat 1
	Sables d'Olonnes GP, F	Cooper-Alta Mk II	5th in heat 2, 3rd o/a on aggregate
15-8-53	Charterhall, F2, Scotland	Coope-Alta Mk II	**PP,** Rtd, fuel injection
	Formule Libre	Cooper-Alta Mk II	Rtd, engine (this time on carburettors)
	500cc race	Cooper-Norton 500 Mk VII	**1st**
22-8-53	Goodwood 9-Hours, GB	Jaguar C-Type	Rtd, engine, after leading — co-driver Peter Walker
5-9-53	RAC Tourist Trophy, Dundrod, NI	Jaguar C-Type	**BPT,** 4th, co-driver Peter Walker, **1st** over-3-litre class
7-9-53	ITALIAN GP, Monza	Cooper-Alta Mk II	13th after terrific run, which ate tyres, on nitro fuel
19-9-53	London Trophy, Crystal Palace, GB	Cooper-Alta Mk II	**1st PP** in heat 1
	London Trophy, Crystal Palace, GB	Cooper-Alta Mk II	**1st PP** in heat 2, so **1st** o/a on aggregate
	Redex Trophy 500cc	Cooper-Norton 500 Mk VII	2nd in heat 1 to Lewis-Evans' Beart Mk VIIA
	Redex Trophy 500cc	Cooper-Norton 500 Mk VII	Rtd, engine blew when running 3rd
20-9-53	Prescott Hill-Climb, GB	Cooper-Alta Mk II	**1st** F2, 46.48″, 2nd *Formule Libre* 46.35″
26-9-53	Madgwich Cup, Goodwood, GB	Cooper-Alta Mk II	2nd in F2 race to Roy Salvacadori's Connaught
	Woodcote Cup	Cooper-Alta Mk II	4th in *Libre* race
	Goodwood Trophy	Cooper-Alta Mk II	Rtd, magneto drive
	500cc race	Cooper-Norton 500 Mk VII	Rtd after running 4th, oil cap opened, spilled oil caused slipping clutch
3-10-53	Castle Combe 500cc, GB	Cooper-Norton 500 Mk VII	**1st** in heat 2, **LR** 81.19mph, DNS final due to injuries in *Libre* race

| | Joe Fry Memorial *Libre* race | Cooper-JAP 1100 Mk VII | Collision with Tony Rolt's Connaught A-Type, SM injured. American driver Bob Said subsequently drove "the Moss Cooper 500" in final Snetterton meeting of the season. |

1954

18/25-1-54	Monte Carlo Rally	Sunbeam-Talbot	15th, with Desmond Scannell and John A. Cooper
7-3-54	Sebring 12-Hours, USA	OSCA	**1st** co-driving with Bill Lloyd
10-4-54	British Empire Trophy, Oulton Park, GB	Leonard-MG	3rd in heat 1
	Oulton Park, GB	Leonard-MG	Rtd in final, engine
17-4-54	Goodwood 500cc race	Beart-Cooper Mk VIIA	7th, engine sick
9-5-54	Bordeaux GP, F	Maserati 250F	4th, debut of new car '2508'
15-5-54	BRDC International Trophy, Silverstone, GB	Maserati 250F	3rd in heat 1
	Silverstone, GB	Maserati 250F	Rtd in final, de Dion tube broke
	Production Touring Car race	Jaguar Mk VII	3rd, **PP**, **=LR** with Ian Appleyard and Tony Rolt, 2:16.0, 77.48mph, starter had jammed, had to rock car in gear on line to get it going!
	500cc race	Beart-Cooper Mk VIIA	**1st FL**
23-5-54	Eifelrennen 500cc, Nürburgring, D	Beart-Cooper Mk VIIA	**1st**
29-5-54	Aintree '200', *Formule Libre* GB	Maserati 250F	3rd in heat 1
	Aintree '200', *Formule Libre*, GB	Maserati 250F	**1st** in final *FIRST VICTORY IN FORMULA ONE CAR*
	500cc race	Beart-Cooper Mk VIIA	**1st, FL**
6-6-54	Rome GP, Castelfusano, I	Maserati 250F	UNC '6th', transmission failed
12/13-6-54	Le Mans 24-Hours, F	Jaguar D-Type	Rtd, brakes, co-drove with Peter Walker, car timed at 172.87mph on Mulsanne Straight
20-6-54	BELGIAN GP, Spa-Francorchamps	Maserati 250F	3rd *FIRST WORLD CHAMPIONSHIP POINTS SCORE*
4-7-54	Reims 12-Hours, F	Jaguar D-Type	Rtd, transmission, after leading
9/16-7-54	Alpine Rally	Sunbeam-Talbot Alpine	*Coupe des Alpes en Or* for third consecutive penalty-free performance, navigated by John Cutts
17-7-54	BRITISH GP, Silverstone	Maserati 250F	UNC '14th' Rtd, transmission when running 2nd near finish
25-7-54	Caen GP, Le Prairie, F	Maserati 250F	2nd, **LR**, 1:25.7, 92.40mph
1-8-54	GERMAN GP, Nürburgring	Maserati 250F	Rtd, engine — *DEBUT AS WORKS DRIVER* using own car

2-8-54	*Daily Telegraph* 500cc races, Brands Hatch, GB	Beart-Cooper Mk VIIA	2nd in heat 4
	Brands Hatch, GB	Beart-Cooper Mk VIIA	2nd in final
7-8-54	Oulton Park Gold Cup, GB	Maserati 250F	**1st, FL,** 1:56.8, 85.11mph, factory car
	Formule Libre race	Maserati 250F	1st **LR,** 1:56.4, 85.40mph
	500cc race	Beart-Cooper Mk VIIA	**1st**
15-8-54	Pescara GP, I	Maserati 250F	**PP,** Rtd, oil pipe, own car, works-entered
22-8-54	SWISS GP, Bremgarten, Berne	Maserati 250F	Rtd, oil pump, fastest during wet practice, noted by Neubauer of Mercedes-Benz
5-9-54	ITALIAN GP, Monza	Maserati 250F	UNC '10th', Rtd with split oil tank, when *LEADING CHAMPIONSHIP GP FOR FIRST TIME*
11-9-54	RAC Tourist Trophy, Dundrod, NI	Jaguar D-Type	18th, oil pressure gone, co-driver Peter Walker
25-9-54	Goodwood Trophy, GB	Maserati 250F	**1st, PP, FL,** 1:33.0, 92.90mph
	Woodcote Cup *Formule Libre*	Maserati 250F	3rd
	Sports car race	Lister-Bristol	2nd, **FL,** behind Roy Salvadori's Maserati A6GCS
	500cc race	Beart-Cooper Mk VIIA	2nd, **LR** 85.88mph, just beaten by Don Parker's Kieft Spl
2-10-54	*Daily Telegraph* Trophy, Aintree, GB	Maserati 250F	**1st, PP, =FL** with Mike Hawthorn (Vanwall), 2:04.8, 86.54mph
	Formule Libre race	Maserati 250F	**1st, PP, LR,** 2:00.6, 89.55mph
	500cc race	Beart-Cooper Mk VIIA	**1st, PP, =FL** with Jim Russell, 2:17.2, 78.72mph — pole time 4secs quicker than next-fastest (Ivor Bueb) *SM's LAST 500cc F3 APPEARANCE*
10-10-54	*Coupe du Salon*, Montlhéry, F	Connaught ALSR	**1st** 1500cc class
24-10-54	SPANISH GP, Barcelona	Maserati 250F	Rtd, oil system
29-11-54	American Mountain Rally	Sunbeam-Talbot Alpine	Team Award, navigated by Ron Kessel

1955

16-1-55	ARGENTINE GP, Buenos Aires	Mercedes-Benz W196	4th, shared car with Kling and Herrmann, MERCEDES DEBUT
30-1-55	Buenos Aires City GP, ARG	3.0 Mercedes-Benz W196	3rd, **FL** in heat 1
	Buenos Aires City GP, ARG	3.0 Mercedes-Benz W196	**1st** in heat 2, **=FL** with Farina's heat 1 time, 2:19.5m, 75.48mph, 2nd o/a on aggregate
13-3-55	Sebring 12-Hours, USA	Austin-Healey 100S	6th, co-driver Lance Macklin
11-4-55	Glover Trophy, Goodwood, GB	Maserati 250F	**PP,** Rtd, injection
	Chichester Cup *Libre* race	Maserati 250F	3rd

	Sports car race	Beart-Climax	Rtd, throttle
24-4-55	Bordeaux GP, F	Maserati 250F	4th **FL,** 1:21.3, 67.67mph
1-5-55	Mille Miglia, Brescia-Brescia, I	Mercedes-Benz 300SLR	**1st, NR** — with Denis Jenkinson
7-5-55	BRDC International Trophy, Silverstone, GB	Maserati 250F	Rtd, engine
	Sports car race	Beart-Climax	Last!
22-5-55	MONACO GP, Monte Carlo	Mercedes-Benz W196	UNC, '9th', pushed car across line after engine trouble when leading
29-5-55	Eifelrennen, Nürburgring, D	Mercedes-Benz 3090SLR	2nd to Fangio
5-6-55	BELGIAN GP, Spa-Francorchamps	Mercedes-Benz W196	2nd to Fangio
11/12-6-55	Le Mans 24-Hours, F	Mercedes-Benz 300SLR	Withdrawn while leading at 1.45am, co-drove with Fangio
19-6-55	DUTCH GP, Zandvoort	Mercedes-Benz W196	2nd to Fangio
16-7-55	BRITISH GP, Aintree	Mercedes-Benz W196	**1st, PP, LR,** 2:00.4, 89.70mph — *FIRST GRANDE EPREUVE WIN*
24-7-55	Civil Governor's Cup, Lisbon, P	Porsche 550	**1st, PP, FL**
7-8-55	Swedish Sports Car GP, Rabelov	Mercedes-Benz 300SLR	2nd to Fangio, **=FL**
13-8-55	Redex Trophy, Snetterton, GB	Maserati 250F	3rd **FL,** 1:56.0, 83.79mph
20-8-55	Goodwood 9-Hours, GB	Porsche 550	Rtd, collision, co-driver Huschke von Hanstein
27-8-55	*Daily Herald* Trophy, Oulton Park, GB	Connaught ALSR	7th o/a 1500cc class
	Sporting Life Trophy	Standard 10	2nd in up to 1100cc class
3-9-55	*Daily Telegraph* Trophy, Aintree, GB	Maserati 250F	Rtd, engine
11-9-55	ITALIAN GP, Monza	Mercedes-Benz W196	Rtd, transmission, **LR,** 2:46.9, 133.95mph
17-9-55	RAC Tourist Trophy, Dundrod, NI	Mercedes-Benz 300SLR	**1st, BPT,** co-driver John Fitch
24-9-55	Oulton Park Gold Cup	Maserati 250F	**1st, LR,** 1:53.2, 87.81mph
16-10-55	Targa Florio, Madonie, Sicily	Mercedes-Benz 300SLR	**1st LR** 43:7.4, 62.25mph, co-driver Peter Collins
9/11-12-55	Governor's Trophy, Windsor Field, Bahamas	Austin-Healey 100S	6th
9/11-12-55	Nassau Trophy	Austin-Healey 100S	Rtd, wishbone

1956

7-1-56	New Zealand GP, Ardmore	Maserati 250F	**1st, PP, LR,** 1:28.0
	Ardmore Sports Car Handicap	Porsche 550	**1st,** handicap 4:47
22-1-56	ARGENTINE GP, Buenos Aires	Maserati 250F	Rtd, engine, while leading on return as Maserati works No 1
29-1-56	Buenos Aires 1,000Kms, ARG	Maserati 300S	**1st,** co-driver Carlos Menditéguy
5-2-56	Buenos Aires City GP, Mendoza, ARG	Maserati 250F	2nd to Fangio's Lancia-Ferrari
24-3-56	Sebring 12-Hours, USA	Aston Martin DB3S	Rtd, engine, co-driver Peter Collins, début as Aston Martin works team No 1

2-4-56	Glover Trophy, Goodwood, GB	Maserati 250F	**1st, PP, LR,** 1:30.2, 95.79mph
	Sports car race	Aston Martin DB3S	**1st, PP, FL,** 1:35.0, 87.45mph
14-4-56	British Empire Trophy, Oulton Park, GB	Cooper-Climax	4th, **FL** in heat, 1:58.0, 84.23mph, in borrowed works Bobtail sports car
	Oulton Park, GB	Cooper-Climax	**1st, FL,** 1:57.0, 84.96mph, in final
23-4-56	Aintree '200', GB	Maserati 250F	**1st** in own obsolescent car '2508'
	Sports car race	Cooper-Climax	5th, own new Bobtail sports car
29-4-56	Mille Miglia, Brescia-Brescia, I	Maserati 350S	Crashed in rain, with Denis Jenkinson
5-5-56	BRDC International Trophy, Silverstone, GB	Vanwall	**1st, PP, =LR** with Mike Hawthorn (BRM P25), 1:43.0, 102.30mph
	Sports car race	Aston Marton DB3S	2nd
13-5-56	MONACO GP, Monte Carlo	Maserati 250F	**1st**
21-5-56	London Trophy, *Formule Libre*, Crystal Palace, GB	Maserati 250F	**1st, PP, FL** in heat 1
	Crystal Palace, GB	Maserati 250F	**1st, LR,** 62.6″, 79.94mph, in heat 2, **1st** o/a on aggregate
	Anerley Trophy	Cooper-Climax	2nd in own Bobtail sports
	Norbury Trophy	Cooper-Climax	**1st, LR,** 64.8″, 77.22mph, Bobtail sports
27-5-56	Nürburgring 1,000Kms, D	Maserati 300S (x2)	**1st,** co-driver Jean Behra, took over sister Taruffi/Schell car
3-6-56	BELGIAN GP, Spa-Francorchamps	Maserati 250F	3rd **LR,** 4:14.7, 124.15mph. Finished in Perdisa's car after own car lost wheel.
24-6-56	Supercortemaggiore GP, Monza, I	Maserati 150S & 200S	2nd, **BPT** before Farina crashed car, started in 150S instead, prop-shaft immediately broke, so took over 200S, co-driver Cesare Perdisa
1-7-56	Reims 12-Hours, F	Cooper-Climax	**FL,** Rtd, overheating, co-driver Phil Hill
	FRENCH GP, Reims-Gueux.	Maserati 250F	5th in Perdisa's car after own Rtd
8-7-56	Rouen GP, Les Essarts, F	Aston Martin DB3S	2nd
14-7-6	BRITISH GP, Silverstone	Maserati 250F	Rtd, **PP, FL,** 1:43.2, 102.10mph, gearbox, led for 68 laps
	Sports car race	Maserati 300S	**1st, PP, FL,** 1:49.0, 96.67mph
22-7-56	Bari Sports Car GP, I	Maserati 300S	**1st, PP, FL,** 2:29.0
28/29-7-56	Le Mans 24-Hours, F	Aston Martin, DB3S	2nd, co-driver Peter Collins — DB3S timed at only 142.66mph on Mulsanne Straight

5-8-56	GERMAN GP, Nürburgring	Maserati 250F	2nd to Fangio
	1500cc Sports car race	Maserati 150S	2nd, **PP, FL,** 10:13.3, 83.15mph
12-8-56	Swedish Sports Car GP, Rabelov	Maserati 300S (x2)	**PP,** Rtd, caught fire in pits, co-driver Jean Behra — took over Villoresi/Schell car, brakes failed
18-8-56	*Daily Herald* Trophy, Oulton Park, GB	Aston Martin DB3S	**1st, PP, FL,** 2:06.8, 78.39mph
	Sporting Life Trophy	Cooper-Climax	**1st, FL,** 2:08.4, 77.41mph, Les Leston's Willment-backed Bobtail sports
2-9-56	ITALIAN GP, Monza	Maserati 250F	**1st, FL,** 2:45.5, 135.50mph, works 'offset' car
3-9-56	Monza Record attempt	Lotus 11	50km 135.54mph
	Monza Record attempt		50 miles 132.77mph
17/23-9-56	Tour de France	Mercedes-Benz 300SL	2nd, with Georges Huel
4-11-56	Venezuelan GP, Caracas	Maserati 300S	**1st, PP, FL**
25-11-56	Australian Tourist Trophy, Albert Park, Melbourne	Maserati 300S	**1st, LR,** 1:55.8
2-12-56	Australian GP, Melbourne	Maserati 250F	**1st, PP, LR,** 1:52.8, 100.26mph
9-12-56	Nassau Trophy, Windsor Field, Bahamas	Maserati 300S	**1st,** Bill Lloyd's car, oldest of its type in the US and said at the time to have 33,000 miles on the clock . . .

1957

13-1-57	ARGENTINE GP, Buenos Aires	Maserati 250F	8th, **PP, FL,** 1:44.7, 81.58mph
20-1-57	Buenos Aires 1,000Kms, ARG	Maserati 450S & 300S	2nd, **FL,** led in 450S co-driven by Fangio until transmission broke, then took over Behra/Menditéguy 300S; diary *"this was my greatest drive"*
27-1-57	Buenos Aires City GP, ARG	Maserati 250F	Rtd in heat 1, heat exhaustion, but accepted for second heat
	Buenos Aires City GP, ARG	Maserati 250F	6th after taking over Carlos Menditeguy's car, 6th o/a on aggregate
24-2-57	Cuban GP, Malecon Highway, Havana	Maserati 200S & 300S	Rtd both cars, 200S was Ettore Chimeri's, 300S was Pinhero Pines', loaned to Harry Schell for this race; both engines failed
24-3-57	Sebring 12-Hours, USA	Maserati 300S	2nd, 4th in Index, co-driver Harry Schell
7-4-57	Syracuse GP, Sicily	Vanwall	3rd, **LR,** 1:54.3, 107.64mph
22-4-57	Glover Trophy, Goodwood, GB	Vanwall	**PP,** Rtd, throttle linkage
12-5-57	Mille Miglia, Brescia-Brescia, I	Maserati 450S	Rtd, brake pedal snapped off after 7 miles, with Denis Jenkinson

19-5-57	MONACO GP, Monte Carlo	Vanwall	Crashed, lap 4
26-5-57	Nürburgring 1,000Kms, D	Maserati 450S & 2×300Ss	5th, **FL** in 450S, 9:49.9, 86.38mph, co-drove 450S with Fangio, but lost wheel, took over Scarlatti's 300S — no good — then Godia/Gould car Rtd, transmission
22/23-6-57	Le Mans 24-Hours, F	Maserati 450S *Berlinetta*	
20-7-57	BRITISH GP, Aintree	Vanwall	**1st, PP, LR,** 1:59.2, 90.60mph, *FIRST GRANDE EPREUVE VICTORY IN BRITISH CAR* Took over Tony Brooks' sister Vanwall
4-8-57	GERMAN GP, Nürburgring	Vanwall	5th, car unsuited to circuit
11-8-57	Swedish Sports Car GP, Rabelov	Maserati 450S (x2) & 300S	**1st** and 3rd, co-driving 450S with Jean Behra/Harry Schell, 300S with Bonnier/Schell/Scarlatti
18-8-57	PESCARA GP, I	Vanwall	**1st, LR,** 9:44.6, 97.87mph
23-8-57	Record attempt, Bonneville, Utah, USA	MG EX181	

1km	245.64mph
1 mile	245.11mph
5km	243.08mph
5 miles	235.69mph
10km	224.70mph

8-9-57	ITALIAN GP, Monza	Vanwall	**1st**
15-9-57	Tour de France	Mercedes-Benz 300SL	4th, with Peter Garnier
27-10-57	Moroccan GP, Casablanca	Vanwall	Practised only, DNS, Asian 'flu
3-11-57	Venezuelan GP, Caracas	Maserati 450S (x2)	**PP, FL,** 3:38.0, collision when leading, took over second 450S from Jean Behra, also Rtd
3-12-57	Nassau Tourist Trophy, Oakes Field, Bahamas	Aston Martin DBR2	24th, lost 3rd place with fuel pump problems
	Governor's Trophy	Aston Martin DBR2	4th, car later rolled twice by Ruth Levy in Lady's race
8-12-57	Nassau Trophy, Bahamas	3.5 Ferrari 290S	**1st,** Jan de Vroom's car

1958

19-1-58	ARGENTINE GP, Buenos Aires	1.9 Cooper-Climax	**1st** — Rob Walker's car, first rear-engined GP win since Auto Union, 1939
26-1-58	Buenos Aires 1,000Kms, ARG	Porsche RSK	3rd o/a, by 9secs behind two works 3.0 Ferraris, **1st** in class, co-driver Jean Behra. SM rated this at the time as *"my greatest race"*, terrorised works Ferraris all day long.
2-2-58	Buenos Aires City GP, ARG	1.9 Cooper-Climax	Rtd, rammed at first corner, heat 1
23-2-58	Cuban GP, Havana	4.1 Ferrari 335S	**1st** race stopped after 5 laps due to fatal accident
22-3-58	Sebring 12-Hours, USA	Aston Martin DBR1	**BPT, LR,** 3:20.3, 93.6mph, Rtd, transmission, led race — co-driver Tony Brooks

7-4-58	Sussex Trophy, Goodwood, GB	Aston Martin DBR2	**1st, PP, LR,** 1:33.4, 92.5mph
	Glover Trophy	1.9 Cooper-Climax	**=LR** with Mike Hawthorn (Ferrari), 1:28.8, 97.30mph, Rtd after stalling at start
12-4-58	British Empire Trophy, Oulton Park, GB	Aston Martin DBR2	**1st** in heat 3
	Oulton Park, GB	Aston Martin DBR2	**1st** in final equallied **LR,** 1:50.8, 89.70mph
19-4-58	Aintree 200, GB	1.9 Cooper-Climax	**1st**
3-5-58	BRDC International Trophy, Silverstone, GB	2.01 Cooper-Climax	Rtd, gearbox
	Sports car race	Aston Martin DBR3	Rtd, engine. Practice time 1:46.0, first 3-litre sports car to exceed 100mph lap speed
11-5-58	Targa Florio, Madonie, Sicily	Aston Martin DBR1	**LR,** 42:17.5, 63.33mph, Rtd, transmission, co-driver Tony Brooks
18-5-58	MONACO GP, Monte Carlo	Vanwall	Rtd, valve-gear
26-5-58	DUTCH GP, Zandvoort	Vanwall	**1st, FL,** 1:38.5, 94.78mph
1-6-58	Nürburgring 1,000Kms, D	Aston Martin DBR1	**1st, LR,** 9:43.0, 87.5mph, co-driver Jack Brabham
15-6-58	BELGIAN GP, Spa-Francorchamps	Vanwall	Rtd, over-revved on opening lap
21-6-58	Le Mans 24-Hours, F	Aston Martin DBR1	Rtd, engine, co-driver Jack Brabham
29-6-58	Two Worlds Trophy, Monza, I	*Eldorado* Maserati	4th in heat 1
	Two Worlds Trophy, Monza, I	*Eldorado* Maserati	5th in heat 2
	Two Worlds Trophy, Monza, I	*Eldorado* Maserati	Crashed in heat 3, steering broke
6-7-58	Coupe de Vitesse, Reims, F	Cooper-Climax F2	Rtd, **LR,** 2:36.7, 118.44mph
	FRENCH GP, Reims-Gueux	Vanwall	2nd
13-7-58	Vila Real Sports Car GP, P	Masterati 300S	**1st, PP, LR,** 88.28mph, from Behra in sister car
19-7-58	BRITISH GP, Silverstone	Vanwall	**PP,** Rtd, engine
	Sports car race	Lister-Jaguar	**1st, PP, =FL,** with Cliff Allison (Lotus), 1:46.0, 99.41mph
20-7-58	Caen GP, Le Prairie, F	2.2 Cooper-Climax	**1st, PP**
3-8-58	GERMAN GP, Nurburgring	Vanwall	**LR,** 9:09.2, 92.9mph, Rtd, ignition
10-8-58	Karlskoga Kannonloppet, S	Maserati 300S	**1st**
15-8-58	Copenhagen GP, Roskildering	Maserati 300S	Rtd in heat 1, engine
	Copenhagen GP, Roskildering	JBW-Maserati	Two **1sts** — Drove this car in two more heats this day, **LR** 46.7″ see next entry
16-8-58	Roskilde, second day	Maserati 300S	Car repaired over night, driven in these three heats, 2nd o/a on aggregate by 0.7sec to Gunnar Carlsson (Ferrari) who had a *very* wide car . . . Individual heat data n/a
24-8-58	PORTUGUESE GP, Oporto	Vanwall	**1st, PP**
30-8-58	Kentish '100', Brands Hatch, GB	Cooper-Climax F2	**PP,** 2nd in heat 1, **=FL** with Jack Brabham's works Cooper
	Kentish '100', Brands Hatch, GB	Cooper-Climax F2	**1st, FL,** 57.4″, 77.77mph, **1st** o/a on aggregate
7-9-58	ITALIAN GP, Monza	Vanwall	**PP,** Rtd, gearbox

13-9-58	RAC Tourist Trophy, Goodwood, GB	Aston Martin DBR1	**1st, PP, LR,** 1:32.6, 93.33mph, co-driver Tony Brooks
19-10-58	MOROCCAN GP, Casablanca	Vanwall	**1st, FL,** 2:22.5, 117.80mph
29-11-58	Melbourne GP, Albert Park, AUS	2.01 Cooper-Climax	1st, PP, FL, 1:53.0, 99.6mph, in heat 1
	Melbourne GP, Albert Park, AUS	2.01 Cooper-Climax	**1st, PP, LR,** 1:50.0, 102.26mph, in final

1959

10-1-59	New Zealand GP, Ardmore	2.2 Cooper-Climax	**PP,** Rtd, half-shaft when leading heat 2
	New Zealand GP, Ardmore	2.2 Cooper-Climax	**1st, LR,** 1:24.8, 85mph in GP proper, started back of grid
21-3-59	Sebring 12-Hours, USA	Lister-Jaguar	**BPT,** DISQ, co-drove with Ivor Bueb. Then shared Briggs Cunningham/Lake Underwood sister car, finished 15th
30-3-59	Glover Trophy, Goodwood, GB	2.5 Cooper-Climax	**1st FL,** 1:31.8, 94.12mph
8-4-59	*GP D'Europe des Micromills,* Palais des Sports, Paris, F	Micromill	see text p 215
	Aintree '200', GB	Cooper-BRM	Rtd when leading, **LR,** 1:58.8, 90.91mph
25-4-59	Syracuse GP, Sicily	Cooper-Borgward	**1st, PP**
2-5-59	BRDC International Trophy, Silverstone, GB	BRM P25	**PP,** Rtd, brake failure, lap 5
	GT race	Aston Martin DB4 GT	**1st, PP, FL,** 1:58.8, 88.7mph
	Sports car race	Aston Martin DBR1	2nd
10-5-59	MONACO GP, Monte Carlo	2.5 Cooper-Climax	**PP,** Rtd when leading, transmission
31-5-59	DUTCH GP, Zandvoort	2.5 Cooper-Climax	Rtd when leading, transmission, **LR,** 1:36.6, 97.19mph
7-6-59	Nurburgring 1000Kms, D	Aston Martin DBR1	**1st, LR,** 9:32.0, 89.16mph, co-driver Jack Fairman
20/21-6-59	Le Mans 24-Hours, F	Aston Martin DBR1	Rtd, engine, after leading — co-driver Jack Fairman
5-7-59	FRENCH GP, Reims-Geux	BRM P25	Rtd, spun and stalled, **LR,** 2:22.8, 130.21mph
	F2 *Coupe de Vitesse*	Cooper-Borgward	**1st, PP, =LR,** with Hans Herrmann (Porsche), 2:33.1, 121.22mph
12-7-59	Rouen GP, Les Essarts, F	Cooper-Borgward	**1st, LR,** 2:24.9, 100.98mph
	Coupe Delamere Deboutteville	Maserati *Tipo* 60	**1st, PP, FL**
18-7-59	BRITISH GP, Aintree	BRM P25	2nd, **=LR,** 1:57.0, 92.31mph shared with Bruce McLaren (works Cooper)
	Sports car race	Cooper Monaco	Rtd, **LR,** 87.66mph, rammed at start, later caught fire
26-7-59	Circuit d'Auvergne, Clermont, F	Cooper-Borgward	**1st, PP, LR,** 3:48.8, 78.73mph
2-8-59	GERMAN GP, AVUS, Berlin	2.5 Cooper-Climax	Rtd, transmission, in heat 1
9-8-59	Karlskoga Kannonloppet, S	Cooper Monaco	**1st, LR,** 1:38.1, 68.37mph
15/16-8-59	Copenhagen GP, Roskildering, DK	Cooper Monaco	**1st** in FOUR heats of six heat race, **1st** o/a, **1st** on aggregate, **LR** shared with David Piper (Lotus), individual result data n/a

23-8-59	PORTUGUESE GP, Monsanto, Lisbon	2.5 Cooper-Monaco	**1st, PP, FL,** 2:05.07, 97.30mph
29-8-59	F2 Kentish '100', Brands Hatch, GB	Cooper-Borgward	**PP,** 3rd in heat 1
	F2 Kentish '100', Brands Hatch, GB	Cooper-Borgward	4th in heat 2, 3rd o/a on aggregate
5-9-59	RAC Tourist Trophy, Goodwood, GB	Aston Martin DBR1	**1st, PP,** changed cars after refuelling fire, co-driver Tony Brooks in first car, then took over Shelby/Fairman car to win. Aston Martin clinched World Sports Car Championship.
13-9-59	ITALIAN GP, Monza	2.5 Cooper Climax	**1st, PP,** Cooper-Climax clinched Formula 1 Constructors' World Championship
26-9-59	Oulton Park Gold Cup, GB	2.5 Cooper-Climax	**1st, PP, LR,** 1:41.8, 97.64mph
10/11-10-59	*LA Times* GP, Riverside, USA	Aston Martin DBR2	Rtd, overheating and oil pressure — race stopped and restarted
18-10-59	Watkins Glen *Libre* GP, USA	2.5 Cooper-Climax	**1st FL,** 1:24.0, 97.1mph, Yeoman Credit team car
27-11/4-12-59	Govenor's Trophy, Oakes Field, Nassau	Aston Martin DB4GT	**1st** in heat
	Oakes Field, Nassau	Aston Martin DB4GT	**LR,** 82.78mph, Rtd in final, brake disc
	Governor's Trophy	Aston Martin DBR2	**1st** in heat
	Governor's Trophy	Aston Martin DBR2	**1st** in Trophy race proper
12-12-59	UNITED STATES GP, Sebring	2.5 Cooper-Climax	**PP,** Rtd, transmission

1960

1-1-60	South African GP, East London	Cooper-Borgward	2nd, **PP, FL,** led until injection pipe split 2 laps from finish
9-1-60	New Zealand GP heat, Ardmore	2.5 Cooper-Climax	**1st, FL,** Yeoman Credit car using engine from Cooper Monaco sports
	New Zealand GP	2.5 Cooper-Climax	Rtd, clutch, **PP, LR,** 1:21.7
7-2-60	ARGENTINE GP, Buenos Aires	2.5 Cooper-Climax	3rd, **PP, FL,** 1:38.9, 88.43mph, took over Trintignant's sister car, voiding Championship points, after suspension broke
28-2-60	Cuban GP, Havana	Maserati *Tipo* 61	**1st, PP LR,** 2:16.0, 81.97mph
19-3-60	Syracuse GP, Sicily	F2 Porsche	Rtd when leading, **PP, LR,** 1:58.8, 103.49mph
26-3-60	Sebring 4-Hours, USA	Austin-Healey Sprite	2nd
	Sebring 12-Hours	Maserati *Tipo* 61	**FL,** 3:18.14, 94.47mph, Rtd, transmission
10-4-60	Brussels GP, Heysel, B	F2 Porsche	**1st LR** in heat 1, 2:04.0, 82.11mph
	Brussels GP, Heysel, B	F2 Porsche	3rd, **PP, FL** in heat 2, 2nd o/a on aggregate points — would have been **1st** if result had been by conventional addition of times
18-4-60	Glover Trophy, Goodwood, GB	2.5 Cooper-Climax	2nd **LR,** 1:24.6, 102.13mph, behind Innes Ireland's new Lotus 18

Date	Event	Car	Result
	Lavant Cup	F2 Porsche	2nd, behind Innes Ireland's other new Lotus 18
	Fordwater Trophy	Aston Martin DB4 GT	**1st, PP, FL,** 84.05mph
30-4-60	Aintree '200', GB	F2 Porsche	**1st, PP**
14-5-60	BRDC International Trophy, Silverstone, GB	2.5 Cooper-Climax	**PP,** Rtd, wishbone
	Touring car race	3.8 Jaguar	2nd, **PP**
22-5-60	Nürburgring 1000Kms, D	Maserati *Tipo* 61	**1st, LR,** 9:37.0, 88.48mph, brilliantly co-driven by Dan Gurney
29-5-60	MONACO GP, Monte Carlo	Lotus-Climax 18	**1st, PP,** on debut of Rob Walker's brand-new Lotus
6-6-60	DUTCH GP, Zandvoort	Lotus-Climax 18	4th, **PP, LR,** 1:33.8, 99.98mph, delayed by tyre burst when challenging for lead
18-6-60	BELGIAN GP, Spa-Francorchamps	Lotus-Climax 18	*Crashed during practice when left-rear hub-shaft broke — SM badly injured*
7-8-60	Karlskoga Kannonloppet, S	Lotus-Climax 19	**1st, LR,** 1:33.3, 69.4mph on comeback in debut brand-new Lotus 'Monte Carlo' owned by Yeoman Credit/BRP
14-8-60	PORTUGUESE GP, Oporto	Lotus-Climax 18	Disqualified for attempting to push-start car against race direction
20-8-60	RAC Tourist Trophy, Goodwood, GB	Ferrari 250GT SWB	**1st, PP, LR,** 1:36.6, 89.44mph
27-8-60	F2 Kentish '100', Brands Hatch, GB	F2 Porsche	11th carburator trouble
	Redex Trophy, Brands Hatch	Ferrari 250GT SWB	**1st, PP, LR,** 1:56.2, 82.09mph
10/11-9-60	Copenhagen GP, Roskildering, DK	F2 Porsche	4th, gearbox problems
18-9-60	Austrian GP, Zeltweg	F2 Porsche	**1st, FL,** 1:16.0, 94.19mph
24-9-60	Oulton Park Gold Cup, GB	Lotus-Climax 18	**1st, PP, =FL** with Bruce McLaren (Cooper), 1:45.4, 94.30mph
2-10-60	Modena GP, I	F2 Lotus-Climax 18	Rtd, valvegear — Parnell team 1.5-litre F2 car. Its brakes failed during practice
9-10-60	Watkins Glen *Libre* GP, USA	Lotus-Climax 18	**1st, PP, LR,** 109mph
16-10-60	*LA Times* GP, Riverside, USA	Lotus-Climax 19	**PP,** Rtd, transmission after leading
23-10-60	Pacific GP, Laguna Seca, USA	Lotus-Climax 19	**1st** in heat 1
	Pacific GP, Laguna Seca, USA	Lotus-Climax 19	**1st, LR,** in heat 2, 1:17.2
20-11-60	UNITED STATES GP, Riverside	Lotus-Climax 18	**1st, PP**
24/25-11-60	Go-Kart race	Go-Kart	13th!
27-11/2-12-60	Nassau Tourist Trophy, Oakes Field, Bahamas	Ferrari 250GT SWB	**1st, FL**
	Nassau International Trophy	Lotus-Climax 19	Rtd, front suspension, after stalling at start
	Governor's Trophy	Lotus-Climax 19	Rtd
17-12-60	Cape GP, Killarney, ZA	F2 Porsche	**1st, PP**
27-12-60	South African GP, East London	F2 Porsche	**1st**

1961

Date	Event	Car	Result
7-1-61	New Zealand GP, Ardmore	2.5 Lotus-Climax 18	**1st, PP, LR,** 1:19.9, 90.1mph in heat 1, Rob Walker's ex-F1 car
	New Zealand GP	2.5 Lotus-Climax	**PP, LR,** 1:20.6, Rtd, half-shaft in GP proper
21-1-61	Lady Wigram Trophy, Christchurch, NZ	2.5 Lotus-Climax	2nd, shunted twice, carbs damaged and wheels skewed, race shortened by 50 miles due to rain
29-1-61	Australian GP, Warwick Farm, Sydney	2.5 Lotus-Climax 18	**1st, PP, FL,** in tremendous heat
24-3-61	Sebring 4-Hours, USA	Austin-Healey Sprite	4th
25-3-61	Sebring 12-Hours, USA	Maserati *Tipo* 61	**LR,** 3:13.2, Rtd, exhaust system broke up — co-driver Graham Hill, took over same Camoradi team's *Tipo* 63 rear-engined V12. Battery flat at start in *Tipo* 61
3-4-61	Lavant Cup, Goodwood, GB	ICF Cooper-Climax	**1st,** Rob Walker's brand-new InterContinental Formula car
	Glover Trophy	1.5 Lotus-Climax 18	·**PP,** 4th, Rob Walker's F1 car revised to new 1.5-litre Formula 1 form
	Sussex Trophy	Lotus-Climax 19	**1st, PP**
	Fordwater Trophy	Aston Martin DB4 GTZ	**PP,** 3rd
9-4-61	Brussels GP, Heysel, B	1.5 Lotus-Climax 18	UNC '15th' in heat 1
	Brussels GP, Heysel, B	1.5 Lotus-Climax 18	8th in heat 2
	Brussels GP, Heysel, B	1.5 Lotus-Climax 18	2nd **FL,** 2:04.7, 81.8mph, UNC '7th' o/a on aggregate points, carburetion problems
16-4-61	Vienna Preis, Aspern, A	1.5 Lotus-Climax 18	**1st, PP, LR,** 1:12.2, 84.57mph
22-4-61	Aintree '200', GB	1.5 Cooper-Climax	Rtd, engine, lap 1 — Lotus 18 on way to Syracuse, used Rob Walker's old Cooper instead . . .
25-4-61	Sports car race	Lotus-Climax 19	**1st, LR,** 2:00.0, 90mph
	Syracuse GP	Lotus-Climax 18	'8th', magneto, Rtd 2 laps from finish
30-4-61	Targa Florio, Madonie, Sicily	Porsche RS60 1.9	Rtd, last lap, differential casing split — co-driver Graham Hill
6-5-61	BRDC International Trophy, Silverstone, GB	ICF Cooper-Climax	**1st, FL,** 1:52.4, 93.75mph
	Sports car race	Lotus-Climax 19	**1st, PP, LR,** 1:39.2, 106.22mph
14-5-61	MONACO GP, Monte Carlo	1.5 Lotus-Climax 18	**1st, PP, =FL,** with Richie Ginther's Ferrari, 1:36.3, 73.13mph
22-5-61	DUTCH GP, Zandvoort	1.5 Lotus-Climax 18	4th
28-5-61	Nürburgring 1000Kms, D	Porsche RS61 1.7	Rtd, took over Porsche Carrera to finish 8th o/a, **1st** 2-litre sports, co-driver Graham Hill
3-6-61	Silver City Trophy, Brands Hatch, GB	1.5 Lotus-Climax 18/21	**1st, PP, LR,** 1:42.0, 93.52mph, UDT-Laystall Team car
10/11-6-61	Le Mans 24-Hours, F	Ferrari 250GT SWB	Rtd, co-driver Graham Hill, ran 3rd o/a
18-6-61	BELGIAN GP, Spa-Francorchamps	1.5 Lotus-Climax 18/21	8th, Rob Walker's car now updated — Possibly SM's only known off-day?
24-6-61	Player's '200', Mosport, CAN	Lotus-Climax 19	**1st** in heat 1
	Player's '200', Mosport, CAN	Lotus-Climax 19	**1st** in heat 2, **1st** o/a aggregate and **FL**

2-7-61	FRENCH GP, Reims-Gueux	1.5 Lotus-Climax 18/21	Rtd, minor collision damage
8-7-61	British Empire Trophy		
	Silverstone, GB	ICF Cooper-Climax	**1st, FL,** 1:35.4, 109.31mph
	GT race	Ferrari 250GT SWB	**1st, PP, LR,** 1:49.8, 95.97mph
15-7-61	BRITISH GP, Aintree	1.5 Lotus-Climax 18/21	Rtd, brake pipe, took over Walker team's 4WD Ferguson P99, DISQ due to push-start after pit stop
23-7-61	Solitude GP, Stuttgart, D	1.5 Lotus-Climax 18/21	'10th', Rtd, gearbox, UDT-Laystall car
6-8-61	GERMAN GP, Nürburgring	1.5 Lotus-Climax 18/21	**1st,** *THE FINAL GRANDE EPREUVE VICTORY*
7-8-61	Peco Trophy, Brands Hatch, GB	Ferrari 250GT SWB	**1st, PP, LR,** 1:54.2, 82.53mph
	Guards Trophy	ICF Cooper-Climax	**PP,** Rtd, transmission — poll time 1:37.4 was 1.4secs quicker than McLaren, next fastest
19-8-61	RAC Tourist Trophy, Goodwood, GB	Ferrari 250GT SWB	**1st** — seventh and final TT win
20-8-61	Karlskoga Kannonloppet, S	1.5 Lotus-Climax 18/21	**1st, FL,** 1:30.4, 74.23mph, UDT-Laystall car
26/27-8-61	Danish GP, Roskildering, DK	1.5 Lotus-Climax 18/21	**1st, PP FL,** 47.0″, 58.23mph in heat 1
	Danish GP, Roskildering, DK	1.5 Lotus-Climax 18/21	**1st, PP, FL,** 42.8″, 63.02mph in heat 2
	Danish GP, Roskildering, DK	1.5 Lotus-Climax 18/21	**1st, PP, FL,** 43.1″, 62.14mph in heat 3 and **1st** o/a on aggregate
3-9-61	Modena GP, I	1.5 Lotus-Climax 18/21	**1st, PP, FL,** 59.2″, 89.40mph, in Rob Walker's car
10-9-61	ITALIAN GP, Monza	1.5 Lotus-Climax 21	Rtd, wheel-bearing, driving Innes Ireland's loaned 1961 Team Lotus works car
23-9-61	Oulton Park Gold Cup, GB	1.5 Ferguson-Climax P99	**1st, LR,** 1:46.4, 93.42mph — Only Formula 1 victory to date scored by 4-wheel drive car
30-9-61	Canadian GP, Mosport Park	Lotus-Climax 19	3rd, **PP, LR,** 1:34.2, 91.71mph, gearbox twice jammed in 3rd, had to be freed, also holed radiator
8-10-61	UNITED STATES GP, Watkins Glen	Lotus-Climax 18/21	Rtd engine, after leading — *SM's LAST WORLD CHAMPIONSHIP-QUALIFYING GRAND PRIX*
13/15-10-61	*LA Times* GP, Riverside	Lotus-Climax 19	16th, leading until brake trouble, no brake fluid in pits . . .
	3-Hour production car race	Sunbeam Alpine	3rd o/a, won class despite gearbox breaking — co-driver Jack Brabham
22-10-61	Pacific GP, Laguna Seca, USA	Lotus-Climax 19	**1st** in heat 1, sticking throttle, duel with Dan Gurney's 19
	Pacific GP, Laguna Seca, USA	Lotus-Climax 19	**1st, FL,** in heat 2, **1st** o/a on aggregate, poor brakes
3/10-12-61	Nassau Tourist Trophy, BA	Ferrari 250GT SWB	**1st, PP,** in heat 2
	Nassau Tourist Trophy, BA	Ferrari 250GT SWB	**1st, PP,** in TT proper
	Governor's Trophy	Lotus-Climax 19	**FL,** 2:56.0, Rtd in heat, rear upright, Team Rosebud entered ex-UDT car
	Nassau Trophy	Lotus-Climax 19	Rtd, broke rear wishbone

17-12-61	Natal GP, Westmead, Durban, ZA	1.5 Lotus-Climax 18/21	2nd, **FL**, 1:24.8, 93.37mph, UDT-Laystall car facing Jim Clark in Team Lotus 21
26-12-61	South African GP, East London	1.5 Lotus-Climax 18/21	2nd, facing Jim Clark in Team Lotus 21

1962

6-1-62	New Zealand GP, Ardmore	2.5 Lotus-Climax 21	**1st, FL,** 1:32.8, 78mph, in torrential rain — no GP preliminary heats this year — Rob Walker's latest car
13-1-62	Vic Hudson Memorial, Levin, NZ	2.7 ICF Cooper-Climax	2nd in heat
	Vic Hudson Memorial, Levin, NZ	2.7 ICF Cooper-Climax	2nd in main race, stopped after 8 laps due to torrential rain. Rob Walker's 1961 InterContinental Formula car
20-1-62	Lady Wigram Trophy, Christchurch, NZ	2.5 Lotus-Climax 21	**1st, =LR** with John Surtees (2.7 Cooper), 1:20.1, 95.1mph
27-1-61	Teretonga Trophy, Invercargill, NZ	2.5 ICF Cooper-Climax	2nd in heat 1
	Teretonga Trophy, Invercargill, NZ	2.5 ICF Cooper-Climax	2nd to Bruce McLaren's 2.7 Cooper in Trophy race proper
4-2-62	Warwick Farm '100', Sydney, Australia	2.7 ICF Cooper-Climax	**1st, PP**
11-2-62	Daytona Continental, USA	Ferrari 250GT *Speciale*	4th o/a, **1st,** GT category
23-3-62	Sebring 3-Hours, USA	Austin-Healey Sprite	3rd
25-3-62	Sebring 12-Hours, USA	Ferrari 250TRI/61	DISQ for refuelling too early, led handsomely — co-driver Innes Ireland
1-4-62	Brussels GP, Heysel, B	Lotus-Climax 18/21 V8	2nd, **FL,** 2:02.0, 83.46mph in heat 1
1-4-62	Brussels GP, Heysel, B	Lotus-Climax 18/21 V8	**FL,** 2:00.0, 84.85mph, Rtd, valvegear in heat 2 so DNS heat 3 — unplaced o/a on aggregate — Rob Walker's V8 'special' made its racing debut in this meeting — previously used only in practice at Monza and Watkins Glen, 1961
14-4-62	Lombank Trophy, Snetterton, GB	Lotus-Climax 18/21 V8	7th, **PP, FL,** 1:33.6, 104.23mph — Walker car in UDT-Laystall colours
	Lombank Trophy, Snetterton, GB	3-lap Mini saloon demonstration — SM and Innes Ireland led massed grid-start in reverse gear	
23-4-62	Glover Trophy, Goodwood, GB	Lotus-Climax 18/21 V8	*CRASHED AT ST MARY'S CORNER, lap 36, PP by 2.0secs from Graham Hill's V8 BRM, =FL with John Surtees (Lola), 1:22.0, 105.37mph*

Index of personalities